Marlboro College

Outdoor Program
Marlboro College

PRINCIPLES OF
WILDLIFE MANAGEMENT

PRINCIPLES OF
WILDLIFE MANAGEMENT

James A. Bailey

Colorado State University

JOHN WILEY & SONS

New York Chichester Brisbane Toronto Singapore

Library of Congress Cataloging in Publication Data:

Bailey, James A. (James Allen), 1934–
    Principles of wildlife management.

    Includes indexes.
    1. Wildlife management. I. Title.
SK355.B34 1984   639.9   83-19766
ISBN 0-471-01649-7

Printed in the United States of America

10 9 8 7 6 5 4 3 2 1

To Ella Maria and Leo Carl,
For hours at Hoffing's, Field's, and West Town;
Thanks to you!

To characters sitting upright,
Jokers by candlelight;
In spite of you!

PREFACE

> The design of a book is the pattern
> of a reality controlled and shaped by
> the mind of the writer. This is
> completely understood about poetry
> or fiction, but it is too seldom
> realized about books of fact.
>
> *John Steinbeck*

All "facts" are opinions, some more widely accepted, at least currently, than others. This is a book of opinions. They are my opinions about what ideas are widely accepted and used as a basis for wildlife management. I have called these ideas *principles* because education in the biological aspects of wildlife management tends to be divided into three parts, commonly referred to as principles, practices or techniques, and life histories of important animals.

The book is intended primarily as a text for an early course in the college curriculum of aspiring professional wildlife biologists. I have assumed the readers will have mastered courses in general biology, both zoology and botany, and a course in ecology. Much of wildlife management is applied ecology, and some of what I have written here will overlap with the contents of many texts in ecology. However, I have found that most texts and courses in ecology do not emphasize the applications of ecology to the management of wildlife populations and habitats. Therefore, some overlap seems necessary.

No chapter provides a complete review of the literature. The papers cited were selected because (1) I was familiar with them, (2) some are considered classics by the profession, (3) many provide good examples, (4) some provide access to numerous additional sources on their subjects, and (5) in total, they demonstrate the great diversity of sources of ideas that are useful in wildlife management.

Those who have contributed to my ideas for this book and to bringing the endless manuscripts into print are too numerous to list entirely. I am grateful for the help, encouragement, interesting discussions, and good times we had along the way. The project began with Professor Ralph T. King. His approach to teaching principles of wildlife management was the major influence on the design and philosophy of this text. Others to whom I am especially indebted are Gene

Hesterberg, who gave the first push toward wildlife biology, Maurice Alexander, Don Behrend, Glen Sanderson, Bill Edwards, Helen Schultz, Doug Gilbert, and Val Geist. Terry May and Mal Coulter, of the University of Maine, and John George, of Pennsylvania State University, provided helpful comments on the last draft of the text. Over the years, Nancy Bowles, Pat Johnson, and Phyllis Turner typed drafts and redrafts of chapters. My wife, Nan, encouraged and nagged me to keep at it, and I am grateful. Many others have influenced my thinking and helped in numerous ways. Not the least of the help has come from several graduate and a few undergraduate students. Without them I would have lost my reasons for getting the job done. Although the contributions of others to this book are recognized, alas, all its flaws are mine.

To the student who uses this text, do not use it as a work of science, for it certainly is not. Anything I have said about any species of wildlife is not nearly the final word on the subject. It is just an example selected to illustrate a principle. Knowledge of species biology requires a review of scientific literature, and the literature is large for many species.

The message of this book lies primarily in its approach to wildlife biology and to the problems of wildlife management. Management is a dynamic activity dealing with a dynamic resource. If you do not continue to observe in the field, to learn from the literature, and to question the conventional wisdom of the day, you will ultimately fail. Your education only begins with your academic education. I hope this text charts the many dimensions of the challenge with reasonable accuracy.

J. Bailey
June 1982
Fort Collins, Colorado

CONTENTS

PRINCIPLES OF
WILDLIFE MANAGEMENT

PART   I

WILDLIFE
CONSERVATION

CHAPTER 1

AN INTRODUCTION TO WILDLIFE MANAGEMENT AND CONSERVATION

> Just when you think "you've got it,"
> good teachers will sometimes seem to
> take an almost sadistic pleasure in
> proving to you that you are wrong.
> Education, not indoctrination, is
> their task.
>
> *Kingman Brewster, Jr.*

DEFINITIONS
WILDLIFE CONSERVATION
PRINCIPLES

This chapter presents a few basic definitions and describes the role of wildlife management as a part of wildlife conservation.

DEFINITIONS

Wildlife includes all free-ranging vertebrates in their naturally associated environments. Other definitions of wildlife are much broader and may include all plants and animals in wild ecosystems. Certainly, wildlife managers are concerned with managing habitats, including vegetation and invertebrates that are foods or disease vectors for vertebrates. But the objectives of most wildlife management programs are to favor or control the abundance or distribution of vertebrate species. Thus, for purposes of this text, our definition of wildlife is limited to vertebrates.

In years past, working definitions of wildlife have been narrower. The emphasis has been on game species, those harvested by recreational hunting. For example, management of wildlife in the United States was for many years based mostly on a text titled *Game Management* (Leopold 1933). With the gradual realization that all wild vertebrates possess important values, including negative values, the narrow definition of wildlife as game was abandoned. Today, biologists are called on to manage predators, song birds, furbearers, and vertebrate pests, as well as game species.

Most wildlife management is directed toward birds and mammals. Fish management has developed quite separately, and amphibians and reptiles have received little attention in wildlife management until the recently increased concern for endangered species. Although most examples in this book concern birds and mammals, the principles illustrated apply to all vertebrate classes, including amphibians, reptiles, and fish.

Free-ranging vertebrates must be unfenced or at least in a very large enclosure. Animals in a zoo are certainly not wildlife, as the term is used here. Animals in a square-mile enclosure might be considered free ranging. If the enclosure is vegetated so that one can enter beyond sight of the fence and the animals may avoid being seen, the inclination is to consider the animals free ranging.

The *naturally associated environment* of a species is the kind of environment in which the species evolved. It is the environment that permits the species to use all its adaptations.

Place white-tailed deer in a square-mile forested enclosure in Michigan, and most people would classify them as wildlife. Put chamois, a goatlike antelope from the mountains of Europe, into the same enclosure to provide exotic trophies for hunting, and the enclosure suddenly seems more zoolike. The chamois are not wildlife, because they are not in their naturally associated environment. The animals are structurally and behaviorally adapted to negotiating narrow ledges and climbing steep cliffs. Without mountains, they cannot use these remarkable adaptations. Like every animal, a chamois is a bundle of adaptations, acquired through natural selection. Without a mountainous environment, a chamois cannot be all that a chamois really is! This ability of an animal to express all of its adaptations is the most important quality of wildness. Wildness is wildlife's most unique and important characteristic.

A species may be transplanted from one part of the world to another and still be in its naturally associated environment. The ring-necked pheasant is an example. This species evolved in prairies and became adapted to intensively cultivated agricultural land in Asia. Transplanted to North America, it exists primarily in the same kinds of environment here.

Wildlife management is the art of making land produce valuable populations of wildlife. It is implied that this definition includes the control of pest populations to limit negative values of wildlife. Wildlife management involves direct population management (control of harvest, transplanting, etc.) and indirect management of populations through habitat manipulation to favor or inhibit target species. Further explanation of wildlife management is delayed until Chapter 19.

In the United States, wildlife is a publicly owned resource. Although many wild animals are produced on privately owned land, they cannot be taken into possession except as specified by state laws and, in the cases of migratory birds, endangered species, and some marine animals, federal laws. Most wildlife-management programs are, therefore, publicly funded to produce a diversity of public benefits. The discussion of management and conservation in this text refers to such public programs. It is assumed that concepts applicable to the more complex public programs are adequate for application to the less complex problems of private wildlife management on shooting preserves and game ranches.

A *principle* of wildlife management is a widely accepted generalization based on abundant and diverse research and experience and having wide application for managing wildlife. Most principles presented in this text are biological principles. Sociological principles applicable to wildlife management are not as well covered.

For example, consider the following principle: Wildlife is an organic resource and can be managed on a sustained-yield basis. This generalization is based on experience with many species of wildlife and other populations. The term *sustained yield* is probably derived from experience in forestry. The generalization embraces concepts of biotic potential, population turnover, density-dependent and compensatory mortality and natality, and ecological density. The principle instructs that all wildlife populations can be harvested periodically without reduction of their breeding stock, which will produce new harvestable surpluses. Like all principles, this one must be applied with judgment. Populations will not sustain all possible levels of harvest, and overharvest can occur. Some small populations, usually in poor and limited habitats, can sustain little or no harvest. Nevertheless, the principle remains broadly applicable.

Simple as the principle appears in its single statement, it rests on the many complex concepts noted above. These concepts are also principles of wildlife management. They are interrelated, and together they support the broader generalization that wildlife can be managed on a sustained-yield basis. Thus, although principles may be simply stated, they may be very complex concepts—to those who understand all their ramifications.

Principles are not rules to follow in managing a wildlife population. "Leave one den-tree per acre in squirrel habitat" is not a principle. It is a rule that is applicable when management objectives specify having at least a modest population of tree squirrels, and it is useful whenever all other habitat requirements of squirrels—besides den-trees—are fulfilled. The rule has very narrow application; but one does not have to understand much biology to successfully apply the rule.

Principles of wildlife management are concepts to consider in formulating management objectives and in reaching management decisions. Principles do not tell the wildlife manager what to do; they are concepts to consider when deciding what should be done. Application of these principles to management requires a knowledge of biology and an ability to think analytically. Rules have narrow application and can be applied by technicians. Principles have broad application and must be applied by biologists.

When concisely stated, principles of wildlife management are difficult to fully comprehend. Examples are necessary to illustrate the principles and are used frequently in this text. The student will further benefit from field trips to wildlife-management areas and research stations where these principles can be illustrated, as well as from reading scientific and semiscientific articles on wildlife populations and their habitats.

Wildlife is a diverse resource. There are many species of vertebrates, even on small areas. Each species population is influenced by its behavior and physiology and by many factors of its environment: foods, weather, soils, predators, and land-use practices, for example. Wildlife management is the application of knowledge about wildlife and about all these other factors. The principles of wildlife management include some that are specific to the profession and many that are shared with other professions and sciences (Fig. 1.1). Therefore, the education of a wildlife manager should include study not only of wildlife biology and management, but also of basic sciences, such as chemistry and meteorology, and applied sciences related to land use, such as forestry, agriculture, and economics (King 1938a).

Principles are neither unchallengeable nor unchanging. They may be widely accepted today and become expanded, modified, or discarded and replaced, as new knowledge provides new insight. Accepted principles such as the earth is flat, atoms are indivisible, and species are immutable have suffered such fates. In wildlife management, it has been widely accepted that large carnivores will control the abundance of deer populations. This principle was based largely on

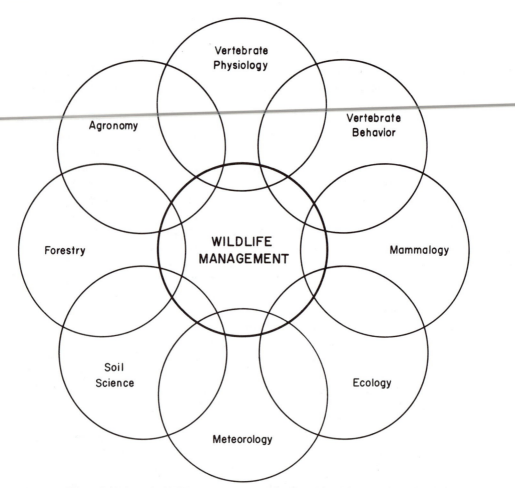

Fig. 1.1   The principles of wildlife management, portrayed by the central circle, include many concepts shared with several sciences and other professions, only a few of which are shown. Wildlife management requires application of an abundance and diversity of information and is one of the most complex of occupations.

experience in northern Arizona and New Mexico, where an eruption of deer followed the elimination of wolves and reduction of puma. The example and concept were used in many ecology texts. Caughley recently challenged these conclusions based on the Arizona–New Mexico experience (1970). Recent studies have shown that large carnivores *may* have little influence on the abundance of ungulates, depending on many population and habitat factors. The concept of predator control of ungulate abundance has now been expanded and complicated by these factors. The old principle has been expanded and modified.

Principles presented in this text should likewise be challenged. These principles are merely the concepts that one person—this author—thinks are important and widely accepted today.

WILDLIFE CONSERVATION

Wildlife management is a part of wildlife conservation. A review of the conservation process clarifies the role of management in the process, its necessary interactions with other conservation activities, and how the limitations and opportunities of wildlife management are usually determined by interactions among several of these activities. Most wildlife managers participate in several activities in the conservation process because some of their efforts involve administration, education, law enforcement, and research.

Wildlife conservation is a social process encompassing both lay and professional activities that define and seek to attain wise use of wildlife resources and maintain the productivities of wildlife habitats. Wildlife managers, research biologists, administrators, extension agents, and also mining company lobbyists and members of the Sierra Club, the Wilderness Society, and local rod-and-gun clubs, among others, participate in this process. I define conservation in this way to emphasize the need for communication among participants in conservation and to emphasize the dynamics of conservation. I believe the success of many wildlife management programs has been limited by deficient communications and by a conservatism that has stifled ingenuity and created resistance to change.

There are other definitions of conservation. Conservation defined simply as "wise use of resources" is inadequate because there are many opinions on what uses are wise. These opinions change as national, state, or local priorities are buffeted by surpluses and scarcities and by crises such as unemployment, a negative balance in foreign trade, or war.

Aldo Leopold once defined conservation as "man living in harmony with the land." I like this philosophical definition, but it is still subject to the different opinions on what constitutes harmony. To one "conservationist," harmony may involve habitat management to produce a harvestable surplus of wildlife on a sustained-yield basis. To another conservationist, wildlife's sole purpose is to exist, to be enjoyed visually, and to be a part of untouched nature; harvest is immoral. Some conservationists reconcile the different opinions by classifying animals as either game or nongame. But people will argue about the classification of species such as doves, cranes, and swans as game or nongame. Both sides of the argument make claims to wisdom and harmony with the land.

Leopold's beautiful writings have served the profession of wildlife conservation well, and our land would be in worse condition today without his influence on our definitions of wise use (1949; 1953). However, his influence also poses a hazard that young professionals must guard against. The beauty of Leopold's writing and philosophy have created, in some, a passionate self-righteousness. The fervor of a natural resources philosophy untempered by reality has led some to unrealistic and unproductive positions on the uses of land. These individuals have not been able to compromise and have lost their opportunity to influence land-use decisions. A symptom of this near-religious attitude has been the sometimes-heard statement "We must do what is good for the resource." The statement is usually followed by someone's opinion of "what is good for the resource." In reality, it is an *opinion* of what is good for some people who use the resource. The resource itself makes no decisions about what is good or evil. It does not know if it is well off or being degraded. Only people have these opinions.

Many laymen and some professionals have developed their philosophy while neglecting a knowledge of biology. Professional biologists should develop both. They should be neither naive poet-naturalists nor technically competent barbarians.

There are two problems with the "wise use" and "harmony" definitions of conservation. First, they allow professional biologists to decide in their own minds what should be "harmony with the land." They then may claim exclusive right to wisdom in dealing with natural resources and, thus, neglect the biases of their backgrounds and educations and fail to see the legitimate claims of others to natural resources. This tendency has produced an authoritarian approach to managing public resources. The public has been told to accept "good" forestry or "good" wildlife management without question. Range managers and wildlife managers, who should have been communicating and cooperating in developing land-management plans, have clung uncompromisingly and often unproductively to their own biased opinions of wise resource use.

Second, these definitions have not described what conservationists do besides having opinions on what constitutes wise use of resources; these definitions have not put the professional conservationist's job in perspective. In contrast, the definition of conservation as a social process emphasizes the historical development of attitudes and practices related to resource use. It emphasizes communication among professionals in the natural resources field, the need for two-way communication with the owners of public resources, and changes that occur in goals, in wildlife habitats, and in our knowledge of wildlife biology. I prefer this practical definition of wildlife conservation in the hope that it will foster an interdisciplinary attitude toward management of natural resources and that it will weaken the stagnation that sometimes grips management priorities and practices. Biologists must be prepared for and participate in change.

Although there are many definitions of wise use and compromises must be made, my definition of wildlife conservation will not accept uses of the wildlife resource that destroy the productivities of wildlife habitats. A piece of land may produce corn and pheasants or grazing and prairie chickens; forest land may lend itself to timber production and deer hunting or wilderness recreation and wilderness wildlife. The products vary, but the productivity remains. However, if land is used for purposes that destroy its capacity for producing wildlife—permanently or temporarily—then wildlife conservation has been disregarded in favor of other uses of the land. There is nothing inherently wrong with this. We do it whenever we develop land for housing or industry or strip-mine land for coal. We will continue to dedicate some lands to these uses. Wildlife conservation returns to the scene if we decide to develop urban wildlife habitat or to revegetate strip-mined land. These decisions are made in the marketplace and through the political process. If democracy works, can our use of the land ever be too far from what the people accept as wise? Yet, there should be limits to what our society can rationalize as wisdom in the use of resources. These limits will result from personal philosophies, ethics, and values, as is discussed in Chapter 2.

The professional activities in wildlife conservation are research, education, administration, law enforcement, and management. I have classified these into the scientific, socioeconomic, and management sectors of the wildlife conservation process for discussing their interrelated roles in conservation (Fig. 1.2).

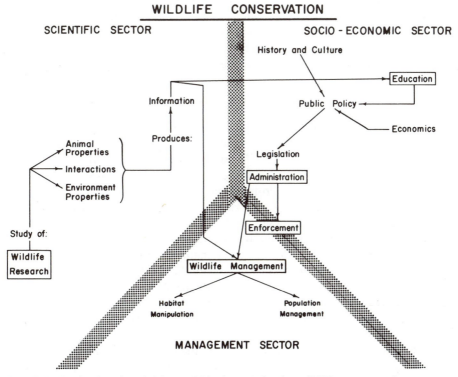

Fig. 1.2 Professional activities (within boxes) in the wildlife conservation process. Arrows indicate flows of information. In the scientific sector, the question "What is possible?" is asked. In the socioeconomic sector, "What do we want?" is asked.

Wildlife research involves study of animals and the environments that, through evolution, they have become adapted to and dependent on. In the scientific sector we ask: What is possible? What are the potentials and limitations of the wildlife resource? What products and services *might* be derived from it? How can these be produced and harvested? What will the cost be? Wildlife research also involves study of people who use the resources. What kinds of people violate game laws? How many hunters can we expect on a Saturday opening day? Research is a continuing process. Answers to questions are often incomplete and change as new research is completed and new questions are asked.

Results of wildlife research serve as a basis for management and administrative decisions, as well as to promote public awareness of the problems and potentials of wildlife. Taking the information to the public is a professional conservation activity. Public awareness enhances the formulation of realistic goals for using resources and the elimination of practices based on incorrect assumptions of the past or practices related to obsolete goals or former circumstances. For example, the American public has set aside certain large wilderness areas, partly in response to resource exploitation of the past and partly on the assumption that most wildlife, white-tailed deer in particular, will thrive and become abundant in undisturbed environments. However, without disturbance, biotic succession may produce monotonous habitat and a wilderness with few white-tailed deer. Whatever the American people's current decision is on how much land should be wilderness, the decision is less wise to the extent that it is based on false assumptions.

In the socioeconomic sector (Fig. 1.2), we ask the questions: What do we want? Considering the biological possibilities, what products and services do we choose? What are we willing to pay for them? How will we distribute the benefits and the costs? In this sector, wildlife conservation overlaps with other social processes. Other goals compete with the goals of wildlife conservation for our attention and financial support. Professional wildlife conservationists working in the socioeconomic sector are educators and administrators. Wildlife education includes the training of professionals to work in conservation and also the extension of information to the public, for purposes noted above.

Public policy determines the goals for managing public wildlife. Agencies responsible for the management of wildlife should communicate frequently with the public they serve. People should be informed of their options for using the public resource. The agency should be aware of public sentiment and priorities. This two-way communication maintains public support for agency programs that serve the public's will.

Awareness of wildlife problems and potentials is not the only influence on public policy. Other resources are considered and, in most places, take precedence over the production of wildlife. On agricultural land, wildlife is a secondary product. Most wildlife values are luxuries, available when people limit their demands on natural resources so that concessions can be made for producing wildlife. When people allow strip mining of land and pollution of rivers and bays, they are expressing their priorities, and wildlife values are set aside in many places. Those who deplore such results must communicate their disgust, seeking to change priorities.

History and culture have great and often unrecognized effects on public policy. Public reactions to land-use problems create laws, programs, and attitudes that tend to persist after the problems disappear. In America, the conservation movement gained lasting influence out of the rebellion against irresponsible lumbering, unlimited commercial hunting, uncontrolled forest fires, and dust storms during the period from about 1900 to 1935. Among the results of this influence were rigid programs of wilderness protection, abhorrence of all forest and range fires, and unwillingness to harvest female big game.

In New York, the Adirondack wilderness was created in reaction to forest exploitation. It persisted despite recurring proposals for multiple use of Adirondack resources. Although most New Yorkers favored having places to hike and camp, hunt deer, and harvest timber, the attitude persisted that forest land could not be used without resource destruction. New Yorkers mistrusted multiple use. They had not seen it successfully applied. Some remembered past irresponsible uses of land. Others had learned of past abuses. A culture opposing multiple use persisted, even among people who had given the concept little serious thought or study.

Until recently, our policy regarding fire on forest and range lands was quite rigid: All fires were bad—every fire, and everywhere. This policy was a reaction to an era of destructive, uncontrolled fires. Despite growing evidence of the value of controlled fire in many biotic communities, it has taken half a century to weaken the antifire policy.

The tradition for bucks-only deer harvests grew out of the rebellion against overharvesting and the disappearance of game in earlier days. This tradition has been reinforced by many aspects of our culture, such as urban living, which favors acceptance of unrealistic, anthropomorphic books and films about animals. Furthermore, a tradition has developed that it is somehow more honorable to harvest a buck than to harvest a doe.

The study of history helps us understand the conservation policies of today and serves as a guide to the future. Awareness of conservation history demonstrates that priorities and practices have not always been what they are and that they can be changed again. Thus, the perspective of history can be a stimulus for change when change is needed. Without that perspective, the professional conservationist finds stagnation more comfortable. The history of the land illustrates what it once was, is becoming, and could be under a different management program. Whoever is unaware of the land's past is not aware of all its potentials.

Administration is central to the conservation process. More than other professionals, administrators need to communicate with other participants in the process—the public, research biologists, wildlife managers, educators, enforcement personnel, and people in agencies responsible for resources other than wildlife. Administrators continuously evaluate public sentiments and needs, arrange priorities, and plan for achieving publicly defined goals. They set broad goals and budgets for wildlife managers.

The art of wildlife management is practiced in the third sector (Fig. 1.2). Given a set of goals, wildlife managers strive to attain them. They use knowledge that is obtained by research yet they are limited by budgets and because knowledge of wildlife ecology is incomplete in areas and subjects needing further research. Wildlife managers must communicate their needs for more knowledge to the researchers and their needs for more financial support to the administrators. They may succeed in gaining what they need, or they may have to adjust their practices to the realities of these limitations.

Law enforcement exists on the boundary between the management and socioeconomic sectors of conservation (Fig. 1.2). Enforcement of laws to protect wildlife populations is a management-type function. But prevention of wildlife-law violations is also largely an educational process. Potential violators should be informed about wildlife laws and their purposes. An informed public may develop attitudes favorable to wildlife, and this can be the most important deterrent to violations.

This description of professional activities in the wildlife conservation process is simplified and may seem obvious. I have presented it to emphasize the dynamics of priorities and practices and to show how these changes occur. I have seen too many wildlife managers doing what they have always done, only because they have never thought of doing anything different. I have also emphasized the need for communication among participants in wildlife conservation. Professionals have often neglected their constituency. They have not explained their agencies' goals to the public, and they have not assured themselves that agency goals were in fact public goals. A well-informed and interested public is necessary, if professionals are to make their maximum contribution to society. Professionals have often neglected each other. They have not communicated with other agencies, and redundant or conflicting agency programs have resulted. They have not communicated within their own agencies. Researchers have published results in esoteric journals, expecting managers to find them; and managers have made no effort to seek new information or to communicate their research needs. I hope the above description of wildlife conservation will help the professional—be he or she a manager, enforcement officer, or whatever—realize that wildlife conservation is a team effort. A failure anywhere in the scheme presented in Fig. 1.2 will limit performance elsewhere. Communication is one key to overall performance. This includes reading scientific and management-related journals, participation in professional societies, especially The Wildlife Society, and attendance at workshops and short courses.

EXAMPLE 1.1   Conservation of White-tailed Deer in Region II, Michigan

A brief history of white-tailed deer in the northern half of the lower peninsula of Michigan illustrates the conservation process (Bartlett 1950; Jenkins and Bartlett 1959). The example clarifies the role of management in the larger conservation process. It illustrates the complexity of wildlife conservation and the diversity of opinions and motivations of professionals and laymen who participate in determining the fate of wildlife resources. Similar histories of any wildlife resource can be valuable to management biologists who need to understand the causes of their current management problems. A knowledge of history can be useful in finding solutions to current problems.

Pristine Conditions Before 1850, forests of pine and hardwoods dominated northern lower Michigan. In the shade of these tall old trees, there probably was little food within reach of deer. Fires occasionally and locally destroyed the forests, initiating temporary communities of herbs, shrubs, and young trees that fed deer and caused their temporary and local abundance. These areas were no doubt favorite hunting grounds of Indians, fur trappers, and wolves and puma. But much of the land supported few deer, being stocked with tall white pines and hardwoods that attracted lumbermen.

Exploitation Early logging replaced the occasional natural fires of pristine times and created many areas of low-growing food and cover. By 1870, deer had become plentiful and were hunted for meat and hides during a five-month-long season, August through December. Market hunting peaked around 1880, when more than 100,000 carcasses were shipped by rail. The herds could not withstand such exploitation and declined despite increasing restrictions on the taking of deer. In 1881, the season was limited to two months, and deer could no longer be taken in water or with traps. Deer were to be used for food, not for hides alone, and carcasses were not to be shipped out of state. In 1883, the season was reduced to one month, and in 1887, hunting with dogs was outlawed. In 1895, the first bag limit—five deer—was imposed. The number was reduced to three deer in 1901, when market hunting was banned. In addition to excessive harvests, forest fires caused by carelessness became so frequent and widespread that the previously beneficial effect of fire on deer habitat became a destructive force. The deer population declined to a low around 1900 to 1910. The wolf and puma appear to have been extirpated from lower Michigan by this time.

In 1884, a group of wealthy businessmen established the Turtle Lake Club on 25,000 acres of Alpena County. Most members were from Detroit, and a visit to the club included a boat trip on Lake Huron and a wagon ride to the area. This seemingly unrelated event was to have much influence on deer management in Region II.

Public Reaction Exploitation similar to that in Michigan occurred throughout the eastern United States before 1900. Public reaction to denuded forests, devastating fires, and extirpated or scarce game resulted in laws, programs, and attitudes that persist today. Major changes occurred during 1900 to 1925. In northern lower Michigan, some of the ravaged land came under public ownership. Quite successful control of forest fires was achieved by 1915. Whereas about 2 million acres burned annually in

Michigan in the late 1800s, only about 200,000 acres burned each year in the 1920s, and the figure was further reduced to about 5000 acres per year in the 1950s. The "buck law," restricting harvesting to deer having at least 3-inch antlers, was instituted in 1921. In that year, only 4 out of 27 counties in northern lower Michigan were open to deer hunting.

The Deer "Explosion" Events prior to 1925 created a utopia for deer in the northern lower peninsula during the 1920s. Major predators were gone. Harvest was limited to males, having no effect on that part of the herd producing annual crops of fawns. Fires had created vast areas of low vegetation, ideal habitat for deer, and fire control was permitting these habitats to persist as long as young trees remained within reach of hungry deer. By 1925, deer numbers and deer hunting had improved greatly. There seemed to be deer everywhere. The success of Turtle Lake Club as a deer-hunting preserve for its limited membership attracted others to establish private clubs nearby. Eventually, 90 percent of a 500-square-mile area in northeastern lower Michigan became privately owned "club land." Club members limited access to these lands and thus limited possibilities for harvesting more than very few deer.

In 1928, Felix Salton published a book having as much influence on deer management in Michigan as any previous or subsequent text. The book was *Bambi*.

The club lands were first to show evidence of too many deer for the forage resources—as early as 1930 (Fig. 1.3). Some forage plants appeared heavily used and damaged. Deer starved to death in severe winters. The problem area spread during the

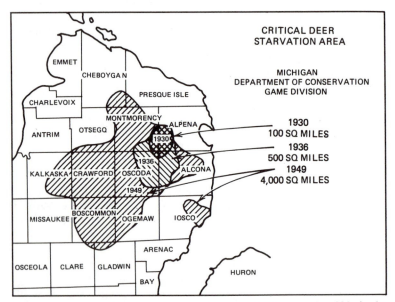

Fig. 1.3 Losses of Michigan deer to malnutrition began in the 1930s in the "club lands" area where few deer were harvested because of abundant private ownership and limited public access. From Bartlett 1950, courtesy of Michigan Department of Natural Resources.

1930s and 1940s. Not only was the loss of deer a problem, the abundant, foraging deer damaged orchards, agricultural crops, and tree plantations. The conservation of deer became intimately related to the conservation of other natural resources.

Early management of the deer problem proved unsuccessful. As early as 1927, trees and shrubs were planted to replace browsed-out food supplies. Poor planting sites limited their survival, and the abundant deer consumed the remaining plants. Feeding deer with hay proved impractical. Most wintering areas were inaccessible, preventing feeding at reasonable costs. Where feeding was possible, it did not eliminate starvation. If feeding did carry more deer through some winters, these animals merely added to the already serious damage being done to the natural forage plants. Cutting timber in overbrowsed wintering areas to stimulate new growth within reach of deer produced limited results. In Region II, there was little commercially valuable timber at this time. Harvest areas were small and scattered. Deer nibbled off the new growth before it could produce much food.

The deer problem led the Michigan Department of Conservation into deer research in the 1930s. A study of deer food habits began in the Cusino wintering area of the upper peninsula at this time. Simple but important concepts of deer biology were learned. White-tailed deer have traditionally used wintering areas, called yards, and will return to them annually despite the scarcity of suitable forage. Not all vegetation is suitable forage. Preferred forages are nutritious to deer, but many plants are eaten only if necessary, and deer cannot survive on them. It became clear from the study that habitat management must be directed at a certain few of the many species of plants in deer yards. Fire control was permitting reforestation of vast areas where forage was growing out of the reach of deer. Thus, the abundant deer herds of the 1930s and 1940s were existing on a declining forage resource. the most malnourished deer produced the fewest fawns (Fig. 1.4). Studies of deer hunting showed that, with a bucks-only hunt, many unantlered deer were shot and left in the woods, a wasted resource. However, conservation department budgets could not provide adequate law enforcement to alleviate this waste.

These concepts were the basis for new proposals for managing deer. It was becoming increasingly evident that herds should be reduced to a level in balance with food supplies. Experience showed that the herds could not be reduced with bucks-only harvests.

In 1941, Felix Salton's *Bambi* was made into a children's movie. Meanwhile, Michigan had become an urban state. Most of its people lived in cities and had little contact with the land. They were unaware of what every farmer knows: Too many cattle in a pasture will destroy the pasture and soon become an unproductive, sickly herd. Urbanites seldom saw Michigan's deer in winter. They did not know the ugliness of malnutrition, the barrenness of the deer yards, the destruction of trees, crops, and deer forage. Their views were easily influenced, mostly by unrealistic and sometimes anthropomorphic presentations of wildlife in books and movies such as *Bambi*. Sentimentalist attitudes grew, and opposition to harvest of antlerless deer resulted.

In 1941, each camp of four hunters was allowed to harvest one unantlered deer. This was a token approach to controlling the herd. The citizens of Michigan opposed the harvest of does; some opposed hunting of any kind. The most vocal accused the Department of Conservation of lying about the condition of the herds; a sellout to the timber companies was sometimes implied. Memories of the era of exploitation lingered. However, one ecologist suggested that if the herds could not be controlled by

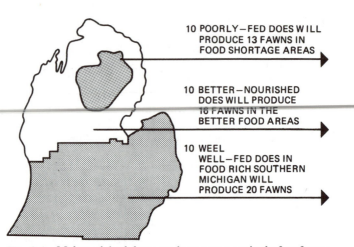

Fig. 1.4   Malnourished deer produce comparatively few fawns. A hundred poorly fed does from the food-shortage areas would produce as many fawns as would 65 well-fed does from southern Michigan. Reducing deer numbers to levels balanced with supplies of good forage can result in increased rates of reproduction. This increase could support larger annual harvests. From Jenkins and Bartlett 1959, courtesy of Michigan Department of Natural Resources.

hunting, timber industries could control deer by cutting the conifer forests needed by deer for winter cover.

The Department of Conservation took its case to the people. As early as 1939, the extension division of Michigan State College sponsored 4-H Club studies of winter deer yards (Welch and Kettunen 1939). Department personnel led "show-me" trips to expose sportsmen to the realities of deer ecology in winter. Teachers and community leaders were told of the deer situation at club meetings and at the Higgens Lake Training School. The history of Michigan's deer and their habitat was presented in booklets in 1950 (Bartlett) and again in 1959 (Jenkins and Bartlett). The latter publication, illustrated by Oscar Warbach's clever cartoons, was especially designed to reach the public (Fig. 1.5).

In the late 1950s American Boxboard Company, in need of wood for its paper mill at Manistee, contracted with landowners in the club lands, Turtle Lake Club included, to manage their forests and wildlife. By mutual agreement, American Boxboard would buy and harvest aspen from the club lands, would manage aspen on a sustained-yield basis, and would improve habitat for deer and other wildlife. The program was soon in serious jeopardy, however. Deer on the club lands were consuming so much aspen reproduction that the possibility of managing aspen on a sustained-yield basis was in doubt, unless the deer herds could be reduced at least locally and temporarily. Reducing the herds would be difficult. First, there was public opposition to harvesting doe deer. Then, there were club traditions for limited memberships. Last, there was the legal question of the liability of club members if nonmembers who might be allowed to harvest deer on club lands were to be injured while hunting. Legal matters had entered wildlife conservation from an unexpected direction.

Fig. 1.5   Not all plants are good deer forage and not all forage is available to deer during Michigan winters. Evaluation of deer food resources requires knowledge of deer food habits and of winter snow conditions From Jenkins and Bartlett 1959, courtesy of Michigan Department of Natural Resources.

During a 110-year period, public conceptions of goals for managing Michigan's deer changed and diversified. At first, deer were a resource to be taken for meat and hides. When deer became scarce around 1900 to 1910, most everyone wanted more deer again—this time for meat and recreation to be enjoyed by Michigan's now numerous citizens, not by a few commercial hunters. As deer numbers grew, some people wanted sufficient herd control to reduce damage to crops and trees. Others wanted only to maximize harvestable surpluses. Still others wanted to increase hunting recreation hours, not necessarily the harvest. Tourism grew as highways and cars improved, and seeing deer during summer became a new goal. However, deer auto accidents also increased, and highway safety became another goal of deer management. For many people, management methods became intricately involved with management goals—they opposed harvesting doe deer.

The example ends about 1960, for I am not familiar with Michigan deer problems since then. But further description is unnecessary. The interplay of many factors in the conservation process has been illustrated. Consider how public policy was influenced by history (the lasting reaction to the era of exploitation), by culture (*Bambi*, city living), by economics (deer competition with other resources), and by education (extension programs, publications). Consider how management was once limited by a lack of research (for example, of deer food habits), by legal restraints (the bucks-only law, liability laws), and by land ownership patterns (club lands). Actually, the process has been more complex than described, just as Fig. 1.2 was a simplified representation.

Wildlife management is not practiced in a vacuum. It is a part of the complex conservation process that places many constraints on the wildlife manager. Young wildlife managers are often frustrated because problems such as resistance to change, ignorance, or poor professional performance elsewhere in the conservation process hinder their efforts to manage according to their personal goals and convictions. But wildlife managers are not hired to make public wildlife resources into private hobbies. They are hired to produce public benefits, however clearly or unclearly the public has defined its intentions. The conservation process is no more cumbersome than any other democratic process. Wildlife managers must work within this process, must recognize the limitations placed on management, and should encourage and participate in efforts elsewhere in the process. They may become involved in public education, in law enforcement, or in determining and publicizing the economic values of wildlife resources. Their efforts in these areas may be necessary before they can improve their contributions within the management sector of the conservation process.

PRINCIPLES

Pl.1 Wildlife includes all free-ranging vertebrate animals in the naturally associated environments that have determined their evolution.

Pl.2 Wildlife conservation is a dynamic social process that defines and seeks to attain wise use of wildlife resources, while maintaining the productivities of wildlife habitats. This process is strongly influenced by practices and attitudes of the past. It includes the professional activities of management, research, education, administration, and law enforcement. Laymen, especially organized groups, participate in wildlife conservation through a continuous political process that defines and redefines *wise use*.

CHAPTER 2

RESOURCE CONSERVATION AND THE QUALITY OF LIFE

A qualitative conception of progress
is premised on the assumption that
enlarging the range of individual
experience is as important as
enlarging the number of individuals.

Aldo Leopold, 1925

A PHILOSOPHY OF RESOURCE USE

This chapter describes a philosophical basis for resource management. The philosophy is a system of personal ideals, principles, and morals. It is presented for two reasons. First, the definition of conservation presented in Chapter 1 includes the term *wise use*, which cannot be clarified without resorting to personal philosophies. Second, although wildlife managers need to know *how* to manage wildlife, they must also know *why*. If they are to succeed, they must be convinced that the job is worthwhile. Such a conviction arises from personal philosophy. The reader need not embrace the philosophy presented here. I merely suggest that he or she consider it in developing his or her own ideas and ideals.

Wildlife production is intimately related to land use and to other land resources. The philosophy we must consider is one pertinent to all natural resources and all their uses.

Conservation is a form of morality because it is practiced not for immediate personal and material reward, but mainly for future benefits to communities, states, and the nation. Our philosophy must depend heavily on concepts of morality that provide direction and motivation to wildlife managers. Biologists should believe that wildlife management is significant and valuable to our society. This belief is based on a strong appreciation of wildlife values and on a personal commitment to contribute to the quality of life for all our people. The student of wildlife management should develop his or her philosophy of resource conservation. It can provide a basis and motivation for a satisfying career. Without it, wildlife management will be just another job. Another basis for entering the profession of wildlife management is usually a love for animals and the out-of-doors. This basis alone will not sustain and motivate a biologist in all endeavors, because much that is important in wildlife management is practiced indoors and involves negotiations with people.

Wise uses of resources are those that are consistent with or provide progress toward goals of the community, state, and nation. A society having well-defined and widely agreed-on goals can easily define wise use for its resources. Our discussion of conservation must, therefore, include a consideration of goals, in this case goals for the United States. (I have sufficient audacity to think I know something of the motivations of people in my own country—no others. However, other nations may find the American experience useful in charting their own course.) If we can agree on some basic goals for our society, then land-use and wildlife-management decisions can be judged wise or unwise with respect to those goals.

GOALS FOR AMERICA

Does contemporary American society have a fundamental goal against which all actions, public and private, are judged? Are decisions to build a dam or highway, to locate a power plant, to open a mine, or to control a population of wolves related to any basic idea of what's good for our people in the long run? Are legal and social sanctions for abusing the land or wasting resources based on any widely accepted idea of social responsibility that is derived from an American consensus of what is a quality life and a quality environment?

The Sidetracked Society

In 1776, we agreed that governments were instituted among men to secure certain inalienable rights for all men, that among these were life, liberty, and the pursuit of happiness. With this goal in mind, our society was formed. Our goal was freedom; and when we added 10 amendments to our Constitution, it became clear that we meant freedom for the individual. Everyone was to have his or her own right to the pursuit of happiness.

But by 18th-century standards, the United States was an economically depressed area, and freedom is limited when people must spend most of their time procuring the necessities of life. Opportunities to use freedom could be expanded and diversified if our land contained more than small towns, small farms, and wilderness. We needed efficient production of necessities and luxuries. We needed the cultural opportunities of cities—theater, education, music, libraries, sports arenas, and museums. We needed efficient transportation. These would expand the horizons of free people. There was commitment to build these things to add dimension to our national goal of freedom.

So it became patriotic, consistent with the national goal, to develop the land, to be successful in business, and to raise large families and populate the country. Such patriotism could not long be separated from accepted concepts of morality. Growth and development became a new ethic. At first, the goal and the morality were freedom; development of the land was a means to expand the goal. But in time, the means became as important as the goal. To those who could forget our national heritage, development became more important.

As economic growth became an ethic, a morality not to be questioned, it became equal to other concepts of morality (Adams 1931). It was not subservient to or controlled by longer established concepts of morality—not even to freedom. There was, and there continues to be, much rationalization of morality on this basis. We have evolved one set of ethics for interpersonal relations and another set of standards for business relations. We have rationalized the existence of child labor, the economic slavery of company towns and migrant labor camps, resource waste and polluted human habitats—all in the name of economic growth. The perpetrators of these immoralities were not necessarily immoral in their personal and nonbusiness relations. For example, there were both legal and social sanctions on these businessmen to neatly landscape their suburban homes, while all was ugliness at their places of business. This double standard was accepted because economic growth was a separate ethic. How often have we heard, "I know, but business is business"?

Our history illustrates how having a well-defined and widely accepted most-important goal will stimulate efficiency, determination, simplicity, and rapid progress. The primary goal of freedom was sufficiently accepted to permit our 13 poor colonies to resist a more powerful England in 1776 and again in 1812. The widely accepted goal of development—our "manifest destiny"—mobilized our efforts as the United States spread across the continent and became a world power in a remarkably short time.

Today we are faced with immobilization, inefficiency, a lack of determination, tremendous complexity—especially in government, conflicting programs, and nonviolent (usually) obstructionism. We cannot measure progress because we have not agreed where to go. Without a compass, the ship of state luffs and jibes while hands argue to control the rudder.

Our problems are a symptom of our collective search for a new goal upon which to guide our course. We are in the process of abandoning the ethic of growth and development. Perhaps our younger generation already has. We have become sidetracked from our original goal of freedom. We realize that although growth and development have expanded the opportunities for freedom, too much growth and development are now restricting freedom. Our most important task is to redefine goals for America. We need goals that are few in number and widely accepted. These goals must be simple enough for broad understanding and practical application to daily decisions, yet profound enough to encompass our personal aspirations and our moral convictions. Until we find these goals, our efforts at government will remain chaotic and inefficient.

The Ultimate Morality

The obvious choice for Americans is to return to the primacy of the goal of freedom. We have the legal basis for freedom in our Constitution. However, laws only prescribe freedom; they do not guarantee it. Only a productive and diverse environment can permit freedom. I hope Americans will soon recognize this and that public programs and resource-use decisions will be evaluated according to their enhancement or constraint of the environmental prerequisites of freedom.

Productivity and diversity of environments determine the abundance and availability of material and spiritual forms of wealth in the United States. Freedom is access to these forms of wealth. I do not use *wealth* in the strictly economic sense. Material wealth includes the necessities of food and shelter and luxuries like cars and television. There is also spiritual wealth, including privacy, education, man-made and natural beauty, and wilderness and peace-and-quiet. The two kinds of wealth are complementary. We cannot enjoy one kind without some of the other. A minimum of material wealth for survival is necessary if we are to enjoy any spiritual wealth; and the better our basic material needs are met, the more time and opportunity we have to enjoy spiritual wealth. Freedom of thought and expression is a spiritual wealth made more meaningful by the existence of a printing and publishing industry with retail stores and libraries. On the other hand, spiritual wealth may help us to enjoy material things. A fine car is more enjoyable if one has freedom of movement and a scenic place to visit. One can turn up one's stereo if one has the privacy of a home separated from one's neighbors, or one can enjoy the stereo played softly if one has the quiet of a home removed from jet runways and busy streets.

It is a problem that spiritual wealth, important as it is, cannot be measured and is often neglected or inadequately considered in the economic analyses that often determine the character of the environments people live in. As our population grows, we are, ever more frequently, choosing among things of value. A piece of land cannot be a duck marsh and a throughway, too. Florida needed a new, larger jet airport, but its construction would have endangered Everglades National Park. An Illinois city wanted river water for domestic and industrial purposes, including to dilute its growing quantity of sewage-plant effluent. To provide this water so the city could grow, it was proposed to flood miles of river valley, including some of the world's best farm land, an important public park, and most of what little wooded, semiwild land remained in the intensively used, monotonous corn-and-soybean landscape of central Illinois. We need throughways, airports, and water. We also need duck marshes, parks, and wild places. And we need the latter near where people live. But the pressure of population growth and the demands for economic growth on our static resources are forcing us to choose. When we choose, material wealth is often enhanced at the expense of spiritual wealth. It is a symptom of our sidetracked approach to decision making.

Spiritual wealth is often neglected because it is more variable and elusive than material wealth. What some enjoy, others dislike. Some prefer art museums and the theater; others, a wilderness hunting camp. Some a city apartment; others a small-town home. Some prefer campfire smoke in their eyes and the yipping of coyotes to cigarette smoke and rock music. No one should proclaim some types of recreation as being "higher" or "better for the soul of man" than others. (If it turns you on and bothers no one else—enjoy it!) But forms of spiritual wealth held dear by minorities are often lost without much notice by the majority, and our environments thus become less diverse. Is this the ultimate morality of our society?

Our overconcern with material wealth seems illogical, partly because we can use substitutes for material things and be none the less wealthy. Our roof may be made of shingles, impregnated plywood, asphalt, or fiberglass. We can be just as happy with substitutes, so long as the roof does not leak. But substitution does not apply as well to spiritual wealth. If we run out of open space in which to hunt and fish near home, we can go bowling instead. Are we just as wealthy when we might have had hunting and fishing as well as bowling? Is not variety of opportunity one form of spiritual wealth?

If the ultimate morality of our society is to be concerned for the freedom of individuals and, therefore, for the maintenance and enhancement of environments that enhance freedom, we cannot continue to choose with increasing frequency among things of value. We must provide for a great variety of both material and spiritual wealth. Our standard of living and the qualities of our lives and environments should be measured by our success at providing a variety of opportunities for individual self-expression. I can see no other measure, no other ultimate goal for our society. The productivity and diversity of environments are equally important in achieving this goal. But we have been emphasizing productivity and ignoring diversity (Dasmann 1968). If we are to retain meaningful freedom in the United States, we must begin to emphasize the enhancement and maintenance of diversity of opportunities and environments in our land-use decisions.

DETERMINANTS OF THE QUALITY OF LIFE

The diversity and per capita abundance of material and spiritual forms of wealth are determined by five factors: resources, knowledge, attitude, conservation, and population size. Similar classifications of factors affecting the optimization of human life have been discussed by Hawley (1950), Sears (1957), and Duncan (1959).

Resources

I define resources as all the materials and processes in the universe, known and unknown. Materials include minerals, soil, water, gene pools, and space. Processes include gravity, radiation, evolution, biotic succession, and the many ways in which energy may be transferred. This is what we have to work with. We will never have more.

Economists may not consider unknown materials and processes to be resources. According to this point of view, the coal of North America was not a resource to the American Indians, who did not know how to use coal. From this concept, economists point to resources as an economic factor that grows to support our expanding economy. This idea, in turn, has supported open-system economic theory based on assumptions of an infinite cesspool for absorption of wastes. The question is purely semantic, but I prefer to separate knowledge from nature and to emphasize that resources can produce more for the welfare of man* only as man makes the effort to learn more about his resources. This emphasis avoids the complacent impression that resources can grow and places the responsibility for expanding the good life squarely where it belongs—on the shoulders of man.

---

*In using *man*, I refer to *Homo sapiens*, both male and female.

Resources may be concentrated and easily available, or they may be diluted and remote. As our nation has grown, we have degraded and used up some of our most concentrated and available resources. Many wildlife resources have been eliminated. We are becoming more dependent on resources that are attained at greater expense in labor and energy and with greater possibilities of environmental damage. Our options for using resources have diminished.

Knowledge

Knowledge determines our ability to use resources—more specifically, to discover them, to harvest or use them at minimum expense, to make and provide a variety of material and spiritual forms of wealth from them, and to distribute this wealth among our people. Knowledge results from experience, scientific research, and education. These are luxuries of a society with time and capital to spare. A society demanding a rapid expansion of wealth cannot learn from experience how to produce that wealth in the most efficient and safe manner. (If we *must* make widespread use of a new pesticide to keep pace with our large and expanding demand for food, we will have little time to study or test in a limited way the hazards of the poison.) A society that has squandered its most accessible resources must pay the price of using its less available resources and is thereby less able to fund research and education.

Attitude

The manner in which knowledge is used may be more important than the mere availability of knowledge. Efficient use of knowledge is determined by public attitude—a product of the constantly changing philosophies and apathies of our people. Our attitudes either stimulate or permit activities that may increase or decrease our quality of life. On the one hand, our social and economic activities may be purposeful and vigorous. This has been the case through much of U. S. history, as people responded in comparative unity to the challenge of development and expansion in a social climate that fostered a sometimes ruthlessly competitive spirit. On the other hand, we may lack a clear definition of our goals and sink into apathy, the worst enemy of democracy. Our sidetracked society has in recent decades promoted such apathy. The inefficiency of government today, with contradictory programs and layers of agencies that control, analyze, and reconsider, is a symptom of our search for clear purpose and unifying goals. In the decades ahead, we should learn how to maintain vigorous and purposeful social and economic activity without stimulation from easily accessible resources, imprudent resource exploitation, an expanding population, and anti-social, excessive economic competition. We will not achieve this kind of social and economic activity until we have more agreement on what kind of America we are trying to build.

Conservation

Conservation, as used here, is our willingness to maintain the productivities of renewable resources and prevent waste of nonrenewable resources. Conservation in the past has determined the resources available today. Conservation now will determine the status of resources for the future.

Population

Resources, knowledge, attitude, and conservation determine the quantity and diversity of material and spiritual wealth we are able to produce and make available to people. Simply put, this wealth must somehow be shared, and the more people, the smaller the average share. Population size and growth rate also influence our quality of life by their negative impacts on the conditions of resources and on knowledge. Excess numbers of people are associated with wastes and pollutants and with intensive and monotonous use of resources, particularly space. These trends decrease the diversity and productivities of resources. A rapid rate of population growth with rapidly expanding demands for all forms of wealth will limit the time available to expand knowledge by testing methods for management and development of resources. Further, the smaller the average share of wealth, the less surplus will be diverted into research and education that can increase the amount and availability of knowledge. For a more thorough discussion of this topic, see Ehrlich and Ehrlich (1970).

Population growth may restrict our freedom by destroying the productivities and diversities of environments. It also restricts freedom directly. With population growth, it is inevitable that we increase the coordination of our activities by passing laws that now regulate almost everything we do. There is ever less room for individualism. As we create a more monotonous culture, we destroy a source of new ideas—the "cultural slack" that permits divergence from established patterns and progress into new and perhaps better ways of life (Boulding 1968).

Population growth that causes demands for wealth to grow faster than knowledge can be expanded and used to provide the wealth, has forced us to choose among forms of wealth. When we choose between a hydroelectric dam and a free-flowing river, the idealist must ask: If we did not have so many people, might we have had both adequate electric power and the value of a free-flowing river?

Quality of Life Equation

It is convenient to summarize the five determinants in the equation

$$\text{Quality of Life} = \frac{\text{Resources} + \text{Knowledge} \pm \text{Attitude} + \text{Conservation}}{\text{Population}}$$

In this equation, attitude is a plus-or-minus factor, depending on how it influences the efficiency of application of knowledge to achieve our goals.

Considering this equation, it is no surprise that European man has been so successful in North America. We applied knowledge developed in the Old World to the relatively untapped resources of the New World. We applied this knowledge aggressively with unanimity of purpose, and no previous lack of conservation had seriously impaired our resources. There was room for population expansion, providing time to gain experience in using resources. These factors favored production of excess capital to be spent on research and education, which in turn expanded the knowledge base. Quality of life grew rapidly.

In recent decades, all this has been reversed. Concentrated and accessible resources have been used up. Poor conservation practices have degraded renewable resources. We lack unanimity of purpose and must pay for inefficient programs. Although our population growth has slowed, our demands on resources continue to climb rapidly. We seem less inclined to support research, especially basic research, and even education. But the future does not appear bleak for the United States because we appear to be controlling our population growth. If we do control our numbers, improvements in knowledge, attitude, and conservation may then solve our current environmental problems, and we may again expand the diversity of opportunities for experience and self-expression. We may also once again divert more capital toward expanding our knowledge base.

Resources, knowledge, and population were the subject of Malthus's famous 1798 essay and bleak predictions. His essay set economists arguing over which factor, knowledge or population, should be manipulated to improve our welfare. Frank Lorimer noted that after a century and a half of arguing along well-worn grooves to antagonistic positions in the Malthusian controversy, the world is coming to realize that control of population and advances in knowledge are not *alternative* solutions to our problems; they are complementary and mutually dependent (1963).

MEASURING THE QUALITY OF LIFE

If the goal of American society is to provide for the greatest possible variety of opportunities for human experience and self-expression, the quality of life and the qualities of our environments should be measured by our success in achieving this goal. Decisions on how resources will be used should be made according to how achievement of this goal will be affected. Environmental protection should mean protection of productivity and diversity in the environment. Such decision making will require an ability to measure the breadth of opportunities for individual experience and expression. Figure 2.1 suggests a conceptual framework for measuring quality of life and environment in these terms.

We need to measure the relative availabilities of a large variety of material and spiritual forms of wealth that provide for human experiences. These forms of

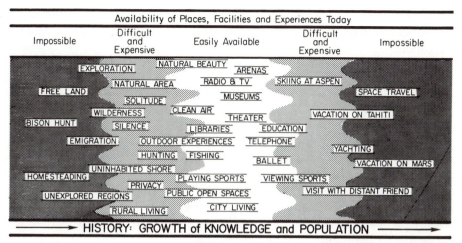

Fig. 2.1 columns and labels:

Availability of Places, Facilities and Experiences Today

| Impossible | Difficult and Expensive | Easily Available | Difficult and Expensive | Impossible |

EXPLORATION · NATURAL BEAUTY · ARENAS
NATURAL AREA · RADIO & TV · SKIING AT ASPEN
FREE LAND · SOLITUDE · MUSEUMS · SPACE TRAVEL
WILDERNESS · CLEAN AIR · VACATION ON TAHITI
THEATER
BISON HUNT · SILENCE · LIBRARIES · EDUCATION
EMIGRATION · OUTDOOR EXPERIENCES · TELEPHONE
HUNTING · FISHING · YACHTING
BALLET · VACATION ON MARS
UNINHABITED SHORE
HOMESTEADING · PLAYING SPORTS · VIEWING SPORTS
PRIVACY
UNEXPLORED REGIONS · PUBLIC OPEN SPACES · VISIT WITH DISTANT FRIEND
RURAL LIVING · CITY LIVING

HISTORY: GROWTH of KNOWLEDGE and POPULATION

Fig. 2.1 Our standard of living in the United States is determined by the breadth of possibilities for variety in human experience and self-expression. The growth of knowledge and of population, in particular, change the relative availabilities of places and facilities for human use, and thus our standard of living.

wealth may be easily available, difficult and expensive to obtain, or impossible to obtain. Figure 2.1 is designed primarily to show past trends in the quality of life in the United States. Favorable changes in knowledge, attitude, and conservation have expanded our quality of life, particularly toward the right side of the figure. In contrast, population growth and unfavorable change in knowledge, attitude, and conservation have been contracting our quality of life, particularly on the left side of the figure. In the United States, the primary determinants have been expansion of knowledge and of population. However, the frontiers of human experience can be expanded in any direction by favorable changes in any of the four variable determinants: knowledge, attitude, conservation, and population.

This concept of quality of life can be a basis for public decision making. We face questions such as: Should a dam or highway be built? Should a town or park be established? Should a city grow larger? Should a deer herd be hunted? Answers should depend largely on how the project or decision will affect the relative availabilities of a diversity of opportunities for human experience. We can quantify these availabilities so that projects and alternatives can be compared more precisely. Development of such quantification methods should be a national research priority.

THE WILDLIFE BIOLOGIST IN ENVIRONMENTAL POLITICS

Wildlife management is important because it produces forms of wealth that are valued by our society. Wild lands and outdoor experiences add importantly to the diversity of our environments and to our breadth of experience. Wildlife are the epitome of wild lands. Experiencing wildlife is often the apex of outdoor recreation.

Wild lands add diversity among areas that are highly developed, intensively used, and often monotonous. Further, wild lands are internally diverse and provide for a great variety of experiences. They are constantly changing in time, variable in space. Wildlife are a part of that diversity, and wildlife management can enhance their values to society.

Many forms of wildlife and many kinds of wild land are in serious jeopardy in the United States today. Many urban dwellers seldom experience wildlife or outdoor recreation—and the proportion of urbanites in our population is increasing. Wildlife management is especially important because wild land experiences are in danger from spreading extirpation and extinction. It is sad that we are destroying opportunities for diversity in our lives. It is immoral that we are destroying these options for future generations.

The wildlife biologist who understands and accepts all that is written in this chapter has good reason for sincere effort in his or her profession. Furthermore, wildlife values are more appreciated and much more important to wildlife biologists than to most other people. Wildlife biologists have worked and studied hard to learn to manage wildlife. They naturally want to apply this knowledge. If the choice were theirs, much land would be dedicated to wildlife production. Budgets for wildlife management would be large. Compromises between wildlife production and other resources would be few.

But the choice is not theirs. Decisions affecting wildlife and habitats are public decisions, made through the political process. Goals for the management of publicly owned resources should be publicly selected goals. Compromises between wildlife, timber, mineral, livestock, and other values must be made. Legislators, commissioners, and other elected or appointed officials determine the emphasis on wildlife production in comparison to other uses of the land. The blend of management goals determined after public hearings and through the political process will almost always include less emphasis on wildlife production than the biologist would like.

In this political process, public input may be sporadic and unbalanced among the various resource users. Wildlife biologists become advocates for wildlife values. They promote wildlife just as miners promote the value of coal production and range managers promote the value of livestock. They best understand the many values of wildlife, and they must interpret them for decision makers and ultimately for the public who elect or accept those decision makers.

Decisions will be made that disappoint the biologist. Mines will be opened, roads will be built, timber will be cut—all in wildlife habitat. Once these decisions are made, it is the biologist's job to develop a mine reclamation plan, request road underpasses for migratory big game, request changes in timber harvesting to favor wildlife habitat. Much wildlife management involves working within the contemporary political and economic system—even if the biologist is unsatisfied with the results of the system. The results are being accepted by the public.

This is a frustrating position, and most biologists are confronted by it. A personal and moral question is posed. How far do biologists compromise their values? At what point can they no longer work within the system? Where must they abandon and challenge the agencies they work for? This brings us back to the question posed in Chapter 1: Where are the limits to what we can rationalize as wise use of resources? Each biologist must find his or her own answer. I suggest the biologist consider the ultimate goals of productivity and diversity. I can accept forgoing wildlife production to produce coal or timber, so long as the land will continue to be productive. Mine reclamation is essential. Timber harvest must be carefully done. I can accept a dam and reservoir for their several values, so long as they do not destroy the habitat of the only remaining herd of bighorn sheep within a hundred miles. To destroy the productivity or diversity of the environment is an injustice to future generations. It is immoral. The biologist should decide whether or not to participate in a project by considering its implications for productivity and diversity of environments.

PRINCIPLES

P2.1   Conservation of wildlife resources is intimately related to conservation of all other natural resources. Conservation is influenced by society's needs, ideals, and morals and by its definition of a quality life for humans.

P2.2   Quality living requires that individuals be free to choose from a variety of life experiences and opportunities for self-expression. A diverse environment, including wild lands and wildlife, is necessary to provide these opportunities. A society's ability to provide a diversity of opportunities for personal experience and self-expression is determined by its resources, knowledge, attitudes, and conservation, all in relation to its population size.

P2.3   Goals for the management of a publicly owned resource are determined through a political process. Wildlife biologists employed by public agencies are expected to predict wildlife responses to land management and to interpret these responses and their implications for realizing wildlife values, so that the public's definition of wise use is not made in ignorance.

CHAPTER 3

WILDLIFE VALUES

The long fight to save wild
beauty represents democracy at
its best. It requires citizens to
practice the hardest of virtues—
self restraint.

Edwin Way Teale

The wildlife manager is responsible for producing wildlife so that several diverse values may be realized. This endeavor requires an awareness of all values of wildlife and of the diverse public and private interests in wildlife.

Most students of wildlife biology do not question the value of wildlife. Wild animals have been important to them—often since childhood—and they may not have given serious thought to questions like, What good are prairie chickens? To a student of prairie ecology, the question at first seems absurd and not meriting an answer. But few Americans see, understand, and cherish prairies anymore. So the question What good are prairie chickens? is asked and must be answered. If wildlife biologists cannot answer clearly and fully, more Americans will fail to appreciate prairies, and none will want to save prairies from plow or bulldozer. Then the question asked will be: What *were* prairie chickens?

More and more in public decisions we see confrontations between wildlife values and the extremely tangible values of reservoirs, highways, subdivisions, and other developments. These confrontations are critical to the future of wildlife. We cannot make the best case for wildlife simply by stating that wildlife values are mostly aesthetic and unmeasurable. Some wildlife values are aesthetic and some cannot be measured—at least not in the common unit of money. Other wildlife values are measurable—even in dollars. If biologists are to argue the case for wildlife against developments that destroy habitats, they must be thoroughly familiar with all wildlife values and some valuation methods (Steinhoff 1971). They must be able to present *both* cases for wildlife—the cold facts of commercial, recreational, biotic, and negative values—and the philosophical, even emotional, side of scientific, aesthetic, and social values. Presenting only an emotional case for wildlife neglects some important values that are commensurable with land development values. Presenting only the cash value of wildlife in a local economy ignores that wildlife values enhance the quality of human life and life is, in essence, an emotional experience. The successful advocate for wildlife will obtain and clearly present statistics on wildlife values and also will communicate what is most difficult to express—the intangible, personal, but real values of wildlife that are especially important to sensitive and perceptive people.

TYPES OF WILDLIFE VALUES

King produced the most complete catalog of wildlife values, and the following discussion is based on his ideas (1966). Wildlife values are (1) commercial, (2) recreational, (3) biotic, (4) scientific, philosophical, and educational, (5) aesthetic, (6) social, and (7) negative.

Commercial Value

The commercial value of wildlife is the capitalized value of the income derived from selling or trading animals or their products, or from conducting a business based on access to wildlife populations. Commercial value can usually be measured in dollars. It includes the value of wild meat and furs harvested in many parts of the world. American deer hunters currently harvest more than $100 million worth of meat annually. Commercial fisheries produce not only meat but fertilizers, livestock feed, and chemicals that support businesses in harvesting, processing, wholesaling, and retailing. Guides, outfitters, sporting goods retailers and wholesalers, motels, restaurants, and transportation industries derive some of their income because people hunt, fish, camp, hike, or otherwise travel and spend money to pursue and enjoy wildlife. Boy scouts in Jackson Hole, Wyoming earned $19,200 in 1973 by collecting elk antlers from the National Elk Refuge and selling them at auction to buyers making jewelry, souvenirs—and aphrodisiacs! A portion of the income of all these businesses and of their employees serves as a basis for measuring the commercial values of the wildlife populations that they depend on.

The local economic impact of commerce generated by wildlife-oriented outdoor recreation is felt beyond the tourist industries directly involved. Dollars spent by recreationists may be exchanged several times in the local economy. For instance, some of the money spent by recreationists on lodging will, in turn, be spent by the motel owner, perhaps on furniture; and the furniture retailer will, in turn, spend some of that income locally. This is called the multiplier effect. It may be as large a factor as 3 or 4. With high levels of tourist spending and because of the multiplier effect, the commercial value of wildlife is great and sometimes critical to the existence of rural communities.

The rate of income production from a wildlife resource is not its capital value. To assess the commercial value of a wildlife resource we must (1) measure the net income from the resource by subtracting business expenses and the value of management's time and labor from gross income, and (2) capitalize the income derived from the resource at some rate of interest normally paid on capital investments. For instance, consider a registered trap line from which the trapper usually sells the annual take of furs for $6000. If his* expenses for equipment and travel average $1000 a year, and if he values his time spent trapping at $1000 a season (perhaps he could earn $1000 working for someone else, if he did not trap), the annual net income from the resource is $4000. (The trapper earns $4000 more than working for someone else *because* he owns access to a productive trap line.) What is the value of access to the trap line—or of the furbearer populations that produce the trapper's extra $4000 annually? If the trapper were to sell access to his trap line, he would have to obtain capital that is capable of producing $4000 annually—or suffer a loss of income. If bank certificates pay 8 percent interest on money deposited, the trapper would have to sell his trap line for $50,000 to maintain his income. Fifty thousand dollars on deposit produce $4000 of income each year—so do the furbearer populations on his trap line. The trap line and its furbearer populations are worth $50,000.

---

*The trapper in this example is male; however, it is recognized that trapping is not exclusively a male profession.

Any business or employment that is dependent on or enhanced by the existence of wildlife realizes a commercial value from wildlife. The total commercial value of a wildlife population is the sum of the capitalized values of all business and employee net incomes dependent on that population.

Recreational Value

People derive benefits of pleasure, adventure, and enhanced physical and mental health from outdoor activities involving the pursuit or sometimes accidental enjoyment of wildlife. These people are hunters, fishermen, bird-watchers, photographers, hikers, campers, and tourists of all kinds. The value they receive is usually measured by their willingness to pay for their outdoor recreation, to the extent that wildlife is wholly, as in hunting, or partly, as in camping, involved.

There have been national, regional, and state surveys of expenditures for wildlife-oriented recreation (for example, U.S. Bureau of Sport Fisheries and Wildlife 1982; Horvath 1974; Nobe and Gilbert 1970). Impressive statistics have resulted (Table 3.1). In addition to about 17 million hunters and 42 million fishermen, there were about 56 million bird-watchers and 12 million wildlife photographers in the United States in 1980. These and other outdoor recreationists spent billions of dollars wholly or partly to enjoy wildlife.

State studies produce similarly impressive data on the importance of commercial and recreational wildlife values. In 1980, fishermen spent $598 million and hunters spent $442 million in Colorado. Capitalizing this value at 10 percent, because Colorado and non-resident sportsmen reap this recreational value every year, the recreational value of hunting and fishing in Colorado in 1980 becomes more than $10 billion.

Since wildlife is a publicly owned resource, people often have to pay less than they *are willing* to pay to see or pursue wildlife. For instance, many people would be willing to pay more for a hunting license than the small fee involved; many

TABLE 3.1   Hunting and Fishing in the United States in 1980

	Number (millions)	Dollars Spent (billions)	Percent of Americans (16+ years old)
Hunters	17	5.6	10
Fishermen	42	10.2	25
Nonconsumptive users	83	14.8	49
All wildlife users[a]	100	30.6[b]	58

[a]Numbers do not total because 65 percent of hunters and fishermen also used wildlife nonconsumptively.

[b]Does not include $9 billion spent for campers, boats, and other special equipment used for hunting and fishing.

Source: *National Survey of Fishing, Hunting and Wildlife-associated Recreation (Initial Findings),* U.S. Fish and Wildlife Service, 1982.

people would pay for hunting access, but hunt for free on public land; and people pay only a dollar to enter a national park, but would be willing to pay more if the park were privately owned by someone intent on maximizing the profits. In these cases, the recreational value of wildlife is underestimated when measured by what people must pay rather than by what they would pay if the price were raised. Krutilla has described a method for estimating public willingness to pay for a publicly owned and price-regulated wildlife resource (1974).

Note that some of the money spent by outdoors enthusiasts in the pursuit of wildlife is used twice in calculating total wildlife value. First, the money is used to indicate the value placed on outdoor activities by recreationists, and second, some of the money becomes commercial value derived from the wildlife resource and realized by local businesses. This is not inflating the value of wildlife artificially, for *both* the recreationist and the business place a value on the wildlife.

Although national, regional, and state studies have demonstrated the immense commercial and recreational value of wildlife, the greatest need is for local studies. Most decisions that can result in loss of habitat and of wildlife values are local decisions. Too often, the value of a local wildlife resource has been poorly considered and, most often, unquantified, when these decisions have been made. The wildlife manager, perhaps in Idaho, who can compare the commercial value of harvesting elk every year with the commercial value of harvesting timber every 50 years, may save elk winter ranges that would otherwise be converted to wood production. Measuring and explaining the value of a local wildlife resource may be a wildlife manager's most important contribution to wildlife conservation.

Biological Value

The biological value of wildlife is the contribution of wild animals to productive ecosystems. Wildlife are part of the complex biotic "machinery" of ecosystems that we rely on for food, water, fertilizer, and aesthetic and recreational values. The activities of wildlife in enhancing the productivity and stability of eco-systems are an enormous service to man. Often these services cannot be replaced by present technology. These services include soil tillage; pollination; seed dispersal and planting; natural regulation of plant and animal populations, including culling of diseased or inferior animals by predators; regulation of water resources; nutrient concentration, transport and recycling; and sanitation through scavenging.

Vertebrates as well as invertebrates, by their fossorial activities, maintain the physical structure of wildland soils, enhancing water infiltration and soil aeration and participating in humus development. In cultivated agricultural fields, where animal populations are limited by monotonous habitat and by direct, often chemical, control, people must till the soil to maintain its structure. The productivity of wildland soils is maintained without costly tillage through this service of wild animals.

Pollination of wild and domestic plants by insects, birds, and mollusks is a service we sometimes carelessly disregard. Our use of chemical poisons may have impaired this service of wildlife—at least locally and temporarily.

Seeds of many plants are designed for transport on or in the guts of animals. Squirrels and rodents, caching seeds for future use, establish new seedlings (Fig. 3.1). These activties are especially important in establishing pioneer species of plants on disturbed areas, such as recently burned forests. In contrast, pioneer plant species are maintained in undisturbed biotic communities because they find suitable mineral-soil seedbeds on sites disturbed by animals, such as at buffalo wallows and prairie-dog towns.

Natural regulation of the quantity and quality of plants and animals by herbivory and predation is a controversial subject among ecologists. Although there have been contrary examples, there are many reports of herbivores overusing and damaging their forage supplies and fewer, but still many, reports of predators limiting the abundance of their prey and selectively preying on the weaker, sometimes diseased members of prey populations. The implications are that wildlife participate in controlling the abundance of pest species and in maintain-

Fig. 3.1   Ten seedlings of limber pine originating from seeds cached in an area less than 2 cm in diameter. On one study area, at least 70 percent of limber pine seedlings originated in such clusters. Photo courtesy of Robert Woodmansee, Colorado State University.

ing the genetic quality and health of prey populations through culling inferior individuals.

Where wild animals enhance soil structure and water infiltration and where beavers build their dams, soil moisture and the rate of release of water from watersheds are greatly affected, usually to man's benefit. Scavenging wildlife alleviate costs of maintaining our beaches and highways by cleaning up carcasses of dead animals.

Many environments are not suited for agriculture or domestic-animal husbandry. Yet wild species adapted to these sites allow man to capture their primary production through harvesting meat and furs. Marine fishes, reptiles, mammals, and birds concentrate nutrients eroded from the continents and carried to the sea. Harvest of these forms and of bird guano allows us to use the productivity of the sea and to return nutrients to the land in the form of fertilizers of marine origin. Soils developed on mineral-deficient parent materials will develop, sometimes after centuries, organic layers containing the deficient minerals. Wild animals transport some of these minerals onto these sites from adjacent soils. Decay of their feces and carcasses enhances the chemical fertility of otherwise infertile areas.

Scientific, Philosophical, and Educational Value

The scientific value of wildlife is the value of wild populations as objects of scientific study. Ecologists, ethologists, physiologists, pathologists, demographers, sociologists, and anthropologists have used studies of wild animals to extend knowledge in their disciplines. The results are valuable to science and also to philosophy because wildlife ecology is the study of life and serves as one basis for speculation on human purposes, values, ethics, and destinies. The educational value of wildlife is realized in the use of wildlife examples in schools and at nature centers and park exhibits to enhance people's understanding of their environment.

The most basic principle of biology, the concept of organic evolution, was conceived and clarified primarily by studying existing and fossil plants and animals, their relationships and distributions. Charles Darwin, in particular, studied wild plants and animals in many parts of the world and formulated the concept of natural selection as part of the principle of evolution. His writings finally brought acceptance of the idea of evolution and upset the previously accepted idea of species immutability. There were immense ramifications in biology, geology, religion, and ethics.

Through the study of wildlife we learn how to better manage plants and animals to our own benefit. We learn methods for biotic control of pests. We gain understanding of epidemiology by studying epizootics in wild populations. Physiological responses of mammals to crowding have been studied in wild animals. The results have implications for human populations. Our awareness of the dangers of chlorinated hydrocarbon pesticides was enhanced when sensitive species of wildlife were affected.

We see the roots of human evolution by studying related anthropoids and by studying the habits of social predators (for man, too, evolved as a social predator). Objectivity in considering man is easier to attain in studying *other* species. Such studies have provided bases for understanding human behavior (Goodall 1965; Howell and Bourliere 1963; Schaller 1972). This scientific value of wildlife should not be underestimated, for man's understanding and management of himself will have ultimate effects on the quality and perhaps even the persistence of human life. The philosophical and educational value of wildlife may be critical to developing an ecological and evolutionary ethic, which Kozlovsky (1974) proposed is the only solution to man's environmental problems.

Aesthetic Value

The value of wildlife and their habitats as objects of beauty or historical significance, and as they become part of literature, poetry, art, and music, is the most personal and variously conceived of wildlife values.

Everyone appreciates the sight of a wood duck or the song of a thrush. This is beauty that meets the eye and ear, and our response to it seems innate. This appreciation is enhanced through identification and understanding of wildlife. One may enjoy the sight of a bighorn ram scrambling up a precipitous slope, head and massive horns held high. But the viewer who knows something of sheep biology sees more than just a majestic ram. He or she may know that rams engage in rutting combat by offering and accepting head-to-head blows of tremendous force; that skulls of rams are intricately designed by natural selection for this combat; that bighorn sheep evolved during ice ages when receding glaciers provided an expanding abundance of summer forage, permitting evolution of nutritionally expensive large horns and aggressive autumn behavior; that older rams spend most of the year in unisexual groups; that young rams mimic ewes in appearance and behavior in order to avoid conflicts with older rams; that bighorn sheep have a great fidelity to seasonal home ranges and, being highly social animals, pass the knowledge of home ranges and migration routes through generations. The viewer who knows these things is reminded of evolution and natural selection and the advances and recessions of glaciers. This is beauty that meets, not the eye or ear, but the educated mind. Aesthetic values thus increase with understanding.

Wildlife species and wild biotic communities provide living historic monuments, equal in inspirational value to any historic building or monument. We have preserved homes of early presidents, old courthouses, and famous battlefields. But where is the environment that challenged the pilgrims—with native vegetation, heath hens and wild deer, bear and turkey? Where can one see again the prairie with grasses taller than the first Illinois settlers? We are concerned about rare and endangered species. But the tall-grass prairie is an extinct *ecosystem*. Nowhere do bison, elk, deer, and prairie chickens live with big bluestem, Indian grass, compass plants, and tall prairie goldenrods. Nowhere does the undrained prairie turn into a marsh each spring, to be celebrated by migrating ducks, geese, and swans. Is not the aesthetic value of the environment that greeted the first white settlers as important as the value of the structures they built?

Wildlife are the subject of literature, poetry, art, and music. One's appreciation of these is more vivid if one has experienced the wildlife portrayed. Jack London's books or the journals of Lewis and Clark are more meaningful if one has heard wolves howl or if one has seen a Montana grizzly bear. Even without these experiences, our appreciation of wildlife art and literature is enhanced just by knowing that wolves still howl on Isle Royale and grizzlies still roam Montana's mountains and that we might someday experience them.

Aesthetic values of wildlife are, I believe, impossible to quantify. They are values that stir the emotions, and they are often the first values that attract people to the cause of conservation. To many of us, who do not depend on wildlife directly for our livelihood, they are the most important value. In these days of compulsion to quantify everything, we must not neglect what is unquantifiable yet, for many, is essential to the quality and even the perception of life. A. Leopold best described the aesthetic value of wildlife in his essay "Goose Music" (1953, Round River Journals, Oxford University Press), which he concludes with:

> I have congenital hunting fever and three sons. As little tots, they spent their time playing with my decoys and scouring vacant lots with wooden guns. I hope to leave them good health, an education, and possibly even a competence. But what are they going to do with these things if there be no more deer in the hills, and no more quail in the coverts? No more snipe whistling in the meadow, no more piping of widgeons and chattering of teal as darkness covers the marshes; no more whistling of swift wings when the morning star pales in the east! And when the dawn-wind stirs through the ancient cottonwoods, and the gray light steals down from the hills over the old river sliding softly past its wide brown sandbars—what if there be no more goose music?

Social Value

When individuals realize commercial, recreational, and aesthetic values from wildlife, there is additional value realized by the community they live in and everyone in the community benefits.

Through the multiplier effect, the community as a whole improves its economic base when money is spent on wildlife-oriented outdoor recreation. This economic base provides for community programs such as schools, libraries, medical facilities, and recreation centers.

An individual's physical and mental health, enhanced by participating in outdoor recreation, is of value not only to oneself, but also to one's neighbors. If individuals are healthy and happy, they are not likely to add to community welfare costs for medical aid, income support, or counseling; nor are they apt to be involved in crimes against the community. There are many reasons why crime rates and welfare costs are highest in our biggest cities; however, crowding and lack of open space and wild natural areas are undoubtedly some of the reasons.

Rural communities and less-developed states cannot compete with cities and heavily populated states in salary offerings to doctors, teachers, surveyors, and other professionals. Yet they can attract competent people who are willing to forgo some income for the privilege of living in a less-developed area with access to hunting, fishing, and other outdoor activities.

Negative Value

The negative values of wildlife are the costs of wildlife damages to crops and other property and the costs of controlling those damages. Where these values can be expressed in dollars, they should be subtracted from the total commercial and recreational value of the wildlife resource.

There are many forms of negative values. Browsing deer may kill tree seedlings and retard forest growth. This may significantly affect a forest industry. Large ungulates, small mammals, and birds damage orchards, consume standing livestock forage, stored hay, and agricultural crops. Roosting birds may be nuisances because of noise and the effects of concentrated guano on desirable vegetation. Beaver may flood stream sides, killing desired trees and jeopardizing cabin sites. Coyote predation can diminish numbers of livestock. The costs of controlling these damages include fencing, poisoning, trapping and removal, use of aversive agents, and extra labor to protect property from potentially damaging wildlife.

TOTAL VALUE AND MITIGATION OF HABITAT LOSS

The total value of a wildlife resource is the sum of all the above values, minus the negative values. However, since the values are not commensurable (not measured in common units) and some are not quantifiable, we cannot produce a single number to represent the total value of wildlife. This makes it difficult to compare the value of a new reservoir or strip mine with the value of the wildlife habitat that would be destroyed in developing these other resources. Since wildlife is a publicly owned resource, what total compensation is due the public when a mine is developed on public land and destroys a wildlife resource? One way to answer this question is to consider the total value of a wildlife resource as the cost necessary to replace it. Colorado has developed this method for calculating the costs of mitigating loss of wildlife habitat (Norman et al. 1975). Replacement costs include those for purchasing and developing new habitat and for improving existing habitat to increase its productivity.

THE VARIETY OF ADVOCATES FOR WILDLIFE

Although wildlife have diverse values, most people do not identify with all of them and some people appreciate very few of them. The diversity of wildlife advocates has resulted in some contradictory wildlife programs, all instituted by well-meaning people, and tends to divide and disorganize public support for wildlife conservation. For example, antihunting and prohunting groups have expended much of their support in attacking each other, while the most common and serious enemy of wildlife—loss of habitat—has continued with all the less opposition. Wildlife managers must communicate with many types of people having diverse interests in wildlife resources. Their ability to unite diverse support for wildlife conservation may be important to the future of the resource.

Laissez-faire Groups

More than 80 percent of Americans live in cities, most of them in very large cities. What will happen to their children's instinctive curiosities for wild living things? Where will their children learn to enjoy nature? If they do not, they will become part of the laissez-faire group—apathetic toward wildlife, uncaring whether or not eagles are being poisoned, uninterested in wild rivers, unaware of wildlife values being lost. The greatest threat to wildlife in the United States is that this laissez-faire group will grow, resulting in declining political support for wildlife conservation.

Countering this trend are the media that convey wildlife values to the public. These are the conservation and nature magazines and the best nature programs on television. But the vicarious enjoyment of wildlife will not suffice to nurture people's concern for wildlife. It has not been enough in many of our biggest, eastern cities, where the greatest apathy toward wildlife values now exists. We must have open spaces with wildlife habitats in and near cities. Waterfowl marshes and floodplain forests provide some of the best opportunities to preserve urban wildlife habitat.

Sentimentalists

Sentimentalists oppose use or management of wildlife on moral principles. To them, wildlife's sole purpose is to exist. Manipulation of populations or habitats is immoral. The most eloquent spokesman for this view has been Albert Schweitzer (1923, Civilization and Ethics, A. and C. Black, Ltd., London).

> Ethics is nothing else than reverence for life. Reverence for life affords me my fundamental principle of morality, namely, that good consists in maintaining, assisting and enhancing life and that to destroy, to harm or to hinder life is evil.

Sentimentalists usually have little understanding of wildlife biology, especially such concepts as population turnover, density dependence, and the complexity of wildlife-habitat relationships. Man cannot exist without using other forms of life or without manipulating habitats. Activities that assist and enhance some forms of life must harm and hinder other forms. If we feed starving deer in winter, we may maintain too many deer that will destroy vegetation and alter the habitat of songbirds. If we control a forest fire or oppose logging, we protect the habitat of species adapted to old-growth forest, and we prohibit the creation of habitat for species adapted to young forest vegetation. Everything we do or do not do with the land and wildlife enhances some forms of life and hinders other forms.

Sentimentalists are sometimes particularly attached to certain species—usually wild warm-blooded species. They show less concern for cold-blooded vertebrates, invertebrates, vegetation, or domestic animals. Their view of the biota and its complex functions is limited. For some sentimentalists, this attitude cannot be changed. Others can broaden their views over a long period of exposure to biology. But sentimentalists are concerned for wildlife. Their support for wildlife conservation will be valuable in proportion to their realization that habitat destruction is the major cause of declining wildlife populations.

Protectionists

Protectionists are concerned mostly for aesthetic values and nonconsumptive uses of wildlife. They are most concerned about maintenance of wild-land resources and view the use of these resources as part of a continuing historical trend of wild land loss and degradation. They tend to oppose use of natural resources. They distrust proposals for multiple use of land. They often favor locking up wild-land resources in parks and wilderness areas.

Protectionists may be knowledgable in biology and in the history of conservation. Their interpretation of history as a continuing assault on renewable resources with loss of wild land and wildlife values is generally correct. But they may ignore some examples of successful wildlife management, such as restoration of deer and elk populations or expansion of Canada goose ranges, as temporary and minor. They are convinced that history has already demonstrated that Americans cannot wisely manage and maintain renewable resources under multiple use, that the only hope is to restrict consumptive use from as much remaining wild land as possible. As a result, protectionists support every politically feasible wilderness proposal, regardless of the multiple-use values lost or the duplication of wilderness resources.

Protectionism is based on a defeatist belief that we cannot learn from past abuses of the land, that truly multiple-use management cannot be achieved, and the users cannot be regulated without elimination of consumptive use entirely. Professional wildlife management biologists cannot base their contributions to wildlife conservation on such a defeatist attitude. We do need some wilderness. We especially need a variety of environments in our wilderness system. But we also need other products of the land—timber, forage, and minerals—and access for some forms of recreation. Wildlife resources have often been neglected in so-called multiple-use programs on public land, but this does not have to continue. Management biologists will make their greatest contribution by participating in multiple-use programs.

Protectionists will continue to influence our land-use policies. History has yet to prove their basic contention, that we cannot achieve good and lasting multiple-use management, to be wrong. That is a task for today's professionals and students—the professional land managers of tomorrow. In communicating with protectionists, much can be achieved if we can convince them that diversity of environments, not quantity of land, is now the most important goal for our wilderness system.

Single-use Adherents

Single-use adherents place one value of wildlife or wild land above all others and are willing to sacrifice all other values. In promoting their interests, most are after personal, sometimes financial, gain. These users are the most zealous hunters, fishermen, miners, lumbermen, livestock producers, and land developers. The wildlife biologist, philosophically oriented toward diversity and unselfish in working toward the common good, is usually unable to communicate with single-use adherents. They usually appear uneducable. The most effective strategy in dealing with single-use adherents is to ensure that all of them contribute their opinions. Single-use adherents often oppose one another, and their extreme positions favoring single uses often balance against each other and define the moderate position of multiple use.

Multiple-use Adherents

Most professional resource managers and many laymen are in this category. An objective of conservation education is to expand public awareness of the many values of land, including wildlife, and to increase the number of multiple-use adherents. These people appreciate a diversity of wild-land values and work sincerely toward management programs that provide an acceptable balance of land uses without degradation of land productivity.

ONTOGENY OF WILDLIFE APPRECIATION

Ontogeny refers to the development of an individual. Here we review the developmental stages of wildlife appreciation, a concept from Leopold (1949), with the aim of enhancing the reader's understanding of the needs and motives of those who use the wildlife resource.

Acquisition: Trophy Hunting

Perhaps all wildlife enthusiasts begin, in their youth, as trophy hunters. Their enjoyment of the outdoors requires that they take home something physical—a duck, a rabbit, a butterfly, or a photograph. The trophy is proof of some physical accomplishment. Its holder has traveled and exercised agility and skill, at least. The trophy hunter may or may not have used knowledge and understanding, and the true trophy hunter has not. The goal is acquisition, nothing more. (The trophy hunter may not know what species of duck has been shot!)

Trophy hunting is rudimentary outdoor recreation. Fortunately, the trophy hunter can progress to other levels of enjoyment. The tragedy is that some outdoor persons do not, and therefore, they cannot realize much of wildlife's recreational and aesthetic values. As a consequence, their advocacy for wildlife is often laissez-faire or single-use adherence.

Recognition: Life-listing

Progress occurs when one expends effort to know and name what one sees. There is suddenly more to look for, and there are more places to look. Classification is the first necessary step toward understanding nature. Millions of Americans reach this stage, scouring the country with field guides, binoculars, and hand lenses. Some make a fetish of recognition, spending thousands of dollars on travel to extend their life-lists of birds identified to over 100, then 200, then beyond anyone else in their local bird club. True life-listers do not understand what they see. Their life-list is their goal. This is unfortunate, for with recognition they would take a great step toward a higher level of wildlife appreciation—perception.

Perception: Ecological Study

Ecologists may be professionals or laymen, and some laymen perceive more than do some professionals. Gaining perception requires additional effort—a willingness to study nature in the field, in books, in museums, and in nature centers. But the rewards are great to the sensitive mind. One's recreation is enhanced, one's aesthetic enjoyments are enlarged, and one's understanding of life and of self is broadened. Many people have found their religion and philosophy in their perception of nature.

Participation: Land Husbandry

Perception can lead to enlightened participation in the conservation process. Participation takes many forms. It includes the care and management of land—soil, water, plants, and animals—to enhance productivity and diversity. This may be done on the farm, range or forest, or in one's back yard. My teacher's yard grew not just zinnias and irises, but also wild trilliums and jack-in-the-pulpits, because he managed his yard for tame *and* wild creatures. His yard had plants with color and ecological processes of interest at all seasons. The variety of birds he attracted were a joy throughout his neighborhood.

Participation includes a willingness to limit one's demands on the land, for our increasing demands reduce land productivity and diversity. Limiting demands includes limiting one's family size, not wasting, and consuming carefully. It includes finding more pleasure in experience and less pleasure in things.

Participation also includes activism—at least, more than apathy—for the cause of maintaining the productivity and diversity of renewable natural resources.

CONSERVATION EDUCATION

Conservation education consists primarily of helping people develop their appreciation of natural-resource values, from acquisition toward participation (Leopold 1949). We must teach Americans to use and enjoy their wild-land resources, or they will never realize much value and will not support programs to produce or maintain the values they do not perceive. The first step is to foster recognition; then comes perception. Once perception begins, participation may follow.

Wildlife management consists of making land produce valuable crops of wildlife. This can be accomplished by producing more wildlife *and* by helping people to realize more value from the wildlife they already have. Every wildlife manager who contacts people has the opportunity to increase wildlife values in both ways.

WILDLIFE VALUES AND WILDLIFE CONSERVATION

There are four major problems involving wildlife valuation and the future of wildlife conservation.

First, we must find better methods to ensure that all wildlife values are considered in decisions affecting wildlife on public land. This will require improved methods for measuring some wildlife values. More important, biologists in field positions will need a broad appreciation of wildlife values and must be willing to communicate these values. Wildlife values are not concentrated and realized intensively by small user groups that will advocate wildlife maintenance. Rather, wildlife values are numerous and dispersed among many people. Although the total wildlife value is large, most recipients of wildlife value are not immensely affected by its loss. Such values, realized by everyone, may have few strong supporters.

Second, although many people reap benefits from wildlife, some without being conscious of it, the hunters and fishermen, through license fees and taxes on their equipment, have been paying the greatest share of the cost of wildlife conservation. Other sources are needed. We are only beginning to find economic support for nongame and noncommercial wildlife. Many states sell special stamps and use some general-fund money to finance wildlife programs. But these programs have been small, and federal general-fund money for wildlife management programs on federal lands has been inadequate compared to the wildlife values received on federal lands by sportsmen, hikers, campers, and tourists.

Third, we must solve the dilemma of public ownership of wildlife produced on private land. The solution probably lies in increasing landowners' ability to profit from the animals they produce. This has worked in Texas where private shooting preserves are numerous (Teer and Forrest 1968).

Pheasants produced on an Illinois farm are public wildlife. No one can harvest them except under public laws concerning licensing, seasons, and bag limits. But farm owners retain control of access to this public property. They produce the pheasants, may suffer damage to seedling crops from them, and reap little benefit from pheasants unless they can lease hunting rights to their land. If the leases bring suitable profits, farmers may provide for the habitat needs of pheasants on their lands. Otherwise there will be few pheasants.

Leased shooting areas will be most common in heavily populated areas with little public land on which to hunt. As human populations grow, access to waterfowl hunting is usually first to be commercialized in this way. To some, hunting loses part of its aesthetic value through commercialization. Checking in and out, and perhaps being restricted to a prescribed blind or hunting area, remove some of the wildness and independence of the experience. Escape from the regulations of everyday life is one reason for hunting. But there seems to be no choice in many heavily populated parts of our country. If much wildlife is to be produced and available on private land, landowners must be compensated for their efforts in producing wildlife and for their trouble in permitting access to it.

Last, we must increase public appreciation that wildlife need habitat. Too often, those who value wildlife do not recognize a threat to wildlife habitat as a threat to wildlife. The old proverb says it well.

> *The law doth punish man or woman*
> *That steals the goose from off the common*
> *But lets the greater felon loose*
> *That steals the common from the goose.*

PRINCIPLES

P3.1 Wildlife have several values—commercial, recreational, biological, scientific, social, aesthetic, and negative. Commercial, recreational, and negative values can be measured in monetary terms. The other values are difficult or impossible to measure. Since wildlife values are not commensurable, the total value of a wildlife population can only be estimated by its cost of replacement.

P3.2 Peoples' perceptions of and attitudes toward wildlife values are highly varied. Attitude groups include laissez-faire groups, sentimentalists, protectionists, single-use adherents, and multiple-use adherents. An effective wildlife management biologist must recognize, understand, and communicate with a diversity of people who influence land management.

P3.3 Personal appreciation of wildlife values develops as individuals learn more about wildlife and ecology. Public realization of wildlife values may be increased not only by producing more wildlife, but also by teaching wildlife ecology, so that people may recognize and appreciate more value in existing wildlife populations.

P3.4 In the United States, four major problems involving wildlife valuation are (1) a need to consider all wildlife values in decisions affecting land use, (2) a need to develop sources of financial support for managing nongame and noncommercial populations of wildlife, (3) a need for methods to compensate landowners for wildlife values produced and realized on private land, and (4) a need for broader public awareness of the importance of habitat as necessary for sustaining wildlife populations.

PART   II

WILDLIFE
BIOLOGY

CHAPTER   4

WILDLIFE BIOLOGY: AN OVERVIEW

Biology is a continuum, but we
biologists, because of our limitations,
divide ourselves into categories, and
we pretend that these categories exist
in the living systems that we study.
From the functional point of view, of
course, an animal is indivisible, and
physiology is not in any sense an
isolatable component of an organism. . . .
[It is] inseparable from morphology
and behavior.

G. A. Bartholomew

Wildlife management involves control of the distribution, abundance, and quality of wildlife. Chapters 5 through 11 discuss the factors determining wildlife distribution, abundance, and quality. These factors are discussed somewhat separately and in considerable detail before a synthesis is presented at the end of Chapter 11. Before proceeding, however, I wish to review briefly some concepts of ecology and to present some definitions. In particular, the concept of evolution by natural selection, which is necessary for understanding wildlife species and their habitat requirements, is emphasized.

Education in zoology tends to emphasize evolution, adaptive radiation, and diversity in the animal kingdom. Zoologists base their understanding of animals on the concept of natural selection and evolutionary histories of species. In contrast, students of wildlife management have been taught characteristics of species without explanation of evolutionary trends and without emphasis on variation among populations. In addition, the profession has sought generalizations that would provide management prescriptions for application to many species in many, often different, habitats. As a result there has not been enough emphasis on evolution as a basis for understanding wildlife and their habitat requirements. Animals are "bundles of adaptations." These adaptations vary among species and also among populations within species. Adaptations determine an animal's responses to its environment and, therefore, its habitat requirements. When we ask, Where did the species or subspecies evolve? What is its naturally associated environment? What selective forces have shaped its adaptations? we are beginning to understand the animal we hope to manage.

VARIETY OF WILDLIFE

It is useful to begin this section with an overview of the complex resource that is the responsibility of the wildlife manager. Succeeding chapters dwell mainly on details. An initial overview should put details into perspective and avoid the danger of underestimating the intellectual task of putting the many interactions of wildlife and their environment into an integrated concept of "what goes on." As a forester cannot manage only trees, a wildlife manager cannot manage only deer. These professionals manage land, that is, ecosystems. The products of primary interest may be timber or deer, but the quantity and quality of the products are influenced by many factors. We must manage the entire "factory," not just the "tail end of the assembly line."

What variety of species must a wildlife biologist deal with on a management-sized area? My example comes from the Huntington Wildlife Forest, about 25 square miles of land and water in the Adirondack Region of New York. It is perhaps an average example. We expect greater diversity from more southerly ecosystems and less from more northerly ones. Of vertebrates, 208 species have been recorded on the Forest. In addition, there are protozoa, coelenterates, sponges, flatworms, and segmented worms, mollusks, arthropods, and a few other minor groups. More than 1200 species of plants have been identified on the Forest, including 108 woody species. These thousands of species, each with its peculiar life cycle, are influenced by numerous physical factors, which vary continuously in space and time.

The many species are interrelated in many ways. We commonly describe interactions within biotic communities as food webs, but these illustrate only a part of the complexity of communities. Animals and plants are interrelated in numerous ways besides foraging, predation, and decomposition. Competition, involving mutual use of resources and the exclusion of animals by antisocial behavior, is one way. Disease relationships, involving direct communication, alternate hosts, and reservoir hosts, is another set of ways. In addition, organisms are constantly altering their environments, to the benefit of some species and harm of others. Beaver alter the habitat of trout, produce temporary habitat for wood ducks, and, when their ponds have filled with silt, create open meadows of value to deer. Porcupines, feeding in the treetops, drop branches and provide extra food for wintering deer. Is a northern forest a better deer habitat because it contains beaver and porcupines? To some degree it is.

The number of potential interrelationships among species increases exponentially with increased numbers of species. There can only be one, or one set, of interactions between two species. Add a third species, and the number of possible connections increases to three. Add a fourth, and there are six connections. Further, the existence and magnitude of all these interactions vary from place to place and daily, seasonally, and annually. The resulting complexity of any ecosystem being managed for wildlife production boggles the mind and has also boggled our largest computers.

Obviously, we cannot measure, we cannot even consider, each aspect of so complex a system. In management, we are forced to concentrate on small parts of an ecosystem and to generalize not only about functions of the ecosystem as a whole, but also about those parts of the system we try to manipulate and monitor. We hope our generalizations are correct most of the time, and we should proceed with humility and caution.

Wildlife managers deal with resources at least as complex as those of any profession. For instance, on the Roosevelt National Forest in Colorado, there are about seven economically and aesthetically important tree species. By comparison, there are at least three times as many wildlife species that are similarly important, even if we group songbirds and furbearers as one species each. Furthermore, most of these wildlife species are mobile and require a diversity of habitat types, and these requirements vary seasonally. Compared to trees, the wildlife are more difficult to study for research purposes or to measure for management purposes. Consequently, if emphasis on wildlife management is to *equal* that usually given to the management of trees (or other resources less complex than wildlife), there will have to be *larger* budgets for both research and management of wildlife than for research and management of trees.

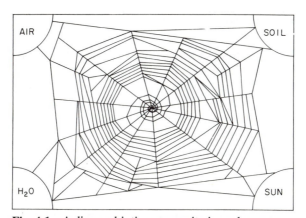

Fig. 4.1   A diverse biotic community is analogous to a complex spiderweb in which each strand represents a plant or animal species. When a strand of the web is broken (species extirpation) or weakened (change in abundance or productivity), every other strand adjusts slightly, and the web continues to function. Similarly, diverse biotic communities .have stability of function despite frequent perturbations in a variable environment. Simple biotic communities, like simple spiderwebs, have less capacity to adjust to environmental variation and are less stable. Further, the functioning of both biotic communities and spiderwebs can be greatly impaired if any of the four "anchor resources" of air, soil, sun, and water are disturbed—as by pollution or erosion.

One generalization that has become an axiom of ecology is that all this complexity favors stability of ecosystem function. The spiderweb analogy illustrates the relationship between biotic complexity and the functional stability of a community (Fig. 4.1). The principle that variety creates complexity and favors stability of function is directly applicable to wildlife management. Wild animals having access to a variety of food and cover resources can, because they live in a diverse environment, compensate for great variation in the physical environment by shifting use among alternative resources. By contrast, if animals depend mainly on one resource for which there is no alternative, the population will suffer whenever events curtail the availability of that one resource. In a diverse environment, wildlife can "stabilize" the quality of their habitat by using numerous alternative food and cover resources that vary in compensating ways with changes in the environment. Maintenance of habitat diversity is, therefore, a goal of most wildlife management programs.

ABUNDANCE OF WILDLIFE

What numbers of wild animals does a wildlife manager deal with? How important are these numbers of animals in biotic communities?

In a census of small mammals on two 1-acre (0.4 ha) plots in northern Minnesota, the populations averaged 116 mammals per acre. There were 32 deer mice, 34 voles, 24 jumping mice, 2 shrews (probably underestimated), 20 chipmunks, 2 pine squirrels, and 2 hares per plot. This equals 74,240 small mammals per square mile. In addition, there were at least 30 other species of mammals, more than 100 species of birds, and a few reptiles and amphibians in the area. So large a number of animals must have a large impact on the ecosystem—including selective consumption of forage, providing food for predators, pollinating flowers, transporting and planting seeds, and soil tillage through digging, mixing soil with organic matter, and transporting nutrients.

To take another example, it was once estimated that 800 white-tailed deer occupied the Huntington Wildlife Forest in New York. Across 21 square miles (54 sq km) of land area, the population averaged 38 per square mile, although deer abundance was not uniform. On a fresh-weight basis, deer consume about 1 kg daily during winter and 2.2 kg daily at other seasons. Assuming a 100-day winter, 38 deer consumed about 26,000 kg of forage per square mile on the Huntington Forest each year. This selective foraging has altered the density and species composition of the forest, including its understory vegetation (Example 6.3).

Wildlife constitute an abundant as well as diverse resource and have large impacts on the structures and functions of ecosystems. Considering the several kinds of wildlife values inherent in each population (Chapter 3), the wildlife resource can produce great benefits for people. It is a resource deserving emphasis in land management.

DEFINITIONS

Ecology is the study of relationships between organisms and their environment. Wildlife management is largely an application of knowledge from this science.

Environment includes all the materials or processes in the surroundings of an organism or population. This term emphasizes the abundance, diversity, and complexity of materials and processes, many of which influence each managed population.

Environmental factor is any one of the materials or processes in an environment. Factors may be groups of materials or processes (soil, food, weather, biotic succession) or may be more specific (temperature, soil moisture, browse, closure of the vegetation canopy).

Habitat is the kind of biotic community, or set of biotic communities, in which an animal or population lives. For example, a marsh is habitat for a muskrat population. Habitat is *not* synonymous with cover (Chapter 7). Suitable habitat provides all the habitat requirements of a species for a season (wintering habitat, breeding habitat) or year-round. *Habitat requirements* are the various types of foods, cover, and other factors needed by a wildlife species for survival and reproductive success. Examples are winter forage and nesting sites. *Habitat resources* are the various acceptable food and cover types that exist in a habitat. These resources usually vary in quality (as there may be good and poor forages and secure nesting sites as well as insecure sites where predation is likely).

Zoogeography is the study of past and present animal distributions, including the evolution, spread, recession, and extinction of species.

Geographic range is the broad area in which a species occurs. Geographic ranges are usually illustrated by irregularly shaped shaded areas on maps. For instance, bighorn sheep occur in western North America.

Ecologic range includes the habitats, within a geographic range, where a species occurs. For instance, bighorn sheep occur in arid and semiarid mountain ranges and canyons of western North America.

EVOLUTION

Species Biology

A first requisite for managing a species population is some understanding of its biology—its habitat requirements, movement patterns, behavior, and patterns of reproduction and mortality. This requires understanding the adaptations that a species has acquired to enhance survival and reproductive fitness in its naturally associated environment. Animal adaptations have been classified as:

1 Anatomical
2 Physiological
3 Behavioral
   A. Instinctive
   B. Learned

For example, consider some adaptations of *Odocoileus virginianus borealis*, the "northern" subspecies of white-tailed deer. Note there are over 20 subspecies of *O. virginianus*, including the comparatively tiny Key deer of Florida. *O. v. borealis* is adapted to forested environments in the northeastern United States and southeastern Canada. Some of its adaptations are:

1 A large body. This is the largest subspecies of *virginianus* in the eastern half of the continent. It illustrates Bergmann's rule, in that large animals have a comparatively low ratio of surface area to body weight. This reduces heat loss in relation to heat production and is an adaptation to cold environments.

2   Long legs. This tall subspecies often has to travel in deep snow.

3   A dense winter coat. This is another adaptation to cold.

4   A reduced metabolic rate during winter. Northern deer reduce energy demands and food requirements during winter when forage is usually scarce, fostering survival through this critical period.

5   Selective feeding habits. Forested environments receive much precipitation and produce an abundance of carbohydrates, especially cellulose. Nutrients, however, are diluted in the abundance of forage. Deer have adapted to feeding selectively on plant types and parts in which nutrients are concentrated, such as new leaves, flowers, and the tips of woody twigs. These forages also provide the most digestible of available carbohydrates. Selective-feeding ruminants have several common adaptations. They tend to be smaller than species with less-selective feeding habits, as deer are smaller than elk or bison. They have a smaller rumen capacity and faster rate of food passage through the digestive tract. They feed more constantly through the day (Hoffman 1968).

6   A propensity for producing twins. Biotic succession proceeds rapidly in forest environments. Following disturbance of old growth forest, as by fire, there is a great but temporary abundance of quality deer forage in the new vegetation. White-tailed deer have become adapted for using this temporary resource by evolving a reproductive potential that responds to forage conditions. With excellent nutrition, does tend to breed at an earlier age and tend to produce twins, even triplets. This permits a deer population to increase rapidly and utilize temporarily abundant forage following forest disturbance. Geist has discussed similar propensities in moose (1974).

7   Small social groups. Ungulates in open, prairie environments tend to aggregate into large herds. The comparatively uniform distribution of prairie forage alleviates a potential for competition among animals, permitting large social groups. Furthermore, the open environment permits visual communication among animals. This permits individuals to spend more time feeding while group alertness to the approach of predators remains high. These factors are reversed in the forest habitat of white-tailed deer. Forest vegetation reduces the effectiveness of visual communication, and there is little advantage to enduring the competition of large social groups. Thus, group sizes average only about two animals in forest white-tailed deer and up to eight animals among whitetails living in more open environments (Hirth 1977).

8   A resistance to brainworm *Parelaphostrongylus tenuis*. White-tailed deer must have had a long history of evolution with this disease. Most northern deer carry adult brainworms with little or no damaging effects. Whitetails are thus considered a normal host for these nematodes, and they are a reservoir of brainworms causing disease problems in moose (Chapter 11).

How is this information on subspecies biology applied in management? First, *O. v. borealis* is designed to withstand the rigors of winter. There is an anthropomorphic tendency to overreact when deer are faced with severe winter weather. Mortality during the severest of winters has adapted these deer to withstand average winters, and winter mortality continues to be the selective force maintaining winter fitness in deer populations. Past attempts to feed deer in many areas during even average winters have wasted public funds.

Second, white-tailed deer populations will increase rapidly whenever forage conditions improve. Forage management can bring a quick return in increased harvestable surpluses. Forage improvement, whether intentional or due to wildfire, windstorm, or timber harvest, can also bring management problems such as crop depredations, increased deer highway accidents, and deer damage to tree reproduction. Furthermore, a temporary increase in forage can result in a large deer population that may ultimately face a declining forage resource due to plant succession. Under these conditions, deer will overuse and damage or eliminate preferred forage plants, and die-offs of many deer will occur in severe winters. Through understanding deer biology, wildlife biologists can predict and respond to these problems and opportunities.

Third, if managers should decide to feed deer (an artificial solution that detracts from wildness—the most unique characteristic of wildlife), a coarse feed with abundant cellulose will not sustain them. Deer have evolved as selective feeders, and their anatomy and physiology requires a quality forage (Schoonveld et al. 1974).

Fourth, the characteristic small group size of forest white-tailed deer has implications for methods of census and for estimating population sex–age structure. For more social species of ungulates that are typically seen in larger groups, one obtains a larger sample of the population from every group observed; however, animal distribution may be less uniform in the habitat. These factors influence the selection of methods for census and for data analysis. Furthermore, if certain sex–age classes tend to occur in the larger groups within a population, and if larger groups are, under some survey conditions, more apt to be seen than are smaller groups, those sex–age classes are expected to be overrepresented in a survey.

Note that some of the adaptations of *O. v. borealis* are subtle, not obvious until one is familiar with literature on the anatomy, physiology, and behavior of the animal and on characteristics of its environment. Nor is the biology of the species fully comprehended until one considers the natural-selective forces that have created it. (See also Examples 4.1 and 8.3.)

EXAMPLE 4.1   Adaptations of Eastern Cottontail Rabbits Reveal Some of the Species Habitat Requirements

It has often been accepted that the best habitat for eastern cottontails consists of an abundance of shrub thickets, briar patches, and brush piles. This idea has perhaps been based on experience with cottontails during autumn and winter, when rabbits have been observed by hunters and when rabbit tracks in snow have produced abundant evidence of rabbit activity. Thus, impressions of habitat requirements of rabbits have emphasized escape cover and winter habitat. Habitat requirements for other functions, such as feeding or nesting, and during other seasons were being neglected.

Cottontails use dense woody cover to escape hunters and their dogs. During periods with snow on the ground, they remain in woody cover where they are at least somewhat camouflaged, and avoid open, snow-covered areas where they would be very visible (Hanson et al. 1969). When rabbits browse on woody twigs, as they often must in winter because other foods are unavailable, the evidence remains on the plant. In contrast, it is very difficult to detect where rabbits have eaten herbage, flowers, and fruits. Biased impressions of cottontail habitat requirements led to management programs emphasizing the establishment of rose hedges, conifers, and patches of woody lespedezas. Often, such management was applied on recently abandoned farmland. The areas produced many rabbits for a few years, but productivity soon declined as dense natural and planted vegetation choked the land.

Research in Illinois suggested that the optimum rabbit habitat, although it contains patches of woody vegetation, also contains abundant open areas with low-growing forage. In the moist climate of areas occupied by eastern cottontails, open areas tend to disappear rapidly because of biotic succession toward woody species. Thus, the most difficult aspect of habitat management is in maintaining open areas, and the planting of woody species is counterproductive.

The behavioral and anatomical adaptations of cottontail rabbits emphasize their use of and need for open areas with low-growing forage. The animals forage nocturnally and may sit in one place throughout a day. Their eyes are set high near the sides of their heads, providing nearly 360-degree horizontal vision and overhead vision as well. Their ears are large and motile. Rabbits are designed to see and hear the approach of predators. They have cryptic coloring. When approached, they remain motionless, expecting not to be detected. Their legs are designed for rapid acceleration and quick changes in direction. These characteristics suggest an animal adapted to rather open habitat with patches of obstacles such as shrubbery or changes in terrain. The predator-evasion strategy of cottontails is to see or hear predators at a distance and become motionless to avoid detection. If that strategy should fail, the rabbits use a burst of speed to get quickly out of sight into cover that may provide a barrier overhead but allows good mobility and visibility at ground level. Thus, the best escape cover for cottontails is patchy and rather open at ground level. In contrast, a habitat with dense and continuous woody cover does not suit the adaptations of cottontails, in that dense cover hinders visibility, hearing, and rapid escape.

Adaptations Are Limitations

Adaptations fit an animal for survival and reproduction within a particular environment or within a limited range of environments. Consequently, the animal is less fit for operating in other environments, to which it is not adapted. Thus, we do not expect ruffed grouse in prairie habitats, pine squirrels in corn fields, or fish out of water. Adaptations that fit a species to its naturally associated environment also limit the species to that environment and to the food and cover resources of that environment.

Some wildlife species are highly *specialized*. They are adapted to a narrow range of environments and have special requirements for food and/or cover. The American woodcock is an example. Its most notable adaptation is its long, slender, prehensile bill for probing soft ground to obtain earthworms and a few other invertebrates for food. Woodcocks are thus limited to moist regions with an abundance of earthworms, the eastern deciduous forests of North America.

Specialized species are usually quite sensitive to changes in their environment. They cannot adjust to habitat change because their specialized adaptations limit them. Woodcocks would be highly sensitive to reduction of earthworms, a potential consequence of using insecticides in deciduous forests. They could not switch to alternative foods. Woodcocks are also specialized in requiring soft, moist soil in which to feed. Any alteration of vegetation or of drainage patterns that causes drying of soils would be detrimental to the birds.

Most rare, endangered, or extinct wildlife have been specialized species. They have been unable to adjust to habitat changes, caused mostly by man. Leopold has noted that specialized species have tended to evolve among wildlife adapted to climax biotic communities, which are comparatively stable, permitting consistent natural selection for a narrow range of adaptations (1966). Species adapted to the always-changing environments of developmental biotic communities cannot evolve a narrow range of adaptations.

At another extreme, some wildlife species are highly *generalized*. Adaptations to a wide range of environments permit them to have large geographic and ecologic ranges. They can use a variety of food and cover resources. They are less sensitive to environmental change. Many generalized species are game animals and many are adapted to developmental biotic communities. They are not expected to become in danger of extinction. The several species of cottontail rabbits are good examples of generalized wildlife. They use a great variety of forages; live in forests, prairies, shrublands, farmlands, and cities; and have a large geographic range.

The concept of adaptations as limitations has sometimes been neglected, resulting in attempts to transplant species into environments in which they could not survive. Ring-necked pheasants, adapted to open, agricultural land, have been tranplanted into forest environments. Pronghorn antelope, adapted to arid shrublands and grasslands, have been transplanted into the moist, dense, and tall grasslands of Florida. These mistakes, opposed by biologists who understood natural selection and evolution, were predictably unsuccessful.

The adaptations and limitations of wildlife populations are often more subtle than those leading to taxonomic separation of species. Taxonomists recognize numerous subspecies, and we expect each subspecies to have somewhat different adaptations that especially fit it, and somewhat limit it, to its naturally associated environment. Ecologists sometimes recognize ecotypes within species. Ecotypes are populations living in, and presumably somewhat adapted to, particular environments. When extirpated populations are to be reestablished, ecotypes similar to the lost populations should be sought for transplantation.

Thus, if bison were to be reestablished in Rocky Mountain National Park, Colorado, mountain-adapted bison would be preferred over plains bison for reintroduction. The most suitable transplant stock apparently would be bison from Yellowstone National Park, Wyoming. This population, though once augmented by plains bison, retains some genes from native mountain bison and has faced several generations of natural selection in a mountain environment.

Dilution of locally adapted gene pools may result from releasing pen-raised strains of animals into the wild. There is little legal control over this practice in some states. One well-intentioned Coloradan released a commercially available strain of "giant" ring-necked pheasants on his property. He expected to augment the local gene pool and produce larger wild birds. Hopefully, the pen-raised birds did not survive long enough to reproduce. Otherwise some dilution of the locally adapted gene pool and a less productive and less viable population seemed inevitable.

It is important to preserve a diversity of gene pools for each species of wildife. For example, Colorado has eliminated most of its populations of bighorn sheep at low elevations in foothills and canyons. Can these populations be replaced simply by transplanting sheep from mountain habitats? Or are there subtle differences between these ecotypes of bighorn? I do not know. But it seems prudent to give special protection to the few remaining populations of bighorn indigenous to low-elevation habitats.

Ecological Niches

The concept of ecological niche relates to evolution, adaptations, and limitations. Ecologists commonly use two definitions of niche. One emphasizes animal functions; the other emphasizes habitat resources.

Functionally, an ecological niche is the role of a species in a biotic community, as determined by its geographic and ecological distribution and by the set of adaptations that separate it from all other species. Feeding functions are usually emphasized in this concept. Thus, we think of niches for grazers, browsers, bark eaters, fruit eaters, and seed eaters among the herbivores of a biotic community. There are also carnivores specialized to catch large mammals, small mammals, birds, insects, and so forth. These carnivores are further subdivided taxonomically, according to body size and according to methods and location of feeding. Thus, the niche of the white-breasted nuthatch is that of a small avian insectivore feeding on trunks of trees in deciduous forests. Similar niches in different geographic regions or biotic communities are termed *niche counterparts*. These are occupied by species termed *ecological equivalents*. In coniferous forests, the red-breasted nuthatch is the ecological equivalent of the white-breasted nuthatch in deciduous forests. Similarly, the large kangaroos of Australia are ecological equivalents of ungulates in other parts of the world. All function as large-mammal herbivores. The main value of the concept of functional niche to wildlife biologists lies in its emphasis on the numerous, often subtle, differences among the diverse species of vertebrates. Because of these differences in sets of adaptations, generalizations concerning the management of one species usually cannot be applied directly to other species.

Alternatively, an ecological niche is the set of habitat resources (foods, cover types, water, etc.) used by a species, as determined by its geographic and ecological range and its adaptations. This definition permits the concept of an empty niche. Habitat resources may be available but unused because of species extinction or extirpation and/or because evolution has not produced an appropriate species to use the resources. Food resources are often emphasized in this concept of niche, because use of foods is often easiest to measure compared to use of other habitat resources. The term *feeding niche* is used to restrict the definition to food resources.

Competition

Competition is the mutual use of habitat resources by two animals or populations when those resources are in short supply (limiting) for at least one animal or population. *Intraspecific* competition occurs between animals of one species. *Interspecific* competition occurs between species and implies *niche overlap*, the occurrence of habitat resources in the niches of two species. Note that mutual use of nonlimiting resources is not competition.

For species occupying one habitat, natural selection has favored the accumulation of adaptations that permit species to avoid interspecific competition. This results in *ecological separation*, the differences between the sets of adaptations of two species, or the differences between the sets of habitat resources used by two species. Ecological separation is the opposite of niche overlap. Species having evolved together tend to be ecologically separated and are not expected to compete under conditions that have been common in their mutual evolutionary history. They tend to have different food preferences and/or different habitat preferences (Fig. 4.2). Disadvantages resulting from interspecific competition have been the natural-selective forces favoring evolution of ecological separation. A fauna of numerous, very specialized species utilizes habitat resources more efficiently than does a fauna of a few generalized species. As a result, a diversity of wild herbivores can use forage resources more efficiently than can a few types of domestic livestock and has greater potential for meat production (Dasmann 1964).

In contrast, intraspecific competition will favor niche expansion. Intraspecific competition is greatest when a species population becomes so abundant that the most preferred habitat resources, often foods, come to be in very short supply. Under these conditions, animals tend to use less-preferred resources that are otherwise used little or not at all. The niche, the set of used habitat resources, "expands." Thus, on "overstocked" ranges, ecological separation tends to break down, and niche overlap and interspecific competition are more likely.

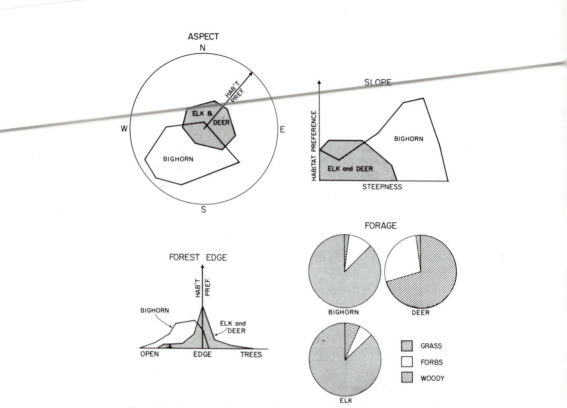

Fig. 4.2 Ecological separation of three ungulate species in an alpine environment of Colorado. Mule deer and elk use similar habitats but have differing forage preferences. Elk and bighorns have similar forage preferences but differing habitat preferences. Data are simplified from Harrington 1978.

PRINCIPLES

P4.1 Wildlife biologists manage land ecosystems supporting a great variety and abundance of plants and animals that are interrelated in many complex ways, including—but not limited to—food webs and competition. The complexity of an ecosystem managed by a wildlife biologist is at least as great as that of any system managed by any profession. This complexity defies complete understanding, limits confidence in predictions, and requires caution in management prescriptions.

P4.2 Wild animals have numerous anatomical, physiological, and learned and genetic behavioral adaptations that enhance their abilities to live in certain ways in certain kinds of environments. Adaptations determine a species' habitat requirements. Adaptations are equally limitations, and some species are highly specialized and, therefore, can exist in only a narrow range of habitat conditions. Such species are especially sensitive to habitat alteration.

P4.3   Competition is mutual use of limiting habitat resources by two animals or populations. Species having evolved together tend to be ecologically separated, so that their functional and resource niches do not overlap completely, and competition is reduced or avoided.

CHAPTER   5

WILDLIFE AND SOILS

The specific ways in which
mineral-rich soils benefit animals...are
by no means well understood. Nevertheless,
one thing stands out clearly:
good soils yield the best crops,
both in quantity and quality, of practically everything
that lives upon them.

Durward L. Allen

SOIL AND ANIMAL QUALITY
SOIL, LAND USE, AND WILDLIFE
  HABITAT

IMPLICATIONS FOR WILDLIFE
  MANAGEMENT
PRINCIPLES

"Life is rooted in the soil" is an accepted axiom. We expect greater production of higher quality agricultural crops—grain, forage, livestock—from soils of higher fertility. There is much data and experience to support this expectation (Albrecht 1956; 1957). Yet, there has been a tendency to assume that wildlife can be produced on the leftover areas, those that are too infertile for satisfactory production of domestic crops. Abundant evidence, however, indicates that poor soil can produce little wildlife. Landowners cannot take satisfaction from leaving the thin soils, rock outcrops, and saline basins for wildlife. They have sacrificed little or nothing for wildlife, for such areas can produce little or nothing of either domestic crops or wildlife.

Soil fertility depends on soil structure and chemistry. These soil characteristics are influenced by the parent material, climate, biota, and age of soil development. The importance of each of these factors in determining soil fertility varies among sites. Parent material is most important in young soils, such as on rock outcrops or on sand plains from which the organic matter has been removed by fire (Example 5.2). As the soil ages, climate and biota become more important factors in determining fertiliity.

In general, soils that develop in a moist climate are well leached of minerals. However, they are highly productive of carbohydrate biomass, usually in forest vegetation. The comparatively mineral deficient soil and the abundant vegetative growth result in large potential forage resources with low concentrations of nutrients. Herbivores adapted to these types of vegetation usually feed selectively on parts of plants in which nutrients are concentrated, such as buds, fruits, or seeds. They may also be adapted to feeding in vegetation resulting from recent disturbance by fire or wind. When forest vegetation is disturbed, nutrients previously bound in the standing crop are released and usually are recycled through the soil into successional vegetation. This process results in temporarily enriched forage resources, and disturbed areas attract many forest herbivores (Sampson 1944; Taber and Dasmann 1958; Leege 1969; Dills 1970). The interaction of climate, soil, vegetation, and disturbance, and its implications for nutrition of animals, particularly ruminants, have been discussed by Dasmann and Dasmann (1963) and particularly by Albrecht (1944; 1957). Livestock and deer have been more productive in the semiarid portions of their geographic ranges where forage is more nutritious. In the more humid portions of their ranges, deer, at least, have been more productive on recently disturbed sites.

SOIL AND ANIMAL QUALITY

Numerous studies have related the productivity of domestic animals to soil fertility, and some results are especially impressive. Steen (1955) noted great differences in cattle production between sites receiving much precipitation and having soils well leached of their mineral fertility and sites receiving less precipitation and retaining soil minerals (Table 5.1).

TABLE 5.1   Productivity of Cattle on Unfertilized Range According to Climate and Resulting Soil Fertility (data reported by Steen 1955 are averaged from records of six experiment stations)

Average Annual Precipitation (inches)	Average Mature Cow (lb)	Average Calf Crop (percent)	Average 8-Month-Old Calf (lb)
20	1000	90	425
60	650	30	225

Specific soil deficiencies and their effects on livestock have often been identified. Morrow described infertility of dairy heifers caused by a phosphorus deficiency that developed from soil depletion by intensive cropping practices (1969). The cows showed poor coats and depraved appetites. After supplementing their diet with phosphorus, the average number of artificial inseminations necessary per conception fell from 3.7 to 1.3. Similar studies with livestock have implicated many areas of the United States where minerals, especially cobalt and phosphorus, are often deficient, or where minerals may be so abundant as to produce toxic forage (Beeson 1941; Fig. 5.1).

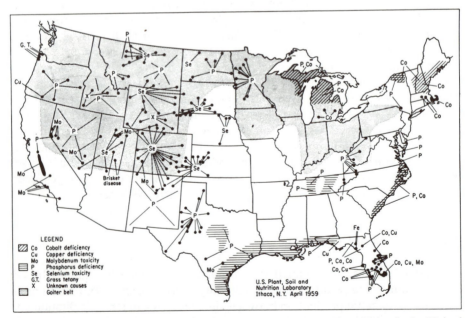

Fig. 5.1   Distribution of studies indicating soil deficiencies and toxicities in the United States.

Wildlife are also affected by soil through nutrition, but they have two advantages over domestic livestock. First, confinement should make livestock more susceptible to problems caused by soil deficiency or toxicity. Wildlife, on the other hand, are often capable of visiting more than one soil type, permitting compensation for local deficiency or avoidance of local toxicity. Second, most wild populations have evolved in the areas where they live. If there are soil problems, we expect wild animals to become behaviorally or physiologically adapted for avoiding those problems. Behaviorally, they may evolve preferences for food items in which soil-deficient minerals are concentrated. For example, Harper and Labisky found that ring-necked pheasants on calcium-deficient soils could selectively ingest the more calcium-rich grit from their environment (1964). Wildlife may also develop traditions for using local soil areas having a greater abundance of the otherwise deficient minerals. In these areas scarce minerals may be obtained from forage or directly, by eating soil in "licks." Physiologically, wild animals may develop tolerances for mineral deficiencies in their environment, perhaps by recycling scarce minerals rather than excreting them.

The productivity of wild populations may be affected by local or regional soil deficiencies or toxicities. However, seldom have data been adequate to demonstrate the existence or absence of specific soil effects on wildlife. Three examples of this situation follow: (1) Several analyses of deer browse have suggested seasonal deficiencies in phosphorus (Swank 1956; Hundley 1959; Dietz et al. 1962; Bailey 1967), but impacts on deer populations have not been proven or disproven. Symptoms of extreme phosphorus deficiency are seldom seen, but deer reproduction could be affected without extreme deficiency. Lack of phosphorus would be accentuated whenever there is a shortage of food, and it would be difficult to separate the effects of poor phosphorus nutrition from those of inadequate feed. (2) The distribution of productive populations of ring-necked pheasants in Illinois is closely related to soil conditions. The birds have existed mostly on younger soils north of the terminal moraine of the Wisconsin glaciation. Older soils south of this line have not supported pheasants. Yet considerable study has failed to conclusively implicate soil factors controlling pheasant populations (Dale 1954; Harper and Labisky 1964; Anderson and Stewart 1969; Anderson 1973). (3) Many populations of big game regularly use soil from licks, suggesting there are mineral deficiencies in forages, but we have not identified deficient minerals in at least most of these populations, nor have we concluded whether or not providing mineral supplements might be a useful management tool in some areas. Salting of big game ranges with mineral-supplement blocks was once routine in some states. But the benefits of these programs, in terms of higher reproduction or survival rates or larger game harvests, were never demonstrated. However, reproduction survival, and harvestable surplus are variables influenced by many environmental factors. Small benefits of mineral supplements in big-game diets would be difficult to detect because the effects of the supplements would be submerged in the variation caused by other factors.

TABLE 5.2   Size and Strength of Femurs of Cottontail Rabbits in Relation to Soil Fertility in Missouri (data from Crawford 1946)

Soil Fertility at Sources of Rabbits[a]	Femur Characteristics			
	Average Weight (g)	Average Length (cm)	Average Thickness of Bone Wall (mm)	Average Breaking Strength (kg)
High	4.2	8.0	0.82	20.2
Medium	3.8	7.9	0.74	16.7
Low	3.4	7.3	0.68	12.4

[a]Femurs were collected from rabbits harvested in many counties. They were grouped according to average soil conditions in each county.

There is general evidence that the quality of wild herbivores is a function of soil fertility in their home ranges (Denney 1944; Steen 1955). When comparing harvested animals from Missouri counties with high, medium, and low soil fertility, Crawford noted that the largest raccoon, muskrats, opossums, and rabbits came from counties with high soil fertility, while the smallest animals came from counties with low fertility (1946). For muskrats and opossums, fur quality was also related to soil fertility. Femur bones from rabbits were bigger and stronger when obtained from counties with high fertility (Table 5.2), and litters of fox squirrels from these counties were also larger. Several studies, recently that of Hill (1972), have demonstrated that litter sizes in cottontail rabbits are positively correlated with increasing soil fertility. Hanson and Kossack found fatness of Illinois mourning doves to be related to soil fertility and resulting land-use practices (1963; Table 5.3). Birds from Hancock County were generally fatter than those from Mason County, where the soils are sandy and low in nitrogen and organic matter. Parts of Mason County support only sparse vegetation, and weed seeds constituted the chief diet of doves there. In Hancock County, where soils are more fertile, much corn was grown and became available to doves, producing heavier birds.

TABLE 5.3   Effects of Soil Fertility and Land Use on Fat Reserves of Immature Mourning Doves Shot in September in Illinois (data from Hanson and Kossack 1963)

County		Percent of Doves in Each Fatness Category			
	Sample Size	No Fat	Little Fat	Moderate Fat	Very Fat
Mason[a]	51	43	49	8	0
Hancock[a]	170	9	42	32	16

[a]Mason County has poorer soil; weed seeds constituted the main dove food. Hancock County has better soil; corn was grown and became available in hog feedlots to doves.

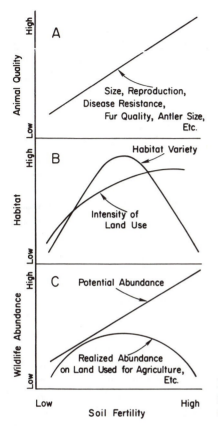

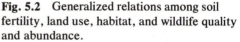

Fig. 5.2 Generalized relations among soil fertility, land use, habitat, and wildlife quality and abundance.

Although soil quality is not the only factor affecting the quality of animals, we can generalize that animal quality is directly related to soil fertility (Fig. 5.2a). We expect to see this relationship expressed in the size, vigor, reproduction, disease resistance, fur quality, antler size, and other characteristics of wild animals. This generalization also implies that the greatest potential for wildlife abundance and productivity lies on the most fertile soils.

SOIL, LAND USE, AND WILDLIFE HABITAT

Use of the land is often tied to the productivity of the soil. Our most intensive agriculture, involving monotonous fields of row crops, is applied on the most fertile soils, especially on the young soils of central and northern Iowa, Illinois, and Indiana (Fig. 5.2b). In these areas, the economic value of corn or soybeans precludes production of hay and pasture, crops of lesser value. There has been strong economic incentive to replace each woodlot, hedgerow, and wide roadside with a few more rows of crops. Weeds and insects are controlled. Fields are very large and harvested with expensive machines. Weather permitting, autumn plowing turns the land bare before winter. This intensive agriculture leaves little wildlife food and cover at some seasons and the large, uniformly managed fields provide little interspersion of habitat resources. Even the ring-necked pheasant, which is adapted to intensively managed agricultural land, suffers from lack of nesting cover and perhaps from lack of winter cover.

It is similar on rangelands and forest lands. Rewards from investing in intensive land management are greatest on the most productive soils. The most productive range soils are most likely to be converted to tame hays and pastures, to be treated with selective herbicides and to be intensively fenced for livestock control. The most productive forest soils are most likely to be planted with selected strains of trees that will be pruned and thinned to remove dead trees and unwanted species. These practices are not always detrimental to wildlife habitat, but they generally produce a more uniform habitat with little interspersion of food and cover. Further, since economic rewards for growing crops other than wildlife are greatest on the most fertile soils, very little of these lands is diverted especially for wildlife production.

Denney concluded that wildlife are often most abundant on soils of medium fertility (1944; Fig. 5.2c). On soils of low fertility, the productivities of herbivore populations are limited by poor nutrition and low population densities result. Although the *potential* for wildlife abundance is greatest on high-fertility soils, intensive land uses designed for other crops result in poor wildlife habitat and small populations (Example 5.1). On soils of medium fertility, wildlife productivity is not so limited by soil infertility, and less intensive land use permits a variety and interspersion of food and cover resources. Sometimes moderate levels of land use *increase* the variety and interspersion of food and cover and improve habitat compared to pristine conditions (Fig. 5.2b). This happened during the early history of the eastern United States, as scattered homesteads opened patches throughout the otherwise continuous forests.

When land is managed primarily for wildlife, opportunities for producing an abundance of quality animals are best on the most fertile soils. However, because of trends illustrated in Fig. 5.2, opportunities for the wildlife manager to influence land-use practices toward providing better habitat are usually greatest on soils of medium fertility where economic competition for the soil is less severe.

EXAMPLE 5.1   Decline in Wildlife Abundance with Intensified Agriculture in Illinois (Vance 1976)

Changing supplies of and demands for agricultural products and advances in agricultural technology, especially in the use of fertilizers and machinery, favored intensification of cash-grain farming in southeastern Illinois during 1939 to 1974. Great changes in wildlife habitat resulted (Fig. 5.3; Table 5.4). Woody fence rows have been removed, fields have been enlarged, and there has been a change from mixed agricul-

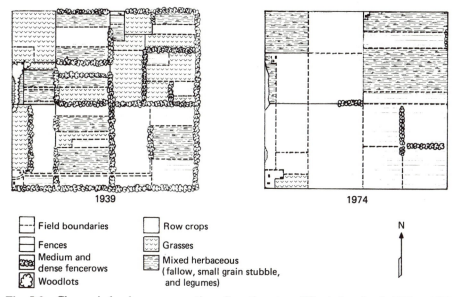

Fig. 5.3   Change in land use on a section of southeastern Illinois farmland, 1939 to 1974. From Vance 1976.

TABLE 5.4   Changes in Habitat and Wildlife During 1939 to 1974 on a Representative Area of Over 2400 Acres in Jasper County, Illinois (Vance 1976)

	1939	1974
Number of fields	236	116
Average size of fields (acres)	10	23
Percent of area		
Corn	19	7
Soybeans	9	69
Grasses	36	0
Pasture	11	1
Stubble, fallow, etc.	8	11
Woodlots	2	1
Roads, farmsteads, etc.	15	10
Fence rows (miles)	54	12
Wildlife abundance		
Prairie chickens (number males on booming grounds)	165	0
Bobwhite quail (number per sq mile)	52	11
Cottontails (number flushed per sq mile)	13	0.5

ture including pasture and grasses for seed and hay to primary emphasis on row crops, especially soybeans. Whereas grasses and pasture once covered 47 percent of a representative area, only 1 percent of that area supported grassy cover in 1974, and this was "overgrazed" pasture.

The loss of grasslands, woody cover in fence rows, and interspersion of vegetation in small fields has deteriorated habitat for many species. Prairie chickens, once abundant on the area, require grasslands for nesting cover. They were extirpated from the area by 1969. Elimination of brushy fence rows, which once provided food, cover, and travel lanes for bobwhite quail and cottontails, has caused these species to decline by about 79 and 96 percent, respectively. Many species of songbirds requiring grasslands and hedgerows also declined during the 35-year period.

Many of the current generation of people in southeastern Illinois are unaware of this land's great potential to produce wildlife. Economics dictates the use of most private land, and there is little economic incentive to provide wildlife habitat, certainly none that can compete with the dollar value of grain crops.

IMPLICATIONS FOR WILDLIFE MANAGEMENT

Wildlife are products of the land, and wildlife managers should be concerned with maintaining and enhancing the fertility of the land. Practices that reduce soil fertility also reduce its capacity to produce wildlife. Some sites and soils are fragile. Their productivities are not inherent in their parent materials, but depend on soil stability, structure, and organic matter that occur only after decades or more of biotic succession and soil development (Example 5.2). Habitat manipulation practices such as prescribed fire or mechanical treatment of vegetation might reduce soil fertility if carelessly applied. Careful application of such practices requires consideration of site factors, such as slope and aspect, and of soil factors, such as erodibility or the consequences of destroying organic matter. In fragile areas, the season and the intensity and frequency of habitat treatment can be varied to reduce or eliminate soil damage.

Soil fertilization has sometimes been used in habitat management. However, the benefits of applying fertilizers have seldom been measured and compared with the costs. Our generalization that more fertile soils produce more and better wildlife does not justify haphazard application of fertilizer mixtures in hopes that wildlife will be favored. Fertilizers have been used in food patches planted for game birds. Sometimes a value of food patches lies in establishing early stages of plant succession, which are valuable to the birds for several years. Soil fertilization may speed succession and reduce this benefit.

Before soil fertilization for wildlife is justified, the population benefits of fertilization must be measured, compared to the costs and compared to potential benefits from other possible management practices. Soil fertilization has, in some instances, increased forage production or increased the concentration of some nutrients in forage. However, these do not prove that wildlife population-limiting factors have been affected or that more animals are being produced.

EXAMPLE 5.2.   Fire and Fragile Soil on the Kingston Plains

The Kingston Plains are one of many sandy areas that produced magnificent pine in northern Michigan. In the early 1900s, the plains were logged by methods no longer sanctioned. Several square miles were clear-cut. Logging slash was not controlled. Carelessness resulted in wildfire following logging. Soil organic matter was turned to ashes, and the released minerals were leached away. Fifty years later, the plains were still unable to grow healthy pine trees (Fig. 5.4).

The sandy parent material of the plains provides little inherent fertility. The sands have little capacity for holding moisture. They are mineral deficient and resistant to weathering, so that minerals are released slowly. In pristine times, a biotic community and topsoil developed on these sands. The biota accumulated scarce minerals in living and dead tissues. Organic matter covered the soil and became incorporated into it. This organic matter became the key to soil fertility. It held moisture above the otherwise well-drained sands. Decaying organic matter became the primary source of minerals needed by plants. Destruction of the organic matter by wildfire meant loss of soil fertility for a century or more.

The once-forested Kingston Plains supported wildlife associated with forest communities—probably a few deer, moose, woodland caribou, bear, marten, and many squirrels and songbirds. After logging and fire, the area was invaded by sharp-tailed grouse, which were native on the prairies to the west. One might argue that loss of soil fertility caused by fire **increased** the land's capacity to produce some wildlife—sharp-tailed grouse. However, grouse were not favored by poor soil, but rather by conver-

Fig. 5.4 The Kingston Plains in 1956. Wildfire following logging of white pine destroyed soil organic matter, the key to fertility. Decades after fire control, much of the surface supports only lichens.

sion of the area from forest to grassland and shrubland. Considering all species of plants and animals on the plains, total biomass production must have been greatly reduced by loss of soil organic matter.

The Kingston Plains is an extreme case illustrating the magnitude and persistence of damage that can occur through careless management of lands with fragile soils.

With respect to soil resources, the United States is overpopulated with people. We are using almost all our most fertile soils to produce our own food. We have forgone the option of producing wildlife on the soils that are most capable of producing many species. We have foreclosed that option for at least many generations of Americans. Our most fertile soil once produced the tall-grass prairie with prairie chickens, bison, elk, passenger pigeons, and seasonally abundant waterfowl. That ecosystem is extinct. Most of its component species persist, but nowhere do all the tall-grass prairie organisms coexist.

The process of relegating wildlife production to the poorest soils continues. New machinery, use of fertilizers, development of new strains of plants, and other new technology are permitting more intensive use of even moderately fertile soils. At the same time, wildlife habitats are being lost to subdivisions, reservoirs, mining, and other developments. We seem to assume that wildlife can always thrive on the "leftover" areas—poor soils, the high-mountain wildernesses, the deserts. We forget that wildlife have specific habitat requirements, and populations are most productive on the best soils within suitable habitats.

PRINCIPLES

P5.1 Soil is our most basic land resource. Soils vary greatly in fertility and fragility. Any land-use practice that degrades soil fertility also degrades its ability to produce any organic resource, includng wildlife.

P5.2 Within suitable habitats, wild animals achieve higher quality, and wildlife populations are larger and more productive on the more fertile soils. As with all organic resources, the benefits of wildlife management can be greater on fertile soils than on infertile soils.

P5.3 Human use of the land tends to be most intensive on areas having the most fertile soils. The intensity of agriculture, forestry, and range management on the most fertile soils usually reduces the variety of food and cover resources available to wildlife and makes these areas less suitable or unsuitable as wildlife habitat. On soils of moderate fertility, extensive agriculture, forestry, and range management often increase the variety of habitat resources and improve wildlife habitat.

CHAPTER   6

WILDLIFE FOODS, NUTRITION, AND WATER REQUIREMENTS

Food shortage appears to be the chief natural
factor limiting the numbers of many birds, of
various carnivorous and herbivorous mammals,
of many larger marine fish, and of certain
predatory insects.

David Lack

When rains come the emerald hills
laugh with delight as bourgeoning
bloom is spread in the sunlight.
When the rains have ceased all the
verdure turns to gold. Then slowly
the hills are brinded until the rains
come again, when verdure and bloom
again peer through the tawny wreck
of last year's greenery.

John Wesley Powell

Our knowledge of food requirements of wildlife begins with studies of food habits, usually of adult animals. In North America, we have begun these studies for most wild species but much remains to be learned about variation in food habits among sex- and age classes of animals, among geographic regions, and among seasons. Beyond food habits, we have used captive animals to make detailed studies of nutritional needs associated with physiological functions such as reproduction.

SCOPE OF WILDLIFE NUTRITION

Obviously, food is important to all wildlife. Animals having good nutrition throughout their lives grow larger and are more vigorous and healthy than animals having experienced poor nutrition during part or all of their lives (Fig. 6.1). Size, vigor, and health are measures of general physical condition. Animals in good condition generally have higher rates of reproduction and are more resistant to all forms of mortality than are animals in poor condition. Thus, nutrition affects birth rates and death rates and is important in the dynamics of managed populations.

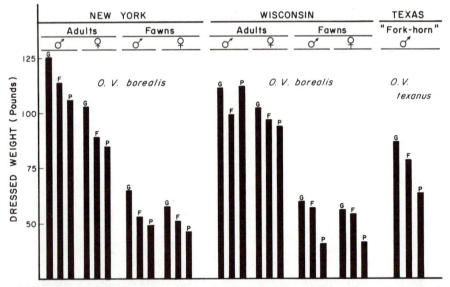

Fig. 6.1   Effects of nutrition on size of white-tailed deer *(Odocoileus virginianus)*. Samples are from populations existing on good *(G)*, fair *(F)* or poor *(P)* range. The subspecies *texanus* is inherently smaller than *borealis*. Data are from Severinghaus 1955, Dahlberg and Guettinger 1956, and Teer et al. 1965.

TABLE 6.1   Reproductive Success of New York Deer on a Range Providing Good Nutrition (Western New York) and a Range Providing Poor Nutrition (Central Adirondacks) (after Cheatum and Severinghaus 1950)

	Western New York	Central Adirondacks
Percent of adult does pregnant	94	79
Mean number of embryos per pregnant adult doe	1.8	1.3
Percent of fawn does pregnant	32	3

EXAMPLE 6.1   Nutrition and Deer Reproduction

Many populations of North American ungulates on overpopulated and overbrowsed winter ranges exhibit poor reproductive success due to poor nutrition. Compare reproductive success of white-tailed deer from western New York, where the quality of winter forage has been adequate to excellent, with success of deer from the central Adirondacks of New York, where overpopulations of deer have subsisted on foods low in quantity and quality (Table 6.1). In western New York 100 adult does produce 169 fawns, whereas in the central Adirondacks 100 adult does bear only 103 fawns. The prevalence of fawn breeding in western New York further differentiates the reproductive rates of these two herds. Furthermore, fawn survival might be higher in western New York. A study of penned white-tailed deer suggests that winter and spring nutrition of female deer may drastically affect the survival of their fawns (Table 6.2). Does on poor nutrition produced small, weak fawns that could not nurse. Often these does did not lactate. Their fawns usually died within two days after birth.

EXAMPLE 6.2   Nutrition and Fox Squirrel Populations

Widespread effects of malnutrition were exhibited by Michigan fox squirrels during failure of mast crops in 1940 (Allen 1943). The years 1937 through 1940 were increasingly

TABLE 6.2   Effect of Nutrition on Reproductive Success of White-tailed Deer (after Verme 1962)

Plane of Nutrition				
Diet	Winter	Spring	Fawns Born Per Pregnant Doe	Fawn Mortality (percent)
1	High	High	1.6	7
2	Moderate	High	1.6	6
3	Low	High	1.4	35
4	Low	Moderate	1.6	54
5	Low	Low	1.3	93

favorable for Michigan fox squirrels. Populations increased and an abundant crop of acorns in 1939 provided for a peak breeding population in early 1940. However, in 1940 both black and white oaks failed to bear acorns and, in areas where acorns were the main winter food, malnutrition followed in the winter of 1940–41. Squirrels averaged 3 to 8 ounces below their weights of the previous winter. Mange caused by scabies mites was unusually common. On one study area, only 2 percent of 52 observed female squirrels were pregnant in the spring of 1941, wheras 81 percent of 139 observed females had been pregnant the previous year. Many squirrels were found dead in nests, dens, and on the ground. Failure of the 1939 acorn crop was not disastrous in agricultural areas of Michigan where grain crops provided alternative winter food. Nevertheless, the statewide success of squirrel hunters declined from 4.5 squirrels harvested per hunter in 1940 to 3.8 per hunter in 1941.

FOOD COMPONENTS

All animals must obtain water, energy, and various nutrients from their environment.

Water is necessary for digestion and metabolism, to carry off body wastes and for evaporative cooling. Wild vertebrates may obtain water (1) from free water in lakes, ponds, and streams, (2) from succulent vegetation, (3) by utilizing dew, or (4) from metabolic water produced in metabolizing fats and carbohydrates. Animal requirements for water and the management of water in wildlife habitat are discussed last in this chapter.

Animals require energy for basal metabolic processes and need additional calories for daily activities. Basal requirements for energy are related to body surface area, a function of body weight (Fig. 6.3). Carbohydrates, fats, and proteins may be digested, absorbed, and metabolized for energy. Among these, digestible fats provide the greatest amount of energy per gram—about 2.25 times as much as carbohydrates.

Animals may store fat for periods when energy demands are high, as during migratory flights of birds, or for seasons when foods are in short supply. However, existence in the wild often requires great mobility for obtaining daily and seasonal needs and for escape from predators. Thus, in some wild species, natural selection has not favored evolution of large fat reserves that might add weight and hinder mobility. For example, fat comprised only 5.5 percent of the weights of the skinned eviscerated carcasses of mule deer collected from mid-December through April (Anderson et al. 1969). African impala, gazelles, and kob are less than 5 percent fat, while gnu and eland are 2 to 10 percent fat (Ledger 1968). In contrast, domestic sheep and cattle average 20 and 26 percent fat, respectively (Maynard and Loosli 1962).

Special nutrients are required to regulate body metabolism and for growth and maintenance of tissues. Nutrients are proteins, vitamins, essential fatty acids, and minerals.

Proteins are especially important for growth, reproduction, and disease resistance. In general, foods having plenty of protein are apt to provide adequate amounts of other nutrients as well. For herbivores, plant materials containing adequate concentrations of protein are often succulent and highly digestible. For these reasons protein levels in foods are especially meaningful, and there has been a tendency to evaluate the qualities of wildlife foods on the basis of their protein levels. Although protein is a good general index to food quality, it must be remembered that the value of a food may be limited by many other factors, such as palatability, digestibility, or toxicity, or by lack of some nutrient such as a vitamin or trace element.

Vertebrates require small amounts of vitamins and certain fatty acids in their diet because they are metabolically unable to synthesize these compounds. Deficiencies of these nutrients may occur in domestic animals restricted to artificially produced feeds. In wild animals on good habitat, such deficiencies are less apt to occur because the animals have access to a great variety of foods. In ruminants, vitamins and fatty acids are synthesized by symbiotic rumen bacteria and can be absorbed by the animal. There has been little study of vitamins and essential fatty acids in the nutrition of wild animals. Deficiencies of these nutrients are most apt to occur in conjunction with food shortages or when available foods are generally poor in quality—that is, deficient in protein and relatively indigestible.

At least 13 elements are essential in vertebrate physiology (Maynard and Loosli 1962). Among these, calcium, phosphorus, magnesium, sodium, potassium, chlorine, and iron are major mineral nutrients. Others, like copper and cobalt, are needed in trace amounts.

In studies of wildlife nutrition, phosphorus concentrations and the ratios between calcium and phosphorus concentrations in big game foods have received much attention. Studies with domestic animals have shown that calcium and phosphorus in food are poorly utilized when the ratio between their concentrations is less than 0.5 or more than 2. Yet analyses of browse used by wintering deer in many parts of North America have indicated low levels of phosphorus and high calcium–phosphorus ratios. The significance of these studies is not clear. Deer may obtain phosphorus from sources other than browse, or they may have unusual abilities to compensate for deficiencies. Or perhaps the reproductive rates and/or mortality rates of many deer populations are being affected by inadequate amounts of phosphorus in their winter diets.

Wild animals fulfill their nutrient requirements by using a great variety of foods. They may also consume soil, grit, afterbirth, urine, and feces. They may adjust to nutrient deficiencies by seeking foods that best satisfy their needs. There have been few field studies of wildlife nutrition, and these have seldom, if ever, demonstrated conclusively that a population was suffering a deficiency of one nutrient. That is, nutritional problems in wildlife have not been specific. Rather, foods have sometimes been seasonally in short supply and also low in protein and relatively indigestible. Sophisticated field studies of wildlife nutrition may yet uncover nutritional problems that can be resolved by providing a certain nutrient, such as phosphorus, in the habitat; but it is likely that nutritional deficiencies in wildlife populations will most often be deficiencies of many nutrients. These deficiencies may be chronic, or they may become important only in periods of population stress—as in years when weather conditions reduce the available supply of food, or when the wildlife population is challenged by an outbreak of disease or parasitism.

FOOD REQUIREMENTS: A VARIABLE

The amount and quality of food required by wildlife may vary among species, between the sexes, among age classes, with physiological function and season of the year, with weather, and among geographic locations.

Most carnivores are opportunistic feeders, adapted to catching certain types of prey (fish, birds, small mammals, large mammals), but generally feeding on any species that is available and vulnerable. These carnivores do not exhibit marked food preferences. Their food, raw meat, provides a high-quality diet, and almost any raw meat suffices. As a result, nutritional problems of wild carnivores are problems of food quantity and availability, not of food quality.

Food Preference Hierarchies

In contrast, herbivores exist on comparatively crude foods, mainly carbohydrates with low concentrations of proteins and other nutrients. Herbivores feed mainly on plant species and parts of plants (buds, leaves, flowers, fruits) in which nutrients are concentrated. They exhibit strong preferences for certain high-quality plant foods. Nutritional problems of wild herbivores are usually due to a lack of foods of adequate quality. Animals may be malnourished or starving in a habitat where, superficially, food appears to be adequate because vegetation is available. However, a biologist familiar with the wildlife species and its nutrition might recognize that preferred foods are absent and that the animals are subsisting on unpalatable and poorly digestible foods.

Because herbivores usually have marked food preferences, their food habits are usually described in a hierarchy of food classes. Some foods are preferred and of high quality. Others are emergency foods, less preferred and usually of mediocre quality. Emergency foods become especially important when all preferred foods have been used. They may sustain a herbivore population through a critical period of food shortage. Still other foods are starvation foods, of inadequate quality and eaten only when other foods are absent. Use of starvation foods indicates that the habitat is inadequate and cannot support the number of animals present.

EXAMPLE 6.3   Impact of Selective Foraging by Deer on Vegetative Composition

A stand of northern-hardwood timber in the Adirondack Mountains, New York, was harvested in 1954 (Tierson et al. 1966). After this commercial harvest, the remaining noncommercial trees were poisoned in 1961. These site-disturbing activities were designed to regenerate the commercial forest. However, early stages of secondary succession following disturbance in northern hardwoods also provide an abundance of shrubs and young trees, which are browsed by white-tailed deer.

This Adirondack forest supported a large population of deer. There were so many deer that their selective browsing on young trees had altered the composition of the forest, favoring abundance of American beech, which deer seldom ate and which had little commercial value. Deer were thus a major factor in Adirondack forest economics. Deer were also a major factor determining their own food supply. Their persistent browsing almost eliminated some preferred browse species from the habitat.

The logged and poisoned northern-hardwood stand contained a large deer enclosure. The effects of deer browsing on forest regeneration and on availability of deer foods were evaluated in 1963 by observing vegetation on 48 milacre plots, 24 within and 24 without the exclosure. On each plot, the number of stems at least 3 feet tall of trees and shrubs were counted. This criterion indicates the rate of stocking of trees that might grow beyond the reach of deer and establish a new commercial forest. It also indicates the abundance of trees and shrubs tall enough to provide deer browse during the critical winter period when snow may be 1 to 2 feet deep.

Woody vegetation over 3-feet tall was abundant and varied within the deer exclosure (Table 6.3). Most trees were commercially valuable yellow birch, white ash, and sugar maple. There was also an abundance of high quality deer browse, both young trees and shrubs.

TABLE 6.3   Availability of Eight Species of Browse in a Regenerating Adirondack Forest with a Dense Population of White-tailed Deer

Browse Species	Browse Preference Rating	Resistance to Browse Damage	Number of Stems 3 Feet and Taller on 24 Milacre-Plots[a]	
			Within Exclosure	Without Exclosure
Trees				
Yellow birch	High	Low	20	0
White ash	High	Low-moderate	24	3
Sugar maple	High	Moderate	82	2
American beech	Starvation	Little-used	16	35
Shrubs				
Scarlet elder	High	Low	12	0
Alternate-leaved dogwood	High	Low	11	0
Striped maple	High	Moderate	18	0
Witch-hobble	Medium-high	Very resistant	55	14

[a]From Tierson et al. 1966.

Outside of the enclosure, the abundance of trees and shrubs over 3-feet tall was primarily dependent on the feeding habits of deer and on the resistance of some plant species to damage caused by browsing (Table 6.3). In 1963, it was apparent that the stand would someday be composed mostly of beech. Also, with 1 to 2 feet of snow on the ground, deer would have little choice of diet. They would have little or none of the highly preferred, and presumably nutritious, yellow birch, scarlet elder, alternate-leaved dogwood, and striped maple. They would have a little white ash and sugar maple, but would have to subsist mostly on witch-hobble. The deer could eat American beech but almost never browse this species. The selective feeding of deer had virtually eliminated four plant species from the habitat and drastically reduced three others. By selective feeding, deer eliminated competition and favored beech, which became about twice as abundant without the exclosure as within.

The situation is similar in other forest types throughout the central Adirondacks. Whereas beech is especially abundant in northern hardwood types, at lower elevations the most abundant tree regeneration is red spruce, also a starvation food for deer. To the superficial observer, touring the Adirondacks by car during summer, deer forage appears abundant. The trained observer, visiting areas used by deer during winter and knowing the food habits of deer, understands why central Adirondack deer are small (see New York "poor range," Fig. 6.1) and have a low reproductive success (Table 6.1).

Comparative Nutrition

Food habits and nutritional requirements obviously vary from species to species according to each animal's array of structural, physiological, and behavioral adaptations to its environment. This fact seems so obvious that the above statement may appear unnecessary. Yet management practices have sometimes neglected differences among nutritional capabilities of species. Coarse hays, capable of sustaining domestic livestock, have been fed as emergency winter food to starving deer. These feeding operations have failed at least partly because deer are less capable of digesting coarse, fibrous hays than are cattle. Stockmen have complained that pronghorn antelope compete with cattle and sheep for range forage. Yet on ranges that are not overstocked, cattle and sheep consume mostly grass, whereas antelope eat mostly forbs and browse. There have been unsuccessful attempts to introduce ring-necked pheasants into primarily forested regions of the United States. These pheasants are adapted to agricultural lands, and much of their food consists of seeds of annual weeds and crops. They are not adapted for feeding in forest habitats and cannot adjust their inherent capabilities in order to survive anywhere they may be introduced by well-meaning persons.

A discussion of some structural, physiological, and behavioral adaptations related to wildlife nutrition will emphasize interspecies differences in nutritional capabilities.

Carnivores, adapted to using easily digested foods in which nutrients are concentrated, need only a simple digestive tract for digestion and absorption.

The vampire bat is a prime example in that its food, blood, is most concentrated, and its digestive tract is little more than a short tube through the animal.

In contrast, herbivores utilize a comparatively less-digestible diet. Compared to carnivores, herbivores may (1) masticate or otherwise grind their food more thoroughly, (2) feed more continuously, (3) have larger, longer and more complex digestive tracts, and (4) pass food through their tracts more slowly and, in some cases, more than one time. These structural and functional adaptations favor digestion of coarse, relatively indigestible materials and permit animals to utilize large volumes of food, thereby substituting food quantity for food quality. The degree to which these adaptations are developed varies greatly among herbivores. Some herbivores, fruit- and seed-eaters, eat comparatively high-quality plant materials. Others, grass- and bark-eaters, eat materials that are difficult to digest. Browsing animals occupy an intermediate position by selecting leaves, buds, and twigs in which nutrients are somewhat concentrated.

Many herbivores have evolved special digestive organs in which physical and chemical conditions serve to maintain populations of symbiotic microorganisms that digest plant materials and synthesize proteins and vitamins, benefiting the host animal. The rumino-reticula of deer and other ruminants and the ceca of peccaries, beaver, rabbits and hares, many game birds, and a variety of other animals are examples of these organs.

Ruminants rely on microbial digestion for survival. Without bacteria in their rumino-reticula, they could not adequately digest the vegetation on which they feed. Ruminants adapted to using coarse and comparatively indigestible foods, such as mature grass, are called grazers or roughage-eaters. Ruminants using the most nutritious and digestible plant parts are called browsers or selective-feeders (Hoffman 1968). In general, roughage-eaters have larger rumino-reticula for their body size than do selective feeders. This permits consumption of more food, substituting quantity for quality, and perhaps a slower rate of food passage through the tract, thus providing more time for microbial digestion. For example, the contents of the rumino-reticulum of a domestic cow amount to 12 to 18 percent of the cow's weight; the contents of the rumino-reticulum of a deer amount to 4 to 7 percent of the deer's weight. The cow will eat browse and green forbs when they are available, but it can also utilize dried grass and coarse tame hays. Deer, on the other hand, require higher quality foods. They eat grass primarily in seasons when it is green and succulent. When fed dry tame hay, they prefer to select leaves and refuse stems. Deer have evolved as selective-feeders, utilizing seasonally nutritious forbs, grass when succulent, and the buds and small twigs wherein nutrients of trees and shrubs are concentrated.

A.S. Leopold provided a similar example of structural-functional adaptations related to food habits in game birds (1953). The ceca and intestines are longer (relative to body size) in grouse that browse on leaves and buds than in quail, partridges, pheasants, and turkeys that rely on comparatively nutritious seeds and fruits (Fig. 6.2). In grouse, the longer digestive tract and cecum appear to enhance digestion of coarse foods and may also provide for microbial synthesis of needed nutrients.

Energy requirements of warm-blooded animals are related to body surface area, which varies in proportion to the three-fourths-power of body weight. More important, the basal metabolic rate *relative to body weight is* is far greater for small animals than for large animals (Fig. 6.3). The small animal, relative to its size and presumably to the capacity of its digestive system, burns energy at a faster rate than does a large animal. Consequently, small homeotherms must eat very often and must have a readily digestible diet that can be rapidly converted to usable energy. This accounts for the food habits of some species. Most grazing ruminants, utilizers of comparatively indigestible grass, are large like cattle, elk, and the African eland and wildebeest. Small ruminants like deer, pronghorn antelope, and the African suni feed selectively on more digestible plant parts. Among birds, there are no small "browsing" game birds (Fig. 6.2). The smaller game birds, like quail, must feed on more concentrated and digestible foods such as seeds and fruits.

These examples illustrate that the food habits and requirements of herbivores are not merely matters of food availability. They are products of evolution, intimately involved with the anatomy, physiology, and behavior of each species.

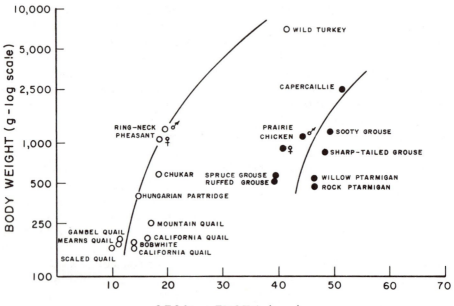

Fig. 6.2 A comparison of cecal lengths in species of browsing grouse of the family *Tetraonidae* and seed-eating quails, partridges, pheasants, and turkeys of the families *Phasaianidae* and *Meleagrididae*. From Leopold 1953.

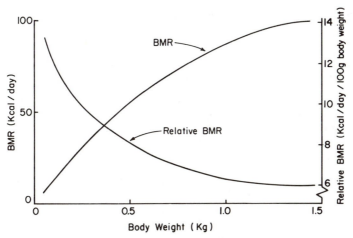

Fig. 6.3 Relationship between body weight and basal metabolic rate (BMR). Relative to body size, and to the capacity of the digestive system, small homoiotherms have greater energy requirements than do large homoiotherms.

Our ability to provide adequate food in the habitat of any wild species will increase in proportion to the depth of our knowledge of the species', or even subspecies', nutritional physiology.

Within-Species Variation

Whereas food requirements vary greatly among wildlife species, there is also much variation in food requirements within species. This variation is associated with the sexes and ages of animals and with seasonal and weather-related changes in physiology. Additional within-species variation in food requirements occurs among regions within geographic ranges.

Sex- and Age-class Requirements Males and females of the same species usually exhibit similar, but not necessarily the same, food habits. In some species sexual dimorphism permits the sexes to use somewhat different food resources, reducing intersexual competition for food. Female sharp-shinned hawks, averaging 171 g, tend to prey on somewhat larger birds and mammals than do male sharp-shinned hawks, averaging 99 g (Storer 1966). The average prey item of these males weighed 18 g; the average prey item of the females weighed 28 g. Selander discussed sexual dimorphism leading to separate feeding niches in several birds, including some woodpeckers (1966). In the Hispaniolan woodpecker of Haiti and the Dominican Republic, the bill of the female is 21 percent shorter than the bill of the male, and the horny, barbed tip of the female's tongue is 34 percent shorter. Related to this sexual dimorphism, the longer billed males spent 34 percent of their feeding time probing to capture insects in crevices and to find seeds and insects within large fruits. The females spent only 9 percent of their feeding time in probing activity, but they spent more time gleaning small insects from the surface of tree limbs than did the males.

In some vertebrates, males and females must use separate food resources because the sexes are geographically separated during part of the year. This occurs in many birds (Selander 1966) and in seals. Male ptarmigan winter above treeline near the breeding grounds, whereas females migrate into open areas within the boreal forest. During the nonbreeding season, male and female grackles may feed in different habitats. In Texas, male flocks of great-tailed grackles tend to feed in city parks and about cattle pens, whereas female flocks tend to forage in agricultural fields (Selander 1965).

Intersexual differences in food requirements also result from nutrient demands for sex-related functions (discussed below), such as pregnancy or antler growth.

Young growing animals, being small, have a higher metabolic rate relative to body size than do adults (Fig. 6.3). They also require extra energy, protein, and other nutrients for rapid growth, often necessary for survival. Young animals usually compensate for their relatively (compared to body size) greater require-ments for energy and nutrients by eating more continuously than mature animals and also by eating easily digested foods in which nutrients are concentrated. Thus, foods adequate in digestible nutrients for mature animals may not suffice for young, growing animals.

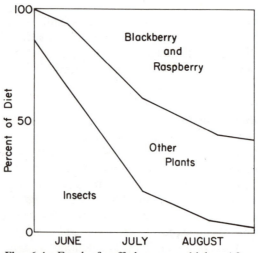

Fig. 6.4 Food of ruffed grouse chicks. After Bump et al 1947, courtesy of New York Depart-ment of Environmental Conservation.

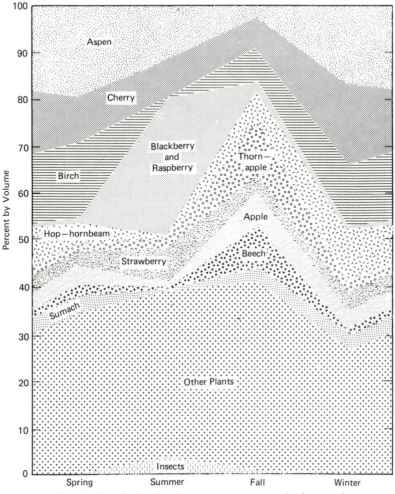

Fig. 6.5 Seasonal variation in the amount consumed of some important foods of 1093 adult grouse in New York. From Bump et al. 1947, courtesy of New York Department of Environmental Conservation.

Whereas adult grouse are primarily herbivorous, 60 to 85 percent of the food of grouse chicks, up to 2 weeks old, consists of insects such as ants, spiders, and caterpillars. The proportion of insects in the diet of chicks declines rapidly as the birds grow larger (Fig. 6.4), and by late summer only 5 percent of the diet of young grouse is insects. In contrast, adult birds seldom eat more than 5 percent insects at any season (Fig. 6.5). Insects are concentrated foods, high in protein and presumably highly digestible. Like grouse, many herbivorous species of birds are insectivorous during the first few weeks of life.

There is evidence that young cottontail rabbits likewise require foods more digestible and nutritious than those required by adult rabbits (Bailey 1969). Adults consume some grass at all seasons, even though grasses are less digestible than many forbs. Young rabbits in cages do poorly on grass diets and, during summer when the plants mature and are especially indigestible, grass diets will not sustain young rabbits. The young, rapidly growing cottontails require highly digestible food, which can be provided by whatever palatable forbs are succulent at any season.

Food for Seasons and Functions   Food habits of vertebrates vary with seasonal changes in the availabilities and qualities of food types, as well as with seasonal changes in the animals' physiologies and nutrient requirements (Fig. 6.5). This variation in food habits may involve foods that are used intensively during one season, yet are unable to sustain the animals at another season. During early spring, deer use the new growth of grass, which may be the first vegetation to become green and nutritious. However, at other seasons when grasses are not in a stage of vigorous growth, deer require succulent forbs and leaves of woody plants (Klein 1970).

The quantities of energy and nutrients required by an animal depend on nutritional demands of functions like pregnancy, growth, lactation, moulting, antler development, and energy-storage prior to hibernation or migration.

Quantitative demands for nutrients are small in early pregnancy but increase severalfold toward late pregnancy. About half the protein and more than half the energy storage in the products of pregnancy occur during the last fourth of gestation. Even larger proportions of calcium and phosphorous are required during late gestation. Further, the stomach capacity of a pregnant female mammal may be reduced during late gestation, as the volume of the uterus increases and prevents complete distention of the stomach. These factors affect the quantity and quality of food required by pregnant animals.

The National Research Council report "Nutrient Requirements of Dairy Cattle" suggests that mature cows can be maintained on a diet of 3.6 to 3.9 percent protein, that lactating cows receive a diet of 6.5 percent protein, and that young, growing heifers receive a diet of 22 percent protein (1958). Similar function-related demands for nutrients occur in wild animals.

Weather may also affect the food requirements of animals. Above or below the thermal-neutral zone, a homeotherm must burn extra food to maintain its body temperature (Fig. 6.6). Within this zone, the animal adjusts to changes in the temperature of its environment by varying its posture and surface area to alter heat loss through its fur or feathers. This adjustment requires no extra energy. However, below the lower critical temperature, the animal must burn extra food to produce heat-energy; and above the upper critical temperature, the animal must facilitate evaporative cooling, usually by panting, a process that also requires extra energy.

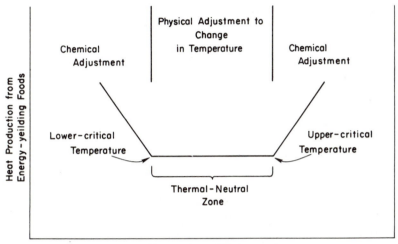

Fig. 6.6 Metabolic response of a homoiotherm to changes in environmental temperature. Outside the thermal-neutral zone, additional energy is required to maintain body temperature.

Geographic Variation in Requirements   Within species, food habits of wildlife often vary among geographic regions. Thus, the preferred browses of northeastern white-tailed deer are white cedar, hemlock, several species of maple, mountain ash, and sumac. Different plants occur in the east-central region, where whitetails prefer blueberry, greenbriar, sumac, sassafras, and tulip poplar, among other species. Still other browse plants are used by whitetails in the southeastern and western regions. There is additional variation in food habits of deer within these regions. Occasionally, studies will show a species of browse to be heavily used by deer in one state but only lightly used in other states. Thus, accurate provision for the food needs of wildlife requires a knowledge of food habits based on local studies.

FOOD SUPPLIES: A VARIABLE

Use of foods by wildlife may depend on the changing availabilities and qualities of food-species in the environment.

Food Availability

For predators, the availability of prey items varies greatly with seasonal and year-to-year changes in abundance of prey. These changes may cause periodic shifts in food habits of predators, which opportunistically utilize whatever prey species is most abundant and available. However, in simple biotic communities, where there are few species of prey, this flexibility is not possible, and predators may suffer malnutrition or emigrate in response to periodic scarcities of necessary prey. Thus, during cyclic declines in abundance of snowshoe hares in northern coniferous forests, populations of Canada lynx also decline. Likewise, when rodent populations are low in Canadian forests, there are "invasions" of snowy owls and other raptors into the United States.

For herbivores, food availability depends first on the abundances and distributions of plant species. Other factors affecting food availability are weather, persistence of plant parts, dependability of forage production, and plant resistance to damage caused by excessive herbivore use.

Thorough discussion of the factors affecting abundances and distributions of plant species would require a textbook of plant ecology, and wildlife biologists should be educated in this subject. In manipulating wildlife habitat, the most successful means for influencing plant communities have involved maintenance of vegetation in desired stages of succession, either by protection of climax communities or by periodic site disturbance, usually by logging, burning, chemical spraying, or mechanical methods. Effects of succession on wildlife habitat are discussed in Chapter 13.

In areas subject to periodic droughts, growth of wildlife foods may show large year-to-year fluctuations. During a dry year, prairie marshes may go dry, eliminating both food and cover for muskrats and ducks. In arid areas, each year's production of vegetation and seeds may depend on the amount of precipitation during the previous fall and winter. Wet winters are often followed by springs in which deserts "bloom" with productivity. But winter moisture may be unreliable, and the resulting availabilities of green forage, especially forbs, as deer food and of seeds as quail food vary greatly from year to year. The reproductive success of deer herds in the arid southwest varies greatly from year to year, presumably in response to these weather-caused changes in the abundance of nutritious foods. Likewise, abundance of desert quail varies greatly from year to year with peak abundance following years with above-average precipitation.

Deep or crusted snow may reduce availability of wildlife foods. On severely browsed winter ranges of deer, the most nutritious and preferred browse plants, having been browsed for many years, are often shortest and first to be covered as snow depth increases.

In periods of deep snow, shrubs and trees with persistent fruits—fruits remaining on twigs rather than falling to the ground in early winter—may be especially important to some wild species.

Dependability of food crops involves the above-mentioned year-to-year variation in plant productivity. It also involves fluctuations in seed and mast crops produced by trees. Good production of seeds by one tree species cannot be depended on every year. In some years, called "seed years," large crops of seeds occur. In other years, few seeds are produced. In oak forests, populations of deer and of squirrels may increase following years of good acorn production. These populations may become too large for the amount of food available during years when acorn crops fail, and crises may occur because acorn crops are not dependable. Dependability of wildlife foods is usually increased when the variety of food species is increased. Thus, in Example 6.2, Michigan fox squirrels were drastically affected by failure of an acorn crop in areas where few alternative winter foods were available.

Persistent use of plants by herbivores may eliminate preferred species or at least reduce their abundance in the plant community (Example 6.3). Overuse of a plant may kill it or at least create a disadvantage in competition with non-preferred and little-used plant species. Among browse species, some are more resistant to persistent browsing than others. In general, opposite-budded woody plants like maple and witch-hobble are more resistant to browse damage than are alternate-budded woody plants.

Food Quality

For herbivores, food quality varies with the chemical and physical compositions of plants and of plant parts. Thus, the quality of wildlife nutrition may be affected by plant genetics, by factors of season, weather, and site, and by the portion of the plant being consumed.

Genetics   Plant composition obviously varies among plant species, but we must also expect variation among geographic races or ecotypes within species. Leopold (1933, p. 273) and Squillace and Silan (1962) noted marked differences among palatabilities of races of ponderosa pine grown on a common site. These differences were presumed due to different chemical compositions of the races. Highly nutritious varieties of domestic plants such as high-lysine corn have been selected or produced by hybridization. In the future, such racial variation in composition of wild or domestic plants may become useful in manipulating habitats for wildlife. Our scant knowledge of wildlife nutrition and especially of plant composition precludes this at present.

Season and Weather   Plant composition varies among phenological stages of plant growth. Generally, plants are highest in protein and most digestible during stages of vigorous growth. As grasses mature and produce seed, protein levels decline in stems and leaves, while levels of cellulose and lignin increase, reducing the digestibility of the grass (Fig. 6.7). In general, browses show less seasonal variation in composition than do grasses (Fig. 6.7), although large variation among seasons may occur in deciduous species as leaves die and are shed (Fig. 6.8; serviceberry and Gambel oak). These variations are related to the phenologies of plants, not to dates on the calendar. Within plant species, the rate of phenological development may vary among years according to weather conditions and also may vary with site conditions such as exposure, aspect, and soil moisture.

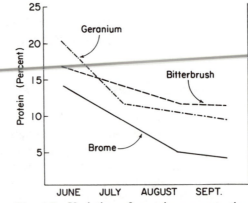

Fig. 6.7 Variation of protein concentration during the growing season in a grass (brome), a forb (geranium), and a shrub (bitterbrush). After Stoddart and Greaves 1942.

Site Factors   Site factors affecting plant composition are primarily those affecting availability of and competition for soil nutrients and/or affecting rate of plant growth.

As growth is limited (for example, by insufficient light, water, or phosphorus), plants may store excesses of some nutrients that are not limiting growth. In browse species, some of these nutrients are stored in small twigs. Consequently, slow growing shrubs on shaded sites sometimes produce browse in which nutrients are slightly more concentrated than in browse from shrubs producing

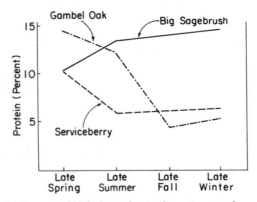

Fig. 6.8 Variation of protein concentration among seasons in browse from three shrubs. After Dietz et al. 1958.

long shoots of annual growth. In the latter cases added growth involves the production of extra carbohydrates and consequent dilution of stored nutrients. For example, in one New York study, witch-hobble plants on six shaded sites produced an average of 270 browse tips, containing an average of 7.4 percent protein, per milacre (Bailey 1967a). Witch-hobble plants on four exposed sites produced an average of 546 browse trips, containing an average of 6.7 percent protein, per milacre. In this comparison, browse quantity was 50 percent less on the shaded sites than on exposed sites, whereas browse quality in terms of protein was 11 percent higher on shaded sites than on exposed sites. It appears that reduction in browse quantity by factors limiting plant growth can be, to a small degree, compensated by an increase in nutrient concentration within the browse.

Although site factors can account for minor variation in chemical composition within plant species, there is far more variation in chemical composition among species. When habitats are manipulated to provide wildlife foods, first consideration should be given to favoring plants that are inherently nutritious.

Plant Part   The chemical and physical compositions of plants vary greatly among structures (seeds, flowers, leaves, stems) and to a lesser degree among positions of structures (top or bottom of crown, north or south side of crown) on the plant. For browsing animals, diet quality is usually best when animals can eat only the terminal portions of twigs, as they do when plenty of food is available. Since most of the nutrients in browse occur in the buds and terminal-most portions of the stems, this provides good nutrition. However, as food becomes scarce, animals are forced to consume more of the stem portions of the browse. This increases the proportions of cellulose and lignin (reducing digestibility) and decreases the proportions of nutrients, including protein, in the diet (Fig. 6.9). When examination of the range indicates that deer or other ungulates are eating unusually large portions of the stems of woody plants, consuming much wood and bark, a food shortage and perhaps critical malnutrition is occurring.

STUDYING WILDLIFE NUTRITION

Studies of wildlife nutrition range from food-habit investigations to research on metabolic pathways and nutrient-turnover rates in wild animals. They also include studies of forage use and availability and analyses of forage quality. Management biologists should be aware of methods and limitations in nutrition studies for two reasons. First, they may have to assess availabilities and qualities of foods in the habitats they manage, and/or they may have to assess the nutritional status of a wildlife population. Second, if they are to utilize knowledge gained by wildlife research as a basis for management decisions, they must be able to interpret scientific journals.

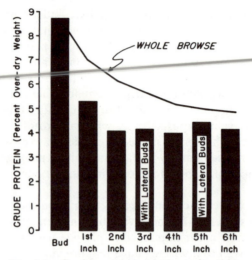

Fig. 6.9   Crude protein in portions of a witch-hobble twig. Bars indicate protein levels in terminal-bud and stem portions. The curved line illustrates concentrations of protein in pieces of browse that include all portions below and to the left of any point on the line. (Bailey 1967b).

Forage Examination

Forage Surveys   Wildlife habitats may be examined to determine the production, availability, or utilization of various wildlife foods. Since wildlife habitats and wildlife foods are so diverse, a great variety of methods has been devised for these field studies. Several methods are described in the *Manual of Wildlife Management Techniques* (Schemnitz 1980). A method most suited for local conditions can be selected from the literature. Often, methods must be revised or new methods must be devised for local conditions. One's ability to select or devise methods of forage measurement will be improved by experience with methods used in plant ecology and by a knowledge of statistical aspects of sampling theory. The chosen method should provide (1) objective, rather than subjective, measurement of forage conditions; (2) biologically and statistically meaningful data; and (3) efficiency.

Subjective evaluations of forage—such as "lightly browsed," "moderately browsed," or "heavily browsed"—are difficult to interpret and analyze and involve variation among biologists making the surveys. Objective measurements—such as noting the percent of available twigs having been browsed—are preferred.

The forage survey should provide information about nutrition that is expected to be critical to productivity of the target wildlife population. For instance, if evidence indicates that the hunting-season abundance of grouse on a shooting area is determined primarily by survival of chicks through the spring and summer, there would be little value in obtaining extensive data on availability of seeds and fruits to the birds during November. For management purposes, it would be more meaningful to obtain data on food availability to grouse chicks in brood habitat.

Forage surveys almost always involve sampling to contend with variation in forage conditions (i.e., if the quantities of forage are measured on a series of milacre plots, each plot usually provides a different estimate of forage abundance per milacre). As a result, samples are almost always taken at random, and they should be numerous enough to provide whatever precision is required by management objectives. Whenever possible, the management biologist should consult with a statistician in designing forage surveys.

Wildlife managers always have limited funds for obtaining information on the habitats and populations they manage. They require efficient survey methods to obtain the most usable information for the least amount of time and money.

Forage-quality Measurement   The traditional method for partitioning food into physical–chemical components has been the proximate analysis. This analysis separates food into five components, usually reported in percentages of dry matter. The following discussion provides a needed minimum knowledge of the significance of each component in wildlife nutrition.

1 Crude protein. Protein-rich foods are *generally* very digestible and provide adequate amounts of important nutrients.

2 Crude fiber. This component contains mostly indigestible carbohydrates such as cellulose and lignin. Foods high in fiber content are usually poor foods because they are comparatively indigestible. Recent advances in forage analysis include new methods for measuring and partitioning fiber (Van Soest 1967).

3 Crude fat. This component consists of a variety of oils and fats and includes fat-soluble vitamins. The significance of crude-fat levels in wildlife foods cannot be determined without additional data. Digestible fats can be especially good sources of energy. On the other hand, some oils are not digestible, and some such as those in sagebrush browse can, when sage is overly abundant in the diet, inhibit the forage-digesting activity of rumen bacteria (Nagy et al. 1964).

4 Ash. Minerals are contained in this component. Ash is significant only when there is further analysis to separate it into the various major and trace elements.

5 Nitrogen-free extract (NFE). This component contains mostly digestible carbohydrates, such as soluble sugars and starches. Foods high in NFE content are good sources of digestible energy. This component is not measured directly, but is obtained by difference, requiring analysis for all four other components.

In analyzing wildlife forages, most emphasis has been on the concentrations of protein and fiber, and when deficiencies have been suspected, on the levels of minerals, especially calcium and phosphorus, in the foods. New methods for determining fiber contents of forages have been developed and are replacing the traditional crude-fiber analysis. Among these are the acid-detergent method for determining fiber and the method of determining the levels of cell-wall constituents and of lignin in the forage. The importance of these methods lies in their ability to provide data for accurate prediction of the digestibilities of forages.

Wildlife Studies

Studies of the nutrition of wild animals include food-habit investigations, feeding and digestion trials, and studies of specific nutritional disorders that demonstrate symptoms that may be used to detect food deficiencies in the wild.

Food Habits and Preferences   Seven methods have been used to study food preferences of wild animals. Each method has limitations, being applicable to some, but not all, species or seasons of the year and involving possibilities for biased results.

1   Feeding-site observations. This usually involves observation of feeding herbivores, often at a distance with field glasses. The location of feeding is noted; then the observer inspects plants at this "feeding site" to see which have been fed upon. The method cannot be used for animals that are difficult to observe, and it is often difficult, on site inspection, to determine which plants have been fed upon. Some plants may be eaten completely and provide no evidence of use. Other plants, such as shrubs, or plant parts, such as fruits, are conspicuous and use may be observed accurately at a distance. As a result, use of conspicuous foods may be overestimated.

2   Observation of the digestive tract. This method involves collecting animals and noting foods present in crops or stomachs. Probably the most commonly used method, its disadvantage lies in the need for collecting animals. There is also the possibility that the most easily digested and presumably most nutritious foods will be more difficult to identify in stomach contents than will the least digestible foods. Thus, biased results are possible.

3   Observation of feces. Feces of both carnivores and herbivores may be examined for undigested food particles. In carnivore scats, these are hair, bones, and feathers. In herbivore feces, microscopic examination of the fecal material is usually required. Fecal analysis involves a possibility that highly digestible foods may be underrepresented in resulting food-habits data.

4   Observation of regurgitated pellets. Many birds, notably owls, hawks, herons, and gulls, regurgitate indigestible hair and bones from their food. Regurgitated pellets may be collected, especially around nests where they may be

numerous, and the remains of food items identified. Biased data may be obtained when some prey items are completely digested and unrepresented in regurgitated pellets.

5 Observation of food remains and sign. Partially eaten carcasses of prey often accumulate at dens or nests. Tabulation of these items provides food-habits information during a limited season of the year. During winter, trails of carnivores such as foxes, bobcats, and fisher have been followed in snow to note the frequency of their predation and, by examining sign, to identify the species of prey taken.

6 Measurement of forage use. Food habits of herbivores may be evaluated by quantifying the evidence of grazing or browsing on naturally available plants. The value of this method is reduced when there are two or more herbivores whose feeding signs cannot be differentiated. To obtain food-preference ratings, plant species are usually compared by considering the intensity of use on each species relative to its abundance in the habitat. This method often produces results differing from those obtained by observing only the intensity of use on plants. A highly preferred plant may constitute a small part of the forage consumed only because the plant is rare in the habitat.

7 Preference trials. Animals in captivity may be presented with two or more food items. In each trial, the item most eaten is rated as preferred over less-eaten items. In the field, free-ranging or tame animals may be followed to observe their food preferences. Esophageal fistulas have been used with tame domestic animals to obtain samples of ingested foods, and this method may soon be used with tame wild animals.

Animals held captive for preference trials are usually maintained mostly on commercial feed. The quality of this staple diet may affect food preferences exhibited by captive animals when test-food items are presented, providing preference ratings differing from the food preferences of free-ranging wild animals.

Feeding and Digestion Trials In feeding trials, captive animals are fed selected forages or prepared artificial diets (such as a phosphorus deficient ration). Diet qualities are then evaluated by noting normal or abnormal functions, such as weight gain or loss, reproductive success, antler growth, or even survival. Qualities of wild forages are compared in this manner.

With artificial diets, animals are subjected to deficiencies that might occur in the wild. An experiment may be designed to determine function-related requirements of the animal for certain nutrients. For example, the levels of phosphorus necessary for normal antler growth may be determined. These data may then be compared to levels of phosphorus in natural deer forage.

Experiments with artificial diets may also be designed for studying and quantifying physiological and perhaps pathological responses of animals to deficiencies. These characteristics of experimentally malnourished animals may then be used as symptoms of specific nutritional disorders when wild populations are examined.

Digestion trials are extensions of feeding trials, requiring measurements of food intake and feces production. These data permit evaluation of food digestibility (food digested = food intake − feces produced). Digestibility may be measured for dry matter, for calories, for protein, or for any food component (Example 6.4). Digestibility data often explain differences among qualities of wildlife foods. Foods that appear nutritious because they contain high concentrations of protein and energy will have little value if they are comparatively indigestible.

EXAMPLE 6.4   A Digestion Trial

A young cottontail rabbit is fed a test forage for 12 days, beginning with a 5-day adjustment period during which all pretest foods are assumed to have been eliminated from the rabbit's tract. During the last 7 days the following data are collected.

> Average daily food intake: 50 g dry matter
> Average daily feces production: 15 g dry matter
> Forage analysis: Energy = 4 Kcal per g dry matter
>   Protein = 30 percent of dry matter
> Feces analysis: Energy = 4.5 Kcal per g dry matter
>   Protein = 15 percent of dry matter

Calculate the digestibilities of dry matter, energy and protein (digestion coefficients) in the forage and the concentrations of digestible dry matter, energy, and protein in the forage.

1 Average daily intake:
  Dry matter = 50 g
  Protein = 50(0.3) = 15 g
  Energy = 50(4) = 200 Kcal

2 Average daily feces production:
  Dry matter = 15 g
  Protein = 15(0.15) = 2.25 g
  Energy = 15(4.5) = 67.5 Kcal

3 Average daily digestion:

	Intake	Feces	Digestion
Dry matter (g)	50	15	35
Protein (g)	15	2.25	12.75
Energy (Kcal)	200	67.5	132.5

4 Digestion coefficients:
  Dry matter = 35/50 = 70 percent
  Protein = 12.75/15 = 85 percent
  Energy = 132.5/200 = 66 percent

5 Digestible components in dry forage:
  Protein = 12.75/50 = 25.5 percent
  Energy = 132.5/50 = 2.65 Kcal per g

In comparing studies of food preferences with results of feeding and/or digestion trials we find that the preferred foods are high-quality foods. This is not surprising, considering natural selection. Animals should evolve preferences that are most valuable to their reproduction and survival.

INTEGRATION: PROVIDING FOODS IN WILDLIFE HABITAT

To maintain productive wildlife populations, for harvesting or otherwise enjoying, management must provide habitat that fulfills the food requirements of both sexes and all age-classes of animals throughout the year. Ideally, the management biologist knows exactly what these requirements are and is also able to assess the availabilities of all required nutrients in the habitat throughout the year. In practice this is almost never true. Wildlife literature provides food-habits data for many species, but these data are often for mature animals only and are often applicable to but part of the year. Qualities of foods have been compared or measured for only a few wild species. Further, the management biologist usually has little time and money for assessing supplies of all foods in the habitat or for detecting nutritional deficiencies in the animals. Because of these limitations of knowledge and of economics, management is seldom precise in providing wildlife foods.

This does not justify haphazard habitat manipulation such as the creation of expensive food patches of domestic plants when there is little evidence that the target wildlife population will use or, more important, is in short supply of such foods. When management must be based on limited information of species biology and, for economic reasons, is unable to assess the nutritional status of the target population or its habitat, wildlife management is extensive. As information becomes available in scientific literature and as management funds increase, management becomes more intensive. Management biologists should continue to search and interpret scientific literature that may have management application. They should use their own resources to obtain information on the nutritional status of populations being managed. Four procedures for supplying foods in wildlife habitat follow. The first two procedures can be used in extensive management. As management becomes more intensive, there should be more emphasis on the third and fourth procedures.

1   Provide vegetation types and successional stages to which the species has adapted via evolution. The animals have evolved means for fulfilling all their needs in such vegetation. For example, in the Lake states ruffed grouse are adapted to midsuccessional stages within the hardwood-conifer forest. (Sharp-tailed grouse are adapted to earlier stages; spruce grouse to later stages.) Management must provide periodic disturbance, such as logging, to maintain the middle stages of forest succession.

2   Provide a variety of vegetation types. Since food requirements vary within wildlife species, and food supplies vary seasonally and among vegetation types, the probability of having an important food deficiency declines as variety increases in the habitat. Any deficiency in one vegetation type may be alleviated in another vegetation type.

3 Provide foods known to be preferred and of high quality. Concentrate on foods needed for apparently critical seasons or functions, such as the staminate flower buds of aspen, birch, alder, and hazel for ruffed grouse. Recent studies suggest that supplies of these foods are especially important to over-winter survival of grouse and may determine densities of grouse populations (Gullion 1966).

4 Watch for symptoms of deficiencies. In extensive management this may be noting winter starvation losses (shortage of persistent late-winter foods), observing a rapid decline in brood sizes of grouse (perhaps a shortage of food for chicks), or noting excessive use of preferred food plants. As management becomes more intensive, animals may be observed or forage may be measured in a systematic way to evaluate food adequacy at a critical season or for one age class of the population.

WILDLIFE WATER REQUIREMENTS

Water is a necessary dietary component, participating in many chemical and physical processes in animals. In addition, animals require water for evaporative cooling in hot environments. Water requirements of a few wildlife species have been studied in controlled environments (Wesley et al. 1970; Turner 1973; Schmidt-Nielsen 1964) and by noting the frequency of visitation of marked, free-ranging animals to water holes (Turner 1973; Leslie and Douglas 1979). In addition, the stresses of dry seasons have been indicated by concentrations of animals around water sources and by increases in mortality during drought. However, for most species, we know surprisingly little about their water requirements for survival or their probably greater requirements for successful reproduction (Swift 1955).

Wildlife respond to water deprivation in three ways. Elephants will dig in dry river bottoms, exposing water for themselves and other species. Mobile species, like doves, will migrate to water sources. But some wildlife must abandon waterless ranges during dry seasons, concentrating around surface waters. Such concentrations are usually disadvantageous because local forage supplies may be overused or trampled, the numerous animals may attract predators and may be forced to use habitats where predators have advantages, and concentration may facilitate transmission of disease and parasites.

Water Requirements: A Variable

We are sometimes unrealistic and anthropomorphic in assuming animals in arid environments are water stressed. Water requirements of animals will vary with weather conditions and according to the seasonal pattern of physiological functions. Water intake must be increased in hot weather to replace that lost by evaporative cooling. The demands of reproduction can also increase water requirements. However, although field observations have indicated poor reproductive performance by wildlife during drought, the relative roles of inadequate water and of poor nutrition, common during drought, in depressing reproduction have not been clear.

Water requirements vary greatly among species since some animals are adapted to arid environments. Adaptations to aridity include:

Nocturnal or Fossorial Habits Many desert-adapted species avoid the demands of evaporative cooling by confining activity to times and places with lower temperatures and higher humidities.

Concentrating Excreta Desert adapted species produce dry feces and have powerful kidneys that concentrate urine, reducing water loss for these functions.

Labile Body Temperature Some species normally allow their body temperatures to rise during the heat of day. The excess heat is lost at night by convection, conduction, or radiation. This reduces water requirements for evaporative cooling.

Morphology A large body size and abundant insulation can prevent heat uptake and provide mass for "thermal inertia." In mammals, insulation is usually greatest on the back to protect skin from the sun. Other body parts may be scantily haired to enhance heat loss by convection. These body parts may be enlarged, like jackrabbit's ears, to expel heat; or they may be associated with mobile appendages or hair patterns that increase air movement, enhancing heat loss by convection.

Use of Metabolic Water Oxidation of carbohydrates and fats produces water to augment intake.

Water Storage Some species are physiologically adapted to withstand temporary reductions in body fluid levels. They may also be able to rehydrate quickly at a source of water. Ruminants have an advantage in that water can be stored in the rumen. Desert bighorn sheep can withstand losing 30 percent of their body water, mostly from the rumen, and can rehydrate quickly by refilling the rumen (Turner 1973).

Mobility Birds have the advantage of flight in visiting water sources distant from their feeding, roosting, or nesting sites. Doves may migrate daily to water.

Patterns of Reproduction The reproductive seasons of most desert wildlife are timed to avoid the driest period of the year. This usually enhances reproductive success in that both water availability and forage quality are best at a critical time. A capacity to produce numerous young in occasional years of good moisture is also an advantage in deserts.

Water Supplies: A Variable

Water sources include surface water (fresh water, salt water, and snow), dew, succulence, and metabolic water. Salty or brackish water can be used only by species having mechanisms for excreting excess salts. Succulence is water in foods. Some plants may contain 90 percent water.

In deserts, water availability may vary greatly among years and among seasons. Although deserts tend to have one or two seasons when precipitation is expected, some years pass without moisture. Man is another primary influence on water availability. Historically, men have concentrated around water in arid areas. Springs have been diverted or developed for livestock or for human use. Roads have followed streams, and housing has been built along rivers. These developments have deprived wildlife of access to water. In the southwestern United States, perhaps desert bighorns have suffered most. On the other hand, some water developments for livestock, or specifically for wildlife, have benefited wild animals.

Management of Water

Numerous cisterns and catchments, traditionally called "guzzlers," have been constructed to accumulate and store water for desert wildlife. These structures usually include a wide, impervious apron to catch water from occasional precipitation. The apron directs water into a cistern (Fig. 6.10) that is usually covered to reduce evaporation. Wild birds and mammals may enter the cistern to drink or the water may be directed to a trough where flow is controlled by a flotation valve.

Guzzlers have been constructed primarily for game birds, such as chukar partridge and desert quail, and for desert bighorn sheep and deer. Enthusiasm for constructing guzzlers has been high because the projects have provided physical evidence of accomplishment. Guzzlers can be photographed. Numbers of guzzlers built can be tallied in annual reports. However, many attempts to improve wildlife habitat by constructing guzzlers have not been followed by evaluations of their effects on wildlife abundance or productivity. Several studies have failed to find evidence that guzzlers enhanced wildlife populations, especially game birds (Gullion 1966; Shaw and Low 1971).

If the construction of guzzlers is to benefit wildlife, (1) the stored water must be accessible to the animals, (2) water must be a limiting factor in their habitat, and (3) there must be no other equally limiting habitat requirement. These constraints have been neglected. Guzzlers have been constructed near roads, which eases construction problems but does not necessarily provide water

Fig. 6.10   Water development, or "guzzler," constructed by the Arizona Game and Fish Department. The concrete apron directs rainwater into a 10,000-gallon covered storage tank. Level of water in the trough is controlled by a float valve. Photo courtesy of James Witham.

where wild animals will use it. For example, water will be most usable to desert bighorns if it is near suitable escape terrain and is in an area of low vegetation providing good visibility. Guzzlers have been constructed within sight of open surface water, where it was hard to imagine water was a limiting factor for mobile species. Gullion suggested that, whereas water may not have been limiting to desert quail, the abundance of certain food resources definitely was limiting (1966). Thus, even if water was limiting to quail, provision of water would accomplish nothing if food resources continued to limit quail abundance.

This is not to conclude that providing water for wildlife is never a useful management tool. But the three constraints listed above should be considered before investments are made in water developments; and management should include evaluation of projects for efficacy in enhancing wildlife abundance or productivity.

PRINCIPLES

P6.1   Good nutrition enhances wildlife reproduction and reduces wildlife susceptability to many forms of mortality. Quality wildlife foods are digestible and provide water, energy, and several required nutrients.

P6.2 The quantities and qualities of foods required by wildlife are highly variable among species of wildlife, among the sex-age classes of animals, among seasons and related physiological functions of animals, and among weather conditions and geographic regions. Food shortages are not uncommon among carnivores. Herbivores have strong forage preferences related to forage quality. Herbivores tend to experience nutritional problems, not for lack of forage, but whenever available forage is of poor qualilty.

P6.3 The quantities and qualities of food available to wildlife are highly variable among areas, seasons, and years. Food quantities are influenced by weather and many site factors. For herbivores, forage qualities are influenced by weather, site factors, genetics of plants, and the parts of plants eaten.

P6.4 Full understanding of the nutritional dynamics of wildlife requires periodic assessment of food abundance, analysis of forage qualities, study of food habits and preferences, and study of the nutritional physiologies of wildlife species. Biologists seldom have full understanding of the nutritional dynamics of wildlife populations they manage.

P6.5 Most wildlife fulfill their nutritional needs by using a variety of foods that support both sexes and all age classes during all seasons and weather conditions. To encourage certain wildlife populations, biologists develop habitats providing this variety of foods. Without a full and detailed understanding of the nutritional dynamics of a desired wildlife population, biologists develop habitats that (1) emphasize the naturally associated environment of the species, (2) provide a diversity of potential foods, (3) provide foods known to be preferred, and (4) provide foods that will alleviate any detected nutritional deficiencies.

P6.6 Water may be a serious limiting factor for wildlife populations in arid areas. Seasonal concentrations of wildlife around limited water sources can result in local damage to forage resources and can enhance transmission of disease. Wildlife may also be compelled to use water sources in areas where their vulnerability to predation is great.

P6.7 Wildlife exhibit a variety of adaptations to arid environments, and water needs vary greatly among species—with weather conditions, and according to seasonal water requirements for reproductive functions. Water supplies vary greatly among years, seasons, and areas.

P6.8 Enhancement of water supplies can be a successful habitat management tool if water is a limiting factor, if any other equally limiting factors are also alleviated, and if the enhanced water supply is acceptable to the animals.

CHAPTER 7

WILDLIFE COVER REQUIREMENTS

> . . . by backtracking a wolf, I found a freshly
> killed male lamb. The tracks in the snow
> plainly told the story. The wolf was following
> a trail . . . within the edge of the uppermost
> timber. Suddenly he came upon five or six
> sheep feeding among the trees. . . . If the
> sheep had been feeding in the open as they
> almost always do, the wolf probably would
> have been discovered before he was close to
> them.
>
> *Adolph Murie*

Wildlife habitat requirements include structural as well as nutritional aspects. Whereas food requirements are a matter of animal nutrition, requirements for habitat structure are a matter of animal behavior. We know more about wildlife foods than about wildlife requirements for cover because the study of wildlife behavior is in its infancy. Information on the requirements of wild species for structural arrangements within habitat is sparse, and there has not been a consistent use of terminology.

COVER

In his classic text, Leopold referred to cover as the kinds of materials making up vegetative or other shelter for wildlife (1933). This definition illustrates the once prevalent emphasis of shelter and of vegetation in the concept of cover. This narrow concept of cover has proved inadequate. Animals often respond to habitat structures that are not vegetative; they use habitat structure for many purposes in addition to shelter. Animals may even respond to habitat structures that themselves are never used, but that are correlated with an abundance of appropriate foods, nest sites, or water. In fact, *cover* has become an unfortunate choice of word. Perhaps it should be replaced by *structural resources*. In this text, the term cover is used because it is so commonly accepted, but it must be remembered that cover may be any needed structural characteristic of the environment.

Definition

Cover is defined as any structural resource of the environment that enhances reproduction and/or survival of animals by providing for any of the natural functions of the species. This definition is a bit ponderous, and I have relied on many examples to illustrate the many forms of cover.

Vegetation is not the only structural component of the environment that influences wildlife. Thus, a large body of open water may be important in the habitat of diving ducks (the factor of openness is needed, perhaps, for visibility). Cliffs are important in the habitat of bighorn sheep (the factor of steepness or "ruggedness" is needed to escape predators). South-facing slopes (the factor of aspect) may be important as winter feeding and resting places for deer, because such slopes are warmer and free of food-covering snow. Vegetation may also be cover, but often it is the structure and not species of vegetation that is important (Stebler and Schemnitz 1955; Harris 1952), as illustrated by the fact that a cottontail may seek to escape a predator in a raspberry patch, a rose hedge, or an overgrown brush pile.

Animals have evolved their requirements for cover by gaining anatomical, physiological, and behavioral adaptations that permit them to use structural resources of the environment in ways that enhance reproduction and/or survival. Structures of the environment that are not related to these demographic parameters are not required by the animals.

In addition to providing shelter, cover may favor the welfare of animals by providing for any natural function such as breeding, feeding, travel, escape, nesting, or resting. Examples involving resting, escape, and feeding have been given above and a few more examples follow. Breeding cover for prairie chickens is the booming ground where males perform courtship displays. Booming grounds are special places in prairie chicken range. They are used traditionally and usually have certain physical characteristics: sparse or low vegetation and elevated topography. Feeding cover for a predator may be concealment from which to ambush prey. In contrast, cover, for any function of a prey species, may be poor cover when it affords concealment for predators.

Thus *cover* is only as general a term as is *food*. It conveys little information unless we use the term with the name of some species function that is enhanced. The cover requirements of prairie grouse have been classified as nesting cover, brood cover, escape cover, courtship cover, roosting cover, and daytime resting cover (Yeatter 1943; Grange 1948; Amann 1957; Hamerstrom 1963; Jones 1963). This list emphasizes the species' functions that are enhanced by needed structural resources.

EXAMPLE 7.1   Winter Cover for Ruffed Grouse

It has been accepted that conifer cover is an essential part of ruffed grouse winter habitat (Bump et al. 1947). This conclusion has been based on frequent sightings of grouse using conifer trees during winter and perhaps on assumptions that grouse require evergreen vegetation for concealment or for shelter from severe weather.

Studies in northern Minnesota suggest, however, that conifers may not be necessary in grouse habitat and that, depending on the forest structure, the presence of conifers may reduce survival of birds by favoring raptor predation (Gullion and Marshall 1968). Gullion and Marshall noted that of 133 instances of raptor predation upon grouse, 89 percent were in places where a background of conifer foliage could have screened the silhouette of a predaceous bird. They believe that cover for concealment is not so important to grouse as is open cover permitting constant surveillance of the surroundings, because the birds rely on their cryptic coloration and their ability to detect nearby predators.

When leaves of deciduous trees have fallen, owls and goshawks are conspicuous in the overstory—unless tall conifers are present. Among the conifers, tall pines are especially poor habitat for grouse and good winter feeding cover for raptors. After pines are 15 to 25 years old, the lower branches self-prune, resulting in a high evergreen crown for raptor concealment and an open understory in which they may swoop down on their victims. In contrast, young pines and spruce and fir trees (which do not self-prune so readily) lack the structural factors favoring raptor predation. Gullion and Marshall conclude: "It is the growth form or physical characteristics of the trees rather than the species of trees that affect grouse survival in a forest habitat. Thus the growth form of pines as they mature makes them 'ecological traps' for grouse. Spruce and balsam fir are less dangerous and hardwoods provide the best forest cover. . . ."

EXAMPLE 7.2   Escape Cover for Bighorn Sheep

A common denominator of habitat for mountain sheep seems to be steep, rugged, and open topography. Sheep spend most of their time near cliffs or bluffs. They tend to avoid dense timber. Their learned migratory routes between seasonally suitable ranges usually skirt patches of trees (Geist 1967).

The adaptive value of this behavior is illustrated in Murie's descriptions of Wolf–Dall sheep interactions in Mt. McKinley National Park, Alaska (1944). Cliffs served as escape cover for sheep because wolves could not match the sheep's agility over steep terrain. When wolves were scarce within the park in the early 1920s, Dall sheep increased and used areas lacking the escape cover of cliffs. However, as wolves increased in abundance after 1925, the sheep population declined, and its range was constricted to areas with steep terrain. Murie notes that sheep "were confined to more rugged habitats where they could cope with the wolf" (p. 142) and that "sheep numbers are dependent on the extent of cliff protection and the degree of wolf pressure" (pp. 83–84).

Wolves have been eliminated from many ranges of mountain sheep, yet the animals continue to strongly prefer mostly open, steep country. Coyote predation may be a factor. Smith notes, "Ordinarily, a group of a half dozen or more (bighorn) sheep would watch nearby coyotes. . . . if approached directly, the sheep would band together before fleeing to the nearest cliffs. . . . (Smith 1954, p. 79)" Another factor may be that mountain sheep behavior is designed for the transfer of habits through succeeding generations (Geist 1967) and that traditional ranges near steep topography continue to be learned and used while very limited exploration of new territory occurs. In any event, habitat for mountain sheep, from California to Alaska, is characterized by open, rugged landscape.

Although sheep restrict themselves to food supplies on or near open steep terrain, they must often compete with deer, elk, and domestic livestock that are less restricted. This must be a disadvantage to the sheep. When food resources are overutilized by several species on suitable mountain sheep habitat, the other ruminants may move to different habitats, whereas the sheep must subsist on the remaining overutilized vegetation. When big game ranges have been abundantly populated by mountain sheep, deer, elk, and also by domestic livestock, the wild sheep populations have been first to decline. It is not entirely clear why wild sheep are such poor competitors, but their requirements for and self-restriction to areas providing steep terrain for escape cover seems to be involved.

Cover and Habitat Selection

Animals may identify and select their appropriate habitats (those to which they are adapted, in which they best survive and reproduce) by responding to nutritional or structural factors. However, most studies of the mechanisms of habitat selection have emphasized animal responses to structural factors (Lack 1933; Klopfer and Hailman 1962; Wecker 1964).

Habitat selection is specialization, for a species selecting a certain type of habitat is restricting itself to that habitat and will gain adaptations especially suited for using the food and cover resources of the selected habitat. Habitat

TABLE 7.1   Results of Two Experiments on the Nature of Habitat Selection by Vertebrates

Chipping Sparrow[a]	Number of Birds Spending Most Time in Pine	Number of Birds Spending Most Time in Oak
Wild-trapped birds	9	1
Nestlings raised without foliage	5	1
Nestlings raised in oak foliage		
2−3 month old birds	5	5
4−6 month old birds	4	3
12−14 month old birds	3	1

Prairie Deer Mouse[b]	Number of Mice Spending Most Time in Field	Number of Mice Spending Most Time in Woods
Wild-trapped mice	11	1
Wild stock raised in laboratory	10	2
Wild stock raised in wooden pen	6	1
Lab stock, over 12 generations	6	7
Lab stock raised in field pen	13	0
Lab stock raised in wooded pen	4	4

[a]Data from Klopfer and Hailman (1962).
[b]Data from Wecker (1964, "Habitat Selection." Copyright © by Scientific American, Inc. All rights reserved).

selection, therefore, favors niche isolation and is reinforced by interspecific competition (Svardson 1949).

From the management point of view, the literature on habitat selection is valuable in demonstrating how rigidly a species may adhere to its preferences for habitat structure. Although learning, perhaps in the form of imprinting to the natal habitat, may affect habitat preferences, these preferences may be largely innate. This is indicated by two experiments (Table 7.1): one with chipping sparrows, which normally use conifer-tree habitat, and another with prairie deer mice, a subspecies that uses fields and avoids forest habitats. In both experiments wild-trapped animals and animals having had experimental habitat experiences in early life were tested for habitat preferences. The sparrows were exposed to pine and oak foliages in a laboratory; the mice were permitted to choose portions of a pen extending across a forest-field border. In both species, the respective habitat preferences appeared largely innate, though preferences for pine foliage by chipping sparrows might be temporarily reduced by early-life experience with decidous foliage.

In habitat selection, some vertebrates respond to the life form or physiognomy of their habitat, rather than to the presence of particular plant species. An example would be the horned lark, which selects open areas of low vegetation, be they farm habitat in Illinois, grasslands in Colorado, or Rocky Mountain tundra. Habitat selection may also be a preference for the microclimate associated with some structural factors of the environment, as illustrated in Example 7.3.

Animals may be just as obligated to their evolved requirements for cover—structural aspects of their environment—as they are obligated to their needs for certain foods. Some species are generalized, not limited by the availability of some kinds of cover. Other species are specialized, having rigid cover requirements.

EXAMPLE 7.3   Winter Cover for White-tailed Deer

Winter cover for white-tailed deer in northern forests usually consists of mature stands of conifer trees (Verme 1965). A densely stocked even-aged stand provides the best snow conditions for travel (Fig. 7.1). Compared to other forest types, these stands exhibit narrow diurnal ranges of temperature, are generally warmer during cold weather, permit less wind movement, and provide less depth of a more compacted snow (Ozaga 1968). In severe weather, deer choose such sites, called *deeryards*, despite their comparatively low supplies of forage (Fig. 7.2). It is cover, not food, that defines winter habitat. Integrated management of timber and white-tailed deer winter range in the north presents planning problems that Verme has addressed. Management must provide for harvest and regeneration of the timber as well as ensure that some parts of each deeryard will always provide suitable winter cover for deer. This is accomplished by planning the sizes, locations, and frequencies of timber harvests so that whenever mature timber is harvested, other stands are approaching maturity, replacing them as winter cover. If the timber rotation is 100 years, this planning must be done 100 years in advance, with perhaps one fifth of the deeryard programmed for harvest each 20 years. Winter habitat for deer can thus be produced on a sustained-yield basis. Verme's paper is a fine example of how a wildlife biologist often must become aware of goals, methods, and jargon in another land-use field, in this case silviculture, in order to promote habitat management under a multiple-use regime.

COVER REQUIREMENTS: A VARIABLE

Cover requirements of wildlife vary among species although some overlap occurs. Occasionally various species of birds, mammals, and even reptiles have been found using the same nesting or denning cover in holes in trees or in the ground. However, variation among species is more common. For instance, cavity-nesting forest birds express preferences for nesting cavities at certain heights above ground (Fig. 7.3).

Within species, the needs for cover will vary with functions of the animals (such as feeding, resting, or travel), with seasons, among sex-age classes, according to the prevalence of predators or pests, with weather conditions, and among geographic regions.

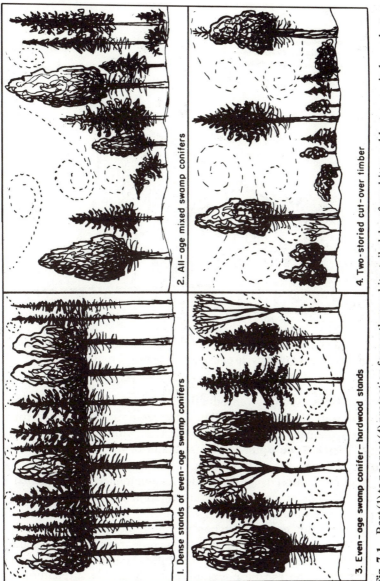

1. Dense stands of even-age swamp conifers

2. All-age mixed swamp conifers

3. Even-age swamp conifer-hardwood stands

4. Two-storied cut-over timber

Fig. 7.1 Best (1) to poorest (4) protection for northern white-tailed deer from bitter cold, strong winds, and snow hindering travel is supplied by stand structures illustrated above. From Verme 1965.

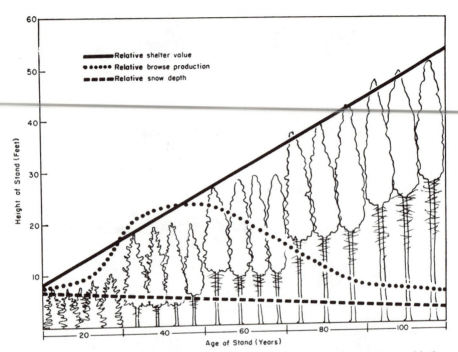

Fig. 7.2 Optimum quantity and quality of browse or shelter for deer is provided at different stages in the rotation cycle of even-aged timber. From Verme 1965.

Species functions, such as reproduction, often occur seasonally and may involve only certain sex-age classes. Thus, the requirement of grouse for brood cover occurs seasonally and involves only hens with young chicks. Grouse brood cover seems to be a not-too-dense stand of forbs having a vegetation canopy to conceal the birds but permitting easy travel by chicks among the stems of plants. Such vegetation usually provides an abundance of soft-bodied insect food for chicks, illustrating that natural selection has influenced food—and cover—preferences simultaneously.

Escape cover is not necessary when predators are absent. Thus, the Dall sheep of Mt. McKinley Park were able to occupy areas lacking escape cover when wolves were scarce (Examle 7.2). In artificial conditions, wildlife may be grown with little or no escape cover by controlling their predators. This is common practice in fish hatcheries where the ponds and runways are devoid of cover, but herons, kingfishers, and sometimes mammalian predators are trapped. The practice of predator control has sometimes been extended to shooting preserves and to waterfowl refuges where production is a paramount goal. This may reduce the need for escape cover and permit dedication of more habitat to shooting areas or to brooding and feeding areas. However, some of the value of wildness is lost when wildlife are viewed or shot for sport under these somewhat artificial conditions. Parts of the animals' naturally associated environment (the escape cover and the predators) are missing, and the animals cannot express some of their evolved adaptations, namely methods for escaping predators, including the hunter.

Are places where wildlife may escape or evade insect pests a habitat requirement? Biologists have interpreted the use of wind-swept ridges or windward sides of lakes by ungulates as attempts to escape biting, warble, or nostril flies. Insect pests may affect reproduction or survival of ungulates, as indicated by Kelsall (1968, p. 272). Therefore, places providing escape from seasonally abundant insect pests qualify under our definition of cover.

An animal's need for shelter from severe weather coincides with the occurrence of such weather. As a result, observations of the animal's use of cover may lead to incomplete knowledge of its cover requirements unless some observations are made during severe weather. For example, radio-tagged cottontail rabbits on an Illinois study area failed to exhibit much preference for cover types during 16 nights with normal winter weather, including little or no snow on the ground (Hanson et al., 1969). However, on a night with 4 inches of snow on the ground, the rabbits restricted themselves entirely to areas with an overstory of

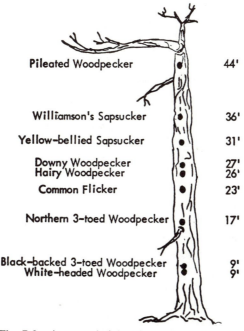

Pileated Woodpecker .... 44'

Williamson's Sapsucker .... 36'

Yellow-bellied Sapsucker .... 31'

Downy Woodpecker .... 27'
Hairy Woodpecker .... 26'
Common Flicker .... 23'

Northern 3-toed Woodpecker .... 17'

Black-backed 3-toed Woodpecker .... 9'
White-headed Woodpecker .... 9'

Fig. 7.3 Average height of nest hole. The figures are averages of 217 mentions in the literature of heights of nest holes. From Jackman 1974.

woody cover and with tall herbaceous vegetation. On a night with blizzard conditions, they showed preference for areas with dense herbaceous vegetation that offered protection from wind and drifting snow. This illustrates that although some components of the habitat—food or cover—may not be used constantly or even frequently, their availability during critical times may be essential to the maintenance of productive populations.

Within species having large geographic ranges, populations in different regions may be adapted to very different environments and may have evolved very different cover requirements. Whereas northern white-tailed deer require the winter cover of old-age conifer forests (Example 7.3), the white-tailed deer of southern Florida never see snow and occur in an environment that is mostly aquatic. Critical periods for these Florida deer are not periods of deep snow but periods of deep water (Loveless 1959). Abnormally wet periods occur once in about five to seven years, sometimes because of hurricanes. At these times the deer are concentrated on islands of high ground. Here, they first consume the best and most palatable forage. If high water persists, they must eventually turn to less nutritious plants, and losses due to malnutrition may exceed 30 percent of the herd. Thus, it is the structural factor of topography, specifically the abundance of elevated sites, and the forage on these sites that determine habitat quality of Everglades marshes for the subspecies *(Odocoileus virginianus seminolus)* of white-tailed deer that inhabits them. The point is that familiarity with the cover requirements of a species in one part of its range may not suffice in other parts of the range. There is even variation in cover requirements within the ranges of subspecies. The coniferous deeryards of the northern white-tailed deer *(O. v. borealis)* described in Example 7.3 are characteristic of the northern part of its range: southeastern Canada and northern parts of Minnesota, Wisconsin, Michigan, New York, and New England. The same subspecies winters principally in deciduous-forested river bottoms in agricultural areas of Illinois, Indiana, and Ohio and on deciduous-forested south aspects of Pennsylvania (Taylor 1956).

COVER AVAILABILITY: A VARIABLE

Cover resources may vary with land-use practices, with site disturbance or biotic succession, among seasons, or with weather conditions. Examples of these variables follow.

The coming of mechanized agriculture to the Midwest changed the habitat of prairie chickens into habitat for the exotic ringnecked pheasant. At first, pheasants prospered, for the early farms provided excellent pheasant habitat. Hay fields provided nesting cover. Unused field borders, roadsides, and ditch banks grew up to jungles of sunflowers, ragweeds, and other forbs or supported hedgerows of osage or elm. These provided resting, escape, and winter cover, as well as seeds and other foods. But intensification of agriculture has since reduced the quality of pheasant habitat. The hedgerows have been removed. Field borders have been cultivated. Ditch banks and roadsides are often mowed or burned to provide a "neat" appearance or to control weeds. In some areas the hayfields are gone, the emphasis turning to high-value row crops like corn and soybeans. Weeds are absent from the fields. Weather permitting, the fields are plowed in autumn and provide little cover through the winter. These changes in land use affecting food and cover for pheasants have resulted from economic and technological change. The food surpluses of the United States had become depleted, widening the margin between the value of an osage hedgerow and the cash value of a few more rows of corn. Government subsidies for retiring land to hay fields had ended. New machinery permits plowing fields without leaving unused corners, and new chemicals are used to control weeds. These changes in land use had immense impacts on cover resources for pheasants, requiring changes in wildlife management programs, such as the development of roadside nesting cover (Example 7.4).

Change in the structure of vegetation in an abandoned midwestern field illustrates the effects of succession, season, and weather on cover for cottontail rabbits. At first the field produces a stand of forbs—weeds to most farmers. There are milkweeds, ragweeds, sunflowers, and many other species growing tall with stout stems. One finds numerous rabbit trails among the stems beneath the herbaceous canopy. By the end of the summer-long breeding season, the animals may be very abundant. Once the growing season has ended, however, this cover can only deteriorate. Heavy, wet snows and wind tend to break down the overstory of forbs, reducing both shelter and concealment for the rabbits. In early years of succession, the forbs are so abundant that much cover remains, unless the damaging snows are especially frequent. In later years, the forbs are usually replaced by grasses. These do not stand erect and do not permit rabbits to travel under the herbaceous cover. When grasses become especially dense, they become a barrier to travel. They also lie down under heavy snow. This deterioration of cover may be compensated in still later years by development of shrubs and young trees in the field. Woody vegetation again provides cover, and its shade reduces the density of grasses near the ground. The structure of vegetation in the abandoned field thus changes yearly, seasonally, and according to weather conditions.

EVALUATION OF COVER QUALITY

Preference and Success

In order to evaluate cover quality, we must restrict our thinking to cover that is used for some one function, such as nesting, brooding, or escape. A method analogous to a study of food preferences involves measuring the animals' preferences among various available types of cover. This may be done in the field (Example 7.4) or in a pen or laboratory where the presentation of cover arrangements to the animals is better controlled. Previously cited examples illustrate controlled experiments (Table 7.1). The assumption of this method is that preferred cover is high-quality cover.

Cover quality may also be evaluated by measuring the animals' success in functioning within various types of cover. This method is analogous to a feeding trial. We might compare survival of animals with access to different types of shelter from weather or access to different types of escape cover. In Examples 7.4 and 7.5, nesting success was measured. A high degree of success in some cover type is evidence of its high quality. As in Example 7.4, we usually find animals have a preference for those forms of cover in which they enjoy functional success. This is expected since natural selection will favor those animals that select forms of cover in which success in survival or reproduction is enhanced. Natural selection will likewise eliminate animals that prefer cover providing little chance for success. The assumption noted above is therefore supported experimentally and through deductive reasoning from the principle of natural selection.

EXAMPLE 7.4 Pheasant Nesting Cover

Joselyn et al. studied the feasibility of manipulating roadside vegetation to augment the dwindling supply of nesting cover for ring-necked pheasants in central Illinois (1968). Pheasants had nested primarily in grass-legume hay fields, and at one time east-central Illinois produced some of the nation's best pheasant hunting. But with increasingly intensive agriculture, hay fields were being converted to row crops, primarily corn and soybeans. Row crops are seldom used by pheasants for nesting. With the disappearance of hay fields, a lack of nesting cover became the area's most significant habitat deficiency for pheasants (and also for prairie songbirds, such as dickcissels and meadowlarks).

A partial solution to this problem would involve production of good pheasant nesting cover along roadside ditches. However, most Illinois farmers had a passion for neatness and kept their roadsides mowed like golf courses. A roadside vegetation both attractive to nesting pheasants and aesthetically satisfying to Illinois farmers was required. Joselyn et al. established roadside seedings of grass-legume mixtures. These provided a uniform physical appearance and were relatively free of weeds that might spread to adjacent fields. The roadsides, mowed once after the pheasant nesting season each year, satisfied most landowners.

But were roadside strips of grass-legume vegetation quality nesting cover for pheasants? A four-year study (Joselyn et al.) of nest abundance and nesting success along roadsides and in other cover types indicates that grass-legume seeded roadsides were more attractive to nesting pheasants than any other available vegetation and that nest success on these roadsides was comparable to or better than nest success in other vegetation (Table 7.2).

TABLE 7.2   Quality of Nesting Cover for Ring-Necked Pheasants in Some Central Illinois Vegetation Types as Indicated by Preferences (Nests Established per Acre) and by Success (Percent of Nests Successful) (Data are from Joselyn et al. 1968)

	Grass-legume Seeded Roadsides	Unmowed Unseeded Roadsides	Mowed Unseeded Roadsides	Unharvested Grass-legume Hay Fields	Pastures	Small Grain Fields
Nests established per acre	3.0	2.0	1.2	1.7	0.7	0.3
Percent nests successful	27	21	16	24	29	33
Hatched nests per acre	0.8	0.4	0.2	0.4	0.2	0.1

EXAMPLE 7.5   Artificial Nesting Cover for Wood Ducks

Natural cavities used by nesting wood ducks are products of wood decay, usually in mature and overmature hardwood trees (Hansen 1966). Bellrose et al. studied the characteristics (structural components) of natural cavities preferred by wood ducks and related nesting success to these characteristics (1964). Preferred cavities had relatively small (14 to 19 sq in.) entrances, were less than 5000 cubic inches in volume, less than 50 inches deep, and more than 30 feet above ground.

Fungal decay may enter a tree through fire scars or other wounds, through insect borings, and perhaps through woodpecker drillings or squirrel gnawings. Trees of sprout origin are more subject to decay than are those from seed. The forest manager can maintain nesting cover in key areas for wood ducks by retaining some overmature trees, by encouraging resprouting, and by favoring those tree species, such as sycamore, silver maple, and black ash, that develop good nesting cavities. However, silvicultural and economic goals may not permit these practices if landowners are little interested in wood ducks. Once a mature forest is harvested and the stand is converted to fast-growing young trees, nesting cavities for wood ducks may be absent for decades. Cavity formation is a slow process. An even more serious problem for wood ducks has been the conversion of many bottomland forests to farmland.

The loss of forests with natural cavities prompted many researchers (including Bellrose et al. 1964; Bellrose and McGilvrey 1966) to investigate the suitability of wooden nest boxes for wood ducks. It was found that properly constructed (Fig. 7.4) and erected wooden boxes were acceptable to the ducks and produced reasonable nesting success (Table 7.3). However, losses due to fox squirrels and raccoon entering the boxes and destroying the nests were fairly high, especially with poorly designed wooden boxes that did not discouage these predators. The problem was especially acute in areas with abundant squirrels or raccoon and in the southern United States where the normally smaller raccoon could not be discouraged by the minimum entry size acceptable to wood ducks. A galvanized metal nest house was therefore designed and tested (Fig. 7.4). These houses were initially less acceptable but once ducks became accustomed to them, nest success was high (Table 7.3). The metal house is especially difficult for mammals to enter.

Fig. 7.4 Artificial nesting cover for wood ducks. Courtesy of Illinois Natural History Survey.

Cover Components

Knowledge of the cover preferences of, and success of, a species in various cover types is often sufficient for describing the animal's cover requirements and for managing its habitat. However, we may not be satisfied with this level of empirical knowledge. We may ask: Why is the species more successful in some form of cover? To understand the special attributes of quality cover we must

TABLE 7.3   Fate of Wood Duck Nests in Natural Cavities, in Wooden Boxes, and in Metal Houses in Illinois (from Bellrose et al. 1964)

| | No. Nests | Nest Success (percent) | Causes of Nest Losses (percent) | | | | | |
			Desertion	Fox Squirrel	Raccoon	Snake	Bird	Other
Natural cavities	158	40	6	18	29	2	2	3
Wooden boxes	1579	36	10	26	19	5	—	3
Metal houses	574	73	11	1	8	—	8	—

measure its structural or microclimatic components. This approach is analogous to forage analyses in animal nutrition. The structural components that matter may be: vegetation form (grass, forbs, shrubs, trees), vegetation density, snow or water depth, topography, slope, aspect, lake size, suitability of soil for digging dens, among others. The microclimatic components that matter may be: temperature, humidity, wind, light intensity, among others. Structural and microclimatic components of cover are related. For example, we would expect vegetation density to influence temperature, wind, shade, and humidity. Verme and Ozaga have explained the quality of mature stands of conifers as deer winter range in terms of the structural and microclimatic components of this cover (Example 7.3).

MANAGEMENT OF COVER

As with food requirements, a productive habitat must fulfill the cover requirements of both sexes and all age-classes of animals throughout the year. However, our knowledge of cover requirements of many species is not great. We tend to understand the cover needs of species that (1) are diurnal, (2) use open habitats, and (3) have specialized cover requirements. There are reasons for this. Diurnal species in open habitats are visible and their use of, and functions in, various types of cover are more easily observed than are the activities of species that are noctural and/or use dense vegetation. Observations of species with specialized cover requirements are easier to explain because the animals are consistent in their use of certain forms of cover. In contrast, the cover needs of generalized species are fulfilled by a variety of forms of cover, and it is difficult to learn much about them. For instance, the nests of cottontail rabbits may be in pastures, roadsides, suburban lawns, or trees—where one has been found. Does the species not have special requirements for nesting cover, or is there some common microclimatic or structural denominator in all these nest sites?

In wildlife management, it is important to recognize that the distribution and abundance of wildlife species are determined not only by the abundance of food in the habitat but also by structural and related microclimatic components of the environment. These often condition the animal's habitat selection and provide for its survival and reproduction. Comments in Chapter 6 concerning the provision of foods in wildlife habitat also apply to the management of cover. When management must be extensive because of lack of funds or lack of knowledge of species biology, rules 1 and 2 apply. These are (1) provide vegetation types and successional stages to which the species has adapted via evolution, and (2) provide a variety of vegetation types. This empirical approach is likely to fulfill the cover needs of the species. With more intensive management, the cover needs of the species can be more clearly defined, and cover deficiencies of the target habitat may be detected and rectified.

PRINCIPLES

P7.1 Cover for wildlife can be any structural resource of the environment that enhances reproduction and/or survival by providing for any natural function such as breeding, escape, travel, or visual communication.

P7.2 Cover requirements of wildlife vary among species, among sex−age classes of animals, with seasons and weather conditions, according to the prevalence of predators or pests, and among geographic regions. Some species are specialized in their evolved requirements for cover and, therefore, are limited, at least seasonally, to a narrow range of cover conditions.

P7.3 The cover resources of a habitat vary with land-use practices, because of natural disturbance and biotic succession, and with seasons and weather conditions. A complete habitat for a wildlife species provides the various cover resources needed for all natural functions by all sex−age classes throughout the year and during all weather conditions.

P7.4 Cover resources vary in quality. Animals have evolved preferences for types of cover in which they function most successfully. Biologists evaluating cover accept rates of preference and success as measures of cover quality. Cover is also analyzed by measuring structural and/or microclimatic components that are correlated with cover quality.

CHAPTER   8

WILDLIFE MOVEMENTS

Is the whole Pacific a grid in the genes
and brain of the golden plover, do you think?
Are the skies of the whole earth mapped by
season and time of day in the mind of the arctic
tern? That is what the celestial-navigation
theory suggests, and what students have not even
begun to explain.

Archie Carr

LOCAL MOVEMENTS   ZOOGEOGRAPHY
MIGRATORY MOVEMENTS   PRINCIPLES

Preceding chapters discuss three major habitat requirements: foods, water, and cover types. Here, we consider how animals travel over the landscape to fulfill their habitat needs. Concepts related to wildlife movements are discussed according to the extent and frequency of the movements: (1) local movements associated with home ranges, (2) migratory movements, and (3) zoogeographic changes in the distributions of populations over long periods of time.

LOCAL MOVEMENTS

Home Range

A home range is the area traversed by an animal or population in its normal daily activities. An animal must find all its habitat requirements within its home range; otherwise it must extend the home range. Abnormal movements, such as the path of a deer harassed by wild dogs, may go outside the home range.

Sedentary animals may have only one home range. Some species normally have several home ranges that are used seasonally, perhaps in conjunction with an annual migration. Bighorn rams, for example, may have from two to six home ranges (Geist 1971). The six possible home ranges of bighorns are the autumn prerutting, rutting ground, winter, spring, salt-lick, and summer home ranges. Bighorn ewes may have up to five home ranges (Fig. 8.1).

By definition, travel or migration routes between home ranges are not parts of home ranges because movements along these routes are not daily activities. Seasonally used home ranges do not fulfill year-round habitat requirements, only seasonal habitat requirements.

Sizes of home ranges vary among animals (Sanderson 1966). Generally, carnivores have larger home ranges than do herbivores of the same body size. Home ranges are often larger for males than for females of the same species. Home ranges may be much reduced in some seasons, for example, when demands of reproduction tie animals to a den or nest, or when deep snow restricts the movements of ungulates. We expect home ranges to be smaller in good habitat than in poor habitat because animals do not have to travel as far to fulfill their needs. Similarly, we expect home ranges to be smaller for high-density populations because they occupy good habitat and because their social interactions may limit movements.

Since many factors cause variation in home-range sizes, there may be limited value in measuring the sizes and shapes of home ranges (Stumpf and Mohr 1962) unless additional variables are measured. Many studies have involved marking, releasing, and relocating animals producing many simple maps of home ranges. Development of radiotelemetry equipment has provided opportunities for obtaining abundant data on animal movements. But some telemetry studies have produced little more than maps of home ranges similar to those produced by earlier studies involving visual markers on animals. Little is learned about the reasons for animal movements unless weather, habitat conditions, or social

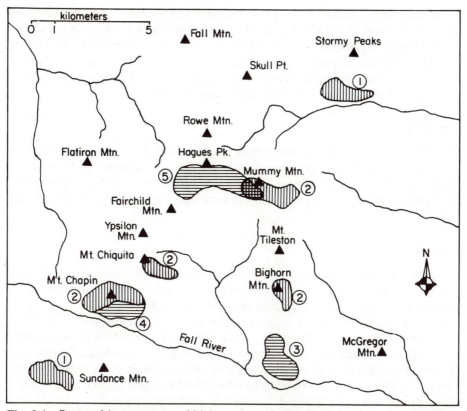

Fig. 8.1 Seasonal home ranges of bighorn sheep in the Mummy Range, northeastern Rocky Mountain National Park, Colorado: (1) ram winter ranges, (2) winter ranges of ewes and immature sheep, (3) salt-lick range, (4) lambing area, and (5) prerutting range. The sheep range widely over the Mummy Range during summer, and rutting-season activity has occurred in at least two areas. Locating seasonal home ranges is necessary for censusing the sheep, for evaluating range condition and trend, and for assessing potential impacts of human activity and recreation development on the population. Data from Bauman 1978 and Goodson 1978.

contacts are measured at each relocation, or unless home-range characteristics are compared between populations in different environments.

Critical Areas

Critical areas are parts of home ranges where limiting habitat resources are located. They have also been termed *key areas*. Examples of critical areas are the areas near water sources on which desert wildlife may depend in dry seasons, winter ranges of northern ungulates, and nesting areas where habitat resources determine the success of bird reproduction.

Locating critical areas within the home range of a wildlife population is usually a necessary part of wildlife management. Maintaining a productive population depends on protecting critical areas from degradation or destruction. Monitoring habitat condition depends on periodic observation of limiting resources on critical areas to see if forages are overused, if water is depleted or polluted, if nesting sites are declining in abundance, and so forth.

Territory

A territory is part or all of a home range that is defended to the exclusion of other animals, especially conspecifics. Territories may be defended by individuals, breeding pairs, or social groups, either year-round or seasonally. Territorialism is important in population regulation of some species and is discussed in Chapter 10.

Dispersal

Dispersal is synonymous with emigration. It refers to permanent abandonment of home ranges and movement, perhaps wandering, in search of suitable habitat for a new home range. (Dispersal is also used by zoogeographers to indicate the spread of a species or other taxon over the surface of the earth.)

Dispersal of juveniles from the home ranges of their parents is a normal seasonal occurrence in many species, for example, woodchuck, beaver, and foxes. This dispersal is in response to social intolerance. It limits population size in occupied home ranges and tends to keep all suitable habitats occupied because there are excess animals annually seeking new home ranges.

In contrast, dispersal has been uncommon in bighorn sheep. They have strong traditions for remaining on their home ranges, and juveniles remain with their parent population. Lack of dispersal by bighorns, at least under current conditions of bighorn abundance and habitat, requires far different management strategies than those used for other big game.

Cruising Ability

Cruising ability is an animal's maximum ability to traverse an area in search of its habitat requirements. King used the term *cruising radius* in this sense, but the term has recently been used in other ways (1938). To avoid confusion, *cruising ability* is preferred and more descriptive of the concept intended.

Cruising ability is determined by the limits of the physical abilities of the species or individual and by the difficulty of terrain. No home range can be larger than the animal's cruising ability because the animal cannot extend itself beyond this limit. Most home ranges will be smaller than the species' cruising ability.

Cruising ability varies among species, with terrain and weather that may inhibit travel. It varies seasonally as animals may remain near a nest or den or may be limited by low mobility of juveniles within a group.

Cruising ability is an important concept because all of a species habitat requirements must exist within an area determined by the cruising ability of the animals. Otherwise, a habitat cannot be occupied. King termed this necessary proximity of habitat requirements *juxtaposition* (1938). It is the minimum geographic interspersion of habitat requirements that must occur if a habitat is to be barely suitable for a species. Further interspersion of habitat requirements will improve the habitat for the species, as discussed in Chapter 12.

There has been surprisingly little study of cruising abilities of species. It is generally accepted that habitat requirements of cottontail rabbits must be fulfilled on a small area, whereas nesting cover, feeding areas, and water may be more widely dispersed in the habitat of mourning doves, since doves are more mobile. But at what limit of dispersion does the habitat become unacceptable to doves?

Homing

Homing is the ability to return to a home range when displaced from it. Homing involves methods of navigation that, for some species, we do not understand. It is especially prominent among migratory species.

Many migratory species return seasonally to their natal areas, wintering areas, and other home ranges along their migration routes. Anadromous fishes return almost unerringly to breed in the same freshwater streams in which they were hatched. Sea turtles cross the open ocean and find tiny islands, breeding and laying their eggs on the same beaches used by their ancestors for centuries. Birds return to the same marsh or the same suburban yard to nest each year.

In some species, the attachment to the natal area results from imprinting, a form of learning. Imprinting is the acquiring of a stable preference for food, cover, objects, or—in this case—location, which results from exposure to them for a short time during early life. A bird, shortly after hatching, is imprinted with the location of its birth. It may migrate to other areas but will return to its natal area to breed.

Imprinting permits the establishment of new breeding populations of animals in suitable, unoccupied habitats. The Canada goose is one of the most successfully managed species in North America because its breeding range has been greatly expanded by this method. To accomplish imprinting, wild geese have been captured, pinioned to prevent their migration, and kept on unoccupied habitats where they have bred and produced young. Their offspring, imprinted to their natal area, developed a new breeding population. Another method has been to collect eggs from occupied breeding habitats and hatch these under foster parents, perhaps domestic ducks, on the transplant sites. Clearing of forests, development of agriculture, and construction of reservoirs has produced much suitable nesting habitat for Canada geese in the United States, and the original nesting range of these birds has been expanded far to the south by imprinting hatchlings to new areas. Carr has attempted to reestablish breeding colonies of sea turtles on once-used beaches by this method (1967). For sea turtle eggs, which incubate buried in warm sand, foster parents are unnecessary.

When imprinting is considered as a management tool for establishing new breeding populations, one should consider why the proposed transplant site is not already being used by the proposed transplant species. If the area was once occupied, but the animals have been extirpated, perhaps the habitat is still suitable. If the area was never occupied by the proposed species, it may be suitable because of recent changes of habitat. In this case, the area may not have been occupied naturally because there has not been enough time for the species to expand its range to the new area or because the wild population is not producing excess animals and range expansion is very slow. Last, the transplant site may not have been occupied by the proposed transplant species because the habitat of the site is not suitable for the animals. In this case a transplant and forced imprinting would be useless.

Knowledge of homing may be important when problem animals are captured and moved as a method of damage control. Black moved problem black bears up to 43 miles from their trap sites and had to retrap them again at the original sites (1958). One bear returned 32 miles in just eight days. However, five bears released more than 50 miles from their trap sites did not return. These bears moved 15 to 27 miles in random directions from their release points and were recaptured. Based on these results, Black suggested moving problem bears at least 50 miles, if there was to be little chance of their returning to the original capture site.

MIGRATORY MOVEMENTS

Migration is a two-way movement, usually between seasonally used home ranges. In contrast, emigration is permanent abandonment of a home range, and immigration is movement into a previously unused home range. Migrations are often latitudinal or altitudinal movements between climatic zones. These include not only the well-known migrations of birds but also the migrations of mountain big game to winter ranges at lower elevations. The more local concentrations of white-tailed deer in traditionally used wintering areas are also termed migrations.

Factors affecting the timing, pathway, and destination of migration are genetics, learning, and environmental factors such as photoperiod, weather, and availability of food (Orr 1970). There is much variation among species in the relative importance of each factor.

Initiation of migration often depends on genetically determined responses to environmental forces such as photoperiod. Migration paths may be learned when young make their first migration with parents. However, in some species juveniles migrate to traditional ranges without their parents, implying that they make instinctive responses to environmental "triggers" along the migration route. Waterfowl may be "short-stopped" in their fall migration if weather and food availability make travel to their southernmost winter range unnecessary (Example 8.1).

Variation in the timing of migratory movements, in the routes taken by migrating animals and in the locations of home ranges established during and after migration, necessitates separating many populations of wildlife into numerous subpopulations for management purposes (Fig. 8.2). Each subpopulation may have particular population and habitat characteristics and problems. In any year, a subpopulation may face severe weather, habitat changes, exposure to harvest, or other hazards on one of its breeding, wintering, or migration ranges. Ideally, each subpopulation could be considered a separate management unit requiring separate census or other data as a basis for management decisions. Prescriptions for habitat management or regulations for commercial or sport harvest could be formulated for each subpopulation (Example 8.2). Such subpopulations that are sometimes geographically separated, but intermingle at other seasons, occur in waterfowl and commercial fishes. Some big game herds from different summer ranges share common winter ranges. Occasionally, habitat or population management prescriptions for one of a pair of seasonally intermingled subpopulations may be contraindicated for the other subpopulation, complicating management. For example, Cringan noted that success of wood duck management in the eastern United States, permitting liberalization of harvest regulations, could result in overharvest of Ontario-produced wood ducks, which migrate with ducks produced in the United States (1971). The likelihood of this overharvest is greatest in years when Ontario's production of wood ducks is low because of cold spring weather.

In North America, waterfowl migrations generally follow four major flyways. There is much overlap in migration routes and breeding and wintering ranges among birds using these flyways, and there are subpopulations that cross two and even three major flyways (Lincoln 1950). However, for administrative purposes, four flyways are used as a basis for management programs in the contiguous United States (Fig. 8.3). Each year, representatives of federal, state, and provincial wildlife management agencies and of private organizations interested in waterfowl meet to discuss flyway populations and management activities, particularly harvest goals and regulations. Waterfowl banding studies have been used to identify subpopulations within each flyway and to locate areas of overlap between flyway populations.

A system of waterfowl refuges has been established along major flyway routes. These lands, purchased mostly with funds from taxes paid by sportsmen, are managed as breeding, wintering, and migration habitats. They are vital links in the year-round habitat requirements of migratory waterfowl. Continental populations of waterfowl would be far smaller without them, as much other habitat has been drained, converted to agriculture, or otherwise degraded or lost. These wildlife refuges also provide sanctuary for waterfowl, which is one method for controlling harvest levels. Refuges are used by many species of wildlife and provide recreational, scientific, educational, and other values to all people, hunters and nonhunters alike.

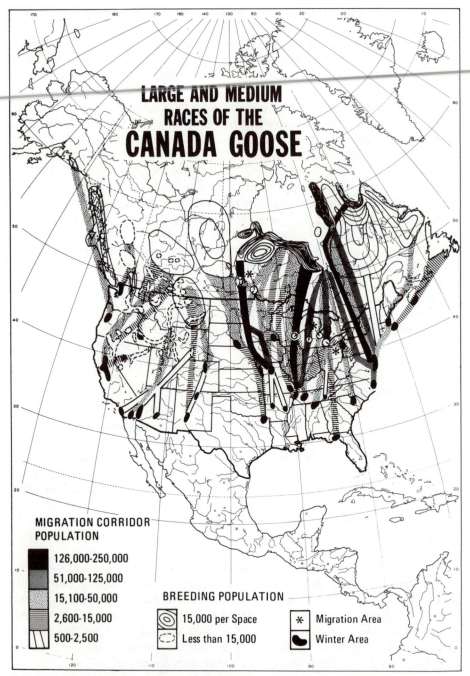

LARGE AND MEDIUM RACES OF THE CANADA GOOSE

MIGRATION CORRIDOR POPULATION
- 126,000-250,000
- 51,000-125,000
- 15,100-50,000
- 2,600-15,000
- 500-2,500

BREEDING POPULATION
- 15,000 per Space
- Less than 15,000
- ✱ Migration Area
- Winter Area

Fig. 8.2 Migration patterns of subpopulations of Canada geese. Note that many subpopulations intermingle on migration and wintering ranges. From Bellrose 1976.

Fig. 8.3.   In the 48 states migratory waterfowl are managed on a flyway basis: (1) Atlantic; (2) Mississippi; (3) Central; (4) Pacific. Other management areas on the continent are (5) Alaska, (6) Canada and (7) Mexico. From Linduska 1964.

EXAMPLE 8.1   Variation of Migration Patterns of Mississippi Valley Canada Geese, 1900 to 1966

A case study of the Mississippi Valley Canada goose population illustrates the effects of harvest, habitat changes, food supplies, and weather on migration patterns and behavior of waterfowl (Reeves et al. 1968). This population nests near Hudson and James Bays in Ontario and originally wintered in the Mississippi Valley south to the river delta and along the nearby gulf coast (Fig. 8.4). The birds apparently migrated and wintered in widely scattered small groups, particularly along sandbars of the Mississippi River.

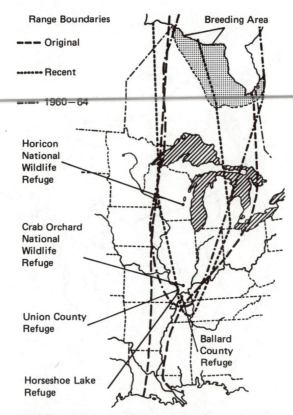

Range Boundaries — Original ····· Recent ·–·–· 1960–64

Breeding Area

Horicon National Wildlife Refuge

Crab Orchard National Wildlife Refuge

Union County Refuge

Ballard County Refuge

Horseshoe Lake Refuge

Fig. 8.4 Original and recent migratory and wintering distribution of Canada geese in the Mississippi Valley population, and refuges that have become important to the population. From Reeves et al. 1968, courtesy of Helen Dwight Reid Educational Foundation.

Market hunters took their toll of geese before 1900. One group of three hunters harvested more than 2000 geese in 1895. Later, sport hunting under few legal restrictions continued the harvest of geese. By 1916, most sand bars along the river were leased for private shooting. In 1918, the season lasted 107 days with a daily bag of eight birds and no possession limit.

Meanwhile, winter habitat for geese along the Mississippi River was being reduced in quantity and quality. The river was channeled. Flood controls prevented scouring of sand bars, and dense brush and trees replaced willow sprouts that had provided browse for geese. Fields were drained for agriculture. A change in agriculture from growing corn to growing soybeans probably reduced food supplies.

In 1927, the Department of Conservation acquired Horseshoe Lake Refuge in southern Illinois. Land around the lake was managed for geese, and the area soon attracted thousands. However, hunters were also attracted, goose hunting was commercialized around the refuge, and overharvest of geese occurred locally.

The number of Canada geese in the Mississippi Flyway reached its lowest level at 53,000 birds early in 1946. Concentrations around Horseshoe Lake were extremely vulnerable. The entire flyway was closed to goose hunting in 1946.

In the next few years, Illinois and the U.S. Fish and Wildlife Service developed more habitat in Illinois and gained experience in managing the harvest of geese. In southern Illinois, Crab Orchard National Wildlife Refuge was established in 1947, and the state acquired Union County Refuge about the same time. These refuges and Horseshoe Lake were managed to attract geese. In particular, land was planted to corn that was left unharvested as feed. These programs were accused of short-stopping geese that once migrated farther south. However, the flyway population of geese climbed steadily to more than 400,000 in 1967.

The decline in numbers of geese that had traditionally wintered south of Illinois on the river and along the gulf first became evident in the 1940s. This decline continued until only remnant flocks wintered in the lower flyway in 1967. Some combination of overharvest of southern subpopulations and less attractive habitat in the south than in the middle of the flyway was responsible. Hazing the birds to encourage their dispersal from Horseshoe Lake did not force the birds to move south. In 1949, it took 183 hours of aircraft flight time, 202 cases of exploding rockets and flares, and crews operating on land and water to disperse geese from Horseshoe Lake to areas where hunters were less concentrated, but these activities did not move birds down the flyway.

The establishment in 1940 of Horicon National Wildlife Refuge in southern Wisconsin further altered the migratory patterns of Mississippi Valley Canada geese. The refuge was established for ducks and was seldom used by geese at first. But migrating geese began to stop at Horicon, at first in small numbers, then by the thousands. Corn in the vicinity of Horicon Marsh gradually held migrating geese longer into autumn and, in mild years, into winter. In 1961 and 1966, more than 12,000 birds were still at Horicon in January. As the numbers of geese using Horicon and their length of stay increased, the numbers of geese reaching southern Illinois, at least during the hunting season, declined after 1957. The birds had been short-stopped again. In some years Wisconsin hunters could harvest the entire harvestable surplus from the flyway population before the birds reached southern Illinois hunters. A quota system has now been established in which Wisconsin's hunting season is closed whenever its designated share of the flyway surplus has been taken.

In summary, changes in migration patterns of geese in the Mississippi Valley have involved (1) near-complete abandonment of southern wintering areas with greater use of areas in Wisconsin and Illinois, (2) later departure and southward movement of the birds, especially in years with mild weather, and (3) aggregation of the once-small migrating and wintering flocks dispersed over wide areas into enormous concentrations of birds, mostly on public areas. These changes resulted from overharvest of southern subpopulations and from vast changes in goose habitat. The changes created new problems for management: local crop depredations on private land; traffic jams of sightseers wanting to see thousands of geese on refuges; commercialization of goose hunting on private lands around refuges and a loss of quality hunting experiences; and problems in allocating the harvestable surplus of geese among various flyway and wintering areas, particularly between Wisconsin and Illinois. Research biologists have also been given a problem to solve: What are the movement patterns of any remnant populations of Canada geese that retain a tradition for wintering south along the Mississippi river, and how can these populations be favored on nesting grounds and along the flyway by habitat manipulation, refuges, and harvest regulations that will increase their reproduction rates and decrease their mortality rates?

EXAMPLE 8.2   Management of Subpopulations of Alaska Salmon

Cooley has described the complexity of Alaska salmon management and the subpopulations that must be recognized if we are to maximize the intensity of salmon management and sustained commercial harvest, an ideal that we work toward but probably will not reach (1963, pp. 8–9). Cooley writes: "For the purpose of conservation each stream must be viewed as a separate unit. Fishing intensity cannot be controlled in a general manner, but must be strictly regulated in each watershed to assure an adequate escapement to each of the tributaries each year. There are about two thousand salmon streams in Alaska which receive significant amounts of spawning salmon. In each of these streams more than one species of salmon may occur and in many three to five do occur. Furthermore, in many streams more than one run of the principal species occurs. Therefore, according to biologists there are approximately 10,000 separate salmon spawning units and there must be a division of catch and escapement sufficient to sustain each unit."[1]

Note the enormous complexity of the management problem. For each of 2000 salmon streams, there is a habitat to monitor. Floods, landslides, logging, dam construction, and oil spills could require a management response on any one of them. For each of 10,000 separate salmon runs, there should be data on which to base an estimate of the harvestable surplus and needed escapement to the spawning areas. For each run there should be regulations to control fishermen to achieve that harvest. This is the biologically indicated ideal, and it is not achieved because of limited budgets that do not allow for collecting needed data and because of limited knowledge. We do not know how to monitor salmon habitats and populations inexpensively, and we do not know how to control fishermen so intensively without eliminating their chance to make a profit. As a result, some subpopulations of salmon may not be identified. Many intermingling subpopulations will be managed under prescriptions that are moderately suitable for each, but probably are not ideal for any.

ZOOGEOGRAPHY

Zoogeography is the study of the evolution, dispersal, recession, and extinction of animal taxa through millions of years of the earth's history. Much knowledge of zoogeography is based on present distributions of animals, their phylogenetic relationships, fossil records, and evidence of present and past climatic and physical barriers to their movements.

---

[1] From: Politics and Conservation. (1963) Harper and Row, N.Y.

Understanding the zoogeographic histories of species frequently provides insights into their ecology that are useful in wildlife management. Zoogeography may explain why some species can exist in a wide variety of environments, whereas other species are successful in only one or a few habitats. Zoogeography is useful in predicting the results of transplanting animals between continents or between continents and oceanic islands. The zoogeographic concept of dispersal and dominance by successful taxa and its antithesis, recession and failure in competition, are especially pertinent to wildlife management.

Dispersal and Dominance

Throughout the history of life, new and dominant forms of animals have evolved and dispersed over the earth replacing forms that had evolved earlier. Reptiles replaced many forms of amphibians. Mammals replaced reptiles (only 4 of 16 orders of reptiles have survived). Placental mammals have mostly replaced marsupials except in the Australian region, where there has been an ocean barrier to dispersal of mammals. The *Artiodactyla* have replaced the *Perissodactyla,* of which only a few species of horses, tapirs, and rhinos remain from a diversity of species extant in Tertiary times. Whereas *Cervidae* apparently evolved in Eurasia in the Oligocene (30 to 40 million years ago) and spread to the Americas, *Bovidae* evolved later in the Old World and dispersed over Africa and Eurasia with a few species reaching North America. Wild bovids have not reached South America, however.

Each of the above taxa has shown characteristics of dominance during its dispersal. These characteristics are wide distribution, radiation into many species, occupation of diverse environments, and ability to replace other forms of animals. Darlington has described this process for each of the five classes of vertebrates (1957).

The dominance of continental fauna over those on oceanic islands has been a consistent zoogeographic pattern (Darlington, p. 569). The introduction of continental species of vertebrates onto islands has usually disrupted native plants and animals, and the replacement of native animals on oceanic islands is to be expected whenever competing, continental species are introduced.

Another consistent zoogeographic pattern has been the tendency for invading fauna to replace rather than supplement native fauna. Thus, intercontinental transplants should not be undertaken without considering possibilities of competition with native animals. Competition is to be expected unless there is evidence of an empty niche for the proposed introduced species.

Recession and Failure in Competition

Adaptations resulting in dominance in competition are sometimes difficult to discern. Homoiothermy obviously conveys an advantage in colder parts of the world, allowing warm-blooded vertebrates to replace amphibians and reptiles.

Placental mammals have likewise replaced many of the marsupials, and presumably have a superior reproductive system. The *Artiodactyla*, having developed rumination and a digestive tract providing for symbiotic digestion of fibrous foods before their passage to the true stomach, presumably have a superior digestive physiology compared to the *Perissodactyla*. But adaptations that explain results of competition between more closely related forms are usually more subtle. Knowledge of the zoogeographic history of a species may aid in understanding its adaptations and limitations and may provide a basis for predicting results of competition (Example 8.3).

Nondominant species may fail in competition because they have lost genetic diversity through specialization and are poor competitors outside their specialized niches. Loss of genetic diversity can result from evolution while in contact with competing species, specialization being a way of avoiding competition. Loss of genetic diversity can also result from selective forces of the environment at a bridge between continents. Thus, the rigorous climate of the Bering land bridge connecting North America and Asia during the Pleistocene should have prohibited all but cold-adapted mammals from crossing. These mammals may be poor competitors in warm environments.

A species should be most successful in competition in habitats to which it is best adapted, habitats usually near the center of its geographic range. Without competition, a species might extend its distribution and use areas, habitats, and food and cover resources that are of marginal value to it. However, the additional stress of competition in these marginal areas can preclude their occupation. Thus, a species may have a large geographic or ecological range only because it has had few competitors in areas to which it is only marginally adapted. The introduction of a competitor may cause recession from these peripheral areas.

EXAMPLE 8.3   Zoogeography, Desert bighorn, and Competition from Exotic Mammals (Bailey 1980)

Geist has described the evolution and dispersal of mountain sheep in North Africa, Eurasia, and North America (1971). He concludes that the most primitive sheep is the Barbary sheep, *Ammotragus*, of North Africa and that Eurasian sheep evolved and dispersed across Asia from an ancestor similar to *Ammotragus*. Sheep crossed the Bering land bridge to North America, perhaps as early as during Illinoisan glaciation, some 125,000 to 275,000 years ago. Thereafter, during interglacial periods, they spread along the mountains of western North America. Wisconsin glaciation, about 10,000 to 125,000 years ago, separated American sheep populations because much of the western mountains was covered by ice. One population was confined to the unglaciated Alaska-Yukon refugium, the other to refugia south of the glacier-covered terrain.

These two major refugia are sources of the two current species of North American mountain sheep. Thinhorn sheep, *Ovis dalli*, evolved from stock in the northern refugium and are represented by Dall's sheep and Stone's sheep in Alaska and Canada today. Bighorn sheep, *Ovis canadensis*, evolved from stock in the southern refugia and are represented by the Rocky Mountain bighorn, the California bighorn, and several races of desert bighorn. Of these, the Rocky Mountain bighorn is most abundant and most widely distributed.

The retreat of Wisconsin glaciers, 10,000 to 15,000 years ago permitted American sheep to reinvade the mountains of western North America. However, populations remained in southern areas, despite climatic changes concurrent with glacial recession. These populations are the desert bighorn sheep. They are distributed from central Nevada to southern New Mexico, in southern California and old Mexico, including Baja California.

How has a mountain sheep, sufficiently adapted to cold environments to cross the Bering land bridge during glacial periods, been able to persist in southern deserts and canyon lands? The answer is lack of competition. There has been no native large grazing mammal better adapted for using these environments. Bighorn are not especially well adapted to desert habitats, but lack of competition has permitted them to persist in these glacial refugia in a limited way. Their habitats have been widely scattered. Bighorn have not been very abundant. They have been very sensitive to changes in their habitat and to competition from domestic livestock and feral burros. Most populations of desert bighorn have declined over the last 100 years.

Why has there not been a native grazing mammal better adapted to these desert habitats? The answer again lies in the Pleistocene period. Martin notes that most of the North American fauna of large mammals became extinct during the Pleistocene, about the time that man reached the New World (1970). In the last 15,000 years, North America has lost 34 genera of large mammals, mostly herbivores, including 17 genera of *Artiodactyla* and *Perissodactyla*. There once were mammoths, camels, horses, and ground sloths, as well as less familiar mammals. This extinction may have been due to predation by man, a new predator to which North American large mammals were not adapted. Whatever the cause of extinction, the early Pleistocene large-mammal fauna has not been replaced, either by radiation of surviving mammals or by invasion of new species from Asia. We recently had about 14 genera of native large mammals, including 9 genera of herbivores, all *Artiodactyla*. (*Equus* was reintroduced only a few centuries ago.) Of the *Artiodactyla*, only *Odocoileus* may have offered competition to bighorn sheep in their southern refugia.

Since the plant communities that supported the once diverse fauna of North American herbivores still exist, Martin contends there are empty niches for large mammals on this continent. Indeed, vast supplies of spruce and fir in the taiga and of mesquite, greasewood, and creosote bush in the Southwest are available for herbivore exploitation. Interestingly, Old World camels, once used by the Army in the Southwest, ate mesquite, greasewood, and creosote. Is this the feeding niche once occupied by North American camels that became extinct?

Efficient conversion of this vegetation into herbivories of value to man will depend on finding and introducing species adapted to these empty niches. The southwestern shrublands, in particular, are poorly used by domestic livestock. Cattle, adapted for consuming grass, do not flourish in these shrublands despite vast investments in range research, water developments, and brush control. Martin estimates there are 10 to 20 million animal units of unused forage in the Southwest, a tremendous resource that could produce human food. However, most introductions of foreign mammals into the Southwest have been with hopes of establishing new game species primarily for their recreation value. At least 20 species of game mammals have been introduced into Texas, California, and New Mexico (Craighead and Dasmann 1965).

These introductions bring the ecology of desert bighorn sheep and the advisability of intercontinental transplants of large mammalian herbivores into common focus. The zoogeographic history of bighorn sheep indicates that they are not well adapted to desert environments and that they will be poor competitors for desert habitats. If desert sheep are to be retained, they must be isolated from competition. They have already declined because of competition from livestock and feral burros that have been introduced from the Old World. In contrast, if efficient use of desert environments by large mammalian herbivores is desired, the desert bighorn is a poor choice of animal.

A serious threat to desert bighorn is the Barbary sheep, which has been introduced into Texas, California, and New Mexico and has been considered for introduction into Nevada (Craighead and Dasmann). Barbary sheep from North Africa have been raised successfully in zoos and parks in Europe and America. Animals from these sources have been released in the wild. Since their native North African habitat is desert mountain ranges, it is likely they are better adapted to desert conditions than are desert bighorn sheep, which are comparatively new to natural selection in desert environments. Indeed, while desert bighorn have been declining, Barbary sheep now number more than 1500 in Texas and more than 1000 in New Mexico. In 1976, more than 200 Barbary sheep were harvested in New Mexico, while only 6 desert bighorn were harvested. How are Barbary sheep better adapted to desert conditions that are desert bighorn? We can only speculate from limited evidence.

Barbary sheep may utilize browse forage more efficiently than do desert bighorn. Seasonal diets of New Mexico Barbary sheep include up to 65 percent browse and average 53 percent year-round. Desert bighorn also use considerable browse. However, shrubs may obscure vision, and bighorn detect predators and communicate visually (Risenhoover and Bailey 1980). It is not clear if desert sheep use browse primarily because preferred herbage is often less available.

Barbary sheep may be better adapted for cooling themselves in hot weather than are bighorn sheep (Ogren 1965). When overheated, they apparently are capable of diverting blood to their horns, which increase in temperature and give off excess heat. Cooling is further enhanced by their habit of digging in wet soil with their horns.

Whereas desert bighorn are obligated to having free water within their cruising ability (Welles and Welles 1961), Barbary sheep seem able to do without free water and are reported to use areas far from water in Africa (Ogren).

The conflict between those who would introduce Old World grazing mammals into the Southwest to better utilize forage resources and those who oppose this idea because of its threat to desert bighorn sheep is a conflict of values. Proponents of the desert bighorn emphasize its aesthetic value as an animal of historic times and its scientific value as a Pleistocene relict. Its value as a game animal is limited by its low productivity despite its trophy horns. Proponents of introductions to fill empty niches emphasize commercial and recreational values possible in producing more human food and game animals. The introduced mammals would have aesthetic and scientific values, too. The aesthetic value of introduced animals is illustrated by the popularity of ring-necked pheasants and wild horses.

Whatever one's preference on the question of introducing large mammals, thorough understanding of the opportunities for introduction and of the precarious ecology of desert bighorn depends partly on knowledge from zoogeography.

PRINCIPLES

P8.1   Wildlife exhibit a great diversity of movement patterns, ranging from sedentary species on small year-round home ranges to species that establish seasonal home ranges, sometimes along migration paths extending thousands of miles. All habitat resources needed by an animal must be juxtapositioned within its home range, but no home range can be larger than an area determined by the animal's cruising ability. Limiting habitat resources often occur in a small but critical part of the home range.

P8.2   In territorial species, animals defend at least part of their home range against intrusion by conspecifics. Usually, the young of territorial species disperse from the territories of their parents. This mechanism limits use of habitat resources within territories and provides an annual surplus of dispersing animals to colonize any suitable, unoccupied habitats.

P8.3   Migratory wildlife have genetic or learned traditions for annually returning to seasonally used home ranges. Imprinting of young animals to new natal areas within suitable but unoccupied ranges has been a successful tool for reestablishing extirpated populations and for extending geographic ranges.

P8.4   Migratory movements of wildlife are influenced by genetics, by learning, and by environmental factors, especially photoperiod and weather and food availability. Management efforts should be coordinated throughout the migration routes of populations, such as the major flyways of birds. Within many species, there are subpopulations with differing migration patterns, creating complex populations that are often difficult to distinguish and measure. Management is complicated whenever these subpopulations intermingle seasonally but are influenced by different environments for part of each year.

P8.5   Awareness of the zoogeographic history of a wildlife species can enhance understanding of its ecological adaptations and limitations, its requirements for habitat resources, and its abilities to withstand competition in various environments. Although natural barriers, especially climate and salt water, have delayed dispersal of terrestrial vertebrates, the dominant pattern of the past has been for successive newly evolved taxa to disperse and replace, rather than supplement, existing fauna. Thus, transplants of competing animals from other continents present a threat of ultimate extinction to elements of a native fauna. This threat is greatest when animals are transplanted from continents onto oceanic islands where faunal diversity and competition have been low.

CHAPTER 9

WILDLIFE REPRODUCTION

A CURLEW'S FAREWELL

I tried but I can try no more
  I cried but I can cry no more
I failed to bring a young chick's cry
  Into this world.

Time now bids me say farewell
  The sun is setting and I must go
But I will come again next year...
  and try
  Until I die.

Julia N. Allen

Reproduction, mortality, and movements determine wildlife abundance. However, many environmental factors may influence these three population characteristics. In a stable population, reproductive success must offset natural mortality. If harvestable surpluses are desired, reproduction must exceed natural mortality. It is, therefore, necessary for wildlife managers to monitor reproductive success and to be aware of and recognize the many environmental factors that may influence reproduction. Most concern in wildlife management has been over the reproductive conditions of female animals because reproductive failures by males have been uncommon.

DEFINITIONS

Fecundity

Fecundity is the ability of an animal to produce eggs or sperm. The major concern in wildlife management has been over the *fecundity rate* of females, or the number of eggs produced per female. Compared to mammals, the fecundity rate of birds may be of less interest because many bird species normally produce eggs that are never incubated, are abandoned, or are destroyed. In mammals, the rate of ovulation is generally more responsive to environmental factors and more indicative of environmental deficiencies. Mammalian fecundity rates have been determined by counting corpora lutea on ovaries of animals collected to assess reproductive status (Cheatum 1949a).

Natality

Natality refers to the production of new individuals by birth or hatching. The *natality rate* is the number of young produced per female. It is often less than the fecundity rate because eggs may not be fertilized or embryos may not survive to birth or hatching. *Potential natality* is the theoretical, genetically imposed upper limit on natality. Potential natality would be observed only in an ideal environment. *Realized natality* is observed in the real world, a less-than-ideal environment, as environmental factors interfere with the reproductive process.

Recruitment

Recruitment usually refers to production of sexually mature animals. *Recruitment rate* is the number of sexually mature animals produced per female or per adult (males and females). Recruitment has also been used to indicate production of self-sufficient animals (regardless of sexual maturity) by a population. The recruitment rate is usually less than the natality rate as environmental factors limit survival of newborn animals.

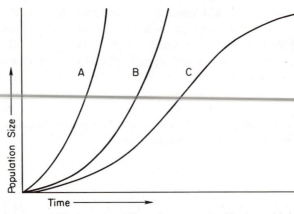

Fig. 9.1 Biotic potential: *A*, for a species having a high rate of reproduction; *B,* for a species having a lower rate of reproduction; *C* illustrates sigmoid, or logistic, population growth for comparison.

Productivity

Productivity is a loosely used word in wildlife literature. It has been used synonymously with fecundity, natality, and recruitment. Here, productivity is the rate at which a population increases or the rate at which harvestable surpluses of animals are produced. Productivity may be expressed as a number of animals per unit of time, or as a percent of the total population. (Harvestable surplus is discussed in Chapter 11.)

Biotic Potential

Biotic potential is the theoretical, genetically imposed upper limit on a population's rate of increase. Biotic potential would be observed with potential natality in an ideal and infinite environment. It results in a geometric increase in population size, regardless of species (Fig. 9.1). Since environments are neither ideal nor infinite, realized population growth is always less than biotic potential and may exhibit a pattern termed *sigmoid* or *logistic* growth (Fig. 9.1).

SEX RELATIONS

Monogamy, the pairing of a male and female for at least a breeding season, is common in birds. It also occurs in beaver and some canid species. Maintenance of an even population sex ratio is important in achieving high rates of reproduction in monogamous species. *Polygamy* includes *polyandry, polygyny,* and *promiscuity*. Polyandry, the pairing of one female with several males, is rare. Polygyny, the pairing of a dominant male with several females, is common in ungulates. Promiscuity occurs in rodents and upland game birds. In polygynous and promiscuous species exhibiting conspicuous sexual dimorphism, it is common practice to harvest many more males than females so that the population sex ratio may depart greatly from unity. Because of their sex relations, such populations have excess males that are not needed to sustain high reproduction. These males are a surplus that may be harvested. Equally important in some species, reducing the population of males may alleviate intraspecific competition and release more and better habitat resources for females, thus enhancing their survival and reproductive success.

PATTERNS OF REPRODUCTION

Wildlife species show large variation in patterns of reproduction (Asdell 1964; Sadlier 1973). Some, especially those in warm climates, breed all year. Other species breed seasonally, and still others do not breed every year. Canids have short breeding seasons, whereas ungulates are polyestrous and have long breeding seasons. The age of sexual maturity also varies among species. Many small mammals can breed as juveniles, less than a year old. Yearling breeding is common in many ungulates, though moutain goats appear not to breed until two years old. Breeding in the large species of bears may begin at an even later age.

While there are large genetic differences among species in the above patterns of reproduction, environmental factors may cause important variation within species, as indicated below (see also Sadlier 1969). Reproductive patterns determine a species biotic potential. The environment, influencing these patterns, determines realized population growth and productivity.

THE REPRODUCTIVE PROCESS

Total annual reproduction by a wildlife population is determined by (1) time of onset of breeding, (2) the number of litters or clutches produced per year, (3) litter or clutch sizes, (4) prenatal survival rates, (5) viability of newborn, (6) parental care, and (7) age at sexual maturity. Each of these seven factors may be influenced by any of several environmental factors, especially poor nutrition, severe weather, crowding and social stress, predation, disease, and parasitism. A failure of reproduction may be caused by a short-term environmental effect on one part of the reproduction process, or it may be caused by a series of environmental effects on several parts of the process. Thus, a biologist may have to measure several aspects of the reproduction process in order to detect the cause(s) of a reproductive failure.

Components of the reproductive process, some environmental factors that often influence them, and some management implications are discussed below. Most of this discussion is based upon Sadlier's reviews, in which original references can be found (1969; 1973).

Onset and Length of the Breeding Season

The length and seasonal timing of breeding activity influence the probability that young will survive, the number of litters or clutches produced in a season, and the potential for early juvenile breeding to contribute to total reproduction.

The annual onset of breeding is often coordinated so that animals breed synchronously. Advantages of synchronous breeding are (1) bringing sufficient numbers of animals into breeding condition simultaneously to enhance fertilization, (2) synchronizing critical stages of reproduction with optimum seasons for birth and survival of young, and (3) in a few species, saturating the environment with more newborn and consequently vulnerable young than predators can consume in a short time. The latter reason for synchronous breeding has been suggested for caribou (Dauphine and McClure 1974) and for cottontail rabbits.

Synchronous breeding may be disadvantageous in years during which severe weather happens to coincide with the time when young are abundant and vulnerable. This happened one March in central Illinois when a severe thunderstorm flooded about half the landscape at a time when most female cottontails had litters in ground nests. The March litter was virtually absent from the juvenile population of rabbits on my study area that year, and there were few rabbits from early in the breeding season to participate in late-summer juvenile breeding (rabbits born late in the season do not breed until after their first winter).

The annual onset of breeding activity is controlled primarily by photoperiod in many wildlife species, though temperature, moisture, and the appearance of green, nutritious forage may also influence the start of a breeding season (Sadlier 1969). Severe weather may force inactivity and delay breeding in some species.

The degree to which reproductive responses to photoperiod are genetically controlled and may vary among local populations has been little studied. Adams noted that deer from southern and from northern Alabama, brought to one site, bred and fawned about one month apart (1960). Leopold desribed a broadening of the otherwise synchronized breeding season when wild turkey populations were diluted with genes from domestic birds (1944); the result was lowered reproductive success. These observations indicate that local populations can carry genes determining a response to photoperiod that optimizes reproductive success under local conditions. These genes may be maladaptive in other locations, particularly other latitudes and perhaps other altitudes, where they may initiate reproduction that is too early or too late for high success. This possibility should be considered whenever transplants are suggested and when local gene pools face extinction.

Early cessation or complete omission of breeding activity can be caused by extremely poor environmental conditions such as drought, poor food conditions, or crowding. In summary, with good weather in good, uncrowded habitats, breeding seasons may begin earlier and last longer, providing greater reproductive output.

Ovulation Rates: Litter and Clutch Sizes

Females experiencing their first pregnancy often have fewer ovulations and smaller litters than do older females. Thus, age structure of a population may influence total reproduction. In lagomorphs, rodents, and some birds, larger litters or clutches are produced in populations living at greater latitudes. In seasonally breeding mammals, ovulation rates and litter sizes are often smallest in the earliest and latest litters.

Nutrition is the environmental factor most often and most clearly implicated as influencing ovulation rates and litter sizes. Allen and Lamming measured beneficial effects of good rutting-season nutrition on ovulation rates in domestic sheep (1961). Similar effects are expected in wild ungulates. In field studies of wildlife, such as that of Morton and Cheatum (1946; Table 9.1), effects of poor nutrition on ovulation rates have been suggested. However, in wild populations, it has been difficult to clearly separate the effects of poor nutrition from direct effects of weather and from the potential physiological effects of crowding on ovulation. Very high or low temperatures for short periods can inhibit successful ovulation by mammals. In experimental populations of rodents, higher population densities have been associated with smaller litter sizes.

Gestation and Incubation: Prenatal Survival

In birds, nest abandonment or destruction may be a cause of reproductive failure. Nest abandonment can result from crowding in dense populations.

TABLE 9.1   Variation of Reproductive Output by White-tailed Deer in Relation to Management Practices, Range Conditions, Soil Fertility and Climate (Morton and Cheatum 1946; Cheatum and Severinghaus 1950)

	Northern New York	Southern New York
Deer harvest	Males Only Few Hunters	Females Harvested Many Hunters
Range	Overbrowsed Poor Soil	Adequate Forage Better Soil
Climate	Deep Snow	Less Snow
Percent of adult does pregnant	78	92
Percent of pregnant adults with twins	18	60
Percent of pregnant adults with triplets	1	7
Percent of female fawns pregnant	4	36

Disturbance of nesting birds is more apt to result in abandonment when the disturbance occurs early, rather than late, during nesting. Nest destruction by predation, flooding, or agricultural machinery is fairly common.

In mammals, prenatal mortality of embryos may account for differences between observed ovulation rates and observed natality rates. Disease, such as brucellosis in ungulates, may cause abortions. Brucellosis is most common in elk herds that are crowded onto feeding grounds, favoring transmission of the disease. Poor nutrition can cause prenatal losses and, at least in rodents, the social stresses of crowding can also cause prenatal mortality (Christian 1964).

Viability of Young

In mammals, nutrition is the environmental factor most often implicated as influencing the size, vigor, and viability of newborn. Example 6.1 illustrates the effects of nutrition, particularly in late gestation, on survival of white-tailed deer fawns. Both mammals and birds are especially vulnerable during the first days or weeks of life. Weather conditions at this critical time, when thermoregulation may be poorly developed, can limit survival and recruitment rates. Predation may also take a heavy toll of young animals.

Parental Care

The environment may influence the quality of parental care for offspring. Poor maternal nutrition may result in reduction or failure of lactation. Failure of lactation and failure of maternal behavior, even cannibalism, have been correlated with extreme crowding in rodent populations. In birds, feeding and brood behavior are usually very intensive. However, high rates of nestling mortality occur because of weather, predation, and parasitism. Starvation may occur in nestling avian predators when prey are scarce. In some raptors, one of a pair of hatchlings is routinely larger and, owing to nestling competition, only one of the pair survives when, owing to scarcity, few prey are brought to the nest. This mechanism tends to balance reproductive success against food resources.

Age at Sexual Maturity

Poor nutrition can delay sexual maturity in mammals (Table 9.1). In addition, several studies have shown delayed sexual maturity because of the social stresses of crowding. Most of these studies have involved rodents, though the effects of density on rabbits and elephants have also been reported. In most studies of wild populations, the effects of crowding on attainment of sexual maturity have been confounded with effects of poor nutrition.

POPULATION SIZE AND REPRODUCTION

Environmental factors that may influence the reproduction process, namely nutrition, weather, crowding, predation, disease, and parasitism, often have more severe impacts on reproductive success when wildlife populations are large rather than small. Why? In larger populations there is more competition for both quantity and quality of foods and cover types. Thus, when populations are large, at least some animals are depending on relatively poor habitat resources. These animals may have poor nutrition. They and their offspring may be more susceptible to severe weather, predation, and disease. In addition, larger populations may attract predators. Disease and parasites are often transmitted more readily among animals in larger populations. Crowding is directly related to population size. Crowding results in behavioral and physiological processes that reduce reproductive success (Chapter 10).

Density-dependent Reproduction

Population density is the number of animals per unit of land area, such as deer per square mile or mice per acre. Since environmental factors influencing the reproduction process often become more severe as populations increase, reproduction rates are often density dependent (Fig. 9.2). When reproduction

No. of Does	Fawns/Does (fawns at 4 months old)	Total Production
50	1.80	90
100	1.77	177
150	1.70	255
200	1.50	300
250	1.30	325
300	1.05	315
350	0.70	245
400	0.10	40

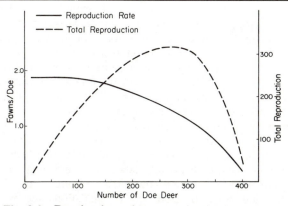

Fig. 9.2 Density dependent reproduction for a hypothetical deer herd. Note that maximum total reproduction, or population "yield," occurs with intermediate density and rate of reproduction.

rates decline with increasing density, total reproduction will assume a dome-shaped relationship to density, with greatest total reproduction at intermediate levels of density (Fig. 9.2). When maximum harvestable surplus is a population-management goal, maximization of total reproduction is necessary so that young animals will be available to replace harvested animals. Note in Fig. 9.2 that maximum total reproduction does not occur with the highest population density, nor with a maximum rate of reproduction. As density increases, the initial slight decline in the reproduction rate is more than compensated by increased numbers of breeders, and total reproduction continues to increase. Thus, when maximum harvestable surplus is a management goal, population density is maintained so that animals are not in optimum condition and do not have maximum reproduction rates.

Furthermore, if a density-dependent decline in reproduction rate is due to effects of the increasing population on forage resources, maximum harvestable surplus occurs with a population density that has measurable effects on the condition of forage resources.

In summary, maximum harvestable surplus does not occur with a maximum density of breeding animals, nor with maximum animal condition and reproduction rates, nor with minimum impact of the animals on habitat, especially forage.

Example 9.1   Density-dependent Reproduction in Antarctic Fin Whales (Gulland 1970)

Concern over declining stocks of whales resulted in establishment of an international Whaling Commission in 1946. The commission set limits on the total Antarctic catch of whales. These limits were based on little knowledge of sustainable harvest levels and did not distinguish among species populations. When the quota was introduced, fin whales had been only moderately exploited. Because of depletion of more preferred blue whales, fin whales became the preferred object of whaling during 1955 to 1965. Antarctic fin whale populations were overexploited and declined by about 65 percent during 1946 to 1964.

Detection of any density dependent increases in reproduction (or declines in natural mortality) that might have occurred was important in calculating sustainable harvest levels for fin whales. Some aspects of reproduction in whales are quite rigid, providing little opportunity for increased reproduction as a response to lowered population levels. Twinning is rare, accounting for about 1 percent of the births. The cycle of pregnancy, lactation, and weaning is two years. Thus, a mature female is not expected to exceed an average of 0.5 offspring per year. However, other aspects of whale reproduction are more changeable. Data indicated that the age of sexual maturity in unexploited whale populations was almost nine years. In the reduced, exploited populations, females began breeding at four to five years. Furthermore, pregnancy rates increased coincident with the decline of fin whales during 1946 to 1963 (Fig. 9.3). Using these and other data, Gulland calculated that the average number of young produced per year per mature female whale increased from 0.35 to 0.4 coincident with population decline due to exploitation. These calculations and estimates of other whale population parameters indicated a sustainable harvesting rate of about 8 percent of existing population levels per year.

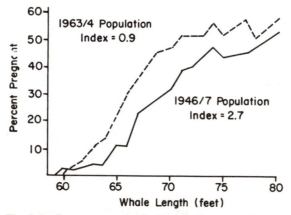

Fig. 9.3 Pregnancy rates for length-classes of Antarctic fin whales during periods with different levels of
population abundance. From Gulland 1970.

Ecological Density and Reproduction

Population density is often used as a measure of crowding, or of social stress, or
to indicate competition for habitat resources. However, density may be a poor
measure of these parameters. For instance, 10 deer per square mile of poor
habitat may be more crowded, more socially stressed, and more deprived of food
and cover than are 20 deer per square mile of good habitat.

Ecological density is the number of animals relative to the quantity and quality
of their habit resources; it is, therefore, the number of animals relative to the
habitat's ability to support animals. Populations at the same ecological density
are equally stressed by crowding and lack of habitat resources, regardless of
differences in densities per unit of land area. Although population density can be
measured, ecological density is a concept and cannot be measured exactly.
However, we often measure the conditions of animals and of their habitat as
indices of ecological density.

When populations occupy habitats of different qualities, we expect different
relationships of reproduction to density (Fig. 9.4a). Thus, a more precise view
is that reproduction rates tend to decline with increases in ecological density
(Fig. 9.4b).

MEASURING REPRODUCTION

Data on reproductive success of wildlife are widely used as a basis for management decisions. Reproduction is a key to maintaining populations and to
producing harvestable surpluses. Reproduction must offset a diversity of kinds

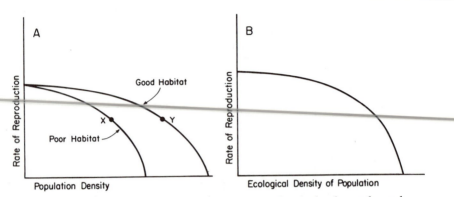

Fig. 9.4 *A* shows the relationship between rates of reproduction and population density on habitats of differing quality. Points *X* and *Y* represent equal ecological densities, because shortages of habitat resources are equally apparent as effects on reproduction. *B* shows the more general case of ecological-density dependent reproduction.

of mortality. Thus, wildlife managers consider any progressive decline in reproduction to be alarming. Reproduction rates are used as indices of trends in ecological density (Fig. 9.4*b*). Total reproduction is often estimated as a basis for calculating allowable harvest levels. Three categories of data on reproduction are (1) breeding rates, (2) litter or clutch sizes, and (3) age ratios.

Breeding Rates

Breeding-rate data indicate the proportion of the female population, or of each age class in the female population, that is participating in reproduction. Pregnancy rates may be determined from special collections or from road-kills or harvested mammals. (Caution is advised, however, since road-kills, in particular, may not provide a representative sample from a population and may produce a biased impression of breeding rates.) A lack of breeding by many animals may indicate early cessation or complete failure of reproduction. Breeding rates by juveniles are often especially sensitive to nutrition and are used as an index to food conditions. For instance, as white-tailed deer populations increase toward limits of their forage supplies, fawn breeding declines detectably before there are noticeable effects on adult breeding rates.

Litter, Clutch Sizes

With mammals, litter sizes are estimated from counts of corpora lutea on ovaries, from counts of embryos within uteri, and from counts of placental scars on uteri of some species. Corpora lutea counts indicate ovulation rates and can be used in early gestation when embryos are small and hard to detect. Embryo counts are preferred because they provide a more accurate estimate of litter sizes at birth. Placental scars can be used to estimate litter sizes, postpregnancy, in some carnivores that have one zonary placenta per embryo. With birds, clutch sizes can be used to estimate total natality for a population of known size and sex—age composition.

Age Ratios

Age ratios are widely used to measure reproduction rates for mammals, especially ungulates. Hence, the familiar fawn—doe, calf—cow, lamb—ewe, and kid—nanny ratios. Age ratios are obtained by observing and classifying a sample of the population, often in fall or early winter. Care must be taken to ensure an unbiased sample, however. Females with young may be more or less visible than females without young, because of social habits of the species. Furthermore, in a few situations, age ratios may be influenced more by adult mortality than by reproductive success (Caughley 1974).

Age ratios are especially valuable for estimating the success of reproduction in that they are obtained late during the reproduction process, after most opportunities for failure in the process have passed. Thus, measuring reproduction by embryo counts may be misleading if many nonviable young are being produced from those embryos. On the contrary, if age ratios indicate a low success of reproduction, they do not indicate what part of the reproduction process has failed and, thus, may provide no clue as to the cause of reproduction failure.

Age pyramids are graphic illustrations of population age structures and may provide evidence of trends in reproduction by a population. Populations with broad bases in their age pyramids are generally considered as increasing, though they may have high rates of mortality as well as of reproduction (Fig. 9.5 *a*). Populations with narrow bases in their age pyramids are generally considered to be declining (Fig. 9.5*b*). (At least reproduction and survival of recent age-cohorts has been poorer than those of previous cohorts.) Missing cohorts occur commonly in population age pyramids (Fig. 9.5*c*). The occurrence of a missing

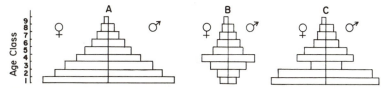

Fig. 9.5   Age pyramids for three hypothetical populations. The length of each bar represents the number of animals in a sex-age class. *A* illustrates a broad-based pyramid characteristic of an increasing population (see text). *B* illustrates a pyramid for a population that has experienced declining reproductive success in the last three years. *C* illustrates a population with a ''missing'' cohort. There was a relative failure of reproduction three years ago in this population.

cohort is often very instructive to a wildlife manager. Characteristics of the year in which the missing cohort failed may provide clues to how the environment influences a population. For instance, the year may have had an unusually wet spring or there may have been unusual disturbance of the breeding animals in that year. Such information is valuable as a basis for management decisions.

PRINCIPLES

P9.1   Reproductive success is critical to the maintenance, increase, and productivity of every wildlife population, and the monitoring of reproductive success is an important management function. There is great variation among species in biotic potential, sex relations, and seasonal patterns and processes of reproduction. Therefore, strategies for monitoring reproductive success and for managing populations will depend on knowledge of the reproduction characteristics of the species being managed.

P9.2   For each wildlife species, the reproduction process has many components that occur in sequence. Numerous environmental factors may influence the process at each stage, so there are many potential causes of an observed failure of reproduction. The relative roles of these factors influencing reproduction can vary among populations and among time periods.

P9.3   Several environmental factors that may inhibit reproductive success may become more intense as population densities increase relative to habitat resources. As a result, rates of reproductive success tend to be ecological-density dependent; that is, they tend to decline as ecological density increases. Under these conditions, total reproduction per year is greatest at intermediate levels of ecological density with intermediate, rather than maximum, rates of reproduction per animal.

P9.4   Breeding rates, litter and clutch sizes, and population age structures are widely used as measures of population reproductive success and as one basis for decisions in wildlife management.

CHAPTER 10

WILDLIFE BEHAVIOR AND PHYSIOLOGY

The study of animals does show what animals
aspire to most. It is not sex. Not by a long
shot. That's second best, at best. Some would
consider it to be a quite satisfactory second
prize, which undoubtedly it would be, were it not
that the second prize goes with the first. So does
the third, fourth, fifth, and so on. The rules
of the game dictate that the winner takes the
cake, and the losers get the crumbs—maybe.
It is true that he who has, gets, no matter
how much we may detest.

Valerius Geist

BEHAVIOR
PHYSIOLOGY
INTRINSIC POPULATION
  REGULATION

MEASURING BEHAVIOR AND
  PHYSIOLOGY
PRINCIPLES

Wild animals have many behavioral and physiological adaptations to their environments. Knowledge of these adaptations enhances the wildlife manager's understanding of wildlife habitat requirements. (For example, see Geist and Walther 1974.) However, this chapter is limited to the major roles of behavior and physiology in intrinsic mechanisms of population regulation.

BEHAVIOR

As natural selection is a process in which the fittest animals survive, we expect aggressive, competitive animals to obtain food and cover and to secure mates and thus survive, reproduce, and extend their genotypes to subsequent generations. This would develop populations of very aggressive, competitive animals and could preclude evolution of cooperative, social behavior. Yet, sociality is common in the animal kingdom, as evidenced by the many terms like covey, flock, herd, pride, school, swarm, band, and family group. Whereas competitive behavior is adaptive, cooperative behavior also enhances survival and is adaptive. Animals in social groups enhance their chances for finding habitat resources, for detecting danger, and for escape from predators or successful defense or confusion of predators. Sociality facilitates the learning of adaptive skills such as feeding and of traditional home ranges and migration routes. Sociality may facilitate breeding and provide group shelter.

Animal populations have retained the adaptive values of both competitive and cooperative behavior through evolution of social systems. These systems, hierarchism and territorialism, control intraspecific aggressive behavior within limits that permit formation and function of social groups.

Hierarchism

In hierarchies, animals assume ranks in a dominance-subordinance system. The two extreme types of dominance hierarchies are the peck order, or straight-line dominance system, and despotism (Fig. 10.1). More complex, mixed hierarchies, blends of these two extreme types, are common.

Dominant animals tend to be older and larger individuals. They are eventually replaced by once-subordinate animals. Dominant animals may possess superior weapons of combat such as horns, teeth, or spurs. Once a dominance hierarchy is established, often mostly through apparently playful combat among juveniles, the ranking of individuals tends to be accepted with infrequent challenge. Energy-expensive and dangerous aggressive behavior is seldom necessary. Subordinate animals defer to dominant animals who retain dominance with threats and displays (Geist 1978). Group cooperation is little inhibited by these competitions, and the survival values of cooperation are retained.

However, the most subordinate animals in a group attain the least and/or poorest of habitat resources. They may also be kept in a state of anxiety that is energetically wasteful and can be physiologically damaging, as is indicated later in this chapter. Thus, in many populations, subordinate animals exhibit poor body condition and low reproductive success and survival.

Competition for scarce resources increases with increased population density, or, more precisely, with increased ecological density of the population. As ecological density increases, an increasing proportion of a population may be experiencing increasing levels of the stresses of competition. Consequently, population parameters such as average animal condition and average rates of survival and reproduction can be inversely related to ecological density, as in Fig. 9.4b.

During periods of environmental stress, dominant animals may continue to find adequate food and cover and maintain good reproduction and survival. Without a dominance hierarchy, all individuals of the population would share equally of limited resources and decline equally in body condition. This situation could be dangerous to survival of the population.

Average animal condition is often used as an indicator of population ecological density. At low ecological density, animals are expected to be in good physical condition. In hierarchial populations at high ecological density, animals should be distributed over a broad range of condition classes, depending on each

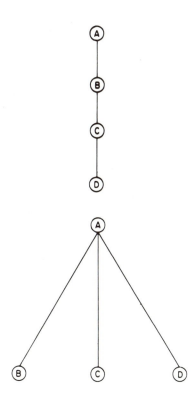

Fig. 10.1 Two extreme types of social hierarchies.

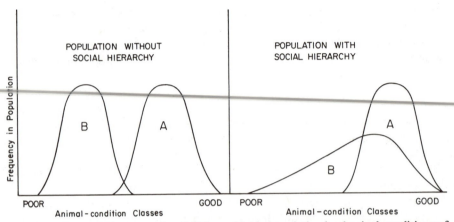

Fig. 10.2 Expected impacts of social hierarchism on variation in physical conditions of animals. Left: Without social hierarchism, all animals decline in condition with a change from low ecological density, A, to high ecological density, B. Right: With social hierarchism, only subordinate animals decline in condition with a change from A to B and even at high ecological density, B, there are some animals (dominants) in good physical condition.

animal's dominance rank (Fig. 10.2). The greater variance of condition data from such populations requires larger samples of animals to obtain desired levels of confidence in measuring average population condition. The variance of condition data may be more diagnostic of a population's ecological density than is the average.

Territorialism

Territorialism is the tendency to defend, or exclude other animals from, part of the home range. It is especially common in birds, but we are becoming increasingly aware of territorialism in many mammal species, especially as we learn more about their use of scent-producing organs (Stokes 1974). Territorialism may be seasonal and is often associated with periods of reproduction. In some species, territories are defended by individuals, in others by breeding pairs of animals, and in still others by social groups. In many species, territorialism results in a seasonal dispersal of juveniles from their natal areas. Dominance of a territorial animal is usually accepted within its territory. As in dominance hierarchies, territorial disputes are often settled by threats and displays, alleviating the need for wasteful and dangerous aggressive behavior. In mammals, territories are often maintained by intensive marking of the area with visible signs and with scents.

Territories may provide for uninterrupted breeding, maternal behavior, and care of young. Territories may assure an adequate food supply for critical seasons. Territories may be moving areas as a male defends the vicinity of a harem of females.

Animals holding territories assure themselves of habitat resources and mates. They tend to be successful in survival and reproduction. In many territorial species, there are excess, nonterritorial animals existing in substandard habitats or constantly moving among occupied territories (Carrick 1963; Carl 1971; Smith 1968). These animals exhibit poor condition, low survival and reproduction rates, and high dispersal rates. Should a territory-holding animal be removed from a population, a nonterritorial animal will usually occupy its territory quickly.

Like hierarchism, territorialism disposes a population to ecological-density dependent reproduction and survival. A habitat of given quality provides a relatively fixed number of suitable territories capable of supporting a relatively fixed number of territorial animals. As a population increases above that number, an increasing proportion of the population consists of nonterritorial animals with low rates of survival and reproduction. Therefore average rates of survival and reproduction for the entire population decline.

Behavior and Populations

In summary, hierarchies and territories provide for orderly functioning of social groups of wildlife, preserving the survival and reproduction benefits of sociality for otherwise competitive animals. When habitat resources are scarce, that is, when ecological density is high, hierarchies and territories provide for elimination of "surplus" animals without endangering those animals that are dominant. Subordinate animals are eliminated by forced dispersal, by their greater risk of mortality, and by inhibition of their reproduction. This process will have eugenic effects if dominant animals are genetically better adapted for success in their environment. The process produces a balance between animal numbers and habitat resources and limits the potential for overuse and destruction of those resources. The process also functions to keep all suitable habitats occupied and all suitable habitat resources moderately exploited, because there are always surplus animals seeking to use these resources as they may become available through removal of dominant animals or through habitat change.

Behavioral regulation of animal abundance, as described here, is most important in territorial species, especially birds. Although behavior may be less dominant as a population-regulating force in taxa other than birds, it contributes to population regulation in most, perhaps all, warm-blooded vertebrate species. Wynne-Edwards (1965) and Calhoun (1952) have been major proponents of behavior as a population-regulating factor in all homoiotherms.

PHYSIOLOGY

In the past 30 years there has been much study of physiological responses of animals to stressful situations, particularly to stresses resulting from crowding and intraspecific competition. Pioneering research on the physiology of stress was done by Hans Selye (1946; 1950; 1955). For the nonphysiologist, the most readable summary of this work has been published in paperback form (Selye 1956). Selye, a physician and endocrinologist, was most concerned with the implications of stress physiology in human disease. Christian and Davis (1964; Christian 1964; 1971), with considerable research, have demonstrated important roles of stress physiology in population dynamics, particularly of rodents.

Stress

Selye discussed the difficult problem of defining stress (1956, pp. 52−56, 222, 254). A stressor is any stimulus that requires a body to make physiological adjustments in order to maintain homeostasis. Stressors include temperature change, lack of food, the presence of antagonists, competitors or predators, toxic substances, unexpected noise, and the physiological demands of reproduction. One could argue that all stimuli require physiological adjustments, however slight, and that the definition of stressor is so broad as to be meaningless. But some stimuli require greater physiological adjustment to maintain homeostasis than do other stimuli. Likewise, animals may experience low, medium, or high frequencies of stressors at particular times. Thus, some animals are more stressed than others, and stress is far from meaningless.

Stress is the state or condition of an animal when it receives stressors. If all stimuli are at least a little stressful, as argued above, all live animals are in a state of stress, and stress is life. In fact, Selye alludes to stress as "the wear and tear of life." However, some environments certainly produce more frequent and intensive stressors than others, and animals can, therefore, be in states of low, medium, or high stress.

The General Adaptation Syndrome

Selye was led to his life's work on stress by noting, during medical training, that a certain set of symptoms occurred with any form of disease, no matter how variable or unusual the disease. These symptoms were nondiagnostic because they were useless in detection of specific diseases. The symptoms were physiological adjustments in response to stressors—any stressors. Selye termed them nonspecific adjustments because they were not specific for any one type of stressor or disease.

A syndrome is a set of physiological symptoms that tend to occur together. The general adaptation syndrome (GAS) is the set of nonspecific physiological adjustments, made by the body in order to maintain homoeostasis when confronted by stressors. Only a brief outline of the GAS is given here.

Stressors act indirectly upon the pituitary gland, located at the base of the brain. The pituitary is stimulated to release adrenocorticotropic hormone (ACTH). With greater abundance or intensity of stressors (the higher the state of stress), more ACTH is produced. A tropic hormone is one that stimulates another gland. ACTH stimulates the adrenal cortex. The stimulated adrenal cortex increases its release of many hormones, corticoids, which regulate many body functions, including mineral and water balance and glucose metabolism. Corticoids also inhibit development of sex organs, suppress growth, and suppress formation of antibodies, thereby lowering disease resistance.

The classic GAS consists of three phases: alarm, resistance, and exhaustion. The alarm phase occurs when levels of stress are elevated. ACTH causes depletion of cell contents in the adrenal cortex, a condition that can be detected histologically. If the newly elevated levels of stress continue, the adrenal cortex enlarges and maintains production of corticoids. At this resistance stage, the adrenal cortex is large, but not depleted. Continuation of excessive levels of stress causes the exhaustion phase in which the adrenal cortex is both large and depleted. This stage is often associated with hypoglycemia (low levels of blood sugar) and possibly hypoglycemic convulsions ("shock disease"), with kidney damage, and with enteritis (inflammation of the digestive tract) or ulcers. Although an animal may die of these problems, wild animals approaching this condition would be liable to predation or death by infectious disease. The three phases of the GAS are actually points in a continuum of symptoms. An animal experiencing all three phases will gradually decline in condition and gradually increase its liability to mortality. Furthermore, numerous studies have correlated increased levels of stress, or increased ACTH secretion, with failure in all stages of the reproduction process, especially in rodents.

Stress is Cumulative

For ecologists, an important feature of the GAS is that diverse stressors are integrated physiologically within the animal. Thus, food scarcity is more of a problem if other stressors such as harassment, intraspecific strife, or toxins are present. The GAS integrates the entire spectrum of an animal's environment into a level of stress that characterizes the quality of its environment. Any environmental factor present in other than optimum abundance should create some level of stress. This concept is important when considering the problem of limiting habitat resources. We often think of *one* limiting factor, as if only one habitat resource can be in short supply and limit a population. The concept of the GAS indicates that many habitat resources might, in combination, be limiting, each contributing stressors that influence the total level of stress and, hence, reproduction and mortality. Improvement of any one of the combination of limiting resources would alleviate some of the stress and permit improved population performance.

Of course, a single habitat resource may be in such short supply as to be the only limiting resource. A given level of stress may occur anywhere in a continuum between having one, intensive stressor and having numerous weak stressors. This may result from having one severely deficient habitat resource or from having numerous, comparatively minor habitat deficiencies. The problem of detecting limiting factors in relation to this concept is illustrated in Fig. 12.4.

GAS and Population Regulation

As populations increase, stresses due to competition, intraspecific strife, reduced per capita levels of habitat resources, increased transmission of disease, and attraction of predators should increase. Thus, symptoms of the GAS should increase with population density, especially ecological density, causing density-dependent reproduction and mortality and, therefore, population regulation. Has this been demonstrated in wildlife populations? The answer is not often and usually not conclusively.

Most studies of effects of crowding-induced stress on reproduction and mortality have involved laboratory or semicontrolled populations of rodents. Furthermore, population densities used in these studies have usually been greater than densities normally encountered in wild populations. Under these conditions, results have been undeniable. Crowding and other stresses affect reproduction and mortality.

Some biologists have discounted these results as artifacts of abnormal crowding and concluded that the GAS is not a factor in population dynamics. I disagree. So many studies have shown strong responses of rodents to stress that it is reasonable to conclude that the GAS is involved in population regulation in rodents. The GAS may make animals more liable to disease, predation or starvation so that its independent contribution to population regulation is not evident.

There is limited evidence supporting a role for the GAS in nonrodents. Symptoms of the GAS, associated with stress, especially crowding, have been observed in birds, deer, and lagomorphs, at least (Whatley et al. 1977; Christian et al. 1960; Pederson 1963; Wodzicki and Roberts 1960; Griffiths et al. 1960). Although the GAS seems much less important in population regulation of nonrodents, it may be involved in and contribute to density-dependent declines in their reproduction and survival. However, to attribute population regulation to the "stress due to crowding" is not a substitute for understanding. The role of stress physiology in population regulation is not well understood. Furthermore, merely attributing population failures to stress does not identify or quantify specific stressors or relevant environmental deficiencies.

INTRINSIC POPULATION REGULATION

Intrinsic population regulation refers to the determination of population size by behaviorial and/or physiological mechanisms that are inherent characteristics of the animals. These behavioral and physiological processes respond to increasing population ecological density in ways that reduce reproduction rates and survival rates. The mechanism has often been termed a *feedback system,* a term borrowed from endocrinology, in that with increasing population size there is *negative feedback* on reproduction and survival. The process of intrinsic population regulation is described below. All aspects of the process are included, although some aspects are expected to be operative whereas others are absent in any one population.

Suppose a population experiences increasing ecological density. This can occur because of population increase or because of decline in habitat quantity or quality. The increased ecological density may be of seasonal occurrence so that the mechanisms of population regulation may not be evident year-round.

Increasing ecological density results in a stressful situation and the various stressors are cumulative, as described above. Social stresses are mediated by hierarchies and/or territorialism. There are environmental stresses due to decreased per capita supplies of foods and cover types. Disease transmission and predator harassment may increase as the population must concentrate around limiting resources. Stresses are intensified during periods of severe weather. The increasingly stressful situation induces behavioral and physiological responses.

Intraspecific competition may cause more frequent aggressive behavior within social hierarchies (Petocz 1973). Dispersal of juveniles from the population may increase. However, displacement of subordinate animals from quality habitat resources should also occur. Such displacement has been difficult to measure in wild populations, but should influence reproduction and survival of subordinates. Aggressive behavior may also result in injuries and disrupted breeding behavior. If the species is territorial, increasing ecological density can result in a larger proportion of nonterritorial animals in the population, a situation reducing average rates of reproduction and survival.

Social and environmental stresses provoke symptoms of the GAS. As noted above, growth, sexual maturity, and all stages of the reproductive process may be impaired as part of the GAS. Lowered resistance to disease, kidney disease, enteritis, and hypoglycemia may reduce viability of animals.

Some combination of the above behavioral and physiological responses to increasing ecological density cause decreased reproduction and/or increased mortality. As a result, the population declines and ecological density also declines. The stress of high ecological density is relaxed, as are the behavioral and physiological responses which limit reproduction and survival. Intrinsic mechanisms thus respond to ecological density and produce a dynamic balance between numbers of animals and ever-changing habitat resources, including space.

Note that intrinsic mechanisms of population regulation may operate in combination with extrinsic factors, such as disease, predation, and malnutrition, which may also respond to changes in ecological density. The importance of intrinsic mechanisms in population regulation varies greatly among species. Intrinsic mechanisms are well-developed in birds and at least some squirrels (behavioral mechanisms) and rodents (physiological mechanisms). In contrast, intrinsic control mechanisms are poorly developed in ungulates. As a result, ungulates frequently overuse forage resources and extrinsic factors of population regulation have frequently been reported for them. However, intrinsic mechanisms are not absent in ungulates. They display hierarchism and, in a few species, territorialism (Buechner 1961; Bromley 1969). Dispersal, especially of males, from large populations is common. Symptoms of the GAS have occurred with increasing population densities of deer (Christian et al. 1960).

MEASURING BEHAVIOR AND PHYSIOLOGY

It is useful for wildlife managers to detect trends in ecological density of a population. At high ecological densities, animals tend to be in poor condition. Geist labeled these low-quality populations (1971). Since characteristics of behavior and physiology respond to changes in ecological density in some species, these characteristics may be used as indices to ecological density. Such measures of ecological density have not yet been widely used in wildlife management but may become so.

Several behavioral parameters have been suggested as indicative of ecological density in ungulates (Geist 1971; Petocz 1973). In high-quality populations at low ecological density, the frequency and intensity of dominance displays by adults and of play by juveniles may be high. These energetically costly activities may be replaced by increasingly aggressive behavior as ecological density increases. At low ecological density, maternal behavior may be pronounced and suckling periods long, frequently terminated by the satiated offspring. In contrast, at high ecological density, maternal behavior is less frequent, suckling periods are short and usually terminated by the adult female. Average group size and spacing of individuals are other parameters that may respond to variation in ecological density.

Symptoms of the GAS, especially adrenal size and histology and blood constituents, have been suggested as indices to levels of stress on animals and, therefore, to ecological densities of populations. However, there is great variation in physiological parameters associated with sex–age classes and with seasonal trends in physiology, especially reproduction. As a result large samples of animals must be collected at appropriate seasons in order to detect trends in ecological density. Such samples have not been possible for populations of high value. However, symptoms of the GAS may find more use as indices to ecological density for less valuable populations, such as pest species, in the future.

PRINCIPLES

P10.1 Intraspecific competition is mediated by either hierarchism or territorialism in many wildlife species. Subordinate or nonterritorial animals tend to have lower rates of reproduction and higher rates of mortality.

P10.2 Stresses resulting from any environmental factors that are other than optimum and from intraspecific competition are cumulative and cause a set of physiological responses known as the general adaptation syndrome (GAS). The role of the GAS in wild populations is not well understood since its effects will be confounded with similar direct effects of environmental inadequacy. However, the GAS occurs with reduced reproduction and increased mortality rates in laboratory populations and probably also in wild populations.

P10.3 Levels of intraspecific competition and stress are positively correlated with population ecological density. Their negative impacts on rates of reproduction and mortality form an intrinsic mechanism of population regulation in response to varying ecological density. The importance of these behavioral and physiological mechanisms in regulating population size varies greatly among species.

P10.4 Since animal behavior and physiology respond to changes in ecological density, wildlife biologists can measure trends in behavioral and/or physiological parameters as indicators of trends in ecological density.

CHAPTER 11

WILDLIFE MORTALITY

. . . as more individuals are
produced than can possibly survive,
there must in every case be a struggle
for existence.

Charles Darwin

Whenever the death of one or more wild animals is observed, there are obvious implications for wildlife abundance—a population has been reduced. In contrast, failure of reproduction is less frequently noticed, especially by lay-persons, but has equally important implications for wildlife abundance. However, as death is an emotional subject, many people overreact to wildlife mortality and are unable to view the subject objectively. The wildlife management biologist must have a less emotional and more thorough understanding of the complex subject of wildlife mortality.

MORTALITY IS ABUNDANT

Species that have high reproductive rates characteristically have high mortality rates. As a result, mortality tends to equal reproduction, and most wildlife populations exhibit relatively stable levels of abundance. However, very many animals may be expected to die every year. In populations of small game, such as rabbits or quail, mortality rates for newly born or newly hatched young are often more than 90 percent in the first year. Most of this mortality occurs in the first few weeks of life. Laypeople often are quite disturbed over any evidence of wildlife mortality. However, for species with characteristically high rates of reproduction and mortality, the wildlife biologist is usually unable to infer anything concerning population status or trend from the casual observation of some dead animals.

NORMAL MORTALITY

Normal mortality includes those rates and types of mortality that have been common in a wildlife species' evolutionary history. A species is adapted to this mortality. It has evolved a potential natality rate that tends to balance normal mortality rates. It has evolved an anatomy, behavior, and physiology that enhance resistance to diseases and to predators and other types of mortality that have been common in the species' evolutionary history.

Most observed wildlife mortality is normal. Normal mortality is, in one sense, good for wildlife populations. It is a mechanism of natural-selection, removing inferior animals, maintaining genetic quality of the population, and forcing continued adaptation of the population to environmental change.

ABNORMAL MORTALITY

Abnormal mortality includes those rates and types of mortality that have not been common in a species' evolutionary history. A species is not adapted to this mortality. Therefore, abnormal mortality, perhaps an introduced disease or predator, can be disastrous, reducing a wildlife population well below expected levels of abundance, even to extinction.

Examples of abnormal mortality include:

1   Man-caused destruction of wildlife by intensive harvest, trapping, and poisoning. Wild animals may lack adaptations to these types and rates of mortality.

2   The new introduction of predators or diseases, for example, of mongoose into the West Indies and rinderpest into Africa (Branagan and Hammond 1965).

3   Abnormal abundance of reservoir hosts for a disease, such as the recently increased abundance of white-tailed deer in the northeastern United States and southeastern Canada. The deer population there has fostered increased levels of brainworm infection in woodland caribou and moose (Anderson 1965). The disease contributed to a decline of caribou and moose and their extirpation from some areas.

4   Abnormal abundance of predators supported by an abnormal food resource. The food supplied to wild predators by garbage or to household pets intentionally may support a density of predators capable of eliminating wild prey.

5   Man-constructed hazards that cause accidental deaths of wildlife. These include reservoirs that may trap and drown ungulates (Edwards 1957), radio-transmission towers that somehow attract and kill migratory songbirds, which collide with guy-wires (Stoddard and Norris 1967), and fishnets that snare and drown diving birds (Bartonek 1965).

MORTALITY AND WILDLIFE MANAGEMENT

Since abnormal mortality may reduce or extirpate wildlife populations, and may prevent the achievement of management objectives, it can be a serious management problem. However, solving the problem is often difficult. The solutions will usually require removal of detrimental environmental factors for which the wildlife have no defensive adaptations. This is not always possible. We cannot remove all radio-transmission towers that are hazards to small birds. We cannot discontinue snow removal from roads and railroads so that ungulates will not be attracted and hit by vehicles. We usually cannot remove an introduced disease organism once it has been established. However, situations creating abnormal wildlife mortality can often be avoided by concessions to the wildlife resource during the planning of man's activities. Radio towers might be located away from migratory paths of birds. Roads and railroads can be located away from wintering areas of ungulates. Surveillance of transported animals can prevent the introduction of disease organisms. Technological solutions to problems of abnormal mortality are sometimes possible. For example, power transmission towers have been designed to reduce the risks that perching raptors will be electrocuted. However, the more we alter wildlife environments, the more problems of abnormal mortality we create. Many of these problems can be avoided in planning or solved technologically; but many such problems have never been solved.

In contrast, normal types of mortality are usually less serious management problems. High rates of normal types of mortality are often symptoms of an inadequate habitat. Thus, parasites that are present in all animals may become pathogenic when animals suffer malnutrition, the parasitic disease being a symptom of inadequate food supplies. In the same way, high predation losses may indicate poor food or cover resources that expose animals to predation. For normal types of mortality, the control of mortality rates usually involves providing good habitat in the form of the species' naturally associated environment. This permits expression of the adaptations that have evolved to counteract normal mortality. With good habitat, mortality will still occur, but at normal rates, and harvestable surpluses of animals will usually be available.

In intensively managed wildlife populations, we may want to eliminate as much mortality as possible, replacing all of it with our own harvest. This single-use approach to wildlife resources is practiced on shooting preserves and on some waterfowl production areas. Under these circumstances, even the normal mortality that occurs with good habitat is a management problem. Predator control is applied; artificial nesting structures and foods dosed with drugs to control diseases may be provided. Game may be stocked from pens. These activities artificially remove predators and create an artificially high abundance of game. The commercial value of wildlife is promoted at the expense of all other wildlife values. However, shooting preserves that practice such single use of wildlife near large cities where natural populations of game are scarce or absent have been commercially successful.

TYPES OF MORTALITY

Wildlife mortality includes (1) starvation and malnutrition, (2) harvest, (3) accidents, (4) predation, (5) exposure, and (6) disease. In reality, animals often die for a combination of causes. For example, malnourished animals are susceptible to disease and predation. The *proximate* cause of death is often predation, whereas the *ultimate* cause is malnutrition or disease that debilitated the animal, exposing it to predation. All factors of the environment —food, cover, diseases, weather, and others—affect the physical conditions of animals; and animals in good condition are less apt to die. Therefore, the ultimate causes of a mortality incident may be ambiguous.

Mortality rates are usually expressed as the percent of a population, or sex−age class within a population, that dies within a unit of time. Accurate estimates of mortality rates of wildlife have been difficult to obtain. In a few, intensively studied populations, the death rates (or at least disappearance rates) of recognizable, perhaps marked or even radio-telemetered, animals have been monitored. Mortality rates have also been estimated from data on population age structure, but this method requires the usually unrealistic assumption that recruitment rates and age-specific mortality rates have been constant for some time (Caughley 1966). With few reliable estimates of wildlife mortality rates, mortality concepts such as density dependence and compensation, discussed below, have often been deduced from the patterns of change in wildlife abundance or have been induced as mortality patterns likely to occur when animals are territorial, when food supplies are limiting, or when high population density facilitates disease transmission or attracts predators.

DENSITY-DEPENDENT MORTALITY

Density-dependent mortality involves an increase in mortality *rate* as population density increases. This type of mortality is sometimes termed directly density-dependent mortality (Fig. 11.1). In contrast, density-independent mortality occurs at the same rate, regardless of population density; or, in an unstable environment, density-independent mortality rates may vary with environmental fluctuations, such as drought or severe winter, but are unrelated to the population density of animals suffering mortality. Inversely density-dependent mortality involves an increase in mortality rate as a population *decreases* (Solomon 1958). Inversely density-dependent mortality does not appear to be a common or persistent pattern in vertebrate populations. It has been reported for predation rates and is discussed under that topic in this chapter.

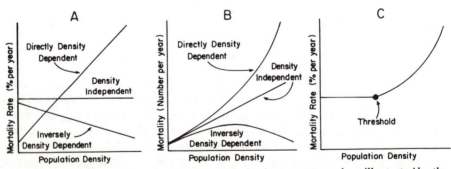

Fig. 11.1 Mortality patterns in wildlife. *A:* The basic concepts are best illustrated by the *proportion* of a population dying per unit of time. Mortality rate may be dependent on density, can be constant regardless of density, or (not illustrated) it may vary, but not be correlated with changes in density. *B:* The *number* of animals dying per unit of time does not illustrate the concepts well. The number dying usually increases with density, even in density independent mortality; and inverse density dependence can cause a peaked relationship between numbers dying and density. *C:* In reality, mortality rates may vary curvilinearly with changes in population density and thresholds may occur, causing abrupt changes in mortality rates as populations exceed or decline below certain critical densities.

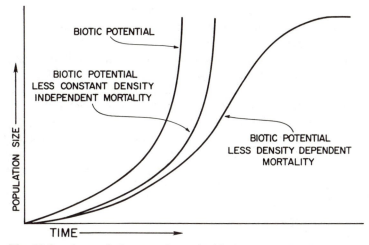

Fig. 11.2.   A population growing at its biotic potential will grow geometrically. Mortality imposed at a constant, density independent rate will delay population growth but will not prevent geometric growth. A directly density dependent mortality rate, however, will cause the population to stabilize.

Since the biotic potential of any species will produce a geometric increase in animal numbers as time passes, and since imposing a constant density-independent mortality rate on the population will slow, but not prevent, the geometric increase toward infinity (Fig. 11.2), it has been deduced that either declines in reproduction or increases in mortality must act in a density-dependent way to regulate animal abundance. It has also been argued that since most populations are relatively stable, always returning toward their long-term average levels of abundance when displaced above or below them, therefore, either reproduction or mortality must react to changes in abundance in a density-dependent manner. These are the two deductive arguments for the existence of density-dependent mortality.

Inductive arguments for density dependence are based on the assumption that with an increasing abundance of animals, there will be a declining per capita availability of habitat resources, an increasing overuse of the best resources, and an increasing intensity of behavioral and physiological mechanisms of population control. There may also be a higher rate of disease transmission and an attraction of predators. These factors should cause mortality to be density dependent.

Beyond the deductive and inductive arguments, mortality rates have been measured and found to be density dependent for some age classes in a few studied populations (cf. Caughley 1970; Sinclair 1977). However, density-independent mortality may also be common, especially in times of stress, such as during severe weather. During a long, cold winter most of the aged and very young animals in a deer population may die, regardless of population density.

Since these two least-viable age classes may comprise about the same percent of a deer population at either high or low density, mortality in such a winter would be density independent.

It is often useful to think of mortality as being ecological-density dependent. Thus, differences in mortality rates between populations exhibiting equal densities may be due to differences in food and cover resources between their habitats. For example, a severe winter may reduce the availability of foods or cover types for animals, increasing the mortality rate above that of previous winters, despite the absence of change in animal density between winters. However, the reduction of food or cover resources while population size is unchanged constitutes an increase in ecological density, and mortality is, in this case, ecological-density dependent.

COMPENSATORY MORTALITY

Compensatory mortality is the combined effect of two or more types of mortality, in which each type may vary in magnitude, while total mortality remains constant. The concept derives primarily from ideas of Paul Errington (1956; 1963). Support for the existence of compensatory mortality comes from an inductive argument and from a few field studies. The argument is based on a belief that habitat resources determine the number of animals that can survive in a population—that excess animals are produced and that these animals must be removed by some forms of mortality. The argument is strongest for species having high biotic potentials, since they are most capable of producing more animals than their habitat can support, and for species having behavior mechanisms that force excess animals to disperse into areas where mortality is likely.

This argument finds support from field studies in which mortality types have been removed or increased, usually by removing predators or by eliminating or increasing harvests, without producing changes in population sizes. The inference has been that rates of some other types of mortality, perhaps losses to alternative predator species, or to disease, have increased to replace the removed mortalities, or have decreased to compensate for increased levels of harvest. In a few studies, compensatory mortality types have been identified and measured (Bellrose et al. 1964, p.667).

Compensatory mortality may be delayed. Thus, if we remove nest predators, increasing nestling survival and the number of successful broods in a bird population, we may make more young birds available to other predators, so that an increase in juvenile mortality compensates for a decrease in nestling mortality.

STARVATION AND MALNUTRITION

Starvation is death or debilitation caused by lack of food quantity, whereas malnutrition is death or debilitation due to lack of food quality. Starvation is more common among carnivores, malnutrition among herbivores. Wildlife nutrition is considered in detail in Chapter 6. A few ideas are reviewed briefly here.

Starvation and malnutrition are usually associated with increased rates of disease and often predation; thus, the ultimate cause of death is sometimes not clear. Starvation and malnutrition usually affect some sex-age classes of animals, especially the very young and very old, more severely than other sex-age classes. These effects may be mediated in social animals by territories or hierarchies, so that subordinate animals suffer most severely. Starvation and malnutrition have been the most obvious forms of mortality in many ungulate populations, especially deer populations.

HARVEST

Harvest Regulations

Sport hunting and commercial harvest are usually legally regulated forms of mortality, although enforcement is variable, and illegal kill appears to be an important mortality factor in some populations (Wright 1980). The number and sexes and ages of animals harvested can be manipulated by regulations controlling:

1 The length of the hunting season. Generally, more animals are harvested in longer seasons, although the rate of harvest usually declines after opening day.

2 The opening and closing dates of the season. Regardless of season length, the vulnerability of certain classes of wildlife to harvest may vary with changes in habitat or weather conditions. For examples, some types of farm game have a low vulnerability to hunting in early seasons before agricultural crops are harvested, eliminating escape cover; species of early-migrating waterfowl might be protected by a delayed opening of the hunting season; late seasons may result in unusually large harvests of ungulates, if early snows concentrate animals in areas of easy access for hunters.

3 The species or sexes of animals that are legal game. In waterfowl seasons, hunters are encouraged or required to harvest certain species and even sexes of certain species of ducks. This practice applies most hunting mortality to the most productive populations and protects less productive populations. A point system is sometimes used to enforce these rules (Table 11.1). For upland game, hunters may be required to take only males or only older males, such as bighorn rams with full-curl horns. Sometimes there are extra, short seasons, or a limited number of special permits are issued, for harvesting a limited number of female animals.

4 The number of animals that can be harvested. Hunters may be allowed to take a limited number of animals per day—the "bag limit"—and to accumulate a limited number of animals over more than one day—the "possession limit."

TABLE 11.1   The 1979 Point-system Bag Limit for Harvesting Ducks in the Central Flyway Portion of Colorado.

Species	Points
Canvasback	100
Mallard hens, redheads, wood ducks	70
Mallard drakes	20
Blue- and green-winged teal, pintails, scaup, gadwall, widgeon	10

Note: A hunter is allowed up to 10 ducks totaling 100 points per day. The daily limit is reached when the point total of ducks taken equals or exceeds 100 points with the last bird taken. This system directs the harvest at certain species and sexes of animals in order to achieve separate management objectives for some populations, yet allows the hunter to make one mistake in identifying species or sexes of birds in the air. The list of species is abbreviated.

All of the above aspects of hunting regulations may be varied among hunting districts or management units within states. A few decades ago, one set of regulations applicable throughout a state was common. Today, most states are divided into numerous management units, especially for big game management (Fig. 11.3). This practice recognizes that management objectives and wildlife productivities may vary among areas within states and that separate regulations are necessary to achieve unique objectives in some areas.

Harvest regulations are established to achieve both biological and sociological objectives (Grieb 1973). They often are a compromise that does not optimize chances for achieving any one objective, but provides for partial achievement of several objectives.

The biological objectives of harvest regulations include: (1) controlling the numbers of animals in a game population so that there are sufficient high-quality habitat resources for all animals, a situation maintaining good animal quality and high rates of reproduction. Without control of numbers, some populations are capable of damaging their habitat resources; (2) altering the sex-ratio of a population so that habitat resources are used primarily by females as is necessary to maximize reproduction; (3) reducing competition among species of wildlife by reducing numbers of a less favored species; (4) influencing the age structure of a population so that older animals of high trophy value are produced; (5) controlling outbreaks of disease in wildlife by reducing the population, lowering the rate at which disease spreads among the animals and potentially to domestic stock; (6) avoiding harassment or harvest of animals during critical times, such as breeding seasons or seasons in which adults care for their young.

The sociological objectives of harvest regulations include: (1) maximizing hunting recreation by providing as many hunters with as many opportunities to hunt as are consistent with other objectives; (2) providing quality hunting. This may include dispersing hunters in time and space to avoid overcrowding the hunting areas. It may include provisions for groups of hunters, including rela-

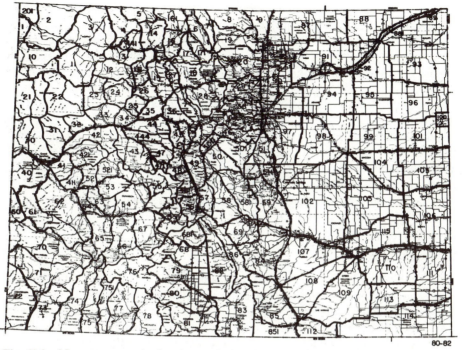

80-82

Fig. 11.3 Management units for deer and elk harvest in Colorado. Regulations can be adjusted to accommodate separate herd and habitat conditions and to achieve unique management goals in each unit. Courtesy of Colorado Division of Wildlife.

tives, to obtain permits for hunting together; (3) maintaining public safety, by requiring hunter-safety education before licensing, by dispersing hunters, by requiring recognizable clothing, and by eliminating hunting in areas where it would jeopardize the nonhunting public; (4) maintaining hunter-landowner relations, by scheduling seasons to minimize damage to property such as crops that would be unharvested during early hunting seasons; (5) reducing local game populations to control game damage to agricultural crops or forest regeneration; (6) providing advance notice of regulations so that hunters may plan their hunts. This may require that decisions on harvest regulations be made before all data on game population status are available; (7) providing understandable and enforceable regulations. For instance, complicated regulations for hunting waterfowl may place too great a burden of species- or sex-identification on hunters.

Sport Hunting as Self-regulated Mortality

Levels of harvest of upland small game tend to be self-regulating, regardless of bag limits or season lengths. Most animals are harvested early in a season. Many of these are the most accessible animals, and they may be especially vulnerable to harvest because of their behavioral characteristics and locations relative to escape cover. Thus, as the hunting season passes, there are fewer animals and they are less vulnerable. The effort required to harvest game increases. As a result, hunter success and hunter interest decline, and fewer game are taken. In this way the harvest of upland small game tends to be self-regulating, preventing drastic reduction of game populations. This self-regulation is a form of density dependence because the rate of harvest declines as animals are removed from the population.

Self-regulation is much less a factor in harvests of waterfowl and big game. Waterfowl, being obligated to concentrate in wetland areas, remain accessible and vulnerable to harvest, despite population reduction by previous harvest. Big-game hunters usually continue their efforts at harvesting an animal despite their failure early in the season when numbers, accessibility, and vulnerability may have provided a greater chance for success.

Harvestable Surplus

Harvestable surplus is the number of animals that can be harvested from a population without affecting the size of the population at some later time, usually the next breeding season or the next hunting season. For small game and waterfowl, which have high biotic potentials, there is a large annual population increase due to reproduction and a large annual mortality that returns the population to about the same abundance each spring (Fig. 11.4a). Harvest is often a *replacive* form of mortality, as it replaces some of the natural annual mortality rather than being *additive* and increasing total mortality. As a result, spring-breeding populations are the same, with or without harvest (Fig. 11.4b). Replacive mortality is compensatory mortality; however, the former term is used especially for hunting whereas the latter may be used for any type of nonadditive mortality.

An earlier opening of the hunting season offers an opportunity for replacing more of the natural mortality and increasing the harvestable surplus. However, objectives other than maximizing game harvest, for instance, allowing for harvest of agricultural crops before hunters enter the fields, may preclude early seasons.

It is unlikely that all fall-winter natural mortality can be replaced by hunting. The greater the level of harvest, the greater is the probability that harvest will become additive (Fig. 11.5). This additional mortality will result in a reduced spring-breeding population. However, a reduced spring-breeding population may not cause a reduction of the population for the succeeding autumn hunting season. If reproductive success responds in a density-dependent manner, a reduced spring-breeding population may produce an autumn population that is just as large as one that would result from a large spring-breeding population. Alternatively, reproductive success during summer may be variable and be unrelated to spring-breeding abundance (Fig. 11.6). It may be influenced primarily by weather during the season of reproduction. In either case, hunting-season (autumn) populations are not directly related to spring-breeding levels of abundance; and larger harvestable surpluses, including additive mortality, are possible if lowered spring-breeding populations are acceptable. In these populations, harvestable surplus is defined as the number of animals that can be harvested without affecting population size at the next hunting season (rather than at the next breeding season).

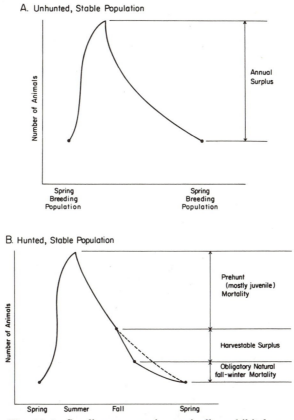

Fig. 11.4 Small game species typically exhibit large annual changes in abundance. *A:* In an unhunted population, a large number of animals is added to the population each breeding season and a large annual surplus suffers natural mortality before the next breeding season. *B:* In a hunted population, some of the annual surplus can be removed as harvest replaces natural mortality.

Hypothetical Data

Harvest	Other (Natural) Mortality	Total (Harvest + Natural) Mortality
0	200	200
25	175	200
50	150	200
75	135	210
100	125	225
125	120	245
150	120	270
175	120	295

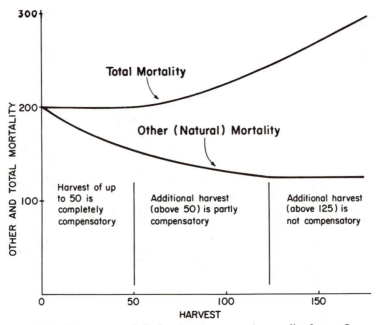

Fig. 11.5 Harvest as a replacive (compensatory) mortality factor. Low levels of harvest tend to be compensatory, but as the harvest rate increases, harvest becomes additive, rather than replacive.

Overharvest

Overharvest is the taking of more animals than is consistent with management goals. It has occurred when legal controls have been inadequate, when animal vulnerability and hunter success have been underestimated, when unexpected weather has increased animal vulnerability, and when population data have been

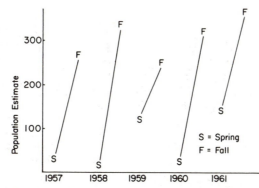

Fig. 11.6 Five years of population estimates for a cottontail population in Illinois. Note the lack of correlation between spring-breeding densities and succeeding fall populations. In mild winters, a large harvest from this population appeared to be an additive mortality and depressed spring-breeding abundance. However, since spring-breeding densities did not determine the abundance of rabbits in succeeding autumns, large harvests did not affect rabbit abundance in succeeding hunting seasons. Data from Lord 1963.

inadequate and caused overestimation of harvestable surplus. Overharvest has been especially common in commerical operations, when objectives have been short-term profits (bison, other ungulates, waterfowl in the past, and whales and commercial fishes in the past and present are examples of overharvested wildlife). Overharvesting by recreational hunting is possible for some game, but regulations are often conservative, especially when population data are poor.

Underharvest

Underharvest is the taking of fewer animals than is consistent with management goals. It occurs when legal restrictions discourage or prohibit hunters, when animal vulnerability has been overestimated, when population size has been underestimated, and when a conservative management seeks to avoid any possibility of overharvest. Underharvest may cause only a temporary failure to realize some wildlife values. However, in ungulate populations, which at high densities may damage their forage resources, underharvest may result in a more lasting loss of habitat and, therefore, of wildlife productivity.

Harvest options are foregone when hunting is prohibited, as on posted private land and in public parks, and when hunter access is limited, as in roadless wilderness areas. Posting of private land occurs especially in heavily populated areas where hunter abundance and a scarcity of wild land create high densities of hunters. Posting is also brought about by inconsiderate hunters who fail to respect property rights. Landowners, who because of American laws and traditions usually gain no profit from allowing hunting on their land, will not accept an abundance of careless hunters and will close their land to hunting. On public land, wilderness and roadless designations may foreclose options for managing wildlife habitat as well as for hunting.

ACCIDENTS

In their naturally associated environments, most wildlife populations exhibit low frequencies of accidental deaths. Few animals are expected to fall from cliffs, break legs, or drown. However, there are exceptions. For instance, Chadwick believed that death in snow avalanches was a major form of mortality in a mountain goat population (1977). Accidental mortality is of greater concern if the affected wildlife population is small, so that a few accidentally killed animals constitute a fairly large proportion of the population.

Abnormal accidental mortality, caused by human modification of the environment, can greatly influence the productivity and even survival of a population. Examples of such mortality and their implications for wildlife management are discussed earlier in this chapter.

PREDATION

Historical Perspective

Attitudes toward predators and beliefs about the roles of predation in controlling prey abundance have, like many ideas in wildlife management, fluctuated between two extremes during the last five decades, before reaching the intermediate position that is widely accepted today. Predator control was one of the earliest methods of game management (Leopold 1933, p. 4). Early in this century, predator control was widely accepted in the United States. Aldo Leopold, who later opposed indiscriminate suppression of predators, favored control and even elimination of some predators in 1920 (Flader 1974). It was public policy to destroy large predators in national parks. Sportsmen casually shot predators, especially hawks and owls, whenever they were encountered. There was, at that time, a tendency to classify all wildlife species as either "good" or "bad," depending on how they appeared, from very limited evidence, to favor or compete with our self-interest. Predators were invariably classed as "bad" and called "vermin." All this antipredator philosophy was due to oversimplified interpretation of casual observations: Predators killed game; therefore, reduction of predators would result in more game. The concepts of density dependence and compensation were little developed and even less well known at the time. No studies had been conducted to test whether predators could be controlled or whether control resulted in increased prey abundance.

At mid-century, our attitudes and beliefs concerning predators and their abilities to control prey abundance swung to an opposite extreme. The shift of ideas was due to overgeneralizing from the results of a few, in particular one, studies of the ecology of predation. Paul Errington studied the effects of predation on quail and especially on muskrats (1946). He found that abundance of these prey was determined by habitat quantity and quality and that each year more animals were produced than the habitat could support and keep secure from predation. This "doomed surplus" was removed by several types of predators and other mortality factors in a compensatory way. Thus, habitat determined prey abundance; predators did not. Overgeneralization of these results led to opinions that all kinds of predators seldom, if ever, controlled the abundance of all kinds of prey in all kinds of environments. There was opposition to all predator control as worthless destruction of animals with important values of their own. We now realize that Errington's results apply best to prey species with high biotic potentials and some intrinsic mechanisms of population control that cause "excess," subordinate animals to become increasingly vulnerable to predation. However, in the 1950s, this limitation of Errington's results was not well recognized.

Meanwhile, reports of large predators controlling abundance of some ungulate populations began to accumulate. Murie had already suggested that wolves were controlling a population of Dall sheep in Alaska (1944). Pimlott (1967), Mech (1966), Jordan et al. (1971), and Bergerud (1971) found evidence of canids and felids controlling ungulate abundance. These authors recognized the complexity of predator-prey population dynamics. Today, few, if any, biologists agree with the extreme positions of the past—that predators either always or never control prey abundance. We recognize that the probability of control depends on the type and abundance of predator, the type and abundance of prey, and numerous environmental factors, discussed below, that determine predator behavior and prey vulnerability. Predator control is considered a legitimate management tool that, under some circumstances, can enhance the abundance of prey animals. In these situations it is worthy of consideration if it is cost-effective and consistent with management goals.

Characteristics of Predation

Predation can be a powerful selective force, shaping the behavior and morphology of prey species (Huffaker 1970). Predation may also influence prey distribution and abundance and may alter population composition by selectively removing animals of one sex or certain age classes or injured, diseased, or otherwise inferior animals.

Quality Control by Predation   Intuitively, we expect predators to be more successful in capturing genotypes of animals that are less alert, less cryptically colored, less quick, or less fit for defense. Over generations of prey, this selection shapes the characteristics of species. We also expect predators to be more successful in capturing injured, sick, or old and weak animals than in capturing prime, healthy prey. This has been termed the "sanitation effect" (Leopold 1933; Mech 1970). In some studies of the characteristics of prey animals selected by predators a sanitation effect has not been detected (Burkholder 1959); that is, there was no evidence that predators were emphasizing the taking of old, weak, or sick animals. However, as in all research, failure to detect an effect does not prove that the effect was absent. A weak tendency by predators to concentrate more on the less-healthy members of a prey population would be difficult to detect and would require large samples of animals suffering predation and of animals escaping predation, as well as precise measurements of the levels of health of the animals in both samples. In other studies, a sanitation effect has been detected (Kolenosky 1972). Mech found that wolves preying upon Isle Royale moose took mostly calves and very old moose (1966). Many of the latter group suffered from tooth infections called lumpy-jaw. The wolf pack would haze all moose they encountered, testing their vigor and willingness to defend themselves. Prime-age, healthy moose that stood their ground were usually abandoned in search of other moose. Of 46 moose tested, only 6 were killed. Such a process has great potential for selecting genetically or otherwise inferior animals from a prey population.

Population Control by Predation   Errington's view of predator-prey dynamics incorporated concepts of carrying capacity, intrinsic population control, density dependence, and compensatory mortality (1946; 1956). Habitat quantity and quality and social intolerance determined prey population size, because subordinate animals were forced into substandard habitat in which they were not secure from predation. Errington termed the population size above which some animals were not secure from predation a "threshold of security." This is a carrying-capacity concept, in that habitat ultimately determines population size. As populations exceeded the threshold of security, predation rates and possibly other mortality rates increased (density dependence and compensation).

Although Errington's concept of four factors influencing predator:prey dynamics was not simple, we now recognize that many more factors influence whether or not predation will control prey abundance. These factors may interact in numerous ways (Holling 1966). In assessing whether or not a predator population controls the abundance of a prey population, we cannot generalize without caution from conclusions based on studies of other populations, even of the same species. Assessment of local predator-prey dynamics should be based on evaluating how the factors listed below may be operating in the local situation.

I.   Factors influencing the ratio of predator abundance:prey abundance. The probability that predators will control prey abundance increases as this ratio increases. For example, Mech concluded that wolves were unable to control ungulate populations when ungulate biomass exceeded about 24,000 pounds per wolf (1970). Six factors influencing the predator-prey ratio are:

A.   The numerical response of predators to prey abundance (Solomon 1949). An increased supply of prey may provide for improved predator nutrition resulting in better reproduction and survival and increased abundance of predators. This is an example of ecological-density dependent reproduction and survival in that an increased food base lowers ecological density for predators.

B.   Prey diversity. Numerous alternate prey resources may maintain an abundance of some predators. In this situation a decline of one prey species does not cause a numerical response (decline) of predators because predator abundance is supported by alternative prey. For the one declining prey species, the predator-prey ratio therefore increases. For example, a high coyote:ungulate ratio may be maintained if coyotes are supported mainly by abundant small mammals. In such a case, the rate of coyote predation upon newborn ungulates may be high, regardless of ungulate abundance.

C.   Biotic potential and longevity of prey and predator. These factors influence the rates at which populations may increase or decrease. A prey population with high biotic potential may increase more rapidly than can a predator population with its lower biotic potential. As long as this disparity persists, the predator:prey ratio declines. On the contrary, the abundance of a short-lived prey species may decline quickly while its longer-lived predators may persist in abundance, even despite failing reproduction caused by food scarcity. This situation would result in an increasing predator:prey ratio until predator abundance finally declines in a delayed numerical response to declining prey abundance. This mechanism can produce inverse density-dependent predation rates during the increase and decrease phases of prey population trends (Fig.11.1).

D.   Geographic concentrations of predators. Predators may be attracted to areas with abundant, vulnerable prey. These areas, such as waterholes, may provide prey with resources that are limited during severe weather or critical seasons. Predator-prey ratios thus increase locally and temporarily.

E.   Intrinsic regulation of predator abundance. Territoriality expressed by predators may limit their maximum population density and thus limit their range of numerical response to prey abundance.

F.   Competition among predators for prey. Such competition may result in poorer predator nutrition, limiting predators' numerical response to prey abundance. Competition may be intraspecific or interspecific.

II. Factors influencing vulnerability of prey. Six factors influencing prey vulnerability are:

A. Habitat quality. Habitat providing poor escape cover, lack of escape cover near other resources, or poor visibility for predator detection exposes animals to predation. Prey may be especially vulnerable during weather or seasons when limited habitat resources force them to use areas in which they are more exposed. This factor may be density dependent if high prey densities overuse and degrade habitat resources in "safe" areas, forcing greater use of "unsafe" areas.

B. Decreased animal quality at higher prey densities. Declining prey alertness and ability for escape or defense may result from extrinsic or intrinsic factors that are density dependent. Extrinsic factors include a relative scarcity of quality food. Intrinsic factors include fighting among and injury to prey and the physiological symptoms of the general adaptation syndrome. In prey species exhibiting dominance hierarchies, these factors will affect subordinate animals most severely. The proportion of subordinate animals in a population may be greater at higher than at lower population density.

C. Dispersal of subordinate prey animals into poor habitats. In territorial prey species, subordinate animals are forced into substandard habitat where they may be more vulnerable to predation. As prey density increases, a greater proportion of the population should be in substandard habitat.

D. The evolved predator-evasion strategy of prey. Prey adaptations limit the effectiveness of normal predators in naturally associated environments. These adaptations may be inappropriate for newly introduced predators or may require environmental characteristics, such as escape terrain or hiding cover, that may be absent when prey are introduced into new areas or when environments are altered by human activity.

E. Increased mutual defense or awareness of predators at higher prey density. Larger groups of prey can, in this way, be less vulnerable to predation than are smaller groups. This factor should operate over a low range of prey density. There should be a threshold above which increased group size provides no additional advantage to prey.

F. Avoidance learning by prey. If changes in prey abundance or vulnerability result in more frequent attacks by predators, prey may learn to avoid the attacking species or places where they are attacked.

III. Changes in predator behavior in response to changes in prey abundance or vulnerability. These factors have been termed "functional responses" of predators (Solomon 1949). Four factors influencing predator behavior are:

A.   Concentration of predator effort. Repeated successful predation may cause predators to concentrate efforts on species of prey or areas of habitat. This increases the rate of prey-predator contact in response to increased prey abundance or vulnerability.

B.   Predator learning. With frequent experience, predators may improve their attack methods, increasing their rate of success per contact with prey.

C.   Predator group facilitation. A numerical response of predators to prey abundance can result in larger groups of predators and these groups may attack with more frequent success than do smaller groups.

D.   Concentration of predator effort on alternative prey species. Abundant alternative prey—termed *buffer species*—may attract predator effort away from a particular prey species. These alternative prey "buffer" the effects of predation upon the particular prey species. For example, Bergerud found less predation by lynx upon caribou calves in years when snowshoe hares were abundant as a buffer species (1971). Note that if predators respond numerically to the abundance of alternative prey (IA above), the buffering effect may be offset by an increased predator:prey ratio (IB above).

IV.   Density-independent processes affecting the above three classes of mostly density-dependent factors. Weather or habitat changes due to flooding, fire, logging, biotic succession, and so forth may alter any effects of the above 16 factors. These processes are termed environmental influences (Chapter 12).

Does a predator population control the abundance of its prey? This would be "control from the top" of the biotic pyramid wherein carnivores control herbivore abundance, and herbivores control vegetation status. Or does the abundance of prey, as a food resource, determine the abundance of predators? This would be "control from the bottom" of the biotic pyramid wherein forage determines the number of herbivores that can be supported, and herbivores support a limited abundance of carnivores. Considering the complex of factors influencing predator-prey dynamics, it seems that control from the top and control from the bottom are not necessarily mutually exclusive. Improvement of habitat for a prey species can stimulate increased prey abundance by supporting greater reproduction and/or survival. The greater abundance of prey may support more predators. (Certainly there would be no predators if there were *no* prey.) This is control from the bottom. However, if predators were removed from the system, more and perhaps poorer quality prey might exist. The additional prey might exist in marginal habitats that could not be occupied if predators were abundant. This is control from the top—in the same system.

Predator Control

In some circumstances control of predator abundance by hunting, trapping, or poisons will result in an increased abundance of prey. If the prey animals have important value, perhaps as game or because they are an endangered species, predator control is an option for management. However, the option should not be selected before considering several questions concerning the local situation.

Will decreased predator abundance cause an increase in abundance of valuable prey? If one or a few species of predators are to be controlled, there appear to be three situations for which the answer may be yes. One is when the predator-prey ratio is unusually high. This may be due to a predator abundance supported by abundant alternative prey, or to a perhaps temporary reduction in valuable prey by severe weather, forage failure, intensive harvest, or habitat losses. This situation would include a population of an endangered prey species. The second situation favoring the possibility of useful predator control results from high vulnerability of valuable prey because of habitat inadequacies. This situation can often be corrected by habitat improvement. A third situation involves artifical concentrations of prey such as livestock or wildlife in rearing pens for artificial stocking.

The possibility of delayed compensatory mortality, negating effects of predator control, should be considered. On wildlife refuges with high densities of nesting waterfowl, control of nest predators has resulted in increased nesting success and more broods of ducks (Balser et al. 1968). However, the survival of ducklings needs to be measured before we can conclude that control of nest predators results in more ducks at the start of the autumn hunting season.

Can predators be controlled effectively? Experience has shown that predators can be difficult to control and that control is seldom long lasting. Often, more than one species of predator use a prey population, and all species may have to be controlled to reduce prey losses. For example, nest predators may include several species of birds, mammals, and reptiles, some diurnal and some nocturnal. Control of this array of predators might require considerable and diverse efforts.

Mortality of predators resulting from control efforts can be compensated by a decrease in natural mortality, so that total mortality is unchanged. This is compensatory or replacive mortality, and we should expect results similar to those expected from hunting (Fig. 11.5). The probability that predator control will be replacive is greater when control efforts are minimal. Thus, a little predator control is apt to be worthless, and considerable control effort may be necessary before any reduction of predators results. However, when predator control is initiated, the most accessible and vulnerable predators are usually removed first. Thus, the cost of control per predator removed will increase as more predators are taken.

When predators are successfully reduced, lowering their ecological density, they often respond with greater reproductive success in the next season. Thus, effective predator control is often short-lived.

The least effective method of predator control has been the bounty system in which a government or private agency pays anyone who submits evidence of having killed a bountied species of predator. Since bounties are paid on predators from any source, many of the animals are killed in areas away from the game populations or livestock that are intended to be protected by the bounty system. Furthermore, some bounty hunters have been more interested in the bounty as income than in protecting prey populations. As a result they have submitted for bounty what they believed was a harvestable surplus of predators, including fox pups dug from a den, whereas they were careful not to destroy the breeding stock, the adult foxes, so that animals could be submitted for bounty in succeeding years. This practice was not conducive to effective control.

Effective and efficient predator control requires a method that selectively removes primarily the offending individuals or species of predators. Such control is usually applied to local areas. Broadcast or indiscriminate methods, such as distributing poisoned baits over the landscape, killing a variety of predators and scavengers over a large area, are unacceptable.

Will predator control be a cost-efficient method of achieving wildlife management goals? The cost of removing adequate numbers of predators is but part of the cost of predator control. The several values of predators, reduced when predator numbers are reduced, should also be considered as a cost of control (See Chapter 3). If any nontarget predators or scavengers are unintentionally reduced, their values also need to be considered.

Can management objectives for increased prey populations be achieved more efficiently by habitat improvement? If habitat inadequacy results in prey vulnerability to predation, habitat improvement may be less expensive and more lasting than predator control and may benefit a variety of wildlife, thereby enhancing several management objectives.

Will the benefits of predator control exceed the costs? What values will be realized from the predicted increase in prey abundance? There may be increased harvest for commercial values, increased recreation, or increased security for an endangered species.

If, after considering the above questions, a management biologist elects to use predator control, the cost, effectiveness, and value of the control program should be monitored. All wildlife management programs are based on assumptions that they are worthwhile; but the assumptions are too seldom tested locally. When the assumptions involve concepts as complex as predator-prey dynamics, they will nearly always be questionable and deserve testing.

EXPOSURE

Wildlife may be killed by the direct effects of severe weather, such as extreme cold, blowing snow, or intense rain or hail. Examples of this mortality are given in Chapter 14. In many cases of severe winter weather, wildlife losses are due to a combination of exposure and malnutrition, because snow makes food resources unavailable. Exposure is often a density-independent form of mortality and is usually most important near the peripheries of geographic ranges of species.

DISEASE

Disease is defined as any deviation of the body from its normal function. The causes of most wildlife deseases can be classified as nutritional, toxic, or infectious. The nutritional requirements of wildlife are discussed in Chapter 6; toxic and infectious diseases are discussed here. Only a few examples are given.

Toxic Diseases

Naturally occurring toxic diseases are rare in wildlife. An exception is "western duck sickness," or botulism (Enright 1971). This disease occurs during hot, dry periods when water in marshes becomes warm, stagnant, and deoxygenated. Under these conditions marsh plants and animals die, and organic matter decays. Anaerobic conditions favor the bacterium *Clostridium botulinum*, which produces potent toxins that may be ingested by waterfowl. Botulism causes paralysis and death unless the birds are removed to fresh-water areas. Losses of waterfowl to this disease have been widespread on western alkaline marshes during drought years. They have been aggravated by water diversions that have reduced flows through marshes and by pollution of waterways with organic matter that provided substrate for anaerobic bacteria. When possible, water control is the main tool for alleviating the disease. Infected marshes can be drained completely, forcing birds to leave, or they can be flushed with fresh water, alleviating anaerobic conditions and diluting the toxins.

Human activities are causing increasingly frequent toxic disease among wildlife. Animals are exposed to lead, pesticides such as DDT, and polychlorinated biphenols (PCBs).

Lead poisoning of waterfowl has occurred when ducks have ingested lead shot from bottoms of marshes where hunting has been abundant. Hunters have recently been required to use steel shot in many of these areas.

DDT and PCBs have insidious effects on wildlife, because these compounds can be concentrated through food chains, exposing predators to unexpected levels of the toxins. Furthermore, these compounds can cause failure of reproduction in ways that are difficult to detect (Hickey and Anderson 1968). DDT is a persistent toxin the use of which has been banned in the United States. Many once-declining populations of wildlife have gradually recovered since the banning of DDT. However, other migratory populations of predaceous birds continue to obtain DDT from winter ranges south of the United States. Some, like western peregrine falcons, exhibit little reproduction and face extinction. Toxicologists have determined the minimum doses of toxins necessary to kill animals. An LD_{50} is a dose that is lethal to half the animals under test conditions. However, animals may be debilitated by sublethal doses of toxins and, therefore, may suffer increased mortality to predation or to other diseases (Friend and Trainer 1974; Friend et al. 1973). Such mortality may go undetected, or, if detected, there may be little evidence to suggest toxicity as a cause of death. As a result, the full impact of chemicals such as pesticides on wildlife is probably underestimated. Toxic diseases are mostly a density-independent form of mortality and, therefore, are capable of decimating populations regardless of their abundance or ecological density.

Infectious Diseases

Wildlife diseases may be caused by a variety of pathogens including viruses, bacteria, fungi, protozoa, helminths, and arthropods. Some are endoparasites, others ectoparasites. A few examples of infectious diseases are presented here to illustrate the potential impacts of disease on wildlife and the complexity of relationships among wildlife and disease organisms.

Normal, Persistent Infections Wildlife have evolved with and are adapted and resistant to the majority of potential pathogens in their environments. All vertebrates carry numerous potential pathogens, usually without disease symptoms. This normal abundance of parasites can become pathogenic when an animal's resistance is lowered by prolonged severe weather or by stresses associated with high ecological density, such as poor nutrition or crowding. Normal types of parasites may also become abnormally abundant when rates of transmission are enhanced by concentration of animals around limited habitat resources. Thus, wildlife diseases caused by normal parasites—those with which animals have evolved—are often a symptom of poor habitat conditions resulting in high ecological densities.

Epizootics Epizootics are widespread outbreaks of disease in a wildlife population. They may be associated with severe weather or high ecological density, but often the causes of epizootics are unknown. For example, outbreaks of tularemia, a bacterial disease in rabbits, beaver, and squirrels, have occurred periodically. These outbreaks have lasted two to three years and have affected large portions of Illinois, Michigan, and other areas. Since tularemia is transmittable to man, hunters and trappers have been advised to exercise extra caution in handling harvested animals. Epizootics of rabies, a viral disease, have likewise exhibited periodic occurrence, especially in skunks and foxes (Anderson et al. 1981).

Epizootics may result during periods when weather or high densities of hosts favor increased abundance or transmission of pathogens. They may also be favored by a gradual loss of genetic or acquired immunity during periods between outbreaks.

Host-Parasite Relationships   Parasites often complete their life cycles in more than one species of animal host. This pattern is common among helminth parasites—the flukes, tapeworms, and roundworms. A *definitive*host is one in which a parasite matures and reproduces. An *intermediate*host harbors immature stages of a parasite. Both vertebrates and invertebrates serve as intermediate hosts. Transfer of a parasite may occur when a definitive host ingests, or is bitten by, an intermediate host. For example, tapeworms exist as immature stages, sometimes called "bladder worms," in the viscera and mesentaries of rabbits, their intermediate hosts. Adult tapeworms develop in the intestines of carnivores, the definitive hosts, when they eat infected rabbits.

A *normal definitive host* has had a long evolutionary association with a parasite and, thus, carries the parasite with little or no debilitation. An *abnormal definitive host* is not adapted to a parasite and, when infected, suffers disease. A *reservoir host* is a normal host that, by its abundance and ability to survive while carrying reproducing parasites, increases the abundance of the parasite to the detriment of other species of definitive hosts in the same environment. For example, in the northeastern United States and southeastern Canada, white-tailed deer are normal definitive hosts for a brainworm, *Parelaphostrongylus tenuis* (Anderson 1965). The intermediate hosts are land snails that become infected by worm larvae passed with deer feces. Although most deer carry the infection, they do not develop disease symptoms. In contrast, moose and woodland caribou are abnormal hosts for the brainworm and exhibit symptoms including loss of vision, weakness, loss of control of the extremities, and fearlessness. If the animals are not killed by predation or accidents, they may die in an emaciated condition. It appears that moose and caribou are new and poorly adapted hosts for *Parelaphostrongylus tenuis* and have contacted the nematode on a broad scale as white-tailed deer have recently extended their geographic range northward. Deer are now a reservoir host for the parasite in areas suitable for moose and caribou.

Abnormal Diseases   In abnormal disease, a wildlife host is not adapted to a disease-causing parasite because their host-parasite relationship is evolutionarily new. Abnormal disease may result (1) when a parasite is introduced into an area where wildlife have had no previous exposure, (2) when a host is newly introduced into an area having parasites to which it is not adapted, (3) when a reservoir host is newly introduced into an area where other disease-susceptible species occur, or (4) when a change of environment results in an increase in infection rate for a parasite that previously had not been an important source of mortality and, therefore, had not fostered the evolution of resistance. Whenever a host species suffers a persistent, high rate of mortality caused by parasitic disease, an abnormal host-parasite relationship is to be suspected. Abnormal diseases of wildlife have been unexpected results of some of man's activities, including the introduction of wild and domestic animals into new lands and habitat modifications favoring range extensions by wildlife. The elimination of large predators may also have favored previously unimportant parasites by allowing hosts to become more sedentary so that reinfection rates have increased. These unexpected disease problems illustrate our inability to predict all the impacts of our activities on wildlife. They suggest that caution and monitoring of results be used whenever we modify wild land ecosystems.

Density Relationships   As noted above, normal diseases of wildlife tend to cause little mortality among wildlife populations existing at low ecological densities. With increased ecological density, animals are in poorer condition and less resistant to disease, and concentration of animals may enhance rates of disease transmission. Normal diseases are, therefore, usually an ecological-density dependent form of mortality.

However, sometimes wildlife diseases are a density-independent form of mortality. Abnormal diseases may cause high mortality rates even in wildlife populations at low ecological densities, because poor resistance to abnormal disease is a genetic trait and not due to poor animal condition resulting from high ecological density. Furthermore, normal diseases of wildlife may tend to be density-independent forms of mortality when intermediate hosts are mobile vectors, such as biting insects, or when a reservoir host is very abundant. In these cases the rates of transmission of the disease to wildlife may remain high even when the wildlife population is at a low density.

Control of Wildlife Diseases

The study of most wildlife diseases has barely begun. Our ability to detect certain diseases is increasing. Parasitologists are gradually uncovering factors influencing parasite abundance, transmission rates, and host susceptibilities. Models of the dynamics of infectious diseases are being developed (Anderson and May 1979; May and Anderson 1979). Normal, persistent infections can be indirectly controlled by maintaining populations at relatively low ecological densities so that animals are not malnourished nor under stress from competition and crowding, both of which enhance disease transmission. Infected animals might be culled. We may also learn to directly control some wildlife diseases, at least locally. Intermediate or reservoir hosts may be controlled directly by shooting or poisoning or indirectly by habitat manipulation. Wildlife may be captured or baited and vaccinated or fed or injected with prophylactic drugs. For example, Colorado bighorn sheep have been treated for lungworm infections in this manner (Schmidt et al. 1979).

It is not clear to what extent control of these parasites should be attempted. Some biologists argue that control of wildlife diseases is inappropriate because it is artificial. They believe that decimation of some wildlife populations by disease is beneficial in perpetuating natural-selective forces that enhance disease resistance and in eliminating especially virulent strains of parasites. They argue that treatment of wildlife diseases will eventually produce artificial populations of wildlife dependent on man for their survival.

Other biologists argue that many wildlife populations are already artificial in that their habitats have been altered, movement patterns have been changed, and parasites and hosts have been introduced into new areas in various combinations. These biologists believe we are already committed to using artificial methods for controlling wildlife diseases, at least in some populations.

PRINCIPLES

P11.1 Wildlife mortality is abundant, equaling reproduction in the long run. Most wildlife mortality is normal, being of types and rates to which wildlife species are adapted. However, some mortality is abnormal, being of types and rates that have not been common during the species' evolutionary histories. Excessive levels of normal types of mortality are usually symptoms of habitat deficiencies that expose or debilitate animals. However, abnormal mortality may drastically reduce wildlife populations, even in habitats providing all the needed resources of the species.

P11.2 The major types of wildlife mortality are starvation and malnutrition, harvest, accidents, predation, exposure, and disease. The ultimate causes of wildlife mortality are often combinations of these types.

P11.3 Mortality rates may be directly or, more rarely, inversely related to population ecological density, or they may be independent of density. Direct ecological-density dependent mortality results in regulation of a population by the quantity and quality of available habitat resources. In compensatory mortality, the magnitude of several types of mortality may vary while total mortality remains constant. This is most common in species with high biotic potentials and with behavioral mechanisms that subordinate "excess" animals to conditions not favoring survival.

P11.4 Starvation and malnutrition are usually associated with increased susceptibility to disease and predation.

P11.5 Harvest is usually a regulated form of mortality. A variety of regulations can by used to control harvest pressure and success so that various biological and sociological objectives might be achieved. Harvestable surpluses can be removed from many populations without affecting the sizes of these populations at subsequent periods. Replacive (compensatory) harvest substitutes for natural mortality and does not affect population size at the next breeding season. Harvest of small, upland game tends to be self-regulating in a density-dependent manner.

P11.6 Accidental death is not frequent in most wildlife populations, but the frequency of accidents may be increased when human alteration of the environment creates new hazards for wildlife.

P11.7 Predation has shaped the behavior and morphology of prey species and continues to influence the distribution, abundance, and composition of populations. In the United States, attutides toward predators have changed greatly as our understanding of the ecology and dynamics of predation has grown. It is now recognized that numerous interacting factors influence predator : prey ratios, prey vulnerabilities, and the functional responses of predators to prey availabilities. These factors vary among sites and periods. Thus, the impacts of predation upon a prey population may be site and time specific. Selective predator control may be an appropriate management tool in some situations where goals, cost-effectiveness of predator control, and local predator : prey dynamics have been considered. However, the complexity of predator-prey relationships dictates that the results of predator control programs should be continually reevaluated.

P11.8 Exposure is often a density-independent form of mortality and is usually most frequent near the peripheries of geographic ranges of species.

P11.9 Wildlife diseases may be nutritional, toxic, or infectious. Most toxic diseases are caused by chemicals from human activities. Infectious diseases may be normal or abnormal and persistent or epizootic in occurrence. Normal, persistent infections tend to cause disease problems when wildlife populations are at high ecological densities. Epizootics are less predictable, and most are not well understood. Trends in weather and in genetic or acquired immunities of animals may account for epizootic outbreaks. Abnormal diseases, in which hosts have not evolved with disease-causing toxins or parasites, result largely from man's activities. Normal, persistent infections can be controlled by maintaining populations at relatively low ecological densities. Direct control of wildlife diseases is a relatively new management tool and involves hazards of circumventing natural selection and obligating wildlife to require continued human assistance for disease control.

SUMMARY

WILDLIFE BIOLOGY

We must never conceal from ourselves that
our concepts are creations of the human mind
which we impose on the facts of nature, that
they are derived from incomplete knowledge,
and therefore never *exactly* fit the facts,
and will require constant revision as
knowledge increases.

A. G. Tansley

The previous chapters of this section describe, quite separately, the factors influencing the distribution and abundance of wild animals. It is beneficial to briefly review and integrate these ideas before proceeding to another subject.

We have used concepts of evolution as an approach to understanding the ecology of wild animals. I hope we have established the value of this point of view. Animals are bundles of adaptations, which are equally limitations. Animals are adapted to live in certain ways in certain kinds of habitats. Yet, some are more specialized in their adaptations and, therefore, more limited; others are more generalized. Specialized animals are quite efficient in utilizing a narrow set of habitat resources, but they are less able to adapt to changes in their environment.

Factors we have considered as influencing the distribution and abundance of wild animals can be illustrated in the following outline.

Habitat Resources
   Foods
   Cover supplies   Quantity   Supplies of:
   Water   Quality   Requirements for:
Reproductive success   Influenced by:
Mortality factors   Behavior
Movements   Physiology

Any one or combination of the above factors can determine the distribution of a wildlife species and the size of a population.

All of the above factors are variables. The relative importance of each factor in determining the sizes or productivities of populations varies greatly among wildlife species. For example, behavior is especially important in territorial species, physiology seems most important in rodents, food quality is very often critical to large herbivores, and water usually limits desert bighorns. Furthermore, within species, the relative importance of each factor in determining the sizes or productivities of populations can vary greatly among populations, among areas, and among time periods. Each population and habitat is at least somewhat unique and changing.

All of the above factors are interrelated. Variation in any one factor will cause changes in other factors. A deficiency in the supply of quality food can result in mortality due to malnutrition, disease, or predation; can reduce reproductive success; can cause animals to abandon areas of secure cover; can produce stress in animals, and can influence competition and behavior. These interactions form population-habitat systems of great complexity. It is often difficult to detect which factors are most primary in determining population size or productivity. Understanding and effectively managing each population and habitat requires careful local observation and analysis.

All of the above factors can respond to changes in ecological density. Thus, habitat change, as it influences ecological density, can alter many aspects of a population, including its productivity. Habitat manipulation is, therefore, a fundamental tool of wildlife management. This observation brings us to the subject of wildlife environments and the next part of this text—wildlife ecology.

PART   III

WILDLIFE
ECOLOGY

CHAPTER 12
HABITAT FACTORS

> When the game manager asks himself
> whether a given piece of land is
> suitable for a given species of game,
> he must realize that he is asking no
> simple question.
>
> *Aldo Leopold*

Numerous factors of the environment affect wildlife habitat. These factors vary in time and space and interact in complex ways to favor or hinder the functions of wildlife. Ecologists often classify environmental factors as:

Biotic	Physical	Edaphic (Soil)
Food Quantity	Temperature	Depth
Food Quality	Precipitation	Moisture
Predation	Snow characteristics	Texture
Disease	Humidity	Chemistry
(Etc.)	(Etc.)	(Etc.)

In texts on ecology, these factors are usually discussed in relation to the concept of limiting factors and Shelford's "law of tolerance" (Kendeigh 1974, pp. 12–13; Fig. 12.1). It is presumed that the reader is familiar with these aspects of plant and animal ecology. The purpose of this chapter is to emphasize their application in wildlife-habitat management.

Physical and edaphic factors, such as those listed here, determine characteristics of wildlife habitats. For example, variations in the temperature and salinity of water often determine the distribution of aquatic plants that are food and cover for many species of wildlife. The study of ecology provides wildlife managers with a necessary holistic view of ecosystems that they manage.

In addition, many wildlife managers must give special consideration to one or a few "target" species that are the primary objectives of their programs. This

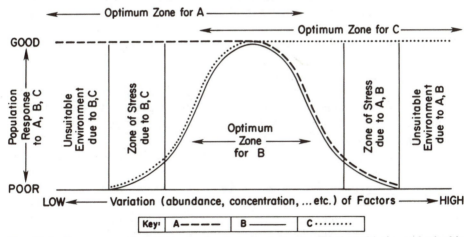

Fig. 12.1 Responses of plants and animals to variation in physical, biotic, and edaphic factors in their environment. Harmful factors (*A*) such as deep snow or predators and diseases have no beneficial effects. Beneficial factors (*C*) such as food supplies have no harmful effects. Other factors (*C*) such as temperature exhibit an optimum range for each species, above and below which the organism is increasingly subjected to stress. Adapted from Kendeigh 1974.

tendency to focus on the environmental relationships of one species of verte-brate has led wildlife biologists to conceptualize environmental factors and processes in the categories described below. This organization of ideas is not an incompatible alternative to the classical categories of biotic, physical, and edaphic factors; it is merely an additional way of conceptualizing environments. Both ways are useful.

LEOPOLD'S "FACTORS OF PRODUCTIVITY"

Leopold viewed wildlife environments as consisting of welfare factors, decimat-ing factors, and environmental influences (1933, p. 25). Welfare factors are the habitat requirements of a species of wildlife. Decimating factors are the various types of mortality. Environmental influences are processes that alter environ-ments. These processes, such as alteration of stream flow, drainage, logging, grazing, cultivation, other disturbances, habitat manipulation, biotic succes-sion, and weather, influence many welfare factors and decimating factors simul-taneously. Thus, an environmental influence that alters vegetation may change foods and cover types for a species and also alter habitat for some of its predators and parasites.

Decimating factors remove animals from a population. Welfare factors sup-port high rates of reproduction and protect animals from decimating factors. The dual role of welfare factors is important when we seek to determine the ultimate factors limiting a population. A lack of welfare factors will limit abundance of animals. For example, inadequate food may result in poor reproduction and deaths of animals by starvation or other mortality factors, perhaps predation or disease. The resulting poor reproduction and increased mortality will limit population increase. Decimating factors also can control abundance of animals. However, since welfare factors can alleviate the effects of decimating factors, as escape cover alleviates losses to predation, the ultimate limitation is often a lack of one or more welfare factors. A decimating factor can be accepted as limiting a population only when provision of sufficient welfare factors to alleviate the effects of the decimating factor is impossible. If sufficient welfare factors can be provided, it is ultimately a lack of those welfare factors that limits the abundance of the population.

This is not to suggest that decimating factors never control the size of wildlife populations. Overharvest of big game, waterfowl, and some commercial fishes; decimations by introduced parasites or predators; and losses due to unusually severe weather are examples of such control. In the cases of overharvest, welfare factors often may not alleviate losses to hunting. In the cases of intro-duced enemies, a prey-welfare factor relationship alleviating the effects of the predator or disease may not be available because it has not evolved. Loss of animals due to exposure may be unrelated to food supplies or cover, especially at the peripheries of species' geographic ranges.

However, we should be cautious in evaluating the roles of decimating factors in controlling populations. Numerous losses of animals to some decimating factor may be a symptom of a defective habitat—a habitat in which a lack of one or more welfare factors limits the population by exposing animals to the decimating factor.

Because of the opposite and interacting roles of welfare and decimating factors in controlling populations, the following terminology is preferred.

1   A *lack* of welfare factors *limits* a population.
2   The *presence* of decimating factors *depresses* a population.

Thus, a population may be depressed, as by harvest, to a level of abundance at which there are no limiting welfare factors. If the harvest were removed, the population would increase until a lack of welfare factors becomes limiting.

WELFARE FACTORS

Welfare factors are the habitat requirements for healthy, productive wild animals. No intensive program of habitat management can begin without some knowledge of he habitat requirements of the target wildlife species. "Management of game range is largely a matter of determining the environmental requirements. . . of the possible species of game, and then manipulating the composition and interspersion of types on the land, so as to increase the density of its game population" (Leopold 1933, p.129).

Lists and descriptions of welfare factors for many animal species are available in wildlife literature. Review of this literature indicates that habitat requirements are sometimes described in broad categories—bobwhite quail require ungrazed or moderately grazed grass, cultivated fields, and brush (Hanson and Miller 1961, p.76)—and sometimes in great detail—the daily winter maintenance requirement for doe white-tailed deer is 158 kcal of apparently digestible energy per kg of body weight $^{0.75}$ (Ullrey et al. 1970). Thus, the structure of thought on habitat requirements of wildlife involves several levels of detail, or resolution, in defining requirements. We shall consider four such levels, (1) basic needs, (2) habitat types, (3) specific welfare factors, and (4) components of welfare factors (Fig. 12.2).

Basic Needs for All Species

At the lowest level of resolution, the six habitat needs of all species are oxygen, foods, cover types, special needs, interspersion, and space.

Oxygen is essential for all wildlife. It is frequently a limiting factor for aquatic animals and is, therefore, important in fisheries management. In terrestrial communities, oxygen is abundant and not limiting.

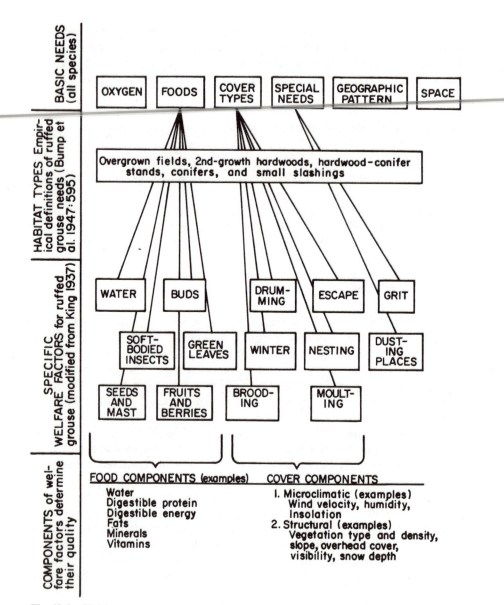

Fig. 12.2   Habitat requirements for ruffed grouse presented at four levels of resolution.

Foods (including water) and cover types are the most frequently considered habitat requirements. They are discussed in detail in Chapters 6 and 7.

The category of special needs contains those minor requirements that vary among species. Leopold listed grit for gallinaceous birds, dusting places for many species, and areas free of biting flies for ungulates as examples of special needs (1933, p.27).

King discussed the importance of the geographic distribution, or interspersion, of welfare factors (1938). He noted that all requirements of a species must be fulfilled within an area determined by the species' cruising ability, or a habitat could not be occupied. King termed this minimum interspersion of habitat requirements *juxtaposition*, noting that it would support a minimum population whereas greater interspersion would support larger populations. He suggested that optimum interspersion of welfare factors occurred when all of the needed kinds of food and types of cover could be found on each unit of range, the size of the units of range being determined by the species inherent limits for accepting crowding. Under these conditions, further growth of the population is limited by an unalterable lack of space. King considered such populations at *saturation point*. Dasmann termed them at *tolerance density* (1964).

Interspersion is certainly a welfare factor. Good interspersion of the food and cover resources of a species is just as important in alleviating the effects of decimating factors and in supporting reproduction as are the food and cover resources themselves. Thus, the fact that escape cover is located near food may be just as important as the fact that escape cover is present. A habitat may be improved without increasing the amount of any food or cover resource, if the interspersion of resources is increased (Fig. 12.3).

Leopold discussed interspersion as *edge effect* (1933, p. 131). He apparently was thinking of welfare factors as a list of vegetation types required by a wildlife species, as shown in Fig. 12.3 Leopold noted that wildlife tended to be more abundant where vegetation types were numerous and well interspersed, providing many "edges" between vegetation types. The edges provide animals with simultaneous access to two or more vegetation types. Where a variety of vegetation types is present and well interspersed over a habitat, it is likely that the several welfare factors required by a species are in adequate juxtaposition at several locations throughout the habitat. The generalization "Provide a variety and interspersion of vegetation types" is a most useful principle in habitat management. Its application will often improve habitat. However, it is a broad generalization that will sometimes fail. If the variety of vegetation types being provided and interspersed over the management area does not include some necessary welfare factor, the habitat will remain unsuitable. Further, a minority of wildlife species, including woodland caribou (Example 13.1), require large blocks of relatively homogeneous vegetation, at least in some seasons.

Providing for variety and interspersion is a rule-of-thumb applied in extensive programs of habitat management, where a limited budget or lack of understanding of a species' habitat requirements does not permit a precise manipulation of

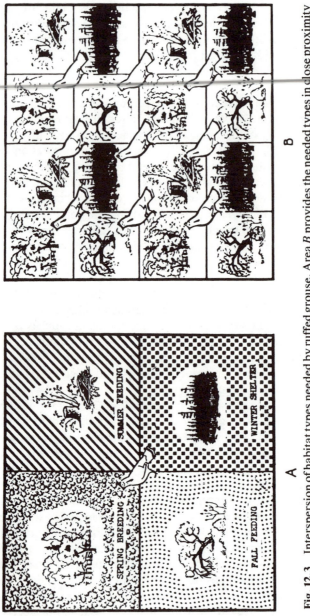

Fig. 12.3 Interspersion of habitat types needed by ruffed grouse. Area *B* provides the needed types in close proximity at nine times as many locations as on area *A* and should support many more grouse. From Bump et al. 1947, courtesy New York Department of Environmental Conservation.

the welfare factors. Where budgets and knowledge permit more intensive management, welfare factors are defined at one of the levels of detail described below, and the abundance and interspersion of these habitat resources are provided for on the land.

Space is another basic need of all animals. Leopold noted that some animal species seemed to exhibit saturation-point populations on optimum ranges (1933, pp. 50–54). Once a saturation-point density has been reached, space is the limiting welfare factor. It cannot be altered unless additional habitat can be managed. Further improvement on existing habitat is impossible.

The concept of saturation-point populations implies intrinsic mechanisms of population control via behavior and/or physiology in response to population density. These mechanisms are discussed in Chapter 10. Remember that the importance of intrinsic mechanisms of population control varies greatly among species and that these mechanisms may be elicited by shortages of and competition for habitat requirements other than space.

Habitat Types: Empirical Definitions of Welfare Factors

The second level of detail involves defining a species' welfare factors as a list of habitat (primarily vegetation) types. These needed types are identified by noting which types are used by the animals for various functions, for instance, for feeding or nesting, and by noting the combination of habitat types present wherever large populations of the animals occur.

Examples of such lists of habitat requirements are as follows (1) Hanson and Miller listed the habitat requirements of bobwhite quail in Illinois as ungrazed or lightly grazed grass, cultivated fields, and brush (1961, p. 76); (2) earlier, Stoddard had listed the requirements of quail as open woodlands, weedy fields, cultivated and fallow ground, and scattered grass or broomsedge areas (1932); (3) the habitat types suggested by Bump et al. for ruffed grouse (1947, p. 595; Fig. 12.2).

This second level of resolution is termed empirical because the list of required habitat types is developed mostly through experience with habitat combinations that produce an abundance of animals. There is no detailed knowledge of the foods used by the animals or of how the animals use the listed habitat types as cover. In other words, we know that the combination of habitat types produces an abundance of animals, but we do not know why the combination is productive.

The empirical approach to defining welfare factors is most useful in extensive programs of wildlife management, where more detailed local knowledge of habitat conditions and of population requirements is not possible. A vegetation-type map is the most useful management tool in such programs (Fig. 18.4). With vegetation maps based on the list of vegetation-habitat requirements, the abundance and interspersion of each habitat type can be evaluated quickly. Suggestions for improving habitats will usually involve increasing the acreage of some scarce but needed vegetation type or subdividing large blocks of homogeneous vegetation.

It would simplify wildlife management if one list of needed habitat types could be developed and used throughout each species' range. However, different lists of habitat types have been useful in different regions. For example, Leopold noted that bobwhite require woodland, brushland, grassland, and cultivated fields in the Southeast and Midwest (1933, p. 130). However, he implied that in the Ozark Moutains where pasturing and cultivation were unimportant, the habitat needs of bobwhite could be defined as dense woodland and open woodland—the open woodland providing brush, grass, and weeds to replace cultivated fields. Further, in Kansas, the habitat needs of quail could be defined as grassland, cultivated fields, and weeds—the grasses, weeds, and cultivated corn being tall and persistent enough to replace woodlands and brushlands on the list of habitat requirements. Thus, we should not expect a single list of empirically defined habitat requirements to be equally useful throughout the entire geographic range of a species. Locally-derived lists will usually be necessary to account for local environmental conditions.

There have been attempts to refine lists of empirically defined welfare factors by specifying the ideal proportions of land in each habitat type (Leopold 1932, p. 133). Thus, perhaps optimum habitat for bobwhite quail is 25 percent cultivated land, 25 percent grassland, 25 percent brushland, and 25 percent woodland. The problem of deciding the optimum proportions of land in each habitat type is again best resolved locally. For example, an optimum habitat may contain less than 25 percent cultivated land if adjacent woodland is sparse with an abundant herbaceous understory or more acres of cultivated land may be necessary if intensive farming allows few weeds and leaves little waste grain in fields. More than 25 percent woodland may be necessary for optimum habitat in regions experiencing severe winters.

The limitation of using habitat types as a basis for habitat management is that broad definitions of habitat requirements may not be adequately precise for detecting and correcting population-limiting factors on many areas. A more intensive program of habitat management will require more detailed definitions of welfare factors. Leopold pointed us in this direction: "Each species requires its own assortment of specialized places. In our present state of almost total ignorance we can list and classify these places only in the most general terms" (1933; pp. 125–126). He also said, ". . . the service rendered by any environment (vegetation) type not only varies by species and season, but is *likely to be contained within a very small fraction of the type*. We must understand something of what these services are before we know what a type is" (p. 128).

Specific Welfare Factors

Specific welfare factors for ruffed grouse are used as an example. This list is based on personal communication with R. T. King and on his published discussion of ruffed grouse management (Fig. 12.2; King 1937). The reader is referred to King's 1937 paper for descriptions of most of the six kinds of food, six types of cover, and two special requirements listed.

Although foods, cover types, and special factors are listed separately, they often occur together. For ruffed grouse, the soft-bodied insects that are eaten by chicks must occur in areas of brooding cover where bare ground without accumulated organic debris and an openness among the bases of concealing herbaceous plants permit chick mobility. Desirable brood cover is often a stand of forbs. It is not coincidental that such stands usually harbor an abundance of soft-bodied insects. Natural selection has favored habitat preferences that solve the food and cover requirements of animals simultaneously.

Components of Specific Welfare Factors

Having a list of specific welfare factors such as that for ruffed grouse, we find that still further resolution of welfare factors is possible (Fig. 12.2). Although buds are necessary winter food for ruffed grouse, we find that male flower buds of aspen are perhaps the best winter food. Although a weedy field may be fair escape cover for a cottontail rabbit, a blackberry patch may be better and a rose hedge still better. This level of resolution involves the quality of foods and the quality of cover types, qualities determined by the components of specific factors.

Components of food welfare factors can be classified in several ways. A simple classification includes digestible energy, digestible protein, minerals, and vitamins. More precise classifications can involve a further breakdown of these components into amino acids, fatty acids, trace elements, and other factors. When the growth of an animal population is limited by a lack of some food welfare factor, certain components of that food are probably more limiting than others. For instance, if the amount of winter browse is critical to a deer population in an area where soils are phosphorus deficient, is it likely that the amount of phosphorus in the winter diet is the component that limits the growth of the population more than any other component of any welfare factor. An improvement in the phosphorus content of the winter browse could result in a larger population even if the quantity of winter browse were unchanged.

Cover welfare factors are described according to their structural or microclimatic components in Chapter 7. Some cover components, such as slope, aspect, and, in some situations, snow depth and quality, cannot be manipulated by management. Others, such as vegetation type, height, and density, can be altered by management.

This last level of detail in defining welfare factors requires much knowledge of species biology. Biologists must know the species requirements for important welfare-factor components within the target habitat. Thus, components of welfare factors will be manipulated only in the most intensive programs of management, those that are least limited by a lack of knowledge of species biology or by a lack of budget for evaluating local habitat conditions.

However, the more extensive programs of management may fail to detect scarcities of welfare factors because these factors are not defined or considered in sufficient detail. Wallmo et al. have shown that digestible energy was the most limiting factor for winter survival of mule deer on a Colorado range (1977). Because of low forage quality, the deer were unable to eat enough to compensate for energy losses during prolonged, severe winters. Winter forage (quantity) was not a limiting factor. Rather, a component of winter forage, digestible energy, was limiting. An extensive program of management may not have detected this problem. However, after more than a decade of research on winter losses of deer and on habitat conditions on this Colorado range, the forage problem has been detected. The research input has been an intensification of the management program. Management may now proceed with attempts to improve forage quality through soil fertilization and vegetation manipulation.

LIMITING WELFARE FACTORS

Up to this point we have considered limiting habitat requirements as those welfare factors that are scarce in the habitat and thereby limit the size of a wildlife population. In this section we consider limiting welfare factors in more detail. Population size is but one aspect of population performance that can be related to limiting welfare factors. For example, we may be interested in factors limiting reproduction, over-winter survival, or harvestable surplus.

Figure 12.2 suggests that each wildlife species is expected to have several habitat requirements. In a given habitat and during a given year, it is unlikely that all these welfare factors are present at levels capable of supporting the *same* number of animals—or the *same* level of some other measure of population performance. It is likely that one or only a few welfare factors limit population performance to levels below what the other welfare factors are capable of supporting. Thus, welfare factors may be nonlimiting, limiting, or minimum.

1   A nonlimiting welfare factor is so abundant that it can support population performance at levels above what some other welfare factors are capable of supporting. Population performance is not limited by any scarcity of this factor.

2   A limiting welfare factor is to some degree in short supply for the wildlife population and to some degree limits population performance.

3   A minimum welfare factor is the one limiting factor that is in shortest supply for the population and limits population performance more than any other welfare factor. In some habitats it may be the only limiting welfare factor.

Shortages of welfare factors may interact to limit population performance. For example, reproductive success in ruminants may depend on rutting-season nutrition, which influences conception rates, and on late-gestation nutrition, which influences the viability of young at birth. A habitat providing good nutrition at both seasons is necessary for a high rate of reproductive success. To offer another example, shortages of food may weaken animals, making them more susceptible to predation or exposure, thus exacerbating the limiting effects of shortages of escape cover or shelter from weather.

The production, availability, and persistence of foods and of some cover types vary seasonally and among years. Further, the animals' requirements for certain welfare factors may vary among seasons and years. Thus, in a given habitat, it is quite likely that different welfare factors will be limiting at different times. Winter food, for example, may be a minimum factor in some years, less limiting compared to other habitat requirements in other years, and nonlimiting in still other years.

Some habitats have obvious, persistent minimum welfare factors (Fig. 12.4a). Consider a northern deer habitat with abundant summer range, adequate winter cover, but a minimum of winter forage every year. It would be easy to detect that among all habitat requirements, winter forage is in shortest supply. Some deer would be lost to malnutrition every year; the survivors would be in poor condition every spring. There would be heavy use, perhaps destructive use, of winter forage every year. Variation among years in abundance and availability of winter forage would be highly correlated with the variation in population performance. All evidence would persistently point to winter forage as the minimum habitat requirement.

We should expect that welfare factors are more in balance in some habitats (Fig. 12.4b). When all welfare factors are capable of supporting about the same level of population performance, year-to-year variation in production and availability of welfare factors will determine which factors are in shortest supply in each year. A factor may be minimum in one year and nonlimiting in the next. These habitats and their populations are perplexing to wildlife biologists. Population performance will not be well correlated with year-to-year variation in abundance of any one welfare factor. Overuse of a welfare factor may occur in some years but not in others. The operation of limiting factors in such a habitat will be difficult to elucidate. Understanding the population ecology in this case will require comparatively large expenditures for measuring population performance and variation in welfare factors.

DETECTING LIMITING FACTORS

The key to efficiency in habitat management for a wildlife species is knowing the habitat requirements of the species and discerning and improving limiting factors in the target habitat. If we do not know species habitat needs, we can only increase variety and interspersion of vegetation types in the hope that limiting welfare factors will be improved. Knowing the habitat requirements, if we improve nonlimiting welfare factors, we waste management effort; if we improve a limiting welfare factor, population performance will be improved; if we improve the minimum welfare factor, we should achieve the greatest population response per unit of habitat improvement.

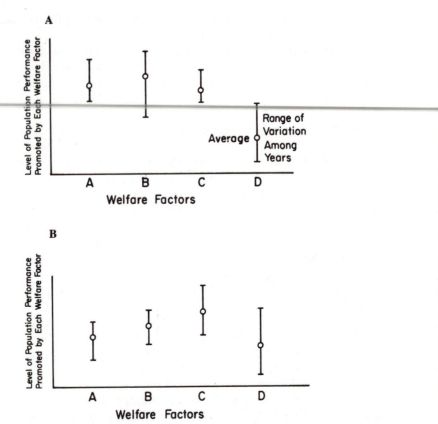

Fig. 12.4 Operation of limiting welfare factors for a wildlife species in two habitats. (*a*) Factors limiting population growth are sometimes easy to deduce from data or other evidence indicating population size, mortality, poor reproduction, poor animal condition, or overuse of some habitat factors. These "easily-understood" populations often have only one limiting welfare factor. Variation in abundance and availability of this welfare factor is highly correlated with performance of the population, and we easily detect the relationship. In this example, population performance is always correlated with abundance of welfare factor D. It is almost always the minimum factor. (Rarely, B is the minimum factor.) (*b*) Factors limiting population growth are sometimes obscure. Data on population performance or habitat condition are not highly correlated with abundance of any one welfare factor. The population may perform well in some years, poorly in others. These "perplexing" populations may have several limiting factors operating. Scarcity of one welfare factor may limit population growth in some, but not all, years—as the abundance of each limiting welfare factor fluctuates from year to year. The operation of limiting factors in such a population will be difficult to elucidate. Considerable information on the population and its environment will be needed, requiring comparatively large expenses for measuring the status of the population and/or its habitat. In this example, any of the four welfare factors may be the minimum factor in any one year.

Detecting limiting welfare factors is, therefore, paramount in habitat management programs. Failure to consider this problem has resulted in some expensive habitat programs that were "just busy-fussing with the landscape in a domineering way" (Egler 1967). Sometimes the habitat deficiencies are obvious, such as the lack of cover for cottontails during autumn and winter on intensively farmed land in central Illinois. Often the deficiencies are not obvious, and wildlife managers must study the animals and the habitat for clues to habitat deficiencies. They will seek correlations between population performance and variation in welfare factors. If there are years or places in which the population performs better, what welfare factors are more abundant in those years or places? What aspect of population performance fails to meet expectations? Conception rates? Birth rates? Juvenile survival? Over-winter survival? What welfare factors are apt to be responsible for the detected failure? Do any welfare factors show signs of persistent heavy use by the animals? Answers to these types of questions are clues to habitat deficiencies.

During the years that may be spent answering these questions, some of the manager's budget will be available for habitat manipulation. What welfare factors should be improved when one is unsure of which factors are limiting? A manager must make the best educated guess. However, it is important that tentative habitat manipulation be designed to help solve the problem of detecting limiting welfare factors. For instance, if it is decided to improve nesting cover, this treatment should be applied to parts of the target habitat and not to other parts. This permits a valid comparison among areas and evaluation of results from improving nesting cover. Haphazard improvement of nesting cover here and there without plans for evaluating the results is still "busy-fussing with the landscape."

The concept of limiting factors, the expected variation among wildlife habitats, and expected year-to-year variation in welfare factors indicate that local decision making is desirable in wildlife habitat management. Biologists who are aware of local habitat conditions, who are aware of performance of local populations during several years with a variety of weather conditions, and who have tested population responses to habitat manipulations are the people most likely to detect limiting welfare factors and apply habitat management most effectively. Administrators of wildlife management programs are sometimes inadequately aware of these considerations. There is a desire to manage a diversity of wildlife habitats with one management prescription from the state or regional office, as if all habitats had the same limiting welfare factors. Increasing availability of aerial photography and even satellite imagery is fostering the illusion that accurate prescriptions for habitat management can be based on habitat maps of comparatively low resolution with little or no local experience and no data on population performance. This is the extreme of extensive wildlife management. I believe it will be an inefficient approach for managing many populations—that is, the management prescription applied to a diversity of wildlife habitats will improve limiting welfare factors in some, but not in others. Further, if there is no local measurement of population performance, the success or failure of the habitat manipulation cannot be evaluated.

PRINCIPLES

P12.1 For wildlife-management purposes, it is useful to classify the numerous and complexly interrelated factors operating in ecosystems as welfare factors, decimating factors, and environmental influences.

P12.2 Welfare factors, the habitat requirements of wildlife species, can be defined at several levels of resolution. At the lowest level of resolution, (1) all species require oxygen, foods, cover types, special needs, interspersion, and space. With increasingly greater resolution, the habitat requirements of a species can be defined (2) empirically as a list of needed habitat types, (3) as a list of specific welfare factors, and (4) as a list of welfare-factor components. Suitable habitat must supply welfare factors for both sexes and all age classes of animals during all seasons and weather conditions.

P12.3 A lack of welfare factors may limit the growth and/or performance of a population. The presence of decimating factors may depress a population to levels below that which welfare factors could support. However, since welfare factors usually can alleviate the effects of decimating factors, welfare factors exert the most fundamental influence upon wildlife abundance and performance.

P12.4 Each wildlife species has several welfare factor requirements. It is unlikely that a given habitat will supply all these welfare factors in perfect balance to a population's needs at a given time. Therefore, it is likely that a small number of welfare factors, perhaps only one, will limit a population at a given time and place. Other welfare factors would be nonlimiting. However, the availabilities of welfare factors vary continuously over time and space. Often different sets of welfare factors will be limiting in different areas and in different seasons and years. When the number of limiting welfare factors is relatively large, it will be more difficult to detect which factors are limiting and which are nonlimiting.

P12.5 Detecting limiting welfare factors is basic to efficient programs of habitat management. Two methods for detecting limiting factors are (1) observing correlations between trends of welfare factors and trends in population performance, and (2) observing symptoms of welfare-factor deficiencies in the animals and symptoms of welfare-factor overuse in the habitat.

CHAPTER   13

ECOLOGICAL SUCCESSION AND WILDLIFE

It takes all the running you can do,
to keep in the same place. If you
want to get somewhere else you must
run at least twice as fast!

The Queen to Alice–in Wonderland
Lewis Carroll

Most changes occurring in wildlife habitats are successional or, conversely, retrogressional. The concept of succession is, therefore, our most useful basis for predicting responses of wildlife to land changes. It is presumed that the reader has mastered concepts of ecological succession (for reviews, see Odum 1971; Daubenmire 1968). However, a brief review of terms and concepts especially pertinent to wildlife management is presented here before further discussion of wildlife in relation to succession.

Ecological succession is the progressive development of a biotic community, involving replacement of species and modification of the physical environment, until a community with a relatively stable species composition is reached. The terminal, relatively stable community is termed *climax*. Characteristics of the climax community may be determined by climate; however, local topography or soils or frequent natural disturbances such as fire are sometimes especially important in controlling the climax community.

In most communities, biotic changes due to succession are most easily recognized and illustrated by considering the flora. But the faunal compositions of communities also change during succession (Figs. 13.1, 13.2).

Succession originating on a sterile site, such as a recent landslide, is termed *primary succession,* whereas succession following most disturbances, such as fire in a forest community, is termed *secondary succession*. Primary succession is comparatively rare and most biotic communities have developed from intermediate stages of community development, such as abandoned agricultural land.

Succession occurs in terrestrial and aquatic communities. Succession on land, termed *xerarch,* proceeds from relatively dry conditions toward a more mesic condition in which moisture is retained on the site and is more available to plants and animals. Succession in aquatic habitats, termed *hydrarch,* proceeds from conditions of abundant water toward a more mesic habitat as lakes and ponds fill in, become shallow, and eventually are invaded by terrestrial organisms. In aquatic succession, young lakes with deep, cold, relatively sterile water and little development of shoreline vegetation are termed *oligotrophic*. In contrast, old, shallow lakes with warmer water containing many organisms and having abundant shoreline vegetation are termed *eutrophic*. Whereas oligotrophic lakes support trout and pike, intermediate lakes may have sunfish and bass, and eutrophic lakes will support suckers and bullheads and, finally, no fish at all.

When a biotic community is disturbed by any force that modifies the physical environment and causes replacement of species toward earlier conditions, the process is termed *retrogression*—change in the opposite direction from that caused by succession. Many types of disturbances cause retrogression and initiate secondary succession. Natural disturbances are fire, landslide, flood, drought, windstorm, outbreaks of plant diseases and insects, and intensive use of forage plants by abundant wild herbivores. Artificial disturbances include prescribed fire, flooding or draining, grazing and trampling of vegetation and soil by abundant livestock or unnaturally abundant wild herbivores, chemical poi-

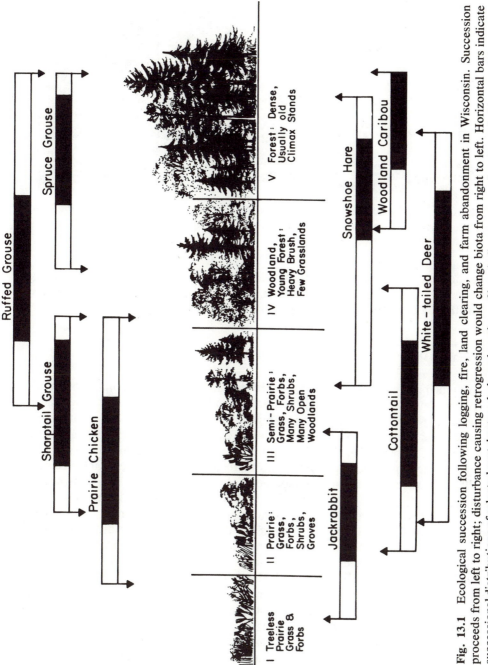

Fig. 13.1 Ecological succession following logging, fire, land clearing, and farm abandonment in Wisconsin. Succession proceeds from left to right; disturbance causing retrogression would change biota from right to left. Horizontal bars indicate successional distributions of selected vertebrates; darkened portions of bars indicate ranges of optimum habitat conditions. The woodland caribou has been extirpated from Wisconsin.

Fig. 13.2   Ecological succession in Wisconsin. From *Wisconsin Conservation Bulletin* 1958, courtesy Wisconsin Department of Natural Resources.

soning of vegetation, and numerous mechanical treatments of the land, including logging, bulldozing, plowing, disking, and chaining. Succession may also be artificially accelerated by planting or fertilizing.

PREDICTING SECONDARY SUCCESSION

Although ecological succession proceeds toward a predictable climax community, the rate of succession and the number and types of developmental stages occurring during succession can be highly variable. Thus, the effects of disturbance and subsequent succession on wildlife populations are not always easy to predict. Compare Fig. 5.4, illustrating slow forest succession, to Fig. 13.3, illustrating rapid succession. Following fire in the subalpine forests of the central Rocky Mountains, any of nine biotic communities may occur in a sequence of from one to three communities before a climax spruce-fir forest develops (Fig. 13.4). The variables determining the rate and direction of secondary succession are categorized as (1) the intensity of the disturbance, (2) the availabilities of plant reproductive materials, and (3) the site conditions for plant growth. These are the major variables considered in predicting results of disturbance and succession. Examples of these variables follow.

The intensity of the disturbance includes the type (light fire, severe fire, logging, etc.), size, and season of disturbance. Severe fires kill all plants and consume soil organic matter; light fires do not and leave residual vegetation and different seed-bed conditions. Logging may vary in intensity from selection cutting to clear-cutting, and varying methods and seasons of log skidding produce great variation in the effects of logging on soils and understory vegetation. Destruction, as by fire or mechanical treatments, of the above-ground parts of plants will produce variable plant responses according to seasonal variation in reserves of plant nutrients in roots. Thus, the burning of shrubs during the dormant season may stimulate resprouting, whereas burning early in the growing season may kill the same plants. The size of a disturbed area in forest vegetation will determine insolation, wind, snow distribution, and availability of seed sources from the edges of the disturbed area.

Availability of plant reproductive materials for reestablishment on a disturbed area is often a function of the survival of the predisturbance vegetation. Seeds of some species persist in the soil. Some conifers may reseed the area from serotinous cones if the predisturbance vegetation consisted of serotinous trees old enough to produce seed. Shrubs and trees, especially aspen, sprout vigorously from roots that may survive the disturbance. A disturbed area may be allowed to revegetate naturally with plants having mobile seeds carried by wind, water, or animals. The type of initial revegetation following disturbance can have long-lasting effects on secondary succession.

There is great variation in growing conditions among and within sites. Some of this variation is associated with climate, soil, aspect, and position on slope. These factors cause much variation in the rates of plant succession following disturbance. Weather conditions in the first few years after disturbance may determine the success of natural or artificial reseeding, altering the rate or direction of succession.

TERMINOLOGY USED FOR CLIMAX COMMUNITIES

Ecological succession has been treated in every ecology text, and differing viewpoints have resulted in a confusion of terminology and at least three primary theoretical approaches to the study of vegetation dynamics. These approaches are the monoclimax concept (Clements 1936; Weaver and Clements 1938), the polyclimax concept (Gleason 1939; Daubenmire 1968), and the continuum concept (Curtis and McIntosh 1951; Whittaker 1975). All three concepts are useful. The monoclimax and polyclimax concepts are similar in that they involve classification of vegetation types according to successional and climax patterns, and both are especially useful in managing vegetation over large areas. The continuum concept does not provide a basis for classifying vegetation into habitat types. It relies on measuring responses of plants to interacting environmental factors on small areas and is especially useful in research on plant ecology.

The polyclimax concept is most useful in wildlife habitat management, especially if applied by biologists who understand the continuum concept and are therefore aware of the limitations of polyclimax ideas. The emphasis in literature on polyclimax has been on classifying stable, usually climax, biotic communities according to the major factors controlling the characteristics of the communities (Table 13.1). These factors have been climate, topography, soils, fire, and the biota, including the effects of vertebrates on communities.

Fig. 13.3 An example of rapid biotic succession following disturbance in western Washington. This area was logged and burned in 1930. Site factors such as topography, soil, temperature, and precipitation have supported rapid plant growth. (Left:

1940 above, 1945 below; Right: 1950 above, 1960 below). Compare to the slow rate of succession illustrated in Fig. 5.4. Photos from Brown (1961) and Weyerhaeuser Company Archives.

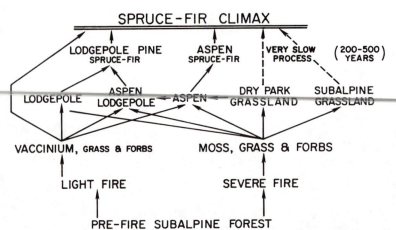

Fig. 13.4 Diversity of trends of secondary succession in conifer forests of Colorado. From Stahelin 1943, Copyright © by Ecological Society of America. Reprinted by permission.

In recent years there has been increased interest in the roles of natural frequencies of fire and natural populations of wildlife in controlling biotic communities. This interest results from recently established goals for national parks in the United States—namely, that where possible, all natural processes such as fire, herbivory, and predation should be reestablished and maintained in the parks (Leopold et al. 1963). Each large park would, therefore, represent a sample of primitive America. The aesthetic and scientific values of natural ecosystems would be paramount among park values. This renewed interest in natural ecosystems has brought increased use of terms for describing disturbance-controlled stable biotic communities, especially when the disturbance is either fire or herbivory. I prefer the terminology given in the right-hand column of Table 13.1. Explanations of these terms follow.

Considering the development of biotic communities over large geographic areas and ignoring local variations, climate is the major factor determining the nature of the climax community. Thus, a continent or state may be divided into climatic climax communities (Fig. 13.5), usually termed *life zones* (Merriam 1898) or *biomes* (Shelford 1963; see also Kendeigh 1954).

However, there is great variation within these large zones, because local, natural geologic conditions prevent attainment of the climatic climax within a reasonable period—centuries or longer. These geologic conditions are topography and soils. A relatively permanent biotic community that persists because topographic or edaphic conditions prevent development of the area's climatic climax community is termed *subclimax*—topographic or edaphic subclimax.

Relatively stable biotic communities, differing from the climatic climax, may also result from frequent or persistent natural disturbance, as by fire, insect

TABLE 13.1 Summary of Terms Related to Climax and Other Relatively Stable Communities, as Used in Some Recent Ecology Texts

Major Factor Controlling Characteristics and Stability of the Community	Weaver and Clements (1938), Oosting (1953)	Daubenmire (1968)	Odum (1971)	Kendeigh (1974)	Willis (1973)	Whittaker (1975)	Terminology Used in this Text
Climate	Climax	Primary climaxes: Climatic Edaphic Topographic	Climatic climax	Climax	Climatic Climax	Climatic or Prevailing Climax	Climax
Other natural factors				Subclimax	Subclimax	Subclimax	Subclimax
Geological				Physiographic Subclimax			
Topographic	Pre- and post-climax					A climax "pattern"	Topographic
Edaphic			Edaphic climaxes	Edaphic Subclimax	Edaphic Climax		Edaphic
Disturbance	Sub- or Ser-climax[a] or disclimax[b]	Disclimaxes:					Disclimax
Fire		Fire	c	Fire Subclimax			Fire
Biotic		Zootic	c		Biotic climax		Zootic
Man-caused disturbance			Disclimax (Anthropogenic)		Anthropogenic climax	Not climax[d]	Disturbed areas
Fire							
Biotic							

[a] From arrest of succession
[b] Usually, from retrogression. Clements also used many other terms.
[c] Fire and biotic climaxes may be "catastrophic" or "cyclic."
[d] This is inferred by emphasis on "natural" areas.

Note: Horizontal lines indicate major distinctions recognized by the terminology.

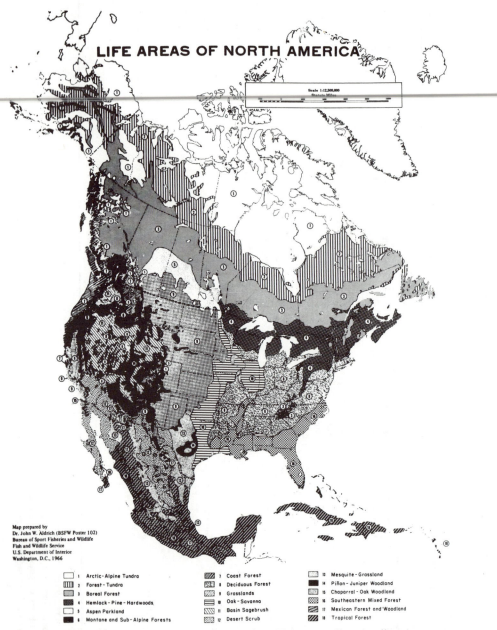

LIFE AREAS OF NORTH AMERICA

Scale 1:12,500,000
Statute Miles

Map prepared by
Dr. John W. Aldrich (BSFW Poster 102)
Bureau of Sport Fisheries and Wildlife
Fish and Wildlife Service
U.S. Department of Interior
Washington, D.C., 1966

1 Arctic-Alpine Tundra	7 Coast Forest	13 Mesquite-Grassland
2 Forest-Tundra	8 Deciduous Forest	14 Piñon-Juniper Woodland
3 Boreal Forest	9 Grasslands	15 Chaparral-Oak Woodland
4 Hemlock-Pine-Hardwoods,	10 Oak-Savanna	16 Southeastern Mixed Forest
5 Aspen Parkland	11 Basin Sagebrush	17 Mexican Forest and Woodland
6 Montane and Sub-Alpine Forests	12 Desert Scrub	18 Tropical Forest

Fig. 13.5   Life areas or biomes of North America. These are climatic-climax communities expected to result from succession under each region's climatic conditions.

attacks, or herbivorous vertebrates. These are termed *disclimax* (disturbance climax) communities. More specifically, they may be termed *fire disclimax* or *zootic disclimax*. (Other natural disturbances, such as accumulation of guano in bird-nesting areas or frequent flooding, also produce disclimax communities.) If the natural disturbance is removed, a disclimax community will succeed toward a subclimax or climatic climax community.

I emphasize that disclimax communities are controlled by *natural* disturbances. Man's activities may increase the frequency of fire, may alter the distribution and abundance of wild herbivores, or may increase the susceptibility of plants to insect attack. In addition, relatively stable biotic communities may result from persistent grazing by livestock or mowing or other mechanical treatments. I prefer not to associate the term *climax* with these communities. I consider them to be communities maintained in unnatural stable conditions by man-caused disturbances.

Often, local areas support subclimax or disclimax communities because of a combination of above conditions. For example, certain south-facing hillsides and ridges within the northern winter range of elk in Yellowstone National Park will not succeed to climatic climax vegetation because: (1) topography creates a xeric microclimate that is harsh for plant development and hinders accumulation of organic litter, (2) parent materials develop into highly erodable soils with little moisture-holding capacity, and (3) the south aspect and windswept locations of the sites preclude snow accumulation and persistence, thereby creating a site attractive to wintering big game, resulting in intensive foraging and trampling (Houston 1976). These areas are termed *topoedaphic zootic disclimax* (Fig. 13.6). (The semantic argument over whether these areas should be termed subclimax or disclimax is useless. Either term will do.)

ZOOTIC DISCLIMAX

Wildlife biologists should be particularly aware of the concept of zootic disclimax. A zootic disclimax community is a relatively stable biotic community, differing from the climatic climax community that is characteristic of the region in which it occurs. Its characteristics and stability are determined chiefly by persistent or frequent effects of natural populations of animals on the vegetation and soils. There are zootic disclimax communities within winter ranges of ungulates in national parks and there are similar communities in other areas, even where the numbers of ungulates are controlled by harvest. In parks, these ungulate herds are maintained as natural herds in natural environments—that is, relatively uninfluenced by man (Cole 1971; Houston 1971; Cayot et al. 1979). Compared to herds and habitats managed to maximize the harvestable surplus of animals, natural herds may have low reproductive rates, at least some animals may be in poor condition during part of the year, and many animals die natural deaths every year. Very many may die in years with severe weather. Preferred

Fig. 13.6   A zootic disclimax site on elk winter range in Yellowstone National Park. This steep south-facing slope tends to shed snow and, therefore, attracts elk during winter and spring. Grasses are grazed largely while dormant. Succession is arrested by topo-edaphic factors influencing soil moisture and temperature and by foraging of elk. Inset: Although plants on the site are widely spaced, they are not unproductive. Photo from Houston 1974.

forage species are not abundant on their critical ranges because past use has reduced these species, and some other forage species are very heavily used, at least locally.

The aesthetic and scientific values of such natural herds in ecosystems relatively uninfluenced by man are great. Aesthetically, the natural herd of animals is not conditioned by sport hunting to avoid people and is, therefore, more visible to tourists. Although the sight of malnourished deer and elk and carcasses near roads on winter ranges is not visually pleasing, it has aesthetic value to the mind that prefers to look more deeply into life's processes, including death. Too many Americans avoid considering death and have unrealistic attitudes toward death, resulting in unrealistic demands for management of all wildlife populations (and probably resulting in human social problems as well).

We know rather little about the functioning of natural ecosystems. The adaptations of North American plants and animals have developed primarily through evolution in ecosystems uninfluenced by European man. Some of these adaptations will not be expressed in managed ecosystems. Natural ecosystems provide opportunities to study those adaptations, permitting a better understanding of the populations we do manage and of the potentials in species we ignore. For instance, what is the value of the carrion produced annually on winter ranges of natural big-game herds to scavenging carnivores and omnivores such as bears, canines, mustelids, and birds of prey? Has the normal seasonal availability of this carrion resulted in the evolution of breeding seasons that are timed so that periods of great demand for food to support reproduction coincide with the availability of winter-killed ungulates? Is the relative rarity of grizzly bears, timber wolves, wolverine, fisher, and perhaps other carnivores due partly or largely to the elimination or unreliability of this seasonal food source because big game herds have been managed to divert natural mortality into harvest? These questions will not be answered without natural ecosystems to study. In the United States it is ironic that whereas we have established many large national parks as natural ecosystems, funding for research on natural processes in the parks has been scarce.

Ungulate management by the National Park Service has been criticized especially by biologists oriented toward herd and habitat management for harvestable-surplus goals (Anon. 1975; Beetle 1974; Ellig 1975). Criticism has been based on a failure to recognize the Park Service goal of naturalness, a contention that naturalness is not possible in at least some parks, and a disagreement over what numbers and distributions of ungulates are natural. Considering the aesthetic and scientific values of natural ecosystems, we should try to reestablish them in some large national parks, despite the first two sources of criticism noted here. As to disagreement over what constitutes a natural ungulate population, it can only be resolved by having uncontrolled populations of ungulates to study.

SUCCESSION AND WILDLIFE

It is useful to classify wildlife species into three categories that describe the relationships between their habitat requirements and ecological succession (Table 13.2).

TABLE 13.2 Classification of Wildlife According to Habitat Requirements in Relation to Ecological Succession

Class	Examples	Habitat Management Prescription
I. Climax-adapted species	Woodland caribou Spruce grouse Snowshoe hare Pileated woodpecker	Protection
II. Species adapted to developmental stages of succession	Bobwhite quail Cottontail rabbit Swainson's thrush	Disturbance: logging, fire, mechanical treatments, etc.
III. Species requiring a mixture of successional stages	Ruffed grouse White-tailed deer Mule deer	Protect or disturb to increase the limiting habitat type

Class I: Climax-adapted Species

Species adapted to climax habitats are hindered and may be extirpated by disturbance that destroys their required climax habitat. Management of their habitat must emphasize protection of climax vegetation, or at least vegetation similar to the climax, from disturbances such as fire or timber harvest (Example 13.1).

There is a tendency for Class I species to be more specialized in their habitat requirements than are species adapted to developmental stages of succession. Presumably, the relative stability of climax communities of Class I species has permitted evolution of specialized food habits and cover needs. In contrast, natural selective forces have been less stable in the more variable and constantly changing developmental communities of Class II species. These forces have favored species generalization, permitting Class II wildlife to use a variety of foods and cover types.

As a result of specialization, many climax-adapted species are less adaptable to habitat changes, and most of our rare and endangered or extinct wildlife have been Class I species (Leopold 1966; Wight 1974). The ivory-billed woodpecker, a bird of mature deciduous forests, is an example.

Until recently, there has been a tendency to neglect Class I species in land-use decisions in the United States. Many climax-adapted species were extirpated or severely reduced early in the nation's development. Consequently, they were mostly disregarded as game species while research and management concentrated on the more abundant Class II and Class III species. It was observed that these latter species were usually favored by interspersion of a diversity of disturbed areas, such as mixed cropland or managed forests with mixed age classes. The generalization developed that disturbance—logging, chaining, burning—is good for "wildlife" habitat because it produces habitat diversity and "productive" successional plant communities. This generalization has limited value because it assumes that all species of wildlife respond similarly (positively) to habitat disturbance under all situations. The assumption, based on neglect of climax-adapted species, is false. Recently, there has been increased concern for species diversity in wildlife populations. This is leading to consideration of the habitat requirements of many species—in contrast to earlier tendencies to lump together all species that presumably were favored by disturbance (Thomas et al. 1975). In forest management, there is increased concern for maintenance of areas with old-growth forest for climax-adapted species like the rare spotted owl in the northwestern states (Zarn 1974) and the woodland caribou of northern Idaho.

EXAMPLE 13.1   Logging, Fire, and Land Clearing, and Caribou Populations

Caribou are climax-adapted animals. The year-round range of woodland subspecies and the winter range of tundra subspecies are climax coniferous forests (Cringan 1957; Kelsall 1968). Both subspecies have declined in abundance and distribution with disturbance of this habitat by fire, logging, and land clearing and with increased harvest of animals, all accelerated with the expansion of human populations in North America. In the eastern United States and Canada, woodland caribou had been extirpated from New York before 1800; Vermont before 1840; Wisconsin, 1850; New Hampshire, 1865; Prince Edward Island, 1873; Michigan, 1906; Maine, 1916; Nova Scotia, 1924; New Brunswick, 1927; and Minnesota, 1942; and their distribution and abundance have declined greatly in Quebec and Ontario (Cringan 1957). Edwards has described the decline of woodland caribou since 1900 in British Columbia (1954). In northern Canada, numbers of tundra caribou have decined since 1900, mostly because of overharvest (Kelsall 1968). The loss of woodland caribou prohibits enjoyment of this interesting animal over a vast area of its former range. The decline of tundra caribou has created serious food shortages for nothern people. The disturbance of climax forests has been important in the decline of woodland caribou and is a threat to the future of tundra caribou.

The critical winter foods of caribou are several species of lichens. These comprise 47 percent of the winter diet of tundra caribou and are also important to woodland caribou (Kelsall 1968; Cringan 1957). Scotter reported the effects of disturbance and succession on production of lichens in boreal forests (Table 13.3), there being little lichen production for 30 years after forest disturbance. Cringan stated that following fire, centuries may pass before an uneven-aged climax forest essential to sustained woodland caribou populations develops. Both authors emphasized forest protection in the management of caribou. Cringan believed that caribou had a limited future in the merchantable forests of Canada where timbering would reduce their habitat; whereas, with fire protection, caribou could be managed successfully in areas supporting non-merchantable timber.

Class II: Species of Developmental Stages

Class II species require vegetation that exists temporarily during secondary succession. Management of their habitat is a constant battle with biotic succession, requiring frequent use of prescribed fire, herbicides, logging, or other mechanical treatment of the land. In contrast, soil fertilization, seeding, tree planting, fire prevention, and establishment of wilderness which precludes timber harvest may be detrimental to their habitat.

TABLE 13.3   Standing crop of Lichens in Forests of Six Age Classes in Tundra Caribou Range, Northern Saskatchewan. (Scotter 1971).

Age Class of Forest (years)	Lichen Crop (lb. per acre)
1−10	3
11−30	104
31−50	312
51−75	469
76−120	423
120+	725

For reasons cited above, Class II species tend to be generalized and adaptable to habitat change. However, there are specialized species in this category, too. The Kirtland's warbler, which requires young stands of pine that normally occur following fire, has become rare because of the disappearance of these stands with forest management and fire protection.

Species of developmental stages flourished with widespread disturbance of biotic communities during the early development of North America by Europeans. Because of their adaptability, they have continued to be abundant in many habitats controlled by human activities. As a result, most animals considered to be important game species are in this class.

A species may be climax adapted in one geographic zone and be adapted to developmental stages of succession in another. Prairie chickens and sharp-tailed grouse, adapted to the climax and fire disclimax prairies of North America, extended their ranges eastward as logging, fire, and land clearing eliminated forests over large areas in Wisconsin, Minnesota, and Michigan (Figs. 13.1 and 13.2). These birds declined as the forest returned (Grange 1948), and only remnant populations remain. Their habitats are maintained locally by prescribed burning to control the encroachment of trees.

Class III: Species Requiring a Mixture of Successional Stages

If we consider the habitat requirements of species in great detail, we will place most species in this class. The habitat requirements of ruffed grouse, illustrated in Fig. 12.2, provide a good example. Ruffed grouse use early stages of forest succession on areas that have lost trees as a result of wind throw, logging, or other disturbances. These areas provide brood cover with abundant insect food, grit, dusting places, green leaves, and fruits and berries. As herbaceous cover in openings is replaced by shrubs and trees, the young forest provides escape cover and molting cover. Older forest growth is used for nesting cover and provides seeds and the buds, especially flower buds of aspen, that grouse rely on for winter food.

Management of habitat for Class III species may involve disturbance or protection, depending on which stages of succession are in shortest supply for the needs of a population. For example, in an area of extensive and dense pinyon-juniper woodland, the creation of small clearings in the trees will increase forage production and enhance mule deer habitat. However, the deer use woodland for cover. In an area of scattered, sparse pinyon-juniper stands among shrublands or grasslands, protection of the remaining cover is necessary to maintain habitat quality for mule deer.

In comparison to the management of Class I and Class II species, management of habitat for Class III species requires more local decision making by a biologist familiar with habitat requirements of the target Class III species and with habitat conditions on the management area. This awareness of the local situation is necessary for identifying limiting welfare factors in the habitat. Without awareness of limiting factors, the effects of habitat disturbance or protection on Class III species cannot be predicted.

Emphasis on Disturbance in Habitat Management

An emphasis on the beneficial results of disturbance in wildlife habitat manipulation has resulted from neglect of climax-adapted species, as noted above, from desires to justify commercially motivated disturbances (logging or vegetation control to enhance livestock forage), and from observations that disturbed areas often produce a diversity and abundance of Class II and Class III species and produce especially nutritious forage for these species.

Succession and Diversity   Along a successional gradient, from a primary sterile site to climax conditions, the diversity of species is certainly very low in the earliest stages of succession and much greater in the climax community. It has been suggested that species diversity will always be greater in the climax community than in any preceeding stage. However, some studies have shown that the greatest diversity of vertebrate species occurs during mid- to late-developmental stages (Bock and Lynch 1970). A problem in studying animal diversity in response to biotic succession is that large areas uniformly in one developmental stage of succession are rare. Most developing biotic communities are mosaics of successional stages.

Three categories of factors determining the rate and direction of secondary succession have been presented. These factors vary within as well as among disturbed areas. Consider a forest fire over a large area. The intensity of the fire may vary greatly among sites within the burn. Most forest fires leave islands of unburned trees within their perimeters. Revegetation of the burned area will vary according to seed sources, patchiness of resprouting by woody plants, and variables affecting seed dispersal and survival. Conditions for plant growth will vary throughout the burned area so that vegetation, once established, will develop toward climax at varying rates. A mosaic of successional stages develops over the burned area.

Thus, regardless of theoretical considerations concerning biotic diversity in relation to ecological succession, it is practical to assume that diversity of wildlife species is usually greatest in some intermediate stages of succession (Fig. 13.7). The mosaic of successional stages that usually develops during secondary succession supports a diversity of Class II wildlife. The mosaic of vegetation is also likely to fulfill habitat requirements of Class III species, and the interspersion of habitat requirements often results in large populations of these species.

Succession and Herbivore Nutrition   Forage produced on recently disturbed sites often contains higher concentrations of nutrients, especially nitrogen and phosphorus, than does forage produced on more developed sites. This has been

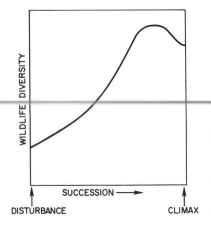

Fig. 13.7 Expected trend of wildlife diversity during secondary succession following disturbance, such as fire, on a large area. The near, preclimax vegetation is usually a mosaic of successional stages and provides habitat for the greatest diversity of wildlife species.

demonstrated for ruminant forages produced on recently burned areas (Cowan et al. 1950; Einarsen 1946; Swank 1956; Taber 1956) and for heather produced on recently burned habitats of red grouse (Moss et al. 1972).

Compared to developmental communities, climax biotic communities support large standing crops of biomass. Much of a site's available nutrients may be incorporated in this organic matter. Disturbance of the community destroys some, often most, of the standing biomass, and nutrients are released as organic matter is burned or decays. These nutrients may be lost from the site in stream outflow, or they may be retained on the site and recycled through vegetation developing in secondary succession. Loss of nutrients from the site in stream or groundwater flow will be enhanced by severe disturbance causing a rapid release of nutrients, by abundant precipitation, and by the presence of steep slopes and light soils. Nutrients not lost from the site in this way, but recycled in secondary vegetation, are partially responsible for the abundant and nutrient-rich vegetation that often follows disturbance of mature or climax biotic communities.

In the northeastern United States, species of trees that are intolerant of competition and shade and typically invade recently disturbed forest sites tend to have higher concentrations of protein in their twigs than do species that are tolerant and normally associated with climax forest types (Table 13.4). This trend may be due to the high availability of nutrients, especially nitrogen, being recycled on recently disturbed sites, or it may be partly a genetic trait of intolerant species of trees.

The production of abundant, available and nutritious forage early in secondary succession has, in many instances, supported an increase in abundance and

TABLE 13.4   Average Protein Levels in Browse of Northeastern Tree Species in Relation to Biotic Succession (data are from numerous sources)

Successional Relationship	Species	Protein Concentration (% dry weight)
Climax-adapted species	Flowering dogwood, *Cornus florida*	5.0
	Sugar maple, *Acer saccharum*	7.2
	American beech, *Fagus grandifolia*	7.5
Species of mid-successional stages	Red maple, *Acer rubrum*	5.1
	Yellow birch, *Betula lutea*	9.8
Species of early stages of forest succession	White ash, *Fraxinus americana*	5.7
	Trembling aspen, *Populus tremuloides*	8.2
	Paper birch, *Betula papyrifera*	8.9
	Black locust, *Robinia pseudo-acacia*	9.0
	Fire cherry, *Prunus pennsylvanica*	9.1
	Choke cherry, *Prunus virginiana*	9.3
	Big-tooth aspen, *Populus grandidentata*	9.7
	Speckled alder, *Alnus rugosa*	10.4
	Tulip poplar, *Liriodendron tulipifera*	10.9
	Black cherry, *Prunus serotina*	13.3

productivity of Class II and Class III game species (Picozzi 1968, Leege 1968, Example 13.2).

EXAMPLE 13.2   Fire, Deer Nutrition, and Abundance in the North Coast Range of California (Taber 1956; Taber and Dasmann 1958)

The climax chaparral of north coastal California is relatively unproductive of deer. Many shrubs, chamise, and live oak, especially, grow so tall that their potential forage is above the reach of deer. Their shade and competition preclude development of a lush herbaceous understory. When chaparral is carefully burned and reseeded, the overhead shrub canopy is reduced and herbaceous ground cover may increase sixfold. Many shrubs resprout from roots that survive fire, and other shrubs seed into burned areas. This community is called shrubland.

Deer increase their consumption of grasses and forbs to 41 percent of the annual diet on shrubland, compared to 9 percent on chaparral. The quality of a diet of herbaceous and woody forages, indicated by its protein concentration, is greater on shrubland than on climax chaparral (Table 13.5). Because of the abundance and quality of forage on shrubland resulting from prescribed fire, deer grow larger, have higher rates of reproduction, become more abundant, and provide a larger harvestable surplus than do populations on climax chaparral.

TABLE 13.5   Production of Forage and Black-tailed Deer on Climax Chaparral and on Frequently Burned Shrubland Sites in Northern California. (data from Taber 1956; Taber and Dasmann 1958)

	Chaparral	Shrubland
Forage (lb. per acre)		
herbaceous	5	86
woody	181	506
Protein in deer diet (percent)	9	14
Deer per square mile	25	60
Annual reproduction		
(fawns per 100 adult does)	62	120
Deer weights, males		
2-year-olds	86	98
3-year-olds	112	122
4-year-olds	130	140
Yield dressed meat (lb. per square mile)		
Bucks only harvest	139	397
"Optimum" harvest	378	861

Caution on Overemphasizing Disturbance in Habitat Management

Although disturbance by prescribed fire, logging, or mechanical treatment of brushlands has often produced beneficial effects on wildlife habitat, as is described above, habitat manipulation by vegetation disturbance should not be applied in all situations. First, some fragile sites are very sensitive to disturbance, and site productivity may be jeopardized by severe or frequent disturbance (Example 5.1). Second, we can expect disturbance to be beneficial to Class II wildlife species because they are adapted to developmental stages of succession. But we must consider that disturbance will be harmful to Class I species and that it may be beneficial, harmful, or neutral to the habitat of Class III species, depending on whether or not limiting welfare factors are affected and in what ways they are affected. Disturbance is no panacea in habitat management. Like all tools of wildlife management, it should be used carefully and with forethought based on a consideration of management goals and local habitat conditions.

SUCCESSION AND HABITAT MANAGEMENT

Control of disturbance and biotic succession is the main habitat manipulation tool of the wildlife manager. Although practices like construction of nesting structures and planting of food patches can produce valuable local effects on wildlife habitat, they are usually expensive relative to the amount of habitat improved. In contrast, prescribed disturbance or habitat protection from disturbance may affect many square miles of habitat at a relatively low cost per acre (Example 13.3).

Much habitat is disturbed annually for purposes other than wildlife management—timber harvest, range improvement, and farming. Wildlife managers can sometimes influence the extent, location, timing, and methods of these disturbances to benefit wildlife habitat. These benefits, often over large areas, can be produced at low cost to the wildlife management program.

EXAMPLE 13.3   Prescribed Fire and Sharecropping in Habitat Management for Midwestern Bobwhite Quail (Ellis et al. 1969)

In the midwestern states, much habitat management for upland game has involved annual planting of cereal grains and legumes and establishment of woody, often nonnative plants like multiflora rose and pines. Biologists of the Illinois Natural History Survey have considered this approach to management to be unnecessarily expensive and often ineffective. They have suggested that more bobwhite quail and other game could be produced at far less expense by manipulating natural vegetation with com-

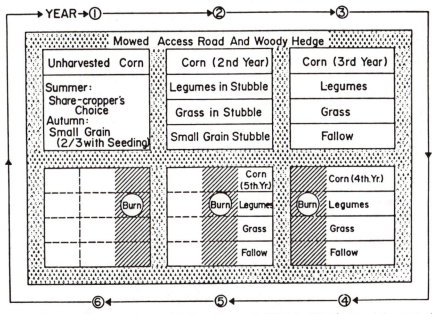

Fig. 13.8   Habitat management for small game in Illinois. Developmental stages of succession are maintained by rotating sharecropping activity and prescribed burning among fields on a six-year schedule. Note the great diversity of habitat resulting when six contiguous fields are in the rotation.

TABLE 13.6   Responses of Bobwhite Quail to Three Programs of Habitat Management in Central Illinois (Ellis et al. 1969)

	Food Patches, Planting of Woody Species	Sharecropping and Prescribed Burning	Prescribed Burning
Quail density per 100 acres	37	96	67
Quail harvest per 100 acres	20	50	33
Management cost per acre	$4.57	$0.16	$0.22
Cost per quail harvested	$22.85	$0.32	$0.66

binations of prescribed burning, sharecropping, and protection. To demonstrate their contention, they compared management costs and quail production and harvest under three management programs: (1) establishment of woody plants and annual planting of scattered food patches, (2) use of sharecropping and prescribed burning to maintain secondary successional communities in cropland fields of 5 to 11 acres and in burned plots of various sizes; (3) use of prescribed burning on a 2-year rotation to maintain secondary successional communities in plots of 1 to 19 acres. In the share-cropping program, local farmers planted one fourth of each field to corn that was left unharvested for wildlife. In return, they were allowed to plant and harvest a summer crop, corn or soybeans, and a winter crop of small grain from three fourths of the field. After the second crop was harvested, a field would not be sharecropped again for three to seven years. However, portions of fields were burned periodically between share-croppings (Fig. 13.8). The main advantages of sharecropping and prescribed burning were in providing inexpensive ways to control biotic succession on large areas of land.

Bobwhite quail, a Class II species, responded well to the management programs based on sharecropping and prescribed burning. The program incorporating both sharecropping and burning was most successful, producing the highest density of quail and the largest harvest, as well as the lowest management costs per acre and per harvested quail (Table 13.6). In contrast, the management program based on food patches and the planting of woody species produced few quail at high cost. Considering this cost, it was likely that bobwhite could have been raised in pens and released before each hunting season at less cost per bird harvested.

SUCCESSION AND HABITAT MEASUREMENTS

Knowing the successional status and trend of a habitat is important to a management biologist because either succession or retrogression may improve or worsen habitat quality for a managed wildlife population (Fig. 13.9). The parameters most often measured to indicate successional trends are vegetation height, species composition of the vegetation, and the proportions of ground vegetated, covered by litter, or bare. Trends in vegetation height indicate when browse plants are growing out of reach of herbivores, usually big game species. Trends in species composition and ground coverage are used to indicate succession or retrogression caused by livestock or wildlife.

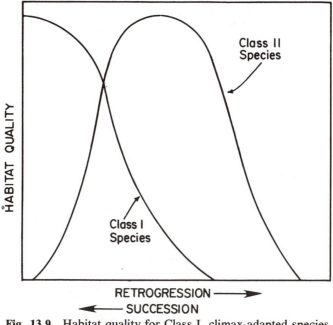

Fig. 13.9 Habitat quality for Class I, climax-adapted species, and for Class II, species of developmental stages, in relation to biotic succession and retrogression.

In the western United States, range managers have been particularly concerned with the effects of grazing as a disturbance affecting species composition, quality, and productivity of range vegetation. Originally, most range managers defined range condition as the state of range vegetation and soils in comparison with vegetation and soils of a similar ungrazed site with climax vegetation (Dyksterhuis 1949). It was assumed that the climax condition was usually most desirable in soil stability and forage. Decline of range condition due to "improper" grazing was then measured as a deviation (retrogression) from climax conditions (Fig. 13.10). Range trend was defined as any decline or improvement in range condition, that is, retrogression or succession.

In this concept of range condition, the climax vegetation consists of *decreasers* (plants that are usually considered desirable forage species but that decline in abundance with heavy grazing) and *increasers* (plants that are less abundant in the climax vegetation but increase in abundance with moderate grazing). Under heavy and continued grazing, decreasers will disappear and even increasers will decline, being replaced by *invaders* that were not present in the climax vegetation (Fig. 13.10). Under severe grazing, total vegetation declines and bare ground increases on the site. With this concept and a classification of plant species as increasers, decreasers, and invaders, range trends can be

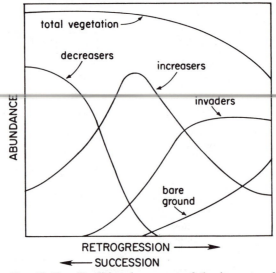

Fig. 13.10   Traditional concept of the impacts of
foraging on vegetation. Increased foraging pressure
causes retrogression to the right; reduced foraging
pressure allows succession to proceed toward the
left. Range trends (retrogression or succession) are
detected by observing changes in the abundance of
increaser, decreaser, and invader species in the vegetation and in the abundance of bare ground.

measured by noting changes in the species composition and ground coverage on
the range.

This concept has not always been adequate for defining and measuring range
condition and trend. The primary problems have been that (1) few areas of
ungrazed climax vegetation remain to serve as a basis for classifying plants as
increasers or decreasers, and the classifications used have, therefore, sometimes been arbitrary; and (2) the assumption that climax vegetation is most
desirable for all range management objectives has been severely questioned. The
concept has, therefore, been refined, though not abandoned. There is an increasing tendency to classify plants as *desirable, intermediate,* and *least desirable.*
Classification is based on local range management objectives, especially the
forage value and productivity of each plant species for the preferred type of
livestock and season of grazing. Since the autecologies of many plant species and
their forage values for all species of livestock are not well known, desirability
classifications may still be somewhat arbitrary, and classifications used in the
field are still influenced by earlier classifications of plants as increasers or
decreasers. Under the refined concept, measurements of range trend involve

noting changes in the proportions of desirable, intermediate, and least desirable species in the vegetation.

This concept of habitat condition and trend is also applied in wildlife management. Vegetation changes can be used as measures of succession or retrogression affecting habitat quality and as measures of habitat disturbance by grazing or browsing wild herbivores. Western wildlife biologists often work with range managers to evaluate trends on ranges used jointly by livestock and wild ungulates. Successful application of the concept for wildlife habitat depends, as in range management, on appropriate classification of plant species as desirable, intermediate, or least desirable. The wildlife biologist should remember that climax vegetation is not most desirable for wildlife species adapted to developmental stages of succession and that plants desirable for livestock may not be equally desirable for wildlife. Furthermore, the biologist should carefully select sites for measuring range condition and trend. Measurements should be replicated at several sites on the range, and zootic disclimax areas should be avoided. Zootic disclimax areas, being so attractive and heavily used no matter what the density of ungulates, are chronically in "poor" condition and will not reflect trends over the entire range.

PRINCIPLES

P13.1   Wildlife habitats are not stable. Much change occurring in habitats is due to biotic succession, retrogression, or to rather sudden natural or man-caused disturbance such as by fire, logging, or flooding. These changes alter food, cover, and other habitat resources for all wildlife species and are fairly predictable. Much wildlife habitat management is, therefore, the management of succession, retrogression, and disturbance.

P13.2   The rate and direction of biotic succession on a site and, therefore, the nature of impacts on wildlife depend on many environmental factors. These factors include (1) those related to the type and intensity of recent disturbance, (2) those determining the availabilities of plant reproductive materials, and (3) those influencing conditions for plant growth. These factors usually vary among sites. Therefore, predicting the results of disturbance and subsequent succession and their effects on wildlife depends on knowing the impacts of these factors on local areas. These factors also vary within sites. As a result, secondary successions following disturbances usually produce a mosaic of successional stages that provide a diversity of wildlife habitat resources.

P13.3   Although succession proceeds toward a climatic climax association of species that is relatively stable, succession may be arrested by local conditions including persistent or frequent impacts of natural or man-caused populations of wildlife. Relatively stable communities that are determined by impacts of natural populations of wildlife are termed zootic disclimax communities.

P13.4 Wildlife species are broadly classified into three categories describing their relationships to ecological succession. Class I species are adapted to climax communities; maintaining their habitats requires protection from disturbance or retrogression. Class II species are adapted to developmental communities, and frequent disturbance is necessary to maintain their habitats. Class III species require a mix of successional stages; maintaining or improving the habitat of a Class III species may require protection or disturbance, depending on which successional stage is most limiting to local abundance.

P13.5 Wildlife diversity increases during primary biotic succession and is greatest in the climax community or in a stage of succession near climax. However, since a mosaic of successional stages usually develops during secondary succession, wildlife diversity on a disturbed area is expected to peak before all of the area reaches climax conditions.

P13.6 Forages produced on recently disturbed areas tend to be of higher quality than forages in old-growth stands of vegetation. The diversity and quality of food and cover on recently disturbed areas has often been observed to produce an abundance of Class II and Class III wildlife, and many of these animals have been game species. Disturbance, for example, caused by logging or prescribed fire, has been recognized as an economical method for enhancing game populations over large areas. However, although disturbance is expected to benefit Class II species, it will be harmful to Class I species and could be harmful to Class III species.

P13.7 At high ecological densities, herbivores can have retrogressive effects on forage resources. Measurement of forage condition and trend is one method for assessing ecological density of a herbivore population.

CHAPTER   14

WEATHER, CLIMATE, AND WILDLIFE

> Management decisions must be made, based
> on past experience, but *no* information
> about the weather forthcoming. A
> manager's success or failure may depend
> on weather he or she cannot foresee. It is
> a serious guessing game. Millions of
> dollars and thousands of hunters are
> influenced. In the aftermath, the manager
> may be blamed, for there is no satisfaction
> in blaming the weather.
>
> *Paraphrased from Robert H. Giles, Jr.*

WEATHER AND WILDLIFE   PRINCIPLES
CLIMATE AND WILDLIFE

The terms *weather* and *climate* should not be used interchangeably. Weather is the condition of the atmosphere at a particular place and during a relatively short period of time. We may refer to the weather "now" or "during a series of years." In contrast, climate refers to weather conditions experienced at a place over a long period of time—decades or even centuries. The climate of an area includes all of its extremes of temperature, moisture, and other weather factors.

Weather is a variable factor capable of large effects on wildlife and habitats. Since it is relatively unpredictable, weather adds much uncertainty to the predictions of wildlife managers and requires frequent review of management decisions. The only certainty is that extreme events will eventually occur and for a time may completely override the effects of management on wildlife populations, perhaps requiring a reversal of management strategies (Example 14.1). Wildlife managers should review weather records for their areas. In the United States these records are compiled by the federal government and are available in major libraries. A review of at least 20 years' records will be necessary to reveal not only averages but expected extremes.

EXAMPLE 14.1   Frequency of Severe Winters in Adirondack Deer Ranges

Severinghaus has described the effects of hunting, windstorm, and severe winters on the abundance of white-tailed deer in New York's Adirondack Preserve during 1900 to 1971 (1972). Nine major declines in the deer population followed seven isolated severe winters, consecutive severe winters in 1909 to 1911, and the trio of consecutive severe winters in 1968 to 1971.

For northern white-tailed deer, the severity of winter can be measured by the number of days with deep snow. In the Adirondacks, serious winter losses occurred when there were more than 60 days with at least 15 inches of snow, or more than about 50 days with at least 20 inches. In such winters, most low-growing forage is covered, excess energy is expended by fawns in moving through 15 inches of snow and by adults in moving through 20 inches, and forage areas outside the wintering areas are not visited because of deep snow.

A windstorm in 1950 had mixed effects on deer habitat. A few wintering areas were mostly destroyed when many tall conifers were blown down. In other areas the fallen timber was replaced by new growth of deer forage near deer wintering areas and on summer ranges.

Hunting was not a major factor determining the number of deer. The harvest of buck deer in 1968, second highest on record, followed several years with high levels of harvest, including 12 consecutive seasons in which does were also harvested. In contrast, the three consecutive hard winters of 1968 to 1971 resulted in a 60 percent reduction in deer numbers. Management strategies were accordingly reversed and the harvest of female deer was temporarily abandoned.

The New York wildlife managers could not have predicted each severe winter. But the records compiled by Severinghaus now permit calculation of the likely frequency of severe winters and the subsequent need to alter management and explain changed strategies to the public. Calculations illustrate the extreme vagaries of weather and how managers who have not reviewed weather records may be deceived by many years of mild-to-moderate weather and be unprepared for what next year may bring.

On average, severe winters occurred every 6 years. However, hard winters were interceded by as few as 0 and as many as 14 years with mild or moderate winters and no widespread losses of deer. There were 12 hard winters in 71 years; thus, the probability of a winter being severe (assuming no climatic trends) is 12/71 = 0.169. The probability of three consecutive severe winters is only $0.169^3 = 0.005$; yet this happened in 1968 to 1971.

WEATHER AND WILDLIFE

Direct Effects of Weather

We expect wild animals to be adapted to weather conditions within their naturally associated environment (Kelsall and Telfer 1971; Koskimies and Lahti 1964). Weather extremes in the past have naturally selected against individuals incapable of withstanding severe weather events, leaving populations of better adapted individuals. However, this natural selection continues, and weather extremes still cause mortality.

Waterfowl nests have been destroyed by flooding (Yocum 1950). Hailstorms have killed individuals of many species over local and occasionally over large areas. Jones reported 50 hawks and owls, 30 crows, 3 doves, 4 cottontail rabbits, and a wood rat, all dead in a single, mile-long shelterbelt after an Oklahoma hailstorm that covered about 110 square miles (1952). Smith described a hailstorm over 700 square miles that apparently killed 36,000 ducks, including 23,000 adults and 13,000 ducklings (1960). He estimated that 150,000 ducks were lost during hailstorms in Alberta in 1953. Birds were killed by large hailstones that crushed skulls and caused massive contusions. Freezing rain, sleet, and snow have caused death to quail, rabbits, doves, songbirds, opossums, muskrat, and ducks in Tennessee (Schultz 1951). Unusually cold and wet weather is a severe problem for nestling passerine birds in the arctic. Of 57 nests containing young birds observed by Jehl and Hussell, only 3 contained live young after a period of cold, wet, and windy weather (1966). The young birds apparently died of hypothermia. Such weather is not too uncommon in the Canadian arctic, perhaps accounting for its relative paucity of breeding passerine birds. Altricial habits of passerine birds make them susceptible to exposure. Of 71 breeding bird species in the Canadian arctic, only 11 are passerine (Snyder 1957).

Very young animals are often especially susceptible to severe weather. Even the precocial, nonpasserine birds can suffer losses if severe weather occurs at a critical time in early life. Marcstrom demonstrated the limited energy reserves of newly hatched capercaillie chicks (1960). They can withstand short periods of cold, wet, windy weather during their first week by drawing on energy reserves and remaining inactive under the brooding hen. But if such weather persists for two to three days, energy reserves, including subcutaneous fat with its insulating value, are lost, and the chicks' inactivity prevents feeding. In addition, insects may be less active in cold weather and less available as chick food. Capercaillie broods are decimated greatly by such weather at this critical time, and other tetraonidae are probably similarly affected.

Indirect Effects of Weather

Weather affects wildlife populations indirectly by restricting their movements; by destroying, making unavailable, or reducing the production of food and cover resources; and by influencing the abundance of competitors, predators, or disease organisms.

In many places snow depth and quality determines the distribution of animals, and snow may cover their food supply. This has often been recorded for ungulates (Gilbert et al. 1970; Pruitt 1959; Edwards 1956; Haugen 1971). In Middle Park, Colorado, mule deer may be restricted by snow conditions to about one tenth of their total winter range (Fig. 14.1), and these concentrations of deer are

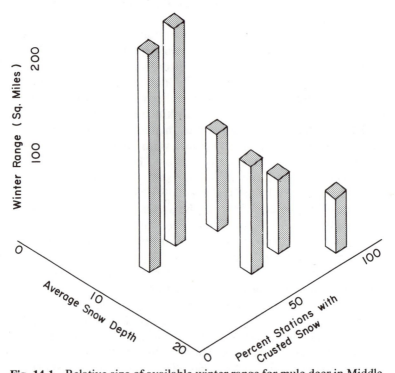

Fig. 14.1   Relative size of available winter range for mule deer in Middle Park, Colorado with varying snow conditions. In open winters, 500 square miles of winter range may be available. Figure adapted from Wallmo and Gill 1971.

TABLE 14.1 Number of Days on Which the Fraser, Colorado Weather Station Reported More Than 20 Inches of Snow on the Ground, January to April, 1961 to 1970

Year	January	February	March	April	Total
1961	0	0	0	0	0
1962	25	28	31	10	94
1963	6	9	13	0	28
1964	0	1	21	0	22
1965	22	28	31	13	94
1966	0	1	0	0	1
1967	6	20	5	0	31
1968	24	9	12	0	45
1969	7	28	13	0	48
1970	15	25	2	1	43

Note: These data indicate large variation in severity among winters. Compare 1961 and 1966 to 1962 and 1965. Although not perfectly correlated with snow conditions on nearby deer winter ranges at lower elevations in Middle Park, the data illustrate the great variation in snow conditions on the winter range. When deer are especially abundant, perhaps following years of good reproduction and low harvest, a severe winter can cause much mortality. This happened in 1965 when 10,000 to 20,000 deer perished out of a population estimated at 30,000 to 40,000 animals.

often on the least productive and most overused areas. Restriction of deer movement and the snow cover vastly reduce available forage supplies. Variation in winter severity for deer is extreme in Middle Park (Table 14.1). The resulting unpredictable variation in winter carrying capacity for the herd creates the most difficult problem in herd management. Each autumn, harvest regulations are adjusted to reduce the herd to the carrying capacity of an average winter. Thus, despite usually good control over deer numbers, many deer die in a severe winter, and during a mild winter the range is capable of supporting more deer than remain after harvest.

In arid regions, particularly in the desert of the Southwest, the quantity and quality of forage production show large variation among years depending on the amount and seasonal distribution of precipitation. Reproductive success in mule deer, Gambel quail, and javelina populations have been correlated with seasonal precipitation patterns (Day 1971; Gallizioli 1965; Shaw 1965; Gullion 1960; Fig. 14.2); and it is presumed that improved forage conditions during years with extra moisture are at least one factor causing higher reproduction (Anthony 1976; Wallmo 1973). Conversely, drought conditions have caused widespread declines in populations of pronghorn antelope (Hailey et al. 1964) and mule deer (Jantzen 1964; Macgregor 1964; Greenley and Humphreys 1964; McKean and Luman 1964; Hancock 1964). The effects of drought on deer may be very complex. Limited forage supplies may affect not only the deer but also small mammal

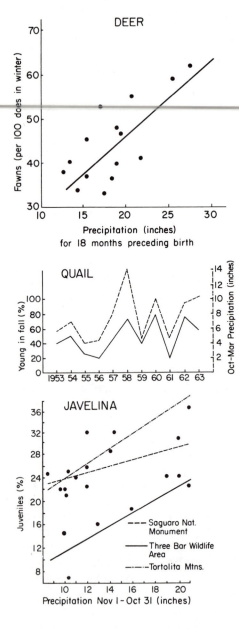

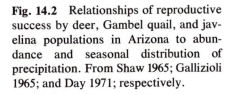

Fig. 14.2 Relationships of reproductive success by deer, Gambel quail, and javelina populations in Arizona to abundance and seasonal distribution of precipitation. From Shaw 1965; Gallizioli 1965; and Day 1971; respectively.

populations. This may result in a shift of coyote predation from smaller mammals to deer, perhaps at a time when comparatively weak fawns are being produced because of the effects of drought on deer nutrition. The less-nourished fawns may also be more susceptible to disease. Diseases, in turn, make animals less resistant to predation.

The effects of weather on wildlife are expected to be more severe on newly acquired geographic ranges or at the edges of geographic ranges (for example, Birch 1958). Siivonen described wide fluctuations in partridge populations at the northern extreme of their range in Finland (1956). In some winters, snow persistently covered food supplies. Partridge numbers and northward distribution expanded in favorable years and contracted in unfavorable years.

Chance Correlations: Wildlife Populations and Weather

When several years' wildlife data have been gathered, such as a series of population indices or a series of data on reproductive success, it is worthwhile to speculate on weather factors that might have influenced the observed year-to-year variation. Hoewever, caution must be used in seeking statistical correlations between wildlife data and several potentially important weather factors. If one tests enough weather factors, one *will* find a "statistically significant" correlation. Using the 0.05 probability level for accepting observed correlations, one should expect *because of chance* to find one "significant" correlation if 20 weather factors are tested. However, the probabilities and the significance values are meaningless in this case, for the data have been allowed to suggest the hypothesis. The correlations themselves are not meaningless; they are suggested hypotheses. They suggest relationships that may exist between weather and wildlife, and biological explanations for the relationships should be sought. The validity of a relationship must be tested with new data, however.

Weather Covariants in Data Analysis

Weather data are often used as a covariant in analyzing time-series data on wildlife populations. Often the effects of manageable factors, such as nutrition or population density, on reproduction or mortality rates cannot be detected until annual variations in these rates caused by weather are accounted for (Example 14.2). Without an ability to account for weather effects, managers will be less able to detect effects due to factors they can control, and they will be slow to realize when control should be applied.

EXAMPLE 14.2   Snow and Age Ratios of Mountain Goats in Colorado

Rocky Mountain goats were introduced into the Sawatch Range of Colorado in 1948. The goats have increased in numbers, particularly the herd on Sheep Mountain, west of Buena Vista. This herd has grown from six animals transplanted in 1949. In 1966, the

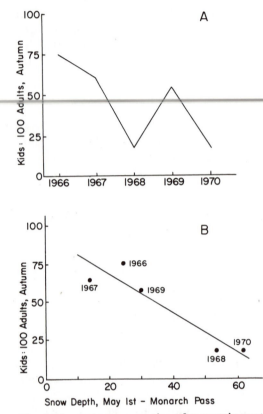

Fig. 14.3   Autumn age ratios of mountain goats on Sheep Mountain, Colorado. The suggested decline in age ratios during 1966 to 1970 becomes less alarming when their correlation with snow conditions at nearby Monarch Pass is considered. Data from Colorado Division of Wildlife and Bruce Johnson.

Colorado Division of Wildlife began counting and classifying goats during September flights over Sheep Mountain. Data accumulated by 1970 were cause for concern (Fig. 14.3).

Although the trend was not statistically significant because of large variation in reproductive success among years, a decline in reproduction might have been occurring during the five years. The highest age ratios were in the earliest years, and two of the last three years produced very low age ratios. Perhaps a density-dependent phenomenon was occurring. The increasing number of goats could have been making greater demands on food supplies, resulting in lower average nutrition and productivity of the animals and perhaps causing damage to the forage resource. These possibilities concerned the Colorado Division of Wildlife. If they were occurring, a management strategy of increased harvest and/or increased trapping of goats for transplantation to new ranges seemed warranted.

But covariant analysis provided an alternative to the hypothesis of density-dependent reproduction. Goat age ratios were found to be correlated with winter-spring snow conditions in the mountains (Fig. 14.3). The years with poor reproductive success, 1968 and 1970, were years when snow lay deep and late. Such conditions could have affected the energy needs of and the forage available to nanny goats during late gestation, a critical time when the viability of offspring is often determined.

Thus, consideration of a weather factor provided a clue to the cause of year-to-year variation in goat reproduction in the Sawatch Range. Once snow conditions were considered, age ratios provided little reason to suspect a density-dependent decline in reproductive success. The effects of snow conditions on goats provided an equally plausible explanation for these data.

However, the population of mountain goats on Sheep Mountain was still increasing in 1970. If a density-related decline in reproductive success were eventually to occur, could data on mountain goat age ratios ever be used to detect the decline? Because of the great variation of age ratios, a time series would be a poor analytical tool for detecting trends (Fig. 14.3a). One would have to observe several consecutive years with low age ratios before concluding that reproductive success had declined. However, covariant analysis would provide a more sensitive measure of trends in age ratios. Large deviations of new points from the regression line in Fig. 14.3b would immediately suggest a change in reproductive success.

CLIMATE AND WILDLIFE

Present Climatic Conditions

Climate controls the distributions of biotic communities. A wildlife population is adapted to the food, cover, and other resources of certain biotic communities and also to the climate of its geographic range. When attempting to explain the distributions of wildlife populations, it is difficult to separate the direct and indirect effects of climate—that is, effects on the animals and effects on their habitat. Adaptations of animals to climate and the animal's ability to withstand weather extremes are especially important when we propose to transplant populations from one area to another for introduction or reintroduction.

Twomey proposed the use of graphic methods for comparing climates among species' ranges and introduction sites (1936). His climographs illustrated mean monthly temperatures and precipitation for sites within the range of Hungarian partridge in Europe and compared these with climates at two sites where partridge had been introduced into the United States (Fig. 14.4). Partridge have been successfully introduced near Havre, Montana, even though its winters are colder than those within the European range (Fig. 14.4). Partridge introductions have failed near Columbia, Missouri. This failure has been interpreted as related to the wetter spring and early summer conditions than in European ranges (Fig.

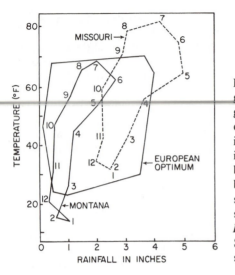

Fig. 14.4 Twomey (1936) compared climographs for Havre, Montana, where Hungarian partridge were successfully introduced, and Columbia, Missouri, where introduction failed, with average conditions in the European partridge range. The numbers 1 . . . 12 represent January . . . December. The "European Optimum" encloses separate climographs for several weather stations within the European range. From *Ecology*, Copyright © by the Ecological Society of America. Reprinted by permission.

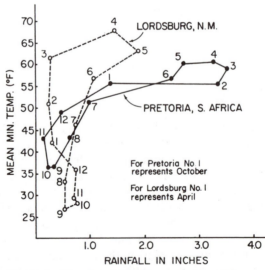

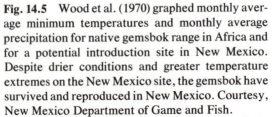

Fig. 14.5 Wood et al. (1970) graphed monthly average minimum temperatures and monthly average precipitation for native gemsbok range in Africa and for a potential introduction site in New Mexico. Despite drier conditions and greater temperature extremes on the New Mexico site, the gemsbok have survived and reproduced in New Mexico. Courtesy, New Mexico Department of Game and Fish.

14.4). A similar approach has been used by Hoffman to explain the northern limits of scaled quail in Colorado (1965).

Although averages of weather factors are important, extremes are apt to have more biological significance. Climographs can be used to illustrate any pair of weather factors including extremes such as mean monthly minimum temperature. Wood et al. used this approach in comparing the climates of the native ranges of gemsbok (Fig. 14.5) and Iranian ibex and potential introduction sites in New Mexico (1970).

Past Climatic Conditions

Over centuries, the climate of the earth has varied greatly. Ice fields and mountain glaciers have advanced and retreated. There have been warm, dry periods and cool, moist periods. The earth's major biotic communities have shifted locations in response to these long-term changes (Darlington 1957). Present distributions of some wildlife populations have been determined largely by these long-past events. Consideration of the zoogeographic history of a species often provides insight into its ecology, its competition with other species, opportunities for transplanting it to new ranges, and its fragility in relation to environmental change. The study of zoogeography is useful background for a wildlife management biologist.

As climates change and biotic communities recede because of deteriorating climatic conditions, some species of a community may be left behind to persist in isolated, small areas that have a microclimate different from the surrounding new climatic conditions. These are relict populations; relict means *left behind*. Relicts of a wetter climate may persist among arid-adapted species by surviving in shaded, moist canyons or in swales where water accumulates. Relicts of a cooler climate may persist among less cold-adapted species by surviving on north-facing slopes in canyons. Many relict populations of the boreal coniferous forest persist in Illinois, Indiana, Ohio, and the Appalachian Mountains. They were established during colder times when ice sheets advanced and the boreal forest moved southward.

Relict populations of wildlife deserve special management consideration. They are usually fragile and very valuable (Example 14.4).

EXAMPLE 14.3   Transplants of Mountain Goats into Colorado

Mountain goats did not occur in the Rocky Mountains south of Wyoming in historic times. Yet there appeared to be suitable mountain habitat to the south, at least in Colorado. Why did goats not occur in Colorado? Fossil evidence of goats has been found south of Colorado (Simpson 1945). Apparently mountain goats disappeared from the southern Rocky Mountains during some period of unsuitable climate, possibly during the warm, dry period that occurred between 4000 and 2000 B.C. Furthermore, high mountain habitat is discontinuous in the Wyoming Rockies, as there is no continuous mountain goat habitat from the northern ranges into Colorado. These considerations indicated that mountain goats could be successfully introduced into Colorado mountain ranges. Transplants of goats from Montana and South Dakota beginning in 1948 resulted in successful establishment, providing a new big game species and an interesting animal in Colorado.

EXAMPLE 14.4   Relict Populations of Prairie Animals in the Northeastern United States

The last great (Wisconsin) advance of Pleistocene glaciers ended about 10 thousand years ago. Since then, the climate of the northeastern states has passed through a cool period, then a warm-moist, a warm-dry, and finally another cool period (Smith 1957). Based on studies of plant pollens preserved in soils, the warm dry period, termed xerothermic, appears to have occurred between 4000 and 2000 B.C. Schmidt suggested that prairie fauna and flora invaded the eastern states shortly after glaciation (1938). However, biogeographers now place this eastward extension of the "prairie peninsula" (Transeau 1935) during the xerothermic period (Smith 1957). Interestingly, there was a mirror-image extension of Eurasian steppe biota westward into Europe after glacial retreat (Schmidt 1938), probably also during the same xerothermic period. In North America, the xerothermic prairie extended at least into western New York, and there is evidence that some prairie species extended as far as the Delaware-Maryland-Virginia peninsula on the east coast. Following the xerothermic period, cooler and wetter conditions forced replacement of the much-extended prairie peninsula by central and eastern deciduous forests. However, some of these forests have soil profiles indicating their prehistoric prairie status (Transeau 1935).

The westward retreat of prairie left many relict populations behind where they persist in bog areas or on small relict prairies, often on sand plains. Indeed, these relict populations are a major evidence of the once eastward extension of prairie. Among the prairie relicts are the ornate box turtle, bull snake, fox snake, plains garter snake, massasauga rattlesnake, and thirteen-lined ground squirrel (Fig. 14.6). Some of these populations exist in small and unusual environments that might easily be altered by human activities, to the destruction of the relict animals.

In Ohio, the plains garter snake survives where the earliest settlers found the most extensive area of relict prairie vegetation in the state (Conant et al. 1945). This land is now intensively farmed except for roadsides, railroad rights-of-way, and a few wet swales where prairie vegetation persists and maintains the relict garter snakes.

The eastern massasauga rattlesnake occurs on the southern Great Plains, and its range extends eastward across the prairie peninsula in Illinois and Indiana to Michigan, Ohio, Ontario, northwest Pennsylvania, and western New York. In the east, the massasauga occurs only locally, being confined to areas of sphagnum bogs (Schmidt 1938). One such area is Cicero Swamp near Syracuse, New York (Kauffeld 1969; Fig. 14.6). Here the snake persists in an area of about 5 square miles. Cicero Swamp lies in the Lake Ontario plain, most of which has been drained for agriculture. Only the wettest areas have escaped.

Relict populations are usually fragile and in need of protection. They are relicts because climatic conditions have changed around them, relegating them to a few unusual places somewhat insulated from climatic change. Such places are often easy for man to change or destroy because they are small. The relict

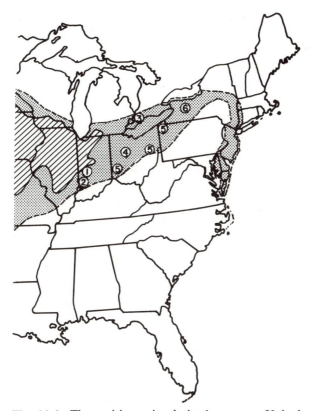

Fig. 14.6 The prairie peninsula in the eastern United States. Solid lines illustrate the general limit of prairie at the time of settlement. After Transeau 1935. Broken lines illustrate the hypothesized maximum extension of prairie during the post-glacial xerothermic period. After Smith 1957. Numbers are locations of relict populations of prairie fauna:

(1) ornate box turtle, (2) bullsnake, (3) fox snake, (4) plains garter snake, (5) 13-lined ground squirrel, and (6) massasauga rattlesnake.

animals, somewhat unsuited to their environment, may not be very productive. A small amount of man-caused mortality—perhaps through turtle collecting or rattlesnake control—could eliminate their populations.

Yet relict fauna have great scientific and educational values. Their existence is important to zoogeography, for they are clues to past changes in climate and in the distributions of biotic communities. They provide natural laboratories where isolated populations can exhibit speciation and help us to understand the mechanics of evolution. Perhaps the educational value of relict populations is greatest. Viewing these populations in their isolated refugia, one may perceive a feeling of ages-old events, of evolution and extinction, of the immensity of time. Only when more people appreciate such concepts will industrialized man fully value and protect his wildlife resources.

PRINCIPLES

P14.1 Weather affects wildlife directly as a cause of mortality and indirectly by restricting animal movements and influencing the abundance and availabilities of habitat resources and the abundance of competitors, predators, and disease organisms. Much direct effect of weather on wildlife results in mortality of young animals. Both direct and indirect effects are often most severe at the peripheries of species' geographic ranges. These largely unpredictable impacts on wildlife abundance and productivity are responsible for much uncertainty in wildlife management.

P14.2 The direct and indirect effects of weather on wildlife are often as great or greater than those of any other environmental influence, including the effects of management. Therefore, it is often necessary to determine and measure the effects due to weather before the effects of other influences, including management, can be detected.

P14.3 Present and past climatic patterns largely determine the distributions of wildlife species. Transplants of species have the greatest chances of success when animals are moved between areas with similar, rather than dissimilar, climates. Isolated, local populations often persist within areas of inhospitable climate as relicts from past climatic regimes. These relict populations have great scientific and educational values.

PART   IV

POPULATION
DYNAMICS

CHAPTER 15

POPULATION DYNAMICS

A realistic basis for building models dealing with the
changes of numbers in populations would include the
following propositions: (a) All populations are constantly
changing in size; (b) The environments of all organisms
are constantly changing; (c) Local populations must be
recognized and investigated if changes in population size
are to be understood; (d) The influence on population size
of various components of the environment varies with
population density, among species, among local populations,
and through time.

P.R. Ehrlich and L. C. Birch

INTRODUCTION

Population dynamics refers to variation in population size and also in sex-age compositions, reproduction and mortality rates, and qualities of animals in populations. It is the study of how this variation results from interactions among animals and between animals and their environment. If we are to manage these characteristics of populations, it is imperative that we have some understanding of how populations operate in variable environments.

Although scientific discussion of some concepts of population dynamics began at least as early as the writings of Malthus and Darwin, most currently accepted concepts in the field stem from publications less than 35 years old (for example, Leopold 1943; Allee et al. 1949; Solomon 1949; Lack 1954; Andrewartha and Birch 1954; Nicholson 1955; Errington 1956; Milne 1957; Wynne-Edwards 1965; Tanner 1966; Pimlott 1967; Wagner 1969; May 1973; Keith 1974; Caughley 1976). Publication in population dynamics was especially active during the 1950s and has again become increasingly active in recent years. Differing points of view on population regulation have been proposed. There have been major differences over the relative importance of welfare factors versus decimating factors and of density-dependent versus density-independent factors in controlling animal numbers. Early workers probably hoped to develop a simple model of population dynamics; but as more populations in a diversity of environments have been studied, the complexities of population regulation have become apparent. In this chapter, I present a conceptual model of population dynamics that has been useful in wildlife management. I believe the several parts of this model are widely accepted by the profession. However, this chapter is not a complete review of the literature on population dynamics. The student of wildlife biology should become aware of contrasting concepts in the rather controversial and recently active literature, some of which is cited above.

In reading this chapter, be aware that my objective of presenting a population model useful to wildlife management has led to three important biases. First, I believe the sigmoid model of population growth is a valid concept useful in management. New concepts of population dynamics should be, whenever possible, integrated into this model. The addition of new concepts, of course, makes the model more elaborate and complex. I believe that communication of the model's concepts is enhanced, for most readers, by graphic rather than mathematical presentation.

Second, I believe a useful population model must include interactions between animals and their habitat, and I prefer a model in which habitat is emphasized as a determinant of population size and characteristics. This bias has two sources. Habitat degradation is our most widespread and serious wildlife management problem in the United States, and we should not get so theoretical as to neglect it. Further, habitat *is* the ultimate factor controlling animal populations. There are many examples of habitat destruction that have caused wildlife populations to decrease and many examples of habitat improvement that have caused increases in wildlife populations. Population models that emphasize decimating factors tend to neglect the role of welfare factors (habitat) in alleviating decimating factors.

Third, I tend to emphasize density-dependent rather than density-independent mechanisms of population regulation. This bias results from the previous two. Density dependence is the mechanism of population regulation in the sigmoid model. Further, since habitat is so important, many population characteristics are dependent on the per capita availability of welfare factors. These characteristics are, therefore, dependent on population size in relation to the quantity and quality of habitat, namely, ecological density. Thus, I stress ecological-density dependent mechanisms of population regulation. This emphasis is most justified for large, homoiothermic animals because they are relatively more capable of responding successfully to density-independent factors of the environment, particularly weather.

THE SIGMOID MODEL OF POPULATION GROWTH

The sigmoid model has long been used as an initial basis for discussing population dynamics. The model has great generality—it incorporates and, therefore, explains many concepts of population dynamics, and it seems to apply to most, if not all, populations. The model describes population dynamics by describing the population and habitat changes resulting after a population is newly introduced into a suitable unoccupied but limited environment.

The sigmoid model has been derived largely from studies of large-mammal populations and their habitats. The model seems applicable to smaller animals, which usually have higher biotic potentials. However, for reasons to be explained later, population changes occur so rapidly in species with high biotic potential that it was difficult for biologists to describe these changes in enough detail to develop a population model. Once the model was developed, however, mostly from studies of ungulates, it also explained fluctuations of other species.

The sigmoid model is based on two assumptions. First, the introduced population is put into a stable limited environment. The physical environment is stable. Weather does not vary among years. No other animal populations influence the habitat. Any habitat changes are caused only by influences of the modeled population as it grows in abundance. Since the environment is limited, population increase must result in increased population density. Either animals cannot leave their environment or emigration must be treated as mortality—the animals are lost from the population. The second assumption is that environmental resistance, expressed in reproduction and/or mortality, is density dependent.

The model proceeds from the concept of biotic potential, the maximum rate of growth of a population introduced into an ideal and infinite environment (Fig. 15.1a). Since the environment is limited, that is, neither ideal nor infinite, the population cannot grow exponentially for long. Environmental resistance is the

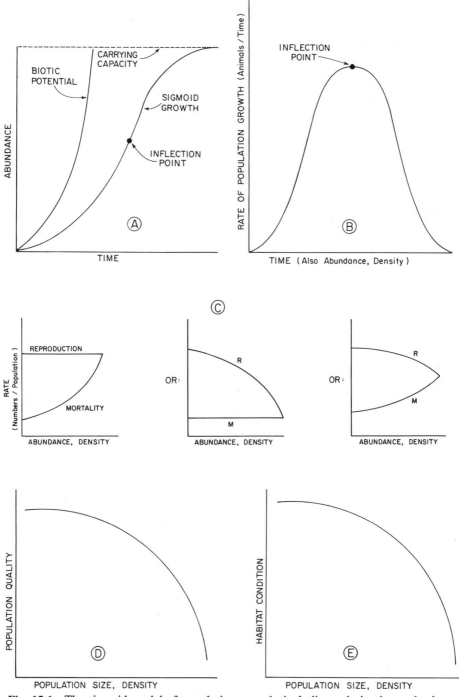

Fig. 15.1 The sigmoid model of population growth, including a derivative and sub-models.

effect of a limited environment on reproduction, mortality, or both. Any combination of welfare factors may become limiting (see Chapter 12). Environmental resistance is measured as the reduction in number of animals born and/or increase in the number that die during each unit of time. Subtracting these animals from biotic potential produces sigmoid population growth (Fig. 15.1a). Population growth accelerates up to the point of inflection and thereafter decelerates until population stability is achieved. The derived graph of rate of population growth over time illustrates this acceleration and deceleration (Fig. 15.1b). The number of animals added to the population per year (or other unit of time) is greatest in the year of the inflection point. It is likewise greatest when population size (also density) is that associated with the inflection point.

Either or both components of environmental resistance, reproduction and mortality, are density dependent (Fig. 15.1c). When reproduction equals mortality, the population stabilizes. These changes in reproduction and/or mortality occur as some or all members of the increasing population are forced to subsist on ever decreasing per-animal quantities and/or decreasing qualities of one or more welfare factors. As a result, an increasing proportion of the animals will be in increasingly poor condition. Thus, population quality declines with population increase (Geist 1971, p. 303; Fig. 15.1d). Population quality may be measured by body size (Fig. 15.2), fat reserves, antler or horn growth, reproductive success, disease resistance, viability, physiological symptoms of stress, or type and intensity of behavior. Decreased population quality may be exhibited by

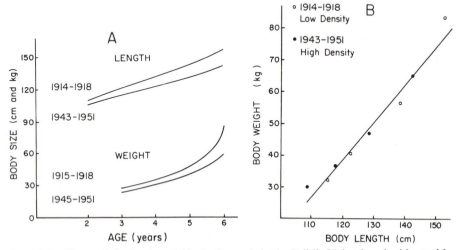

Fig. 15.2 Change in body size of Alaska fur seals in the Pribilof Islands coincident with a 4.5-fold increase in population size during about 30 years. Although both body length and weight declined (A), the relationship between these measurements and, therefore, "body stockiness" did not decline (B) as happens in some mammals. However, the implications remain that population quality declined with increasing population density. Data from Scheffer 1955.

only part of the population because of the apportionment of welfare factors and social stresses according to social status. Decreased population quality may be exhibited primarily in one season of the year, because of limiting welfare factors that operate in that season. Since various low-quality populations of a species will face differing sets of limiting welfare factors, the symptoms of low population quality will vary among these populations.

Many welfare factors that may become limiting are capable of being overused and damaged by the increasingly abundant population. Thus, habitat condition may decline (Fig. 15.1e). Habitat condition may be measured by levels of use on limiting supplies of food or cover, disappearance of preferred food types, retrogression of vegetation and erosion of soil, or abundance of parasites in the environment.

In the sigmoid model, the term *carrying capacity* is used to denote the upper asymptote of the sigmoid curve—the maximum number of animals the environment will support (Fig. 15.1a). In the model, and often in real situations, these animals and their habitat are in poor condition at carrying capacity. Ecological density is the number of animals in relation to quantity and quality of habitat and, therefore, in relation to carrying capacity in the model. *Ecological density* can replace *density* in Fig. 15.1b to 15.1e. The concept of ecological density is essential in application of the model to real management situations. In real environments, we must accept carrying capacity as a variable. Ecological density is influenced by changes in either population size or habitat. Thus, in real situations the responses of the population and habitat illustrated by Fig. 15.1 are not necessarily responses to population size or density; they are, more precisely, responses to ecological density.

Many populations exhibit an annual cycle of abundance with a marked increase during the season of reproduction and a decline through the rest of the annual cycle. Thus, the smooth sigmoid curve of Fig. 15.1 is really a series of "saw teeth" representing annual changes in abundance (Fig. 15.3a). The nature of environmental resistance, namely, the kinds of welfare factors that become limiting, determines the relative importance of lowered reproduction versus increased mortality (Fig. 15.1c) in the annual cycle and, therefore, determines the amplitude of each year's variation in abundance (Fig. 15.3b versus 15.3c).

If we were to hold a population at some level of abundance shown in Fig. 15.1a, what level, that is, what point on the sigmoid curve, would provide the maximum annual harvestable surplus? The nature of environmental resistance, as described above, determines the answer. Environmental resistance causes lowered reproduction and increased mortality. Annual harvestable surplus consists of (1) potential population increase, which can be harvested to return the population to the same breeding-season abundance each year, and (2) that part of natural mortality (caused by environmental resistance) that can be replaced by harvest (Fig. 15.3d). Thus, depending on which welfare factors become limiting, environmental resistance consists of some combination of (1) decreased reproduction, (2) increased mortality not replaceable by harvest (such as juvenile mortality), and (3) increased mortality replaceable by harvest (such as winter mortality that usually occurs after the harvest season). If environmental resistance consists entirely of the first two categories above, maximum annual harvestable surplus occurs at the point of inflection, and Fig. 15.1*b* illustrates the relation between this surplus and population abundance. Annual surplus is entirely the potential annual population increase. As replaceable mortality becomes a more important component of environmental resistance, the point of maximum annual harvestable surplus moves up the sigmoid curve from the inflection point.

The model thus demonstrates that maximum harvestable surplus is unlikely to

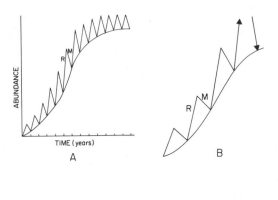

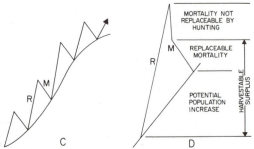

Fig. 15.3 Harvestable surplus in relation to the sigmoid model for a population having one season of reproduction per year. (*A*) Population growth over time showing annual reproduction (*R*) and mortality (*M*); (*B*) segment of the model for a population in which environmental resistance primarily involves density-dependent *M*: (*C*) segment of the model in which environmental resistance primarily involves density-dependent *R*: (*D*) components of harvestable surplus in terms of annual *R* and *M* and potential population increase.

occur when there is a maximum year-round abundance of animals (the top of the sigmoid curve). Nor does maximum surplus occur when population quality, including rates of reproduction, and habitat condition (Fig. 15.1d and 15.1e) are maximum, which would occur far to the left in Fig. 15.1a. Maximum annual harvestable surplus occurs at or somewhat above the point of inflection in the sigmoid model, depending on the nature of environmental resistance.

The sigmoid model has great generality. It incorporates a large variety of information and, therefore, can be used to explain the dynamics of diverse populations in different habitats. The model permits environmental resistance to vary in that any combination of welfare factors may be limiting. If space is considered as a welfare factor so that lack of space may produce environmental resistance, the model applies to intrinsic as well as extrinsic population control. The model incorporates not only the dynamics of a population but the effects on its habitat as well.

However, the model cannot be applied directly to explain the dynamics of real populations because these populations do not exist in stable environments. As a result, the carrying capacity of a population's habitat is constantly changing. Whereas a population cannot be above carrying capacity in the sigmoid model, this can happen to real populations in two ways. First, the carrying capacity of a habitat may be abruptly lowered by severe weather or by human activities that temporarily or permanently restrict production and/or availability of welfare factors. Second, a growing population may temporarily exceed carrying capacity and continue to cause a decline in habitat condition until the population ultimately declines as well. In real populations, the ultimate declines have often been associated with severe weather (Example 15.1), confounding the evidence for causes of exceeding carrying capacity. These populations appear to have caused the carrying capacities of their habitats to decline by their persistent damaging use of food welfare factors.

Since real populations do not exist in stable environments, none achieve the perfect stability indicated by the sigmoid model. All fluctuate, slightly or very greatly, about a constantly changing carrying capacity. There has been a tendency to report histories of populations that have exhibited large fluctuations; however, most populations of wildlife are comparatively stable.

If we use increasing ecological density as the independent variable (horizontal axis) in the sigmoid model, the submodels become those illustrated in Figure 15.4. These permit a population to be above carrying capacity and to decline in response to this high extreme of ecological density. Figure 15.4 explains the fluctuations of real populations about variable carrying capacities. We would predict from the model that a population at a high ecological density will face high environmental resistance, manifested in low reproduction and/or high mortality rates; that it would be a population of low quality; that its habitat would show signs of overuse; that the population would produce few if any animals for harvest or for population increase; and that the population would decline. For a population at low ecological density, we would make opposite predictions.

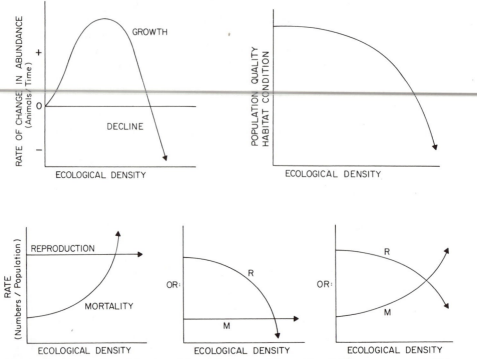

Fig. 15.4   Adaptation of the sigmoid population model used in wildlife management. This adaptation permits a population to be above "carrying capacity" and permits mortality to exceed reproduction.

The sigmoid model is, thus, a major basis for predictions in wildlife management. We predict the population and habitat consequences of changes in population size (resulting from change in harvest strategy, losses due to toxic chemicals, etc.) and of changes in carrying capacity (caused by habitat improvement or destruction, variation in weather, etc.) by considering their effects on ecological density. Furthermore, we use parameters in Fig. 15.4 as indicators of ecological density. For instance, if a population contains poor quality animals, we predict the conditions of the remaining parameters in Fig. 15.4 are also those associated with high ecological density.

EXAMPLE 15.1   The Introduction and Increase of Reindeer on St. Matthew Island (Klein 1968)

A few examples in wildlife literature illustrate early phases of the sigmoid population model. In these examples, some assumptions of the model were fulfilled in that populations were introduced into suitable, unoccupied, and limited environments. The environments, however, were not stable. Reports of the introduction and increase of reindeer on St. Matthew Island in the Bering Sea illustrate biotic potential, density-dependent environmental resistance, and changes in population quality and habitat condition.

Twenty-nine reindeer were introduced onto St. Matthew Island in 1944. Previous to this, the island's only terrestrial herbivore appears to have been one species of vole. Reindeer abundance increased rapidly, making use of an abundant, nutritious, previously unused forage resource that was, however, not very diverse in species composition. The principle foods were lichens and willows. By 1957, 13 years after introduction, the herd numbered about 1350 animals. The average population increase had been about 34 percent per year. Although this average is well below the biotic potential of reindeer, it is a rapid rate of population increase for wild ungulates. During this period, the rate of reproduction was presumably high and predation was absent, as there were no large predators on the island. About 80 reindeer had been harvested by hunting, and a few were collected for study in 1957.

The herd increased to 6000 reindeer by 1963, 19 years after introduction. Average population growth in the intervening 6 years had declined to 28 percent per year, still an impressive rate of gain. A second collection of animals in 1963 indicated increasing environmental resistance since 1957. Reproduction rates and average body size had declined (Table 15.1). Although sample sizes were small, 20 percent of 15 collected animals exhibited lungworm infestations in 1963, whereas none of 12 animals had shown the disease in 1957. Vegetation on wintering areas showed the effect of heavy use in 1957. Lichens had been seriously depleted through grazing and trampling and by 1963 were almost completely eliminated from some areas. Whereas ungrazed lichens may average 10 cm deep, lichens on winter ranges in 1963 were seldom over 1 cm deep. Less palatable grasses and sedges were replacing lichens. By 1963, willows had begun to show deterioration from browsing. These trends in the rate of population growth, reproduction, population quality and habitat condition are similar to those illustrated in Fig. 15.1b to 15.1e.

TABLE 15.1   Population Dynamics of Reindeer on St. Matthew Island (Klein 1968)

	1957	1963
Number years post introduction	13	19
Population estimate	1350	6000
Recent rate of increase (%)[a]	34	28
Reproductive success		
Fawns per 100 adult females	75	60
Yearlings per 100 adult females	45	26
Population quality: body weight (kg)		
Yearling males	103	68
Yearling females	90	68
Adult males	183	128
Adult females	112	79
Population quality: body length (m)		
Yearling males	1.58	1.44
Yearling females	1.58	1.49
Adult males	2.02	1.70
Adult females	1.74	1.62

[a]Average rates of increase for 1944 to 1957 and 1957 to 1963, respectively.

Food resources on St. Matthew could not sustain such numbers of reindeer, and the population crashed in the severe winter of 1963–64. Only 42 of 6000 animals survived. The population crash, of course, deviates from the classic sigmoid model, partly because a severe winter violated the model's assumption of a stable environment. The population decline is consistent with results of increasing ecological density illustrated in Fig. 15.4. The abruptness of the population decline, however, requires further explanation, given later in this chapter.

EXAMPLE 15.2.   The Introduction, Increase, and Decline of Thar in New Zealand (Caughley 1970)

Caughley measured population and habitat trends associated with the introduction, eruption, leveling off, and decline of thar—goatlike bovids—in New Zealand. The population eruption spread from the point of introduction as the geographic range of thar expanded. Thus, thar populations were already declining near the point of introduction at the same time that they were newly increasing at the spreading edge of their range. Caughley observed an increasing population in the Rangitata area, at range edge, and a declining population in the Dobson area, near the point of introduction. He also observed a population that had increased but was leveling off in the Godley area between the other two areas. Differences from Rangitata to Godley to Dobson illustrate population and habitat trends during an eruption and subsequent decline. They also illustrate concepts in the adaptation of the sigmoid population model shown in Fig. 15.4.

Although the density of the declining thar population at Dobson was lower than the density of the predecline population at Godley (Fig. 15.5), ecological density appears to have been higher at Dobson (Table 15.2). As a result, population growth and decline, rates of reproduction and mortality, population quality, and habitat condition showed expected (from Fig. 15.4) relationships to ecological density (Fig. 15.5). In the habitat, herbs greater than 30 cm tall, especially tussock grasses, responded to grazing as decreasers, whereas *Poa* responded as an increaser, in the manner described in Chapter 13.

It is worthy of note that the first obvious signs of high ecological density and impending population decline (derived by comparing data from Godley and Rangitata) would have been: a decline in the kidney fat index for females in summer (31 percent); a decline in pregnancy rates for two-year-olds (60 percent); an increase in mortality of juveniles (43 percent); and marked changes in vegetation. Compared to these changes, reproduction by adults and total reproduction, the latter indicated by age ratios, were not as sensitive to early changes in ecological density. Furthermore, age ratios showed only a small decline between the increasing (Rangitata) and decreasing (Dobson) populations. Obviously, all population and habitat parameters would not have been equally sensitive indicators of trends in ecological density or in population size.

STABILITY OF POPULATIONS

Populations may exhibit great variation in abundance or they may exhibit comparative stability. Highly variable abundance can result from a highly variable

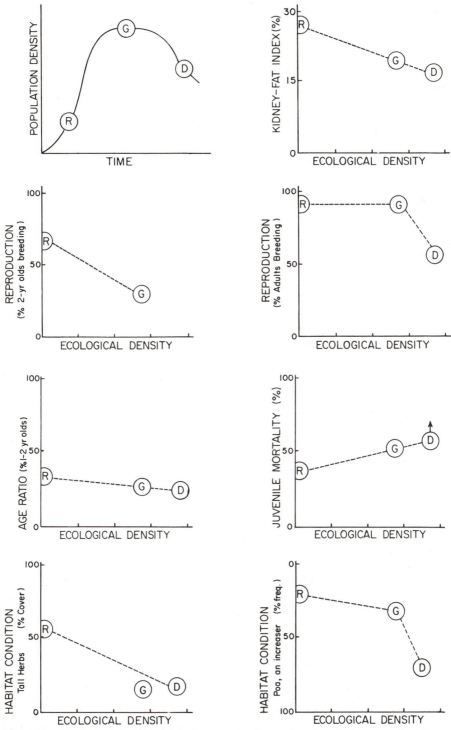

Fig. 15.5 Ecological-density dependent mechanisms related to the increase, leveling and decline of thar populations in New Zealand. Data from Caughley 1970 and Table 15.2. Dashed lines show simplistic trends based on the sigmoid population model.

TABLE 15.2   Summary of Data Extracted from Caughley (1970) Illustrating Population
and Habitat Dynamics During Initial Increase, Leveling, and Decline of an Introduced
Thar Population in New Zealand[a]

Area	Rangitata	Godley	Dobson
Population trend	Increasing	Level	Declining
Population density index (A)	22	100	65
Winter food index (B)	100	18	9
Ecological density index (A/B)	0.2	5.6	7.2
Kidney-fat index ($\female$)	27.0	18.5	17.1
Reproduction			
Percent 2-year-olds breeding	67	27	—
Percent older $\female$s breeding	90	90	75
Age ratio: percent 1- and 2-year-olds ($\female$s)	34	31	29
Mortality: percent ($\female$ juveniles)	37	53	>59
Habitat			
Herbs[b] > 30 cm tall (% cover)	59	16	22
Poa, a short grass (% frequency)	19	29	66

[a]Caughley's data for a fourth area, Hooker, are omitted. Results from this area are less
consistent with concepts of the sigmoid model. However, they are not a strong objection
to the model in that sample sizes for this area were small and because the winter food index
does not include the amount of available browse. Indices to population density and winter
food were obtained from Caughley's Fig. 5. From *Ecology,* Copyright© by the Ecological
Society of America. Reprinted by permission.
[b]Herbs equal grasses and forbs. Caughley apparently used *herbs* as synonymous with
forbs.

environment in which carrying capacity varies greatly because of large changes
in supplies of and requirements for limiting welfare factors. However, some
populations attain comparative stability even in variable environments. Population stability is a function of (1) environmental variability, (2) intrinsic mechanisms of population control, (3) a species' biotic potential, (4) environmental
complexity, and (5) persistence of population and environmental characteristics.
The variability of environmental factors is discussed in earlier chapters. Intrinsic
population control is discussed in Chapter 10. The relationships of population
stability to biotic potential, environmental complexity, and persistence of population and environmental characteristics are discussed here.

Stability and Biotic Potential

Species with high biotic potential are capable of a rapid increase of population in
response to habitat changes that lower ecological density. Similarly, they decline

rapidly in response to increased ecological density. Rapid population response occurs because comparatively small changes in either reproduction rates or mortality rates cause comparatively large changes in abundance for species with high biotic potential. This relationship is best clarified by presenting a few simple life tables.

First, we consider the effect of a small change in mortality rate upon abundance in a species with high biotic potential.

1 Assume there are two pair of quail   =   4 birds.
2 If each female hatches 14 eggs (+28)   =   32 birds,
   the population is now 88 percent juveniles.
3 In a stable population, mortality is (−28)   =   4 birds.
   The mortalilty rate is 88 percent.

If environmental change results in a small (7 percent) decrease in mortality, 2 of the 28 birds would survive (2/28 = 7 percent). The effect on abundance is comparatively large.

1 Start with same two pair of quail   =   4 birds
2 and the same reproduction (+28)   =   32 birds.
3 Mortality is now 81 percent (−26)   =   6 birds.

A small change in mortality rate (7 percent) has resulted in a large change in population size (+50 percent). A 7 percent change in reproduction rate would have caused the same result.

Now we consider the effect of a similar small change in mortality rate on abundance in a species having low biotic potential.

1 Assume there are eight pair of deer   =   16 deer.
2 If females average 1.5 fawns (+12)   =   28 deer,
   the population is now 43 percent juveniles.
3 In a stable population, mortality is (−12)   =   16 deer.
   The mortality rate is 43 percent.

If environmental change results in a small (8 percent) decrease in mortality, 1 of the 12 lost deer would survive (1/12 = 8 percent). The effect on abundance is comparatively small.

1 Start with same eight pair of deer   =   16 deer
2 and the same reproduction (+12)   =   28 deer.
3 Mortality is now 39 percent (−11)   =   17 deer.

A small change in mortality rate (8 percent) has resulted in a small change in population size (+6 percent). If we had reduced mortality by 16 percent (2 more survivors out of 12), the population would have increased by only 12 percent. Corresponding changes in reproduction rates would have produced the same changes in abundance.

Thus, the abundance of a species with high biotic potential responds very quickly to environmental changes that influence either reproduction or mortality. These species may exhibit large year-to-year changes in abundance in a variable environment. Some are characteristically eruptive (Chapt. 17).

Because of this sensitivity to environmental change, species with high biotic potential do not usually "get out of balance" with their habitat for long and seldom seriously overuse and damage their welfare factors. In contrast, species with low biotic potential have become famous in the literature on population dynamics for the many populations that have seriously depleted their habitat (cf. Leopold 1943; Leopold et al. 1947). In these populations, abundance has responded slowly to high ecological density, permitting the population to remain at high ecological density for several years and allowing it to persist in overusing and depleting its welfare factors.

These life tables also illustrate that species with high biotic potentials exhibit high rates of population turnover (the rate at which animals are replaced in the population) and high age ratios (juveniles to adults). Steen observed important management implications of biotic potential for small game animals (1944). He described population turnover by noting that a large majority of small game harvested each autumn are the young of the year. (In cottontails, it is common for 80 to 85 percent of the harvested rabbits to be juveniles.) As a result, the determinants of harvestable surplus in small animals are largely the reproductive success and survival in the spring and summer just before harvest. Over-winter survival from the preceding year is often of little or no importance. Steen admonished management agencies for emphasizing study and management of over-winter survival of small game. A census of spring-breeding density cannot be used alone to predict autumn abundance. Improvement of winter habitat might increase spring-breeding densities but is likely to have little effect on hunting-season populations. Research aimed at the winter season will not provide the information most needed by management. Steen suggested more emphasis on census, management, and research during spring and summer when almost all of the harvestable population was being produced. The implications of biotic potential for population dynamics and management are summarized in Table 15.3.

Stability and Environmental Complexity

In the sigmoid model, gradual approach of population size to carrying capacity (Fig. 15.1a) depends on a gradual increase in environmental resistance resulting in gradual changes in reproduction and/or mortality rates (Fig. 15.1c). The

TABLE 15.3   Some Management and Population-dynamics Aspects of Biotic Potential (BP)

	Species with High BP	Species with Low BP
Examples	Small game	Big game
Longevity	Short	Long
Mortality rate	High	Low
Population turnover rate	Fast	Slow
Age ratio (young:old)	High	Low
Importance of each year's reproduction to havestable surpluses	High	Lower
Response to environmental change such as management	Fast	Slower
Probability of remaining "out of balance" with carrying capacity and depleting welfare factors[a]	Low	High
Rate of return to "normal" density after population decimation in good habitat	Fast	Slower

[a]Probability of attaining and holding levels of abundance that cause depletion of welfare factors is also a function of intrinsic population control and of environmental complexity.

growth rate of the population is very sensitive to density because even small changes in population size result in effective changes in reproduction and/or mortality. This is the mechanism by which perfect population stability is produced in the model.

In contrast, population instability is enhanced if small deviations of the population from carrying capacity (changes in ecological density) cause comparatively large variation in reproduction and/or mortality rates. Ecological-density dependent reproduction and mortality are the mechanisms that balance populations with carrying capacity. These mechanisms may be precise, that is, they may produce just the right amount of change in reproduction and/or mortality to establish balance with carrying capacity quickly after each change in ecological density (Fig. 15.6a). However, these mechanisms might be imprecise, producing changes in reproduction and mortality that are too large or too small to quickly establish balance with carrying capacity following change in ecological density. If ecological-density dependent mechanisms are imprecise, we expect a highly variable population size, a population that is frequently out of balance (at quite high or quite low ecological density) and a population exhibiting *overcompensation* in its responses to changing carrying capacity. Imprecision in responses of reproduction and mortality to ecological density was exhibited by reindeer on St. Matthew Island (Example 15.1). The responses were inadequate to slow the exponential population growth until a threshold was reached when mortality suddenly increased to cause population decline. This pattern is similar to that in Fig. 15.6b. The reindeer herd grew rapidly to point X until a severe winter suddenly increased ecological density to point Y, where mortality increased greatly and the population collapsed.

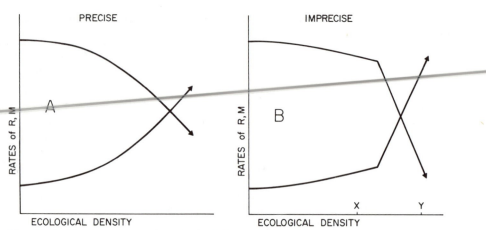

Fig. 15.6 Two patterns of ecological-density dependent responses of rates of reproduction and mortality. X and Y are discussed in the text.

Such imprecise response of reproduction and mortality is due to a scarcity of ecological-density dependent factors affecting the population and is expected in simple environments. These environments lack a diversity of both decimating and welfare factors that can respond to ecological density. Such was the case on St. Matthew Island. The reindeer on St. Matthew had experienced some decline in condition before the population crash of 1964. This was indicated by the reindeer's declining reproduction and decreasing average body size. Animals in declining physical condition should have become more susceptible to predation and disease. However, large predators were absent from the island. Further, most disease species may not have been present or abundant on the island because of its harsh environment and lack of cervid hosts before 1944. As a result, mortality rates did not increase appropriately with increasing ecological density, and rapid population growth continued.

There was a low diversity of food welfare factors on St. Matthew. All plants were low growing, few exceeding 30 cm in height. An emergency forage supply was not available when snow was deep in the winter of 1963–64. Forage supplies changed from adequate to sustain most of the population in the comparatively mild winter of 1962–63 to inadequate to prevent starvation of most of the population the next year. There was an abrupt change in starvation rate.

In contrast to the situation on St. Matthew Island, we expect a diversity of welfare factors to produce more gradual changes in reproduction and mortality rates as ecological density varies. With a diversity of welfare factors, animals respond to change in ecological density by shifting use among more preferred and less preferred food and cover resources. Preferred resources support higher rates of reproduction and survival; less preferred resources result in lowered rates because preferences are correlated with food and cover qualities. A preference (quality) gradient of many food and cover resources thus produces gradients of reproduction and mortalilty rates, as illustrated in Fig. 15.6*a*, when animals are forced to shift use among these resources.

This is not a new concept. Most ecology texts propose that populations tend to be more stable in complex environments that provide an abundance of intercompensating and density-dependent mechanisms to control populations. The discussion here connects this concept to the sigmoid population model.

Stability and Time Lags in Ecological-density Dependence

Population stability can be influenced if rates of reproduction and/or mortality respond comparatively slowly to changes in ecological density, producing deviations from the rates in Fig. 15.6*a*. Slow responses of reproduction and mortality can result from population and/or environmental characteristics that persist from year to year or from generation to generation, despite changes in ecological density.

Suppose a population experiences a change from low to high ecological density. If population and environmental characteristics developed during the period of low ecological density should persist, the animals may be better fit to withstand the problems of high ecological density. Welfare factors may not decline (through excessive use) immediately, and decimating factors may not increase immediately. As a result, rates of reproduction and survival would temporarily remain higher than expected as ecological density increases. This would allow further increase in ecological density.

Conversely, if the effects of high ecological density persist, debilitating the animals and prolonging an inhospitable environment, a change to low ecological density will result in rates of reproduction and survival that are temporarily lower than expected. Deviations from expected rates will persist as long as the carry-over effects last, producing a time-lag in population response to lowered ecological density.

Persistence of Population Characteristics   The literature suggests three types of such carryover in populations. These are (1) the age structure of the population, (2) the physical and physiological conditions of the animals, and (3) the genetic constitution of the population.

The age structure of a population reflects recent rates of reproduction and mortality. A population at low ecological density is expected to have high rates of reproduction and a young age structure. A preponderance of young animals favors continuing high rates of reproduction and survival, even with increasing ecological density, because prime-age animals are usually more fecund and resistant to mortality. In contrast, a population at high ecological density is expected to have an old age structure, and this preponderance of old animals may favor continuing low rates of reproduction and survival despite a change to lower ecological density.

Likewise, the physical conditions of animals tend to reflect their recent ecological density. Body size and energy reserves may be large or small, depending on recent conditions, and may modify an animal's ability to respond to changing ecological density. Larger animals can forage more effectively and can counter predation with more effective escape or defense. Large energy reserves can permit animals to withstand a temporary change to increased ecological density. These factors would delay responses of reproduction and mortality to increasing ecological density. Opposite trends can occur with a change from high to low ecological density.

Christian and LeMunyan, and Herrenkohl suggested that stress due to crowding of parent rodents can cause impairment of reproduction and growth in one or two succeeding uncrowded generations (1958; 1979). They believed that physiological effects in the general adaptation syndrome were transferred during embryonic life.

The persistence of genotypes despite changes in ecological density has also been suggested. A population existing at some level of ecological density for several breeding periods can accumulate genotypes of animals adapted to that level of ecological density. The persistence of these animals can delay ecological-density dependent responses of the population during a change to a new level of ecological density. Time lags in ecological-density dependence due to persistence of genotypes have been suggested in rodents (Chitty 1960; 1967; Krebs et al. 1973) and grouse (Bergerud 1970; Henderson 1977) but may also occur in longer-lived species. Consider the selective forces affecting thar populations during the eruption phase compared to selection during the decline phase (Example 15.2). During the eruption, ecological density was low. Forage supplies were abundant. Genotypes prone to dispersing into new areas with abundant forage and prone to abundant reproduction beginning early in life would tend to accumulate in the population. This has come to be known as r-selection, r referring to the rapid rate of population increase at low ecological densities (Krebs et al. 1973; MacArthur and Wilson 1967). During the decline of thar populations, ecological density was high. Forage supplies were depleted, and all available habitats were occupied by thar. Genotypes prone to a maintenance existence, rather than an expansion existence, would be favored by natural selection. There would be no advantage in dispersal. Animals capable of using forages of mediocre quality and of maximizing digestive and metabolic efficiency and energy storage would be favored. Selection would also favor animals limiting reproduction to more favorable years when chances of producing a viable offspring are greatest. Likewise, animals with behavioral means for limiting competition, such as dominance hierarchies, would be favored. This pattern is known as K-selection, K referring to carrying capacity and the upper asymptote in the sigmoid model. There apparently is no evidence that these changes did occur in the genetics of thar populations in New Zealand. But, theoretically, such changes, however small, should have occurred.

The population genetics of wild populations of large, long-lived animals have been difficult to study. Isolation of the genotypic and phenotypic effects of ecological density has been especially difficult. Genetics has, as yet, found little application in wildlife management. Yet genetic variability and natural selection are basic principles of biology and one day may account for some of the currently unexplained variation in abundance of wildlife populations.

Persistence of Environmental Characteristics The persistence of environmental characteristics can also produce time lags in ecological-density dependent reproduction and survival. Consider a population at high ecological density. Its abundance and vulnerability may attract and support an abundance of predators and may support an abundance of disease organisms. The population may also overuse and damage limiting food and/or cover resources. Assume the population begins to decline in response to these and other ecological-density dependent mechanisms. With precise ecological-density dependence, as in Fig. 15.6a, the rates of predation and disease losses would quickly decrease, slowing the rate of population decline. Further, overuse of food and/or cover resources would decrease with population decline and resulting improvement in food, and cover conditions would likewise slow population decline. In contrast, if predators and disease organisms persist in abundance as the population begins to decline, rates of mortality due to these factors may not be density dependent and would favor continued population decline so long as high levels of predation and disease persist. Keith has suggested that a persistent high population of predators may kill an *increasing* proportion of animals from a declining prey population (1974). This is *inverse* density dependence. Furthermore, if damage to food and cover resources tends to persist after overuse has ceased because of population decline, there will be a time lag before habitat improvement may contribute to slowing the rate of population decline.

The persistence of environmental characteristics during population decline has been documented. Keith presented data showing persistence of predator populations for a few years after each cyclic decline of snowshoe hare populations (1963). He also indicated that damage to plants producing winter browse tends to persist for one to two years after the passage of high populations of hares (1974). Ungulates, especially artificially supported and protected domestic ungulates, are capable of damaging soil and forage resources so severely that recovery may require decades.

Environmental characteristics resulting from low ecological density also may persist temporarily despite an increasing population. Compared to predators, most prey species have high biotic potentials. Although predator abundance may increase in respone to an increasing supply of prey, predators cannot increase as rapidly as can prey numbers. Thus, the ratio of predator numbers to prey numbers may decline until other ecological-density dependent factors slow the rate of prey increase. Likewise, excellent habitat conditions resulting from low ecological density may tend to presist, despite an increasing wildlife population, until ecological density has remained at a high level for a time necessary to initiate habitat decline.

Persistence and Population Stability   The persistence of population and environmental characteristics favors population stability in long-lived species during short-term changes in ecological density. A population and environment that respond slowly to change in ecological density will tend to maintain themselves through the temporary change. Thus, a healthy deer population with a preponderance of young animals in a habitat with abundant emergency foods might withstand one unusually severe winter without much change in population abundance or characteristics.

The persistence of population and environmental characteristics favors instability in long-lived species during long-term changes in ecological density. Consider a deer population that is increasing from a low level of ecological density. If favorable population and environmental characteristics acquired at low ecological density persist for several years, rates of reproduction and survival will not decline appropriately as ecological density increases. The population can, therefore, reach a higher level of abundance because of persisting favorable characteristics. At this level the deer can cause inordinate damage to limiting welfare factors, especially foods. The result is an inordinately high ecological density. This condition has been termed *overshooting carrying capacity*. When reproduction and survival rates eventually decline, they are responding to this inordinate level of ecological density, and the population experiences an abrupt and large decline. The contrasting possibility is that a herd with persisting unfavorable population and environmental characteristics will not respond quickly to lowered ecological density, allowing habitat condition to improve, further lowering ecological density. This eventually permits an abrupt and large population increase.

Persistence of population and environmental characteristics also favors population instability in short-lived species. These species, with high biotic potential, tend to respond quickly to changes in ecological density, as already discussed. However, several studies of small-game species suggest a population "inertia" counteracting the effects related to biotic potential (Keith 1974; Wagner et al. 1965; Bailey 1968). Increasing populations of grouse, hares, pheasants, and rabbits have tended to continue increasing for several consecutive years; or they have tended to remain above their long-term average abundance for several consecutive years. When populations have declined, they have declined or remained below their average abundance for several consecutive years. Biologists have not been able to detect patterns of habitat change or weather to account for these effects. Therefore, the population inertia does not appear to be due to consecutive years of low ecological density favoring reproduction and survival followed by consecutive years of high ecological density causing reproductive failure and mortality. Wagner et al. suggested that characteristics persisting within populations could account for such inertia in rates of reproduction and mortality (1965). Keith suggested persisting environmental characteristics, namely, forage abundance and predator-prey ratios (1974). Thus, a growing small-game population can continue growing despite increasing ecological density, until favorable characteristics no longer persist, allowing reproduction and mortality to respond to high ecological density. Populations of grouse, hares, pheasants, and rabbits have been unstable in the long term, oscillating between periods of abundance and scarcity. Some are cyclic populations. Although this discussion indicates that persistence of population and environmental characteristics can account for such oscillating population abundance, these populations are far from fully understood (see Chapter 17).

PRINCIPLES

P15.1   The sigmoid or logistic model is the most widely accepted and used principle of wildlife population dynamics. The model predicts changes in population productivity, rates of reproduction and mortality, population quality, and habitat condition that occur as a population grows toward a stable carrying capacity. However, the model's assumption of a stable carrying capacity is unrealistic. Therefore, an adaptation of the model in which population processes are determined by ecological density, rather than by density of the population, is necessary for using the model in analyzing populations and in predicting impacts of changes in population or habitat parameters.

P15.2   The sigmoid model demonstrates that wildlife populations, as other organic resources, can be managed on a sustained-yield basis. When a population is habitat limited and environmental resistance is ecological-density dependent, as in the adaptation of the sigmoid model, maximum harvestable surpluses are produced by maintaining the population at an intermediate level of ecological density. This level of population size is below the maximum, sustainable population. At this level, animal quality and habitat condition are at intermediate, rather than maximum attainable, levels.

P15.3   Species with high biotic potentials have high rates of population turnover. Harvestable surpluses for these populations tend to be determined, not by the number of breeders at the start of each breeding season, but by rates of reproduction and survival of juveniles during the season immediately preceding harvest. Species with low biotic potentials exhibit low rates of population turnover. The numbers of breeders present at the start of each breeding season are more important in determining harvestable surpluses for these species.

P15.4   The stability of a wildlife population is supported by (1) existence in a relatively stable environment, (2) any intrinsic mechanisms of population control, (3) a low biotic potential and high longevity of animals, (4) existence in a diverse environment, which generates precise ecological-density dependent reproduction and mortality, and (5) a lack of time lags in density dependence. Time lags in density dependence are due to population and environmental characteristics that respond slowly to changes in ecological density. Such persisting population characteristics are population age structure, the physical and physiological conditions of animals, and the genetic constitution of the population. Persisting environmental characteristics are habitat conditions and the prevalence of predators and disease organisms.

CHAPTER   **16**

CARRYING CAPACITY

I differentiate the two kinds of carrying
capacity by calling the range manager's
version 'economic carrying capacity,' and
the unharvested equilibrium 'ecological
carrying capacity.' Although I know what a
range manager means when he declares a range
overpopulated, I am less certain what a
wildlife manager means. He may be using the
term in either sense.

Graeme Caughley

DEFINITION
APPLICATION OF THE
CONCEPT

VARIATION OF CARRYING
CAPACITY
PRINCIPLES

Perhaps no term in wildlife biology has been used more variously than has *carrying capacity* (Edwards and Fowle 1955). The term apparently was adopted from range management. Range managers usually consider carrying capacity as a measure of land productivity, namely, its *capacity* to support (*carry*) animals. More precisely, range managers usually define carrying capacity as the number of livestock the land can support while providing maximum sustained production (Stoddart et al. 1955; p. 183). This definition recognizes that land resources may support many unproductive animals or fewer, more productive animals. It, thus, recognizes concepts of the sigmoid population model (Figs. 15.1 and 15.4).

The land's capacity to support animals is determined by limiting welfare factors (Chapter 12). In practice, range managers have emphasized forage as the major, often only, factor limiting range carrying capacity. Other welfare factors often have not been considered. Stocking rates above carrying capacity due to variation in numbers of animals or to variation in forage production have been detected largly by observing the effects of animals on forage condition (Sampson 1952, pp. 359–376). This emphasis on forage as the major limiting factor is often justified in livestock production because (1) forage is an especially important welfare factor for most ungulate populations, (2) livestock are often provided with water, and (3) livestock are often protected from decimating factors by control of predators and diseases, by artificial shelters, and by forced movement in response to weather. Water and cover are, therefore, not often important limiting factors. Wildlife managers, on the other hand, must recognize a potential diversity of limiting welfare factors, including cover.

As the term carrying capacity was adopted by wildlife management, confusion over its meaning developed for three reasons. First, wildlife managers were responsible for recognizing not only maximum sustained production of animals, but other goals as well. Their definition of carrying capacity had to recognize the land's ability to support animals for a diversity of purposes. However, wildlife managers have retained the range-management concept that a population at carrying capacity will not cause progressive, continuing damage to its habitat so that the land's ability to sustain the achievement of goals is not progressively reduced.

Second, wildlife managers had a greater concern for decimating factors than did range managers. Thus, whereas some wildlife biologists retain the range-management concept that carrying capacity is a characteristic of a habitat and is determined by limiting welfare factors, other biologists consider carrying capacity to be a characteristic of an ecosystem determined by welfare *and* decimating factors. In the latter view, an abundance of predators may lower carrying capacity for a prey population by removing animals and controlling population size. In the first view, predation *may* depress a prey population to levels *below* the carrying capacity of the habitat. However, if the predation can be alleviated by improved cover and interspersion, the prey population is not depressed. It is at a carrying capacity determined by limiting factors of cover and interspersion. I

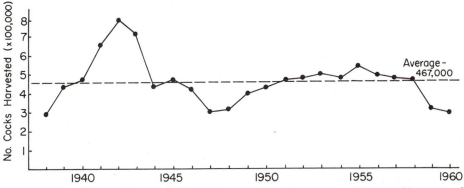

Fig. 16.1 Variation in abundance of Wisconsin pheasants estimated by annual harvests of cocks. From Wagner et al. 1965. Deviations from long-term average abundance are considered due to variation in carrying capacity and to deviations of abundance from carrying capacity. Courtesy Wisconsin Department of Natural Resources.

prefer the first view and retain the concept that carrying capacity is a habitat characteristic determined by limiting welfare factors.

A third source of confusion over the term results from differences of opinion as to the variableness of carrying capacity. In a series of estimates from a relatively stable population (such as in Fig. 16.1), there are annual deviations of abundance about a long-term mean. This long-term mean abundance is sometimes referred to as carrying capacity. In this view, deviations of the population from mean abundance are deviations *from* carrying capacity. They are often ascribed to the effects of weather. The emphasis is on weather that directly affects animals, influencing rates of reproduction and mortality. It is implied that food and cover resources do not vary among years. An alternative view is that deviations of the population from long-term mean abundance are partly, perhaps largely, due to variation *of* carrying capacity. The effects of weather are again considered important. But the emphasis is on the effects of weather in changing supplies of and requirements for welfare factors. In this alternative view, fluctuations in population abundance are due to variation in carrying capacity *and* to deviations from carrying capacity resulting from time lags and imprecision in ecological-density dependent mechanisms of population control (discussed in Chapter 15 under Stability of Populations).

In the extreme of this alternative view, carrying capacity varies constantly as many factors alter supplies of and requirements for limiting welfare factors. The population is seldom *at* carrying capacity, being almost always somewhat above or below carrying capacity. Deviations from carrying capacity produce a continuum of ecological densities. The effects of ecological density are integrated over time to produce responses in the population and habitat indicated in Fig. 15.4. I prefer this alternative view of a variable carrying capacity.

DEFINITION

A suitable definition of carrying capacity should, therefore, include the following concepts. Carrying capacity is a property of habitat. It is determined by limiting welfare factors. Any combination of welfare factors can be limiting. Carrying capacity varies as supplies of, and animal requirements for, welfare factors vary. Carrying capacity is the ability of the habitat to support a number of animals, the quality and productivity of the animals being defined according to management goals. Although habitat conditions may be influenced by the number of animals, it is implied that a population at carrying capacity will not cause progressive, continuing destruction of habitat such that management goals cannot be sustained. Management goals may relate as much to habitat conditions as to conditions of the animals.

Therefore, carrying capacity is the number of animals of a specified quality that a habitat can support while sustaining a specified, but not progressively increasing, level of impact on habitat resources. If management's goals do not specify the quality of the animals or the condition of the habitat, carrying capacity is simply the number of animals the habitat can sustain.

APPLICATION OF THE CONCEPT

Among various wildlife populations and habitats, carrying capacities will be determined by differing sets of limiting factors and can be related to a variety of management goals. No one set of population and habitat conditions will characterize carrying capacity for all types of populations. Dasmann described four types of carrying capacity (1964a). Caughley also differentiated types of carrying capacity (1979). I have found their approaches instructive. The following discussion combines their ideas and borrows their terminologies.

Economic Carrying Capacity

Sometimes management goals are a primary basis for defining carrying capacity. Two such examples are maximum harvest density and minimum-impact density.

Maximum-harvest Density   This concept is usually applied to ungulates. It is the number of animals a habitat will support while producing a maximum sustained harvestable surplus. In terms of the sigmoid model (Fig. 16.2), the population is at or somewhat above the inflection point, as discussed in Chapter 15. The population must be maintained at this level of abundance by harvest. Therefore, no lack of welfare factors prohibits growth of this population. However, a lack of welfare factors may limit productivity of the population; that is, a greater average annual harvestable surplus might be realized if some welfare factor, such as food quality or escape cover, were improved.

At maximum-harvest density, population quality will be very good, though probably not the very best possible. Note in Chapter 9 that some decline in animal condition, particularly in rates or reproduction, can be compensated by increased numbers of animals. Likewise, habitat condition will be good, though not without signs of use and perhaps retrogressed vegetation, especially locally in areas that attract animals and temporarily in years of poor vegetative production or unusual concentration of animals. A botanist might be very unhappy with the results of maximum-harvest density.

The young age structure and high rate of turnover characteristic of populations at maximum-harvest density result in harvest of few large trophy animals. Production of trophy animals may require a population somewhat above maximum-harvest density because some animals, usually males, will be maintained for extra years to achieve trophy size.

Maximum-harvest density is the goal of much wildlife management in the United States. This goal usually requires an annual determination of the number of animals to be harvested, keeping the population from exceeding an optimum size, yet not reducing it so low as to impair total production of young for recruitment into the harvestable-age class. Precise determination of the population size for maximum-harvest density (and of the number to be harvested annually) has been difficult. Many biologists have been attempting to achieve maximum-harvest density by monitoring trends in habitat condition and animal condition, especially reproduction. It has been relatively easy to detect trends indicating population growth far above maximum-harvest density and many big-game herds have been reduced in respone to declining habitat and population conditions. However, trends in habitat and population conditions have not provided a precise basis for achieving maximum-harvest density. When herds have been reduced, biologists have been unsure of how much reduction would be optimum. More precise attainment of maximum-harvest density will require more data and probably will require population modeling with life tables or computer simulations. These population models will be based largely on a

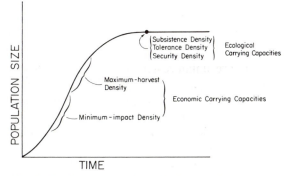

Fig. 16.2   Five types of population regulation in relation to the sigmoid population model.

knowledge of how recruitment responds to variation in population size and to variation in weather and in habitat productivity. This knowledge should be based on local experience and locally collected data because the relationship between recruitment and population size is expected to vary among areas.

Minimum-impact Density   It may be desirable to depress and maintain a wildlife population below maximum-harvest density (Fig. 16.2), minimizing its impact on other wildlife or vegetation without eliminating the population. In this situation management places greater value on the vegetation or on competing or preyed-upon wildlife or livestock than on the population maintained at minimum-impact density. The population may be considered a pest species, one not to be eliminated but to be controlled.

Minimum-impact density is a potential goal for predator populations where predation depresses production of livestock or wildlife. It may be a goal for wild ungulates competing with livestock or with valuable and perhaps less-competitive wildlife. Populations of feral horses and burros on ranges of livestock and game, particularly desert bighorn sheep, are candidates for minimum-impact density.

Minimum-impact density is a very low level of ecological density. Population quality should be very good, perhaps the maximum attainable. Reproduction and resistance to natural mortality will be high, requiring persistent and perhaps abundant harvest of animals to maintain the population at this level. The population's habitat should also be in excellent condition, receiving only minor use from the depressed population.

Although management goals are a primary basis for determining minimum-impact density, limiting habitat resources may also be involved. (Thus this type of carrying capacity, like the other types, is a property of habitat.) The impact of an offending wildlife population on other wildlife, livestock, or vegetation may often be alleviated not only by controlling population size, but also by enhancing alternative habitat resources. This may alter animal distribution or reduce competition and allow the habitat to support the offending population without exceeding an acceptable level of impact on other resources.

Ecological Carrying Capacity

Sometimes populations are unharvested, or normal levels of harvest do not influence population size very much. In these cases carrying capacities are determined only by limiting habitat resources, and it is often useful to distinguish which set of limiting resources is important in determining population size. Three examples of such ecological carrying capacities are subsistence density, tolerance density, and security density.

Subsistence Density   Subsistence density is a term usually applied to ungulate populations. It is the size of an unharvested population limited primarily by forage. In terms of the sigmoid model, subsistence density occurs at the upper asymptote (Fig. 16.2). This is carrying capacity in the model. Subsistence density is the goal for ungulate populations in some large national parks in the United States where the overall objectives are to establish and maintain natural ecosystems, primarily for their recreational, scientific, and educational values (Houston 1971).

At subsistence density, population quality and habitat condition will be comparatively poor because this is the ultimate in ecological density. Reproduction is expected to be low and periodic die-offs will probably occur in years of severe weather. Predation may be an important mortality factor, but subsistence density implies that the primary limitation on reproduction and survival is food. Cole described an elk herd at subsistence density (1972).

We have little experience with ungulate populations at subsistence density in the United States. Almost all our big-game herds are unnatural in that they have been reduced by hunting, their habitats have been greatly altered, and their large predators have been reduced or eliminated. Critics of subsistence density as a management goal have been concerned that progressive deterioration of site productivity, including accelerated erosion, will occur (Beetle 1974). This possibility remains to be demonstrated (Houston 1982; Cayot et al. 1979), but it should not be neglected through lack of research in national parks. Populations at subsistence density will fluctuate in abundance because of weather-caused variation in ecological density. The magnitude of these expected fluctuations is largely unknown. Will there be periodic large population increases followed by massive die-offs that will create much negative public reaction? Or will moderate levels of mortality occur annually without great changes in population size? The persistence of population and environmental characteristics, discussed in Chapter 15, would moderate the amplitudes of short-term changes in abundance. Our inability to answer the above questions emphasizes the need for naturally regulated ungulate populations that permit study that will enhance our understanding of their population dynamics. The resulting knowledge will permit better management of all big-game populations.

Tolerance Density   Tolerance density is the number of animals a habitat will support when intrinsic behavioral and/or physiological mechanisms are dominant in controlling the population. Leopold (1933) and King (1938) termed this conditon *saturation-point density*. In terms of the sigmoid model, tolerance density occurs at the upper asymptote (Fig. 16.2).

Tolerance density is especially important in territorial species. Although space is an important limiting factor, other welfare factors may also be limiting to the extent that there is intraspecific competition for them. Thus, territorial animals protect areas with suitable combinations of foods, cover types, and other resources. However, the habitat may still be improved and support more animals if areas lacking suitable combinations of resources can be improved. Thus, new, suitable spaces are created and can be occupied by the animals.

At tolerance density, all animals may be in good condition or they may be in a hierarchy of condition, with subordinate animals and those not "owning" territories being in poorest condition. These latter animals may have low rates of reproduction and survival (Carrick 1963). Since animals tend to defend resources, there is little or no degradation of limiting welfare factors, and habitat condition is, therefore, good. Populations at tolerance density will produce good harvestable surpluses if there is an abundance of nonterritorial or subordinate animals. Harvest of these animals should have little effect on the productivity of the population. Harvest of territorial or of dominant animals can result in their replacement by others, again with little effect on population productivity.

Security Density   Security density is the number of animals a habitat will support when welfare factors necessary to alleviate predation are limiting. These welfare factors are apt to be escape cover, interspersion, and, for some species, space. If space is a limiting factor, security density is not distinct from tolerance density. This concept of carrying capacity originates from Errington's ideas of a threshold of security for muskrat populations (1945; 1956). In the sigmoid model, security density is at the upper asymptote (Fig. 16.2).

At security density, social intolerance may force some animals out of secure habitat. These animals suffer high predation losses. Reproduction by dominant animals should be high, and these animals should be in good condition. Habitat condition should also be good. Harvestable surplus can be large but there is competition with predation for "excess" animals.

VARIATION OF CARRYING CAPACITY

Carrying capacities depend on environmental factors that vary in space and time. These factors, especially weather, constantly alter the supplies of habitat resources and the requirements of animals for those resources. When explaining population fluctuations or managing the size of a population, a wildlife biologist may have to work with a population that resonds to large variations in carrying capacity. It is, therefore, useful to consider how ecological-density dependent mechanisms of population regulation respond to variation in carrying capacity.

Consider first the implications of sigmoid population theory (Fig. 15.1) for three habitats of relatively low, medium and high carrying capacities. A population introduced into the poorest habitat would grow more slowly and reach carrying capacity at a lower population size than would a population introduced into the best habitat (Fig. 16.3a). Likewise, the expected declines in animal condition, rates of reproduction, and habitat condition would occur with lower density in the poorest habitat (Fig. 16.3b). Lastly, both the rate of population growth and the expected harvestable surplus would be related to population density as indicated in Fig. 16.3c. In poorer habitat, maximum harvestable

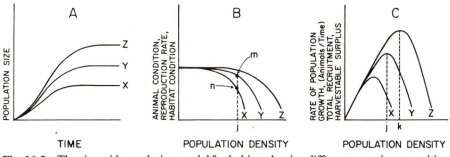

Fig. 16.3 The sigmoid population model for habitats having different carrying capacities: X = poor habitat or year with severe weather; Y = average habitat or an average year; Z = good habitat or a favorable year. See text for further discussion.

surplus would be less and would occur with a lower population density than in better habitat.

The patterns illustrated in Fig. 16.3b and 16.3c may be used in predicting the responses of one population to year-to-year variation in carrying capacity. The density relationships for poor habitat are to be expected whenever the carrying capacity of a given habitat is reduced by severe weather. The relationships for good habitat are to be expected whenever carrying capacity is increased by favorable weather. (However, changes in these relationships may be modified by time lags in density dependence. See Chapter 15.)

The often annual variation of carrying capacity creates special problems for the biologist who intends to manage population size to achieve maximum-harvest density. The relationship of recruitment and of harvestable surplus to density will vary among years with weather-induced fluctuations in carrying capacity. Several years of local data may be needed to illustrate the variation of relationships between recruitment, harvestable surplus, and population size. Weather data may be used as covariants in explaining this variation (Chapter 14). Also, the impacts of variable weather conditions on carrying capacity might be reduced by habitat manipulation. Enhancement of habitat diversity to provide a population with alternative resources for a variety of weather conditions will reduce variation of carrying capacity. However, the wildlife manager may face a complicated decision: Should population size be managed to maximize harvestable surplus in an average year (Fig. 16.3c, point j)? If the year happens to be favorable, harvestable surplus will not be as large as it would be if population size were controlled at point k (Fig. 16.3c). Or, if the population is controlled at j, and the year happens to be severe, the level of use on limiting resources and, therefore, habitat condition will change from point m to point n (Fig. 16.3b). Such an impact on habitat might persist into the following year. These and similar possibilities are very real in wildlife management. Unfortunately, goals for population management are often selected with very little local information on the density relationships illustrated in Fig. 16.3. Management of a variable population in a variable environment will always be difficult. But fewer errors will be made when the consequences of decisions can be predicted with reasonable accuracy. In developing such predictions, there will be no substitute for many years of local data on population and habitat responses to variation in population size and weather conditions.

PRINCIPLES

P16.1   Ecological carrying capacity is a variable habitat characteristic determined by the changeful amounts of welfare factors that limit the size and productivity of a species population. Economic carrying capacity is defined by management goals for population productivity, animal quality, and habitat conditions but is determined by a habitat's variable and limited ability to sustain achievement of these goals. Combining these concepts, carrying capacity is the number of animals of a specified quality that a habitat can support while sustaining a specified, but not progressively increasing, level of impact on habitat resources.

P16.2   Any combination of limiting welfare factors may determine a carrying capacity for a species population. Ecological carrying capacities determined by limiting amounts of forage, of escape cover and interspersion, and of space are termed susbsistence density, security density, and tolerance density, respectively. Economic carrying capacities defined by management goals for population productivity and for population control are termed maximum-harvest density and minimum-impact density, respectively.

P16.3   Since both population size and ecological carrying capacity are variables, populations are often either above or below the carrying capacities of their habitats, and populations fluctuate over a continuum of ecological densities. In the long run, however, population sizes tend to follow trends in ecological carrying capacities because animal quality, rates of reproduction and survival, and habitat condition tend to be ecological-density dependent. When a population is maintained below ecological carrying capacity to maximize harvestable surplus, a precise achievement of this economic goal will depend on understanding the relationship of the population and habitat to variation in population size and variation in carrying capacity of the habitat. Local data will be needed to achieve this understanding.

CHAPTER   17

PERENNIAL PATTERNS OF ABUNDANCE

Had the eccentric adventurer John Hornby,
in the summer of 1926, taken seriously the
impending cyclic low in grouse and hares,
his bones and those of his two companions
would not be interred deep in the remote
Thelon Sanctuary of northern Canada.

Robert A. McCabe

STABLE POPULATIONS
UNSTABLE POPULATIONS
ERUPTIVE POPULATIONS
CYCLIC POPULATIONS

REGIONWIDE-SYNCHRONOUS
    POPULATIONS
PRINCIPLES

Leopold described three patterns of among-years variation in wildlife abundance (1933). These patterns were *flat* (stable), *cyclic*, and *irruptive*. A larger classification of patterns now seems necessary. Wildlife populations may be (1) stable, (2) unstable, (3) eruptive, (4) cyclic, or (5) regionwide synchronous. There is no precise separation among the first three patterns.

STABLE POPULATIONS

Leopold arbitrarily defined stable populations as exhibiting year-to-year changes in abundance of no more than 50 percent (1933). Such changes might not be detected (with statistical significance) by routine extensive methods for monitoring populations. Many wildlife populations exhibit this pattern (Fig. 17.1). Leopold emphasized the role of intrinsic mechanisms of population control in maintaining stable populations. In addition, environmental stability and complexity, low biotic potential, and persisting population characteristics may enhance population stability (Chapter 15). Whereas stable populations do not exhibit large deviations from short-term mean abundance, the long-term trend may be up or down because of gradual improvement or degradation of habitat.

UNSTABLE POPULATIONS

An unstable population exhibits large and essentially random changes in abundance. Arbitrarily, we may define these changes as being greater than 50 percent. A better definition might be that frequent unpredictable changes in abundance are large enough to be of significance for management.

Populations of mule deer in western Colorado have exhibited instability (Fig. 17.2). The management objectives have been to stabilize these populations by

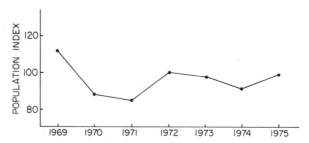

Fig. 17.1. Abundance of Common Flickers in central Ontario and Quebec; an example of a stable population. There are no statistically significant differences among indices. Data from Erskine 1978; Reproduced by permission of the Minister of Supply and Services Canada.

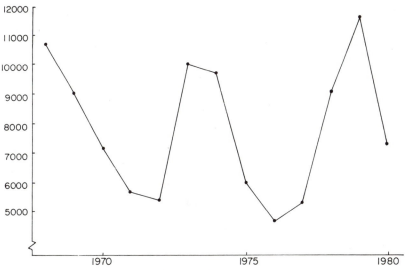

Fig. 17.2 An unstable population: estimates of the numbers of mule deer wintering in Middle Park, Colorado. Data courtesy of Colorado Division of Wildlife.

adjusting levels of harvest to population size. However, the major causes for instability persist. These are a highly variable environment and a lack of environmental diversity.

Western Colorado receives considerable snowfall but its winters can be highly variable, both in intensity and duration (Table 14.1). In some years, early snows force deer onto winter ranges during rutting. This circumstance appears to result in low conception rates, probably because forage quality on winter ranges is below that on summer range. In some years, snow and cold persist into early spring, increasing the energy requirements of deer and making forage unavailable. Persistent winter weather causes deer mortality and also contributes to the production of nonviable fawns. The reproduction and survival of deer thus depend on the highly variable winter weather, and populations tend to be unstable.

Animals may compensate for environmental instability in a diverse environment by shifting use among numerous food and cover alternatives. In Colorado, topographic diversity allows some mule deer populations to always select favorable environments by moving among various slope, aspect, and elevation zones. In addition, an available diversity of forages would favor stabilization of food intake as animals could switch between herbs and browse and between preferred and less-preferred forages to compensate for variable snow conditions. However, many western Colorado winter ranges provide only limited diversity of forages and topography. Sagebrush winter ranges do not provide a great diversity of winter foods for deer. Sagebrush itself is of limited value. When deep and crusted snow cover herbage, there is little for deer to turn to. In Middle Park,

Colorado, topographic diversity is limited because the Colorado River leaves the valley via a canyon that deer do not traverse. The deer are, thus, limited in their ability to seek lower elevations in severe winters. Human use of low elevations on western Colorado winter ranges has further depleted both topographic and forage diversity. These developments include highways, railroads, urban areas, reservoirs, agriculture, livestock grazing, and fencing, which have eliminated lower elevations from winter ranges. Not only has topographic diversity been reduced for deer, unique forage supplies at low elevations, particularly along streams and drainages, have been eliminated or made unavailable. This continuing loss of environmental diversity increases instability in western Colorado deer populations and creates difficult management problems. Where deer are considered, a land management goal should be to preserve remaining habitat at low elevations and to increase diversity of forage resources on these winter ranges.

ERUPTIVE POPULATIONS

Eruptive populations show characteristics of stable populations except for the irregular occurrence of short-term, great increases in abundance. These eruptions appear to be due to occasional release of the population by a brief improvement of a minimum welfare factor, or by occasional escape of the population from effects of a depressing decimating factor. Eruptive populations tend to have high biotic potentials, allowing the populations to expand rapidly, making use of an abundant supply of otherwise unused welfare factors.

Eruptive populations differ from unstable populations only in that they exhibit periods of relative stability between eruptions. The lengths of these periods of stability may vary, providing a continuum of population behavior between unstable and eruptive.

Early literature used the term *irruptive* for these populations. This term seems more appropriate for populations invading new territories. Existing populations that suddenly increase in abundance are more correctly termed eruptive.

Unstable population behavior tending toward the eruptive pattern has been attributed to desert quail (Gullion 1960) and jackrabbits (Wagner and Stoddart 1972). Eruptions have also occurred in big game (Leopold et al. 1947; Caughley 1970). Desert quail eruptions follow years with unusually good fall-winter precipitation, after which the desert "blooms" with a diversity of plant species providing a new abundance of quality foods for quail. Jackrabbit eruptions are described as periods when rabbit abundance and production overcome the effects of predation, allowing the population to expand rapidly until a population decline is again triggered. The jackrabbits then reach a low abundance that is maintained by predation. The mechanism of these eruptions is not entirely clear, and there is some evidence that they are synchronized over large areas. Most deer eruptions in North America have occurred after large predators were removed or reduced coincident with widespread alteration of habitat. The relative roles of predator control and habitat change in stimulating these eruptions are also unclear.

CYCLIC POPULATIONS

References to periodic scarcity and abundance of game in northern North America occurred at least as early as 1708. Fur records of the Hudson's Bay Company provide data on these fluctuations back to 1775 (Keith 1963, p. 5). Periodic outbreaks of small rodents are described throughout European history (Krebs et al. 1973). These fluctuations were largely unstudied until Seton (1911), Hewitt (1921), and Elton (1924) noted the occurrence of cycles of animal abundance in scientific literature.

The term *cycle* has been applied to two sets of populations. Lemmings, voles, and other mammals of like size have been described as exhibiting a *short* cycle with peaks in abundance every 2 to 4 years (Fig. 17.3). Hares, grouse, other game of like size, and their predators have been described as exhibiting a 10-year cycle with peaks in abundance usually every 8 to 11 years. In using the term cycle, biologists have not inferred that the amplitude and interval between peaks have been invariable. However, they have inferred that population fluctuations have been more regular than the random fluctuations of unstable populations. A broadly accepted and precise definition of cycle was not available in the 1920s and 1930s, however.

Only the 10-year cycle is considered in this chapter. An introduction to literature on the *short cycle* is available in the works of Elton (1942), Chitty (1960, 1967), Schultz (1969), Pitelka (1971), and Krebs et al. (1973).

Growing interest in wildlife management stimulated inventory and research on cyclic populations in the 1920s and 30s. In this period, Green and Evans studied

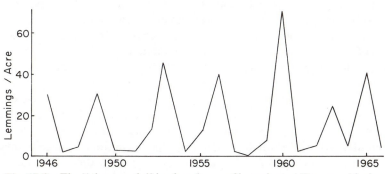

Fig. 17.3   The "short cycle" in abundance of lemmings at Barrow, Alaska. Data from Schultz 1969.

cyclic declines in abundance of snowshoe hares in Minnesota (1940), Grange observed cyclic populations of hares and grouse in Wisconsin (1936; 1949), and R. T. King began to study a cyclic population of ruffed grouse in Minnesota. The latter research has continued for more than five decades, providing one of the few long-term studies of a local cyclic population (summarized once by Marshall in 1954).

Early speculation on the 10-year cycle and its causes was abundant. There were soon "more theories than data." This was not entirely inappropriate. Science progresses only as theories are proposed and tested. But testing was a slow process. Few field stations existed for studying wildlife. Few study techniques had been developed and tested, and the biologies of most wildlife species were poorly understood. Thus, most studies were largely qualitative rather than quantitative. Further, a 10-year study provided a sample size of but one cycle interval. Unfortunately, some biologists confused theory with fact or accepted limited evidence as proof of theory. Worse, some rationalized that cycles existed in many populations, despite the paucity of data on population trends in most of them. Many fluctuations in wildlife abundance, poorly measured and not understood, were casually rationalized as caused by "the cycle," as if this rationalization provided explanation. The profession needed to be challenged to provide a precise definition of population cycle, one that would eliminate the confusion and hopefully stimulate more careful and critical thought. But first, the extremes of thought and publication on population cycles had to descend from science and biology to the fringes of mysticism. Some papers on cycles included speculations that were not testable theories and were supported by careless selections of data (see the short-lived *Journal of Cycle Research*). On reading these, one imagines some cosmic, pulsating force controlling the fortunes of plants, animals, and men in mysterious ways.

In a symposium on cyclic populations, sponsored by The Wildlife Society, Cole challenged biologists by demonstrating that a series of random numbers could be manipulated to provide data equally as "cyclic" as data on abundance of some reputedly cyclic populations (1954). The existence of population cycles was severely questioned. This prompted development of a more precise definition of population cycle and formulation of an objective statistical test for evidence of cyclic fluctuations in animal abundance.

Davis produced the generally accepted definition of cyclic populations, from which I paraphrase (1957): Cyclic populations exhibit peaks and lows in abundance that recur at intervals that are less variable than expected by chance. Based on this regularity, reasonably accurate predictions of abundance can be made. Thus, regularity and predictability are the characteristics identifying cyclic populations. Unfortunately, some biologists continue to neglect this definition. Populations should not be termed cyclic unless there is evidence for regularity of changes in abundance.

With this definition, Keith (1963) extended the ideas of Butler (1953), Cole (1954), and Hickey (1954) to develop a statistical test for evaluating regularity in

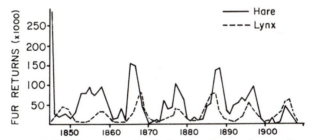

Fig. 17.4   The 10-year cycle in abundance of snowshoe hares and lynx, illustrated by Hudson Bay Company fur returns. Charts from *The Arctic Prairies*. Copyright 1911, E. T. Seton; renewed 1939. Reprinted with permission of Charles Scribner's Sons.

a series of population data. For the 10-year cycle, the test requires at least two decades of annual data. Such series, especially the long records of the Hudson's Bay Company, provided statistically significant evidence that many northern populations were indeed cyclic (Keith 1963). Ruffed grouse populations were fairly synchronized in a 10-year cycle over much of the species range, from Alaska to Quebec. Ptarmigan, spruce, blue and sharp-tailed grouse, prairie chickens, and Hungarian partridge populations were also cyclic, through not in all cases over so large a portion of their range as ruffed grouse. Populations of snowshoe hares exhibited a 10-year cycle geographically and temporally well aligned with that of ruffed grouse (Fig. 17.4). Muskrat populations were also cyclic in parts of Canada. Populations of predators dependent on these prey exhibited similar cycles, especially lynx populations (Fig. 17.4), but also fox, coyote, mink, and fisher populations in parts of these species' ranges. These predators have been labeled *secondarily* cyclic species.

   Keith reviewed the abundant literature on the 10-year cycle (1963). Only a partial summary of his conclusions is presented here. For more detail, see Keith's excellent contribution to our knowledge of the 10-year cycle and also Williams' review (1954).

Characteristics of the 10-year Cycle

The 10-year cycle is characteristic of the northern coniferous forest, or taiga, and its ecotones. The species mentioned above have been cyclic over part, in some cases most, of this vast area. However, grouse and hares do not appear to be cyclic in the southeast and southwest portions of the coniferous biome (the Maritime provinces, northeastern United States, and southern British Columbia).

   Cyclic populations may exhibit enormous changes in abundance. Amplitudes of hare cycles have often been greater than 100 : 1 and may exceed 1000 : 1.

Ruffed grouse have fluctuated less violently with amplitudes up to 34 : 1. Secondarily cyclic populations of predators dependent on cyclic prey have exhibited cycle amplitudes that were generally smaller, though changes in lynx abundance have exceeded 100 : 1.

During peaks of the cycle, snowshoe hares may be incredibly abundant. Keith describes at least 64 hares in 1.5 acres of habitat, a density of at least 43 per acre (1963, p. 74)! In contrast, during lows of the cycle, the land may seem void of hares, giving rise to comments such as "One track seen in five days of snowshoeing" and estimates of one hare per square mile (Keith 1963; p. 75). The largest amplitudes have been observed in large, continuous blocks of habitat, whereas lesser amplitudes have been observed in more discontinuous and varied habitats, usually toward the south of the taiga and its ecotones.

Two characteristics of the 10-year cycle most difficult ot explain have been geographic and interspecies synchrony. There has been a broad synchronization of the 10-year cycle over a vast area from Quebec to Alaska. Over this region, peaks in population abundance have occurred within three to four years. These peaks have been followed by declines, so that lows in abundance have been similarly synchronized. Fig. 17.5 illustrates this synchrony in snowshoe hare populations over all their range in Alberta. Furthermore, grouse and snowshoe hares, taxonomically unrelated and ecologically dissimilar species, have fluctuated in relative synchrony. Declines from peak abundance by sympatric grouse and snowshoe hares have usually occurred within two years. Secondarily cyclic species have usually declined one to two years after the decline of their cyclic prey.

Since Keith's conclusion that population cycles do exist, that they involve many ecologically and economically important species over an immense area, and that we do not understand their causes, there has been little research on population cycles (1963). Keith has provided the major effort (1974). The lack of research on so important a phenomenon is testimony to the recent lack of support for long-term and basic studies in field biology.

Hypothesized Causes of the 10-year Cycle

This discussion is based largely on Keith's review, wherein references to original literature may be found (1963). Proposed causes are mostly discussed separately. However, it is recognized that two or more of these influences may act in combination to produce a 10-year cycle of wildlife abundance.

Meteorological Theories   The occurrence of interspecies and geographic synchrony in cyclic fluctuations of wildlife has led many biologists to propose that *extensive, extraterrestrial,* or *cosmic* forces must provide explanation. Keith grouped these theories as *meteorological.* Direct meteorological effects on animals, as well as effects on their habitats, have been suggested.

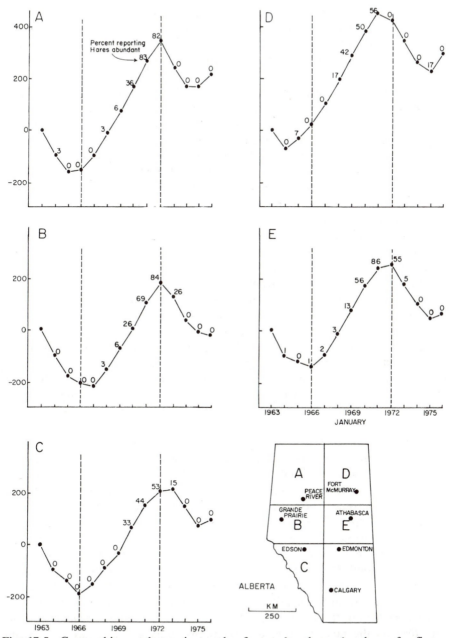

Fig. 17.5 Geographic synchrony in trends of snowshoe hare abundance for five regions of Alberta. Data from Keith and Windberg (1978) are indices based on question-naires.

An early idea was that cyclic peaks in abundance of hares were correlated with the cyclic occurrence of minimum sunspot activity. It was suggested that sunspot activity resulted in variation in the quality of solar radiation, affecting animals directly, affecting plants and therefore the qualities of forages, or affecting the composition of the atmosphere near the earth's poles and, in turn, animals. A later analysis of sunspot cycles found them uncorrelated with the 10-year wildlife cycle. The sunspot theory has few proponents in recent literature.

Another theory was based on observations that lunar phases exhibit a cycle of approximately 9.5 years. Archibald has shown correlations of lunar phases with wildlife populations, but a causal relationship between lunar phases and changes in wildlife abundance has not been detected (1977).

Abnormal weather at critical seasons has often been proposed as an influence on the 10-year cycle. Weather phenomena have been described as influencing animals directly or indirectly through effects on habitat and have been described as beneficial, favoring development of cyclic peaks in abundance, or decimating, explaining cyclic declines in abundance. Although many studies have shown direct and indirect effects of weather on wildlife (Chapter 14), a cyclic weather pattern, expressed all across northern North America, has not been detected. As a result, few biologists have recently suggested weather as a *cause* of the 10-year cycle. However, some suggest that cyclic changes in abundance due to other causes could be synchronized by occasional weather phenomena that are geographically widespread. Thus, if, for whatever causes, populations tend to fluctuate in a cycle of 8 to 11 years, geographic synchronization of those fluctuations can be generated by a widespread, severe, and long winter that reduces all populations to a very low level. Occurrence of such a winter, perhaps once in four decades, might be adequate to generate the observed synchrony.

Overpopulation Theories "The gist of overpopulation theories is that some species increase in density . . . until levels are attained which trigger overpopulation phenomena" (Keith 1963, p. 108). These phenomena might be malnutrition, starvation, predation, emigration, and disease, including the general-adaptation syndrome. They cause population declines to low levels, after which the pattern is repeated. The persistent interval of 8 to 11 years between peak populations is usually rationalized as being due to the fixed biotic potential of each species. However, it is difficult to imagine how so many populations could exhibit such consistent rates of population increase when habitat and weather factors affecting reproduction and mortality vary so widely among years and over thousands of miles of taiga. In a later paper, Keith suggested that local synchronization of the cycle interval is achieved as mobile predators concentrate first on the fastest growing populations, thus allowing slower growing populations to "catch up" (1974).

A criticism of overpopulation theories has been that once population declines have begun, overpopulation phenomena should diminish, halting the decline. However, a persistence of environmental and/or population characteristics could cause the decline to continue, as indicated in Chapter 15. Overpopulation theories generally rely on the existence of an occasional synchronizing weather phenomenon to account for geographic synchrony.

Forage-quality Theories   Laukhart proposed a cyclic pattern of forage quality as a cause of the 10-year cycle (1957). He suggested periodic seed years might somehow be connected to changes in the quality of browse used by primary cyclic species. The theory attracted few proponents. Svoboda and Gullion, however, have suggested a similar idea, proposing that a cycle might exist in the production of flower buds by aspen, an important food of ruffed grouse (1974). Forage-quality theories must rely on occasional weather phenomena to account for geographic synchrony, and it will have to be demonstrated that changes in forage are the cause, not result, of the cycle of animal abundance.

Genetic Theories   Chitty (1960) and Krebs et al. (1973) have proposed genotypic variation as a cause of the 2- to 4-year cycle in small mammals. Bergerud suggested this mechanism as a cause for the 10-year cycle (1970). Simply stated, a growing population would inevitably decline if, while growing, it were accumulating dominant genotypes of animals poorly adapted to reproductive success at high ecological density. Following the decline, the population would consist mainly of the nondominant genotype. However, with regrowth of the population from low ecological density, the dominant genotype would again begin to predominate in abundance until high ecological density again triggered its failure. The authors cited here have suggested patterns that are at least similar to this concept. Genetic theories for population cycles are still viable, and the recent findings of Krebs et al. enhance interest in them (1973). However, it has been very difficult to study genetics in wild populations, and the role of genetics in population dynamics remains obscure.

Keith's Composite Theory   Lloyd Keith recently studied the 10-year cycle in Alberta for over a decade. Since his study appears to be the only recent one of such intensity and continuity, he must be considered a most prominent authority on the 10-year cycle. He has provided tentative conclusions on causes of the cycle (1974).

Keith's proposal is an overpopulation theory that is more complex than those previously suggested. He proposes that hare populations growing toward cyclic peaks in abundance are curtailed by shortages of browse in winter. These shortages are exaggerated by decreased plant production due to impacts of foraging. Losses of hares resulting from malnutrition or starvation occur. In addition, as hare population growth slows and ultimately stops, the rising abundance of predators, responding to an increased supply of prey, begins to remove an increasing proportion of the hare population. The mobility of predators, principally hawks, owls, canines, and felines, tends to synchronize hare abundance locally, as greatest predation is applied to the highest densities of hares, allowing populations of lower density to continue growing after other populations have reached their peaks. Predation and lack of winter browse trigger a population decline, and the decline continues because of the persisting effects of damage to browse plants and persisting high abundance of predators. Inverse density-dependent predation may occur during the decline of hares. Eventually, after the hares reach a low ecological density, browse production improves and predator populations decline, allowing hare populations to increase once more. Hares increase faster in abundance than do predators, until lack of winter browse again slows population growth and the cycle is repeated. Keith relies on an occasional widespread weather phenomenon to explain geographic synchrony. Ruffed grouse provide a far smaller biomass than do hares in the taiga, and secondarily cyclic predators do not rely on them, preying on them incidentally to their predation on hares. However, predation levels on grouse are cyclic because predator numbers rise and fall with the abundance of hares. This causes grouse abundance to be synchronized with hare abundance.

Keith has outlined this theory based on a preliminary analysis of data (1974). He may alter his conclusions, and the theory will undoubtedly be reviewed critically by others. It will have to be tested on other study areas and over many years. At present, it is still a theory; but, recognizing Keith's intense efforts in studying the 10-year cycle and the scarcity of other consequential published research, it is an important theory.

Management of Cyclic Populations

Given the primitive state of knowledge concerning the 10-year cycle, it is difficult to conclude how management should respond to it. Management has not been successful in eliminating the cyclic decline of game abundance. Perhaps management of habitat or populations can increase and/or prolong population peaks or can minimize population declines or hasten returns to abundance, at least in some areas. Considering Keith's theory, one might apply predator control and a heavy harvest of hares to forestall overuse of winter forage. The efficacy of these proposals remains to be tested, however. Given Keith's view of the role of predator mobility in the 10-year cycle, these management schemes seem apt to be of little value if applied on small areas within large blocks of unmanaged habitat.

REGIONWIDE-SYNCHRONOUS POPULATIONS

Like cyclic populations, regionwide-synchronous populations exhibit some degree of geographic synchrony in alternating periods of abundance and scarcity. However, there is little or no evidence that these changes of abundance have been regular in occurrence. Confusion exists in early literature, as some regionwide-synchronous populations have been termed cyclic without adequate evidence of regularity.

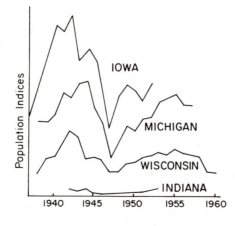

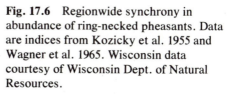

Fig. 17.6   Regionwide synchrony in abundance of ring-necked pheasants. Data are indices from Kozicky et al. 1955 and Wagner et al. 1965. Wisconsin data courtesy of Wisconsin Dept. of Natural Resources.

Bock and Lepthien described synchronous "eruptions" of eight species of boreal seed-eating birds, including nuthatches, siskins, and crossbills (1976). The migration patterns of these birds were synchronized by circumboreal failures of seed crops. In years of poor seed supply, seed-eating birds migrated southward and were seen in above-average numbers in the United States and southern Canada. This created an apparent population eruption when the phenomenon was primarily a synchronized migration pattern.

Regionwide synchrony has been evident in pheasant populations over Iowa, Michigan, Wisconsin, and Indiana during 1937 to 1960 (Fig. 17.6). An analysis of literature and data (Bailey 1968a) indicates regionwide synchrony in abundance of cottontail rabbits on a large area from New York to Minnesota and south to Missouri and Kentucky during 1928 to 1965 (Table 17.1; Fig. 17.7). The literature

TABLE 17.1   A Review of Literature Has Indicated Regionally Synchronized Periods of Abundance and Scarcity of Cottontails from 1928 to 1956, With No Significant Contrary Reports (Bailey 1968a)

Period	Reported Population	States
1928 to 1930	Scarce	New York, Illinois, Indiana, Wisconsin
1931 to 1934	Abundant	New York, Illinois, Wisconsin, Ohio
1935 to 1937	Scarce	New York, Illinois, Wisconsin, Pennsylvania
1938 to 1942	Abundant	New York, Illinois, Wisconsin, Pennsylvania, Michigan, Missouri
1947 to 1948	Scarce	Wisconsin, Indiana, Ohio
1949 to 1950	Abundant	Indiana, Ohio, Michigan, Missouri, Pennsylvania
1952 to 1953	Scarce	Indiana, Ohio, Michigan, Missouri, Pennsylvania
1955 to 1956	Abundant	Indiana, Ohio, Michigan, Missouri, Pennsylvania, Wisconsin, Minnesota

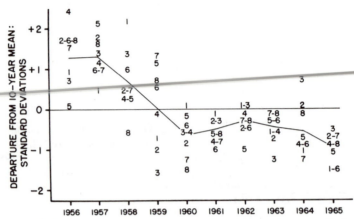

Fig. 17.7 Regionwide synchrony in abundance of cottontails in eight states: (1) Minnesota, (2) Wisconsin, (3) Michigan, (4) New York, (5) Illinois, (6) Indiana, (7) Missouri, and (8) Kentucky. Data are deviations from 10-year mean indices. The line is an average for all states. After Bailey 1968a.

and data did not suggest regularity in the oscillations of rabbit populations, and the fluctuations were not well synchronized with changes in abundance of cyclic ruffed grouse further north.

Aside from geographic synchrony, a characteristic of these populations is their tendency for alternating prolonged periods of abundance and scarcity. The populations exhibit above-average abundance for several years, then below-average abundance for several years. This indicates that regionwide weather phenomena are not alone responsible for geographic synchrony, because weather is not known to exhibit such an alternating pattern. Prolonged periods of abundance and scarcity suggest that persisting population and/or environmental characteristics influence population size (Chapter 15). Regionwide changes in land use affecting habitat might also account for this type of population behavior. A critical investigation has not been made, however, and the causes of region-wide-synchronous population behavior are unknown.

We have long-term data for so few species. One wonders how many species might exhibit regionwide synchrony if more data were available. We have not even looked closely at all the data we have. More important, there have been extremely few long-term studies of local populations. Without them we are unlikely to understand the mechanisms of regionwide synchrony.

During regionwide-synchronous peaks in cottontail abundance, rabbits have seemed abundant in many kinds of habitats. However, during synchronous depressions in cottontail abundance, rabbits have been scarce or absent from most areas, whereas a few habitats have retained at least fair numbers of the animals. This indicates that habitat management is worthwhile for regionwide-synchronous populations, although it is not clear whether habitat improvement will enhance populations during peaks, as well as during depressions, in abundance.

PRINCIPLES

P17.1 Long-term trends in abundance of wildlife populations exhibit five patterns: stable, unstable, eruptive, cyclic, and regionwide synchronous. (Factors favoring population stability or, conversely, instability are considered in Principle 15.4.)

P17.2 Cyclic populations exhibit regularity of long-term trends in abundance, and reasonably accurate predictions of population trends can, therefore, be made. A 2 to 4 year cycle is common in small rodents; a 10-year cycle occurs in populations of hares, grouse, and other northern species in America. Causes of the 10-year cycle are not well understood. Geographic and interspecies synchrony have been two characteristics of the 10-year cycle most difficult to explain.

P17.3 Pheasants and some lagomorphs, at least, have exhibited regionwide synchrony in population abundance but have not demonstrated regularity in these trends. Causes of synchronous trends in these populations are not well understood.

P17.4 Without several long-term studies of local populations, we are unlikely to understand the mechanisms of cyclic and regionwide-synchronous populations.

PART

V

WILDLIFE
MANAGEMENT

CHAPTER   18

THE DATA BASES OF WILDLIFE MANAGEMENT

It is a common pastime in many organizations
to collect vast quantities of data on a
routine basis . . . with the vague intention of
submitting them to analysis one day . . . the
piles of useful stuff in the files get more
comprehensive, and out of date, as the years
go by. Pious intentions to analyze some day
are of litle value. If data are not worth
analysis at a suitable near date they are
rarely worth collection. . . . Data should be
collected with a clear purpose in mind. Not
only a clear purpose, but a clear idea as to
the precise way in which they will be analysed
so as to yield the desired information.

M. J. Moroney

WILDLIFE MEASUREMENTS
DATA AND ANALYSIS FOR
   EXTENSIVE MANAGEMENT

DATA AND ANALYSIS FOR
   INTENSIVE MANAGEMENT
PRINCIPLES

Wildlife management consists of controlling the number, distribution, and quality of wild animals, either directly—as by manipulating hunting seasons—or indirectly—as by manipulating wildlife habitat. Management decisions (perhaps to liberalize hunting regulations, plant food patches, or control-burn shrub fields) should be based on some knowledge of the target population and/or of its habitat. Acquiring the information necessary to make correct decisions is part of the wildlife manager's job. The manager must allocate some time and budget to measuring the abundance of animals, their reproductive success, the quantity and quality of their habitat, or whatever population or habitat characteristics can be expected to provide the best basis for management decisions.

However, the wildlife manager can never know all he or she would like to know about the target population or its habitat. A manager cannot measure everything. He or she may wish to know exactly how many animals are present, and exactly how much food they require, and exactly how much food the habitat provides. But managers may be unable to devise methods for measuring these parameters, or the methods may produce highly variable data or be too costly.

For some management objectives, precise and expensive population or habitat data may be unnecessary. Comparatively crude data may suffice. Rather than knowing the number of animals in a population, it may be sufficient to know if the population is declining, is increasing, or is approximately stable. Rather than knowing the weight of deer browse per acre, it may be sufficient to know that certain key browse plants are, or are not, being overbrowsed and damaged.

Wildlife managers must select the population or habitat parameters to be measured and used as a basis for management. Selecting this data base is one of the most important management decisions. The decision should be influenced by (1) the objectives of the management program, (2) the availability, cost, and precision of methods for measuring various population and habitat characteristics, and (3) the budget of time and money for population and/or habitat analysis. In addition, the data base should have a meaningful relation to management objectives. For instance, if objectives are to provide a maximum sustained harvest from a deer herd, there would be little value in measuring the use or abundance of winter browse in a habitat where winter forage is not considered to be limiting the herd. Or if objectives are to adjust the harvest of waterfowl to annual variations in production of young birds, a census of winter populations may have little value compared to data on breeding-ground populations and nesting success. In this case, both sets of data may be useful, but if there are budget limitations, management should spend its effort attaining the most useful data.

The data gathering process will, of course, provide an estimate of some population or habitat characteristic such as the average number of rabbits per acre or the percent of shrub stems browsed by deer. Most often, it is equally important that some measure of data variation also be obtained. This permits statistical analysis of the data and evaluation of the significance of any observed difference between locations, populations, or years.

WILDLIFE MEASUREMENTS

The data bases for wildlife management are (1) population indices, (2) population censuses, (3) measures of habitat factors, and (4) indices of ecological density of the target population.

Population Indices

Population indices serve as a data base for many state programs of game management. They are also used to monitor changes in the abundance of non-game birds. Common population indices are hunter success data (e.g., percent of hunters killing a deer, number of small game harvested per hunting trip and estimated total harvest of cottontails in a state) and roadside-count data (e.g., number of animals seen per mile along selected routes traveled under standardized conditions, and roadside whistle counts of quail and crow counts of pheasants). Indices provide useful data for extensive programs of management. It is assumed that trends in the index values reflect, with "reasonable" accuracy, trends in abundance of the target population. The validity of this assumption has not always been tested.

The intelligent use of population indices requires an awareness of possible relationships between index values and population abundance (Fig. 18.1). An ideal population index is related to population abundance in a 1:1 ratio (Fig. 18.1a). Thus, a 30 percent change in population abundance causes a 30 percent change in the index value. Further, an ideal index provides consistent data, alleviating the expense of many replications and providing for detection of small changes in population abundance.

Indices may also relate to population abundance in ratios other than 1:1 (Fig. 18.1b). Thus, a 50 percent change in animal abundance may cause only a 10 percent change in the index value. Or the relation between the index and population abundance may not be linear, resulting in indices of little value either at high population abundance (Fig. 18.1c) or at low population abundance (Fig. 18.1d).

The variaton of index values may not be homogeneous over all ranges of population abundance (Fig. 18.1e), reducing the usefulness of the index at some levels of abundance. It is likely that some population indices being used in wildlife management have both a nonlinear relation to animal abundance and nonhomogeneous variance (Fig. 18.1f).

For an ideal population index the relationship between expected index values and population is stable from year to year and from place to place. However, many factors may bias the index-population relationship. These factors should be considered and eliminated if possible. Thus, roadside counts of cottontail rabbits may always be conducted on the same set of roads on windless mornings during the first two weeks of June. This standardization of the roadside count should eliminate some sources of variation that are not consistent among places

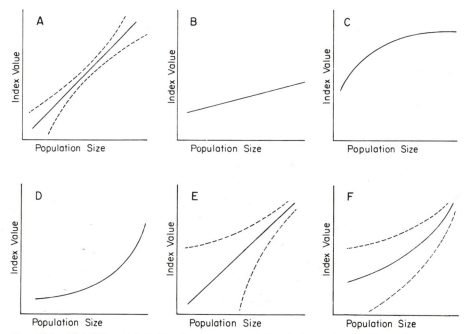

Fig. 18.1 Possible relationships between population-index values and population size. Dashed lines represent magnitudes of variation of index values. See text for further explanation.

or years. But some bias cannot be controlled. Increasingly intensive land use may eliminate cottontail habitat in farm fields, causing a reduction in rabbit abundance. This reduction may not be reflected in roadside counts if roadside vegetation is unchanged and "roadside rabbits" are as abundant as ever. Weather can be an important uncontrollable source of bias. Poor hunting conditions on opening day of the season may cause a drop in hunter success, even during a year of high game abundance.

Despite these serious deficiencies, population indices are important for monitoring trends in wildlife populations, especially trends over large areas and/ or over long periods (Fig. 18.2).

Population Census

A census provides an estimate of the number of animals in a defined population. A population may be defined as a certain class (species, sex, age, alive, or dead) of animal within a certain area at a certain time. Most wildlife populations are difficult and, therefore, expensive to census because most animals are mobile and/or secretive.

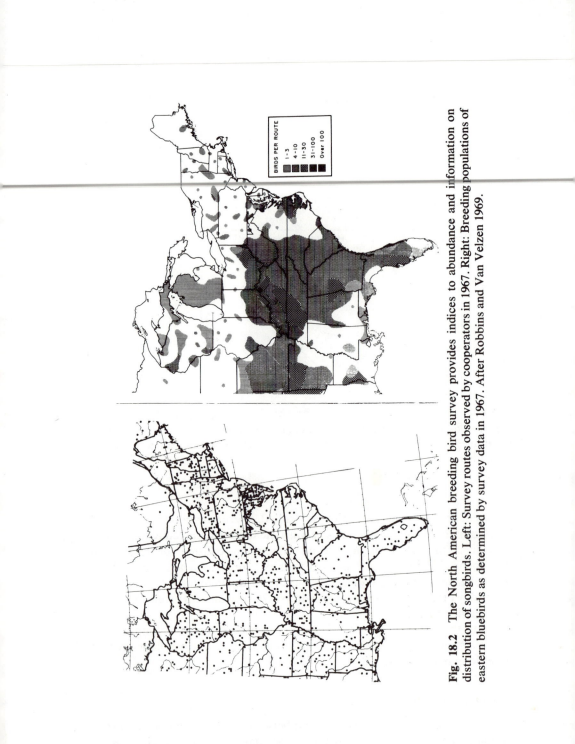

Fig. 18.2 The North American breeding bird survey provides indices to abundance and information on distribution of songbirds. Left: Survey routes observed by cooperators in 1967. Right: Breeding populations of eastern bluebirds as determined by survey data in 1967. After Robbins and Van Velzen 1969.

BIRDS PER ROUTE
1-3
4-10
11-30
31-100
Over 100

Census methods have been reviewed and described in the *Manual of Wildlife Management Techniques* (Schemnitz 1980) and by Caughley (1977). Therefore, only a few examples are described here and much detail is omitted. The reader is cautioned that the assumptions necessary for using some of these methods are not thoroughly discussed. Census methods are classified here as total counts, sample counts, and population-ratio methods.

Total Counts   A drive census requires large numbers of personnel. This method is used to census deer, jackrabbits, and other relatively large animals. Observers must be stationed around the target area to count any animal leaving it. Drivers line up, walk through the area, and drive all animals from it.

A total count of nesting pheasants in agricultural fields or roadside vegetation may be obtained by examining every square foot of ground for nests. Again, many man-hours are required.

The applicability of total count methods obviously varies among species and their habitats. Drive censuses require fairly large, visible animals that can be flushed by the drivers. Nest searches are practical for pheasants because their nests are large. In contrast, a search for meadowlark nests would underestimate the nesting population because these nests are smaller and better concealed.

Sample Counts   Often total counts are conducted on plots randomly selected from within a target habitat. Data from the plots may be used to estimate the population of the entire habitat and also to estimate among-plot variation, thus providing confidence limits for the population estimate. A statistician's advice may be necessary to determine the number and locations of plots, so that adequate precision is obtained, and time and labor are utilized efficiently.

Counts of wildlife sign, such as deer fecal-pellet groups or muskrat houses, may be calibrated by a ratio of sign to animal to provide population estimates. Thus, pen studies show that deer on winter range produce 13 pellet groups per day (Neff 1968). If permanent plots are cleared in the fall and the winter accumulation of pellet groups is counted the following spring, the overwintering population of deer may be estimated from the density of pellet groups on the wintering area and the number of days allowed for pellet-group accumulation (Example 18.1).

In the King strip-census (Example 18.2), the size of sample area on which animals are counted depends on the *flushing distances* at which animals are first observed when walking a transect. The number of animals observed is assumed to represent the population density on an area defined by the length of the transect times twice the average flushing distance for all observed animals. This method was developed for ruffed grouse and has not been accepted for use with species that may skulk away from the approaching observer.

Population-ratio Methods   It is sometimes possible to count all animals in some segment of the population, such as all the animals that have been captured and tagged, all the male animals, or all the harvested male animals. If the percent frequency of these animals in the population can be estimated in an unbiased manner, the number of animals in the population can be easily estimated. For instance, if there are 30 tagged animals and it is estimated that tagged animals are 25 percent of the population, the population is estimated at 4 × 30, or 120 animals. This method using tagged animals has been named the Lincoln Index, although it is not a population index but a census method (Example 18.3).

Several methods for estimating populations from animal-trapping data are population-ratio methods. If all animals in the population have an equal probability of being captured, then continued trapping increases the percent frequency of previously captured and tagged animals in the population in a predictable manner. This is illustrated by the declining rate at which untagged animals are captured. The number of animals present when the entire population would be tagged—if trapping were to be continued—can also be predicted by extrapolating the rate of capture of untagged animals to zero (Fig. 18.3).

Change in a population index caused by removal of a known number of animals provides a basis for estimating the total populaton by a ratio method. Thus, if 15 sets of deer tracks are observed per mile of recently graded dirt road before the hunting season, and if 10 sets of tracks are observed per mile of road after harvest of 50 deer, the prehunt population is estimated at 150 deer, because removal of 50 deer reduced track density, and presumably the herd, by one third.

It is important to consider the assumptions necessary for use of population-ratio methods. If the assumptions are not true, biased population estimates are obtained.

Use of the Lincoln census method requires that the known segment of the population represent a constant proportion of the entire population, at least for a short period. If the known segment consists of tagged animals, (1) there cannot be a loss of tags from animals, (2) there cannot be a difference between mortality or emigration rates for tagged versus untagged animals, and (3) there cannot be recruitment (births or immigration) of untagged animals.

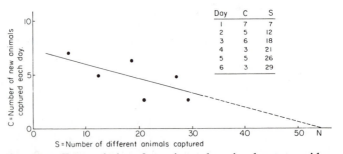

Day	C	S
1	7	7
2	5	12
3	6	18
4	3	21
5	5	26
6	3	29

C = Number of new animals captured each day.

S = Number of different animals captured

Fig. 18.3 Extrapolation of trapping and tagging data to provide a population estimate (N). Results of six days of trapping are provided in the above table. Extrapolation of the regression line, justified if all animals in the population have an equal probability of being captured, provides an estimate of 53 animals in the population.

TABLE 18.1   Hypothetical Data from Pellet-group Transects

Transect	Number of Pellet Groups	Pellet Groups Per Acre	Number of Deer-Days Per Acre	Number of Deer-Days Per Square Mile	Number of Deer Per Square Mile
1	10	100	7.69	4923	49
2	7	70	5.38	3446	34
3	8	80	6.15	3938	39
4	4	40	3.08	1969	20
5	5	50	3.85	2462	25
6	9	90	6.92	4431	44
7	8	80	6.15	3938	39
8	8	80	6.15	3938	39
9	5	50	3.85	2462	25
10	7	70	5.38	3446	34

$$\bar{x} = 34.8$$

Population-ratio methods require some assumption about the probability of capturing or otherwise observing animals or their sign. The Lincoln census method requires obtaining an unbiased estimate of the percent-frequency of tagged animals in the population. Therefore, when this estimate is obtained, tagged animals must have the same probability of being observed and counted as have untagged animals. The method for estimating populations from trapping (Fig. 18.3) requires that all animals have the same probability of capture. The ratio method based on frequency of deer tracks on roads requires that the tendency for 150 deer to use roads before the hunting season is the same as the tendency for 100 deer to use roads after the hunting season. Assumptions regarding the probability of capturing or observing animals or their sign are often unjustified, and ratio methods for censusing wildlife must be used with caution.

EXAMPLE 18.1   Deer Pellet-Group Census

Ten belt transects, each 0.1 acre in size (6.6 ft by 660 ft) are established in deer winter range. All deer fecal groups are removed from the plots in autumn. One hundred days later, in spring, the belt transects are reexamined. The numbers of pellet groups found are presented in Table 18.1.

Calculations for transect number 1 are as follows.

1   Ten pellet groups on a 0.1-acre plot = 100 pellet groups per acre (10 × 10 = 100).

2   Since each deer produces 13 pellet groups each day, 100 groups per acre is equivalent to 7.69 deer-days of use per acre (100/13 = 7.69). Seven deer-days of use may accumulate, for example, with 1 deer present for 7 days or 7 deer present for 1 day. Or, during 100 days, 1 deer spending 7 percent of its time on an acre will produce a use of 7 deer-days on that acre.

3   Since there are 640 acres per square mile, 7.69 deer-days per acre is equal to 4923 deer-days per square mile (7.69 × 640 = 4923).

4   Since the pellet groups accumulated during 100 days, 4923 deer-days are equivalent to an average of 49 deer present per square mile during the 100 days. If the winter range is used by a migratory herd, the peak number of deer present may have been more than 49 per square mile. In this case, during part of the 100 days fewer than 49 deer per square mile were present.

Confidence limits for the population estimate are based on variation of estimates among the 10 transects.

$$\bar{x} = 34.8 \text{ deer per square mile}$$
$$S = 9.1 \text{ deer per square mile}$$
$$S\bar{x} = 2.9 \text{ deer per square mile}$$
$$t, 0.05, df = 9 = 2.26$$
$$tS\bar{x} = 6.5 \text{ deer per square mile}$$

95 percent confidence limits = 28.3 to 41.3 deer per square mile.

Disregarding possible bias (such as uncounted pellet groups), we can say that the *average* number of deer present on the winter range was between 28 and 41 per square mile, or else we have chanced to select a rare sample of transects—one that occurs less than 5 pecent of the time.

EXAMPLE 18.2   King Strip-Census Method

Eight transect lines each 5 miles (four hundred 66-ft chains) long are walked by eight observers. Ruffed grouse are observed and their flushing distances are recorded.

Flushing-Distances (feet) for Ruffed Grouse Observed on Eight Transects

1	2	3	4	5	6	7	8
40	30	50	45	55	35	55	60
30	45	25	20	40	25	25	20
25	50	65	25	25	40	40	25
15	60	20	20	40	35	40	40
50		35	40	60		45	30
		15		45			
				35			

An estimate of grouse density is obtained for each transect. This provides a measure of among-transect variation—a basis for evaluating the precision of the overall population estimate (calculating confidence limits for the estimate). In the following analysis the number of birds observed on each transect represents the density of grouse on an area 5-miles long and as wide as twice the average flushing-distance for the transect. [Note that there are 80 surveyor's (66-ft) chains per mile and 10 square chains are one acre. A square mile contains 640 acres].

Transect number	1	2	3	4	5	6	7	8
No. observed birds	5	4	6	5	7	4	5	5
Mean flushing Distance (Feet)	32	46	35	30	43	34	41	35
Transect width (feet)	64	92	70	60	86	68	82	70
Transect width (chains)	0.97	1.40	1.06	0.91	1.30	1.02	1.24	1.06
Transect area (square chains)	388	561	424	364	519	409	497	424
Transect area (acres)	39	56	42	36	52	41	50	42
Grouse per acre	0.13	0.07	0.14	0.14	0.13	0.10	0.10	0.12
Grouse per square mile	82	46	90	88	86	63	64	75

Statistical analysis of the eight population-density estimates provides an overall estimate of 74 grouse per square mile. The precision of this estimate is obtained by standard methods for calculating confidence intervals.

Mean estimate	74.25	grouse per square mile
Sample size	8	transects
Standard deviation	14.45	grouse per square mile
Standard error of mean	5.10	grouse per square mile
t at $P = 0.05$, 7 degrees of freedom	2.36	
Interval estimate	74 ± 12 grouse per square mile	

If the assumptions of the census method are correct (see Eberhardt 1968) we can say that either the density of grouse on the area is between 62 and 86 birds per square mile, or we have through random sampling obtained a very unusual set of transect data—a set of data occurring by chance less than 5 percent of the time.

EXAMPLE 18.3   Lincoln Census Method

Prior to the hunting season, 75 rabbits are live trapped, tagged, and released on a game management area. During the first week of hunting, 70 rabbits are harvested; 40 of these are tagged animals. What is the estimate of the prehunt number of rabbits?

This problem is solved using the proportion

$$\frac{M}{N} = \frac{m}{n}$$

where M equals the number of animals marked, n equals the number of animals in the second sample—in this case, the harvested rabbits, and m equals the number of marked animals in the second sample. Thus,

$$\frac{75}{N} = \frac{40}{70} \qquad \text{or} \qquad N = 131 \text{ rabbits}$$

The standard error of this estimate is obtained (Bailey 1951) from

$$\text{S.E.} = \sqrt{\frac{M^2 n\,(n-m)}{m^3}}$$

In this case

$$\text{S.E.} = \sqrt{\frac{75^2\,70(70-40)}{40^3}} \quad \text{or} \quad \text{S.E.} = 13.6 \text{ rabbits}$$

The 95-percent confidence limits for the estimate include 2 standard errors above and below the estimate, or 131 ± 27 = 104 to 158 rabbits. Such wide confidence limits are typical for wildlife census data. Small changes in wildlife abundance are, therefore, difficult to detect.

Habitat Measurements

Management objectives may require information on the quantity, quality, distribution, persistence, dependability, or level of use of any food or cover resource in the habitat. Habitat requirements of wildlife are discussed in Chapter 12. Since each wildlife species has a distinct set of habitat requirements, methods used for measuring wildlife habitat are numerous and variable. Only a few examples are discussed here.

If habitat requirements are being considered at the empirical level (Chapter 12), the primary habitat measurement is a habitat-type map (Figure 18.4). A type map is used to evaluate abundance and interspersion of required habitat types. It exposes large homogeneous habitats that provide poor habitat interspersion. These areas might be improved for some species of wildlife by habitat manipulation, such as by locating timber-harvest operations in several small areas within a large stand of old growth forest. A habitat-type map is useful in managing several species on one area.

Most type maps are developed from aerial photographs, or aerial photos may be used as type maps. Photos taken years apart show gross habitat changes due to ecological succession or disturbance or due to changes in land use. Type maps are easy to comprehend and are, therefore, especially valuable in explaining programs to the public.

Examples of measuring habitat requirements at the specific welfare-factor level (Chapter 12) are: estimating the number of pounds of forage available per acre of deer winter range, measuring the abundance of soft-bodied insects available to grouse chicks in potential brood habitat and, evaluating each year's production of mast in tree-squirrel habitat.

Table 18.2 shows annual variation—and therefore dependability—of browse production on a winter range of mule deer in Colorado. Note the great variation among years. If a year of low browse production happened to be followed by a

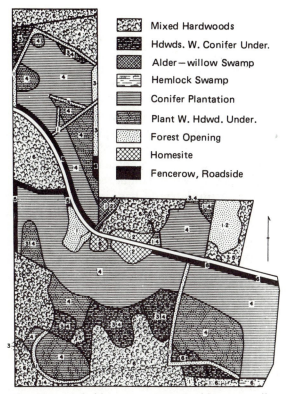

Fig. 18.4 A habitat-type map provides an easily comprehended picture of the abundance and interspersion of empirically defined habitat requirements of wildlife. From Alexander 1959.

severe winter, limiting deer mobility and constricting their winter range, serious food shortages might occur.

The most detailed habitat measurements are analyses of components of food or cover resources. The proximate analysis of foods is described in Chapter 6; examples of cover components are given in Chapter 7.

TABLE 18.2   Browse Production During Three Years at Kelly Flats, Poudre Management Unit, Colorado (Anderson et al. 1972)

| | Browse Production (oven-dry pounds per acre) | |
Year	Mountain Mahogany	Bitterbrush
1962	9.9	43.6
1963	3.1	8.5
1964	5.2	13.3

Indices of Ecological Density

Ecological density of a population is the number of animals relative to the quantity and quality of habitat resources available to the animals. Thus, a population of 20 deer may have a low ecological density in a square mile of good deer habitat. The same animals, however, would have a high ecological density in a square mile of poor habitat. Similarly, 20 deer may have a low ecological density on their winter range during a mild winter, whereas they would have a high ecological density on winter range during a severe winter with deep snow that restricts deer movement and covers forage.

Obviously, the ecological density of a population will change with *either* the number of animals changes, *or* when habitat resources change.

Some species, such as territorial birds, have intrinsic behavioral-physiological methods for adjusting their number to the quantity and quality of habitat available. These populations tend to maintain a constant ecological density.

Other species are less able to control their numbers. Their populations may temporarily exceed the ability of the habitat to support animals, or periodic disturbance such as overharvest may reduce their numbers to a level not fully utilizing the available habitat.

When a habitat is overpopulated, food and/or cover resources are usually in short supply for at least some of the animals during at least part of the year. This results in a decline in the physical condition and quality of the animals. Overuse of limiting foods may occur, resulting in a decline in the condition of forage plants. In contrast, when the animal population is low and not fully utilizing available food and cover resources, the physical condition and quality of the animals are high. No overuse of forage plants occurs and the condition of habitat resources is good (See Chapter 15 for a more detailed discussion of population dynamics in relation to the carrying capacity of habitat).

It is seldom feasible to evaluate ecological density by censusing a population and measuring all pertinent factors of its habitat, so that animal abundance may be compared to habitat carrying capacity. However, indices of ecological density often may be obtained and used as a basis for management decisions. The two types of indices of ecological density are population-condition indices and habitat-condition indices. Most of the examples that follow involve wild ungulates since they are well-studied animals that show large fluctuations in ecological density. This limited discussion is intended only to provide examples. A wildlife manager using any of these methods should become familiar with published literature on their applications and limitations.

Population-condition Indices   Population-condition indices are (1) indices of general animal condition, (2) data on reproductive success or mortality rates, and (3) symptoms of specific nutritional deficiencies.

The most common indices of general animal condition are measures of body size, usually body weight, or measures of body-fat reserves. Body weight is seldom a useful index without additional information such as sex and age or body length. If sex and age data are obtained, weights of animals may be compared within sex-age classes. Figure 6.1 illustrates the effects of ecological density on weights of deer within sex-age classes. In these data *good range* implies a low ecological density and *poor range* implies a high ecological density.

Use of some liner measure of body size, such as body length or foot length, in conjunction with body weight permits interpretation of data in terms of the slenderness of an animal in the same way that human weights are compared within height classes. This interpretation is usually better related to current physical condition than is body weight alone. For instance, as a deer loses weight because of poor nutrition through a winter, its body length or foot length do not change. Therefore, its condition index, based on its weight divided by some function of its length, will decline. The value of using a weight-length ratio as a condition index is that the ratio may be compared among different-sized deer. Comparisions might even be considered appropriate among animals of different age classes. McEwan and Wood analyzed body weights and foot lengths of caribou and suggested that a body weight-foot length ratio be used as a condition index, but only for comparisons within year-classes of animals (1966). Bandy et. al. suggested using a function of heart girth, which correlated well with body weight, divided by a function of foot length as a condition index of ungulates (1956). Bailey used a weight-body length relationship as a condition index for comparisons among age classes of cottontail rabbits (1968; Example 18.4).

Physical conditions of animals are sometimes evaluated by observing them at a distance. Riney noted that loss of fat reserves by an ungulate produces notable changes in appearance of the pelvic area (1960; Fig. 18.5). Albl noted similar pelvic- and lumbar-area changes related to fat reserves in African elephants (1971).

A commonly used condition index, the kidney-fat index (Riney 1955), requires sacrifice of animals. This index is the ratio of the weight of fat surrounding the kidney to the weight of the kidney. An animal with declining fat reserves would have a declining kidney-fat index, as kidney fat disappears and the kidney weight remains approximately stable.

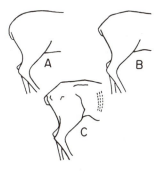

Fig. 18.5 Riney's (1960) sketch of deer in good (*A*), medium (*B*), and poor (*C*) physical condition. Classification of a sample of deer into these condition classes would indicate ecological density of the deer population.

Fat reserves of ungulates are often evaluated by observing the amount of fat in the marrow of a leg bone, usually the femur (Cheatum 1949). Normal bone marrow is solid and white. A red or yellowish marrow, gelatinous in consistency, indicates depletion of body fat reserves. Although factors other than depletion of body fat, such as disease or age of the animal, may also affect marrow color (Bischoff 1954), this method is satisfactory for separating dead malnourished deer from those killed by vehicles or rifles.

In male cervids, poor nutrition due to high ecological density before and/or during antler growth results in stunted growth of antlers. This effect seems most pronounced in young growing animals, such as yearling deer (French et al. 1955). Taber suggested that antler development, especially in yearlings, be used as an index of the physical condition of deer at the onset of antler growth (1958). Antlers measured during the autumn hunting season would, therefore, be an index of ecological density on late-winter range during the previous year.

Many other indices of general animal condition in response to ecological density have been used or at least suggested. Some are: skeletal ratios, especially femur to hind-foot length (Klein 1964); weight and morphology of adrenal glands, which are expected to change with increasing stress caused by increasing ecological density (Hughes and Mall 1958; Christian, Flyger, and Davis 1960); and blood parameters in response to nutrition (Rosen and Bischoff 1952; Browman and Sears 1955; Teeri et al. 1958; Taber et al. 1959). These measurements may find more use in the future.

No method for obtaining an index to population condition is ideal. The characteristics of an ideal index are listed here as a standard for evaluating any index method. (This list is partly after Riney 1955).

1   Index values are objectively measured, as with a calipers, ruler or scale. Subjectively determined values, such as good, medium, and poor fat reserves, vary among observers and may be biased by recent experience.

2   Index values are reproducible among and within observers. Even objectively measured values may vary among observers. For instance, the method used to extend an animal to measure body length may vary.

3   Index values should be obtained inexpensively with a minimum of simple equipment.

4   Index values should be sensitive to small changes in ecological denisty. This will be true if index values change rapidly over a wide range of ecological density and if there is little variation in index values among animals living at the same ecological density.

5   The method for obtaining index values should be usable for all sex-age groups of animals.

6   The method for obtaining index values should be usable with live as well as dead animals.

7   Normal seasonal variation in the index values should be known.

8   There should be good standards available for comparing and interpreting index values. A standard for comparison may be index values from some population known to be in either good, normal, or poor condition and, therefore, known to have either low, normal, or high ecological density. A standard may be index values for a series of experimental animals maintained on diets ranging from poor to good nutritional planes. Lacking standards for comparison, a change in average condition-index values for a target population over a series of years may be interpreted as a change in ecological density.

At high ecological densities, limited resources may not support good levels of reproductive success. These limiting factors are often nutritional, as illustrated (by experiments) in Example 6.1, but competition for space or for any limiting food or cover resource can also trigger behavioral-physiological mechanisms that depress reproduction. Reproductive success of a population is, in these cases, an index to ecological density, low reproductive success indicating high ecological density. Reproductive success may be measured as (1) percent of females breeding, (2) litter or clutch sizes, (3) number of litters or clutches per breeding season, or (4) age-ratios and population age-structures. Methods for measuring these parameters of reproductive success are discussed in Chapter 9.

Likewise, at high ecological densities limited resources may result in unusually high rates of mortality. However, mortality rates of wild populations are difficult to measure and have not been used extensively as indices to ecological density. One exception has been mortality of big game populations due to malnutrition on overused winter range—an obvious evidence of a high ecological density on the winter range.

Deficiency of a nutrient in the diet of a population may be severe enough to cause nutritional disease. Symptoms of the disease are, therefore, an index to the balance between the nutrient requirements of the animals and the availability of the deficient nutrient in the habitat and are an index to ecological density with respect to a specific habitat component. For instance, symptoms of calcium and/ or phosphorus deficiency are the reduction of ash concentration in bones and changes in the structure of bone tissues. In severe cases, the disease osteomalacia occurs. It should be possible to detect deficiencies of calcium and/ or phosphorus in wild animals by analyzing their bones chemically or histologically.

EXAMPLE 18.4   A Condition Index Based on Body Weight and Length

Bailey weighed and measured cottontail rabbits, obtaining the data presented in Fig. 18.6 (1968). The weight-length relationship of each rabbit is a measure of its slenderness or heaviness and is used as a condition index. In the sample of 499 cottontails (Fig. 18.6), a rabbit with average condition would provide weight and length data fitting any point on the curved line described by Weight $= 15.6 + 5.48$ (Length)^3. Solving this

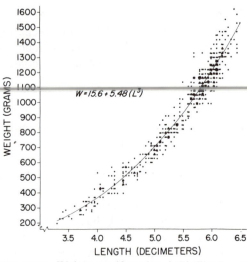

$$W = 15.6 + 5.48 (L^3)$$

Fig. 18.6   Weights and lengths of 499 Illinois cottontails live-trapped during May to November.

equation for the regression coefficient and rounding off the dependent variable intercept produces the equation

$$5.48 = (W - 16)/L^{3.}$$

The right side of this equation is used to compute an index of the physical condition of these rabbits. For example, any animal in Fig. 18.6 with a condition index greater than 5.48 was heavier than average for its length class. Curvilinear regression analysis permits use of the value 5.48 as a measure of average condition for both young (small) and old (large) animals, permitting comparisons among age classes.

Note that if the simple quotient weight/length were used as a condition index, comparisons could not be made among age classes of rabbits. Consider two rabbits, one weighing 366 g and being 4 dm long the other weighing 1199 g and being 6 dm long. Condition indices for these rabbits calculated by $(W - 16)/L^3$ are both 5.48, for their measurements fall on the curved line in Fig. 18.6. However, the former rabbit has a weight to length ratio of 91.5; the latter has a ratio of 200.

EXAMPLE 18.5   Use of a reproductive index as a basis for management decisions

Of 28 adult does collected during 1939 to 1943 on the De Bar Mountain Area of the Adirondack Region, New York, only 57 percent were pregnant, averaging 1.2 embryos per pregnant adult doe. This is poor reproductive performance for white-tailed deer. In addition, winter starvation of deer was a chronic problem in the Adirondacks. All evidence indicated a high ecological density of deer.

Management recommendations called for a reduction of the Adirondack herd through harvest of antlerless deer in 1943. The population in the vicinity of the De Bar

TABLE 18.3   Indices of Reproductive Performance of Adult Female White-tailed Deer on the De Bar Mountain Area, New York During 1939 to 1949 (Cheatum and Severinghaus 1950)

1939 to 1943		1947 to 1949	
Does Pregnant (percent)	Embryos Per Pregnant Doe	Does Pregnant (percent)	Embryos Per Pregnant Doe
57(28)[a]	1.2(16)	100(9)	1.8(9)

[a]Sample sizes in parentheses.

Area was heavily harvested in 1943. In addition, the De Bar Area itself, previously a refuge, was opened to hunting in 1945. This further reduced the deer herd in the De Bar Mountain district. Concurrently, logging operations began in the vicinity of the De Bar Mountain Area in 1946. These cuttings provided deer forage by dropping tree tops and also by stimulating sprout growth. The reduction in deer numbers and improvement in deer habitat constituted a decline in ecological density of deer.

Adult does collected on the De Bar Area in 1947 to 1949 showed markedly improved reproductive rates (Table 18.3) in response to the change in ecological density. (Sample sizes in these data are small. Intensive management of deer would require statistical analysis of data and perhaps collections of larger numbers of deer).

Habitat-condition Indices   At high ecological densities, overuse of limiting habitat resources may occur. If food resources are being overused, one of the first signs of increasing ecological density is overuse of preferred food species, as indicated by their decline in vigor and their ultimate disappearance from the habitat. Example 6.3 illustrates the loss of preferred food species due to high ecological densities of white-tailed deer, and Fig. 13.10 provides a conceptual model of vegetative retrogression due to high ecological density of herbivores.

Many states use surveys of the vigor, condition, and utilization of preferred browse species on winter ranges as indices of the ecological density of large ungulates. Dasmann described some of the methods used and interpretations made (1951). Browse surveys usually involve measuring plants in one wintering area for several years to ascertain trends in forage condition and use. Often browse transects are permanently located and the same plants are observed each year. Overuse of browse plants is indicated by a progressive decline in plant vigor and in declining production and increasing utilization of annual growth, causing a hedged appearance and an increase in the amount of dead material in the shrub crown. Another evaluation of overuse is possible if percent utilization of annual growth can be compared to allowable levels of utilization that do not ultimately cause a decline in plant vigor. Long-term research on the effects of various levels of clipping (artificial browsing) on plant productivity are necessary to determine allowable levels of utilization (for example, Shepherd 1971).

Interpretation of forage-transect data indicating production and utilization

TABLE 18.4 Percent of Serviceberry Browse Leaders Utilized by Deer on the Goat Creek Winter Range, Swan Valley, Montana During 1960–1969. (Hildebrand 1971)

Year	1960	1961	1962	1963	1964	1965	1966	1967	1968	1969
Utilization (%)	46	35	60	38	57	74	78	84	78	85

requires a consideration of normal year-to-year variation of local ecological density of ungulates due to weather patterns. Variation of growing-season precipitation may cause large changes in plant production, altering production to utilization ratios temporarily. Winter snow depths affect ungulate distribution. Browse transects showing heavy use during a severe winter may show little use during a mild winter because the animals wintered elsewhere. In management areas where year-to-year variation in ungulate distribution is large, production or utilization data should be obtained from many key areas within the range and weather data should be used as a covariant in the analysis.

EXAMPLE 18.6 Browse Utilization: an Index to Ecological Density

Hildebrand compiled data from browse transects observed by the Montana Fish and Game Department in the Swan Valley winter range of white-tailed deer (1971; Table 18.4). These data show large annual variations, but a gradual increasing utilization of serviceberry during 1960 to 1969. The indication of increasing ecological density of deer was further verified by evidence of winter starvation losses. More than 20 dead deer were found per square mile of winter range in 1969 and in 1970.

DATA AND ANALYSIS FOR EXTENSIVE MANAGEMENT

The best wildlife management requires continued assessment of the target population and habitat and accurate prediction of the results of management procedures. Many management programs have suffered from insufficient information and inadequate data analysis and interpretation. A prime reason for insufficient data as a basis for management has been the insufficient staffs and budgets assigned to gathering data on wildlife. In some less populated western states, one district wildlife biologist with a small supporting staff may be responsible for all wildlife, including several game species, on more than 10,000 square miles of rather inaccessible land. The district may include 10 or more big-game management units requiring separate management considerations. Habitat management in the district may depend on the biologist's ability to influence decisions of several people in the U.S. Forest Service and Bureau of Land Management and numerous private landowners, both corporations and individuals.

In this situation management decisions will be based on the best information obtainable, but there will always be a great deal of uncertainty about the status of each population and its habitat. Improved staffing may come to the district following growth of human populations and intensification of management efforts. In the meantime the district biologist must seek new ways to obtain information on the wildlife of the district and reduce the uncertainty of management decisions.

This district wildlife biologist typically has a little data on each of several population and habitat parameters. For each deer herd, perhaps there are some check-station data on the ages and conditions of harvested deer. There may be reproductive tracts from a few highway-killed does for evolution of reproductive success. There probably are some forage-survey transects, hopefully observed for several years, to show trends in forage production and utilization. Weather records may be available for interpreting forage production and utilization data. The manager stays informed of activities affecting habitat, perhaps logging operations or grazing practices by public or private agencies. He or she must then ask: Do I need better information for managing this deer herd? (Perhaps there is little public access to and use of the herd and no increase in use is expected for many years. Publicly financed management effort might better be directed elsewhere.) If I need better information, what kind of data would be most useful? Will my budget permit obtaining this data? Would local sportsmen or school groups donate adequate labor to obtain population or habitat information? If the management of one deer herd is important enough, the biologist will spend time and money to improve the data base for managing that herd. He or she will see that meaningful data are obtained and carefully analyzed before making management decisions. If management of another deer herd is considered less important, less effort will be applied to understanding that herd because budgets are always limited. But management should be based on careful analysis of the best information available. Careful analysis includes statistical evaluation of the variability of the data and of the significance of trends. This is especially important when sample sizes are small. Analysis showing large sampling variation usually dictates caution in management recommendations.

Even in extensive programs of wildlife management, there are almost always some data available and some budget for obtaining data for management decision making. Management based on no local data is seldom excusable.

EXAMPLE 18.7   Use of Two Indices of Ecological Density of Deer

This example is primarily speculation. I believe the ideas presented are correct for many deer herds. This example shows the kind of thinking necessary and the many factors to be considered in selecting a data base for management decisions.

Figure 18.7a illustrates a relationship between ecological density of deer and browse-condition indices such as live-crown ratio, percent of twigs browsed, or percent of plants in various form-classes related to utilization (i.e., moderately hedged or severely hedged). Figure 18.7b illustrates a relationship between ecological density of deer and reproduction indices such as average number of embryos per doe or doe-fawn ratios. Dashed lines in both figures indicate variation of the indices among areas within the deer range, among years, among deer, or among browse species.

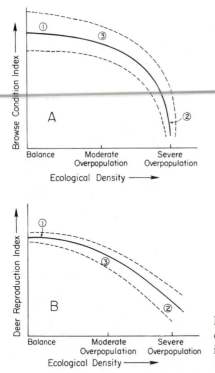

Fig. 18.7   Two indices of ecological density of deer. Dashed lines show expected variability of index values. Further explanation is in Example 18.7.

At point 1 in Fig. 18.7a, browse plants are in good condition. However variation of index-data is large. Overutilization may appear in some locations while browse is little-used in other locations. Overutilization may occur locally during unusually severe winters that concentrate animals more than usual; or it may occur following especially dry growing seasons resulting in unusually low browse production. In all of these cases the most-preferred forage species will show overutilization, while less-preferred species will not.

At point 2 in Fig. 18.7a, all browse plants are in poor condition throughout the range, every year. Browse condition indices are most useful as indices of ecological density of deer when there is severe overpopulation. In this condition variation of the condition indices is low, and few data are required to demonstrate overpopulation.

Many states once based their harvest quotas for deer on browse condition indices. This worked well during severe overpopulations of deer that occurred in most states because of earlier protective bucks-only harvests and declining deer habitats resulting from natural succession and human development on deer range. With severe over-populations, few data and only simple analysis were necessary to indicate that there were too many deer for the range. As range improvement was seldom feasible, the management decision was usually to harvest more deer and reduce the herds. This management often worked—deer herds were reduced. The ecological density of deer was further reduced in some areas by programs of browse management, such as mechanical or pyric disturbance of winter range, by reduction of abundant populations of domestic stock, and by increased growth of deer forage following logging.

With reduced ecological densities of deer, browse condition indices became difficult to interpret. Variation of the data increased. Whereas poor browse condition indicated "too many deer," what did an improving trend in browse condition mean? Too few deer? About the right number of deer? What did overutilization in some years mean? What level of browse utilization corresponded to an ecological density producing the maximum sustained harvest of deer (assuming that to be a management goal)?

At point 1 in Fig. 18.7b, deer are in good condition and reproductive success is maximum. All does show high fecundity in all units of the range. Occasional dry growing seasons or severe winters have little effect on reproductive success.

At point 2 in Fig. 18.7b, reproduction indices are reduced, as most deer are in poor condition. Reproductive success varies considerably among years—a result of the vagaries of precipitation determining forage production and snow depth that affect forage availability and deer distribution. Although forage is overutilized everywhere, in some years and some parts of the range it provides enough nutrients and energy to support fair reproduction. Occasionally ecological density of the population is temporarily reduced by winter starvation. This may be followed by a temporary response in reproductive success—adding to the among-years variation in reproduction indices.

If browse-condition indices become difficult to use as a basis for managing deer herds at ecological densities less than severe overpopulation, are reproductive-condition indices better? The answer to this question turns on three factors: (1) the steepness of lines at point 3 in Fig. 18.7a and 18.7b, (2) the variation of the indices at these points, and (3) the usefulness of reproduction data and of browse-condition data in measuring attainment of management goals. (This assumes that management goals are attained when ecological density of deer is closer to point 3 in Fig. 18.7a and 18.7b than to points 1 or 2 in the figures.

The steepness of slope at point 3 determines the sensitivity of the indices to changes in ecological density. An index is more useful if small changes in ecological density result in large and, therefore, easily detected changes in index values. I know of no data permitting comparison of these indices in this manner.

The foregoing discussion suggests that variation of reproduction indices is less at point 3 in Fig. 18.7b than is variation of browse indices at 3 in Fig. 18.7a. If this is correct, the quantity of data needed to detect important changes in ecological density will be less for the reproduction index than for the browse-condition index. However, the cost of obtaining adequate reproduction data must ultimately be compared to the cost of obtaining adequate browse-condition data.

Lastly, deer reproduction data have utility beyond being an index of ecological density. In intensive management, reproduction data may be used with other population parameters in population modeling to predict harvestable surplus. If maximum sustained harvestable surplus is the management goal, data on reproductive success of deer are more closely related to this goal than are data on browse condition. This emphasizes the importance and value of reproduction data in these programs.

On the other hand, wildlife management programs in the national parks are not aimed at the harvestable surplus of big game. Objectives of management in the parks are to maintain a balance between habitats and wildlife numbers so that examples of pristine ecosystems are maintained. In these cases, data on browse condition may be more closely related to management goals and, therefore, be more valuable than are data on deer reproductive success.

DATA AND ANALYSIS FOR INTENSIVE MANAGEMENT

As management staff and budgets increase, management programs become more intensive. Managers can obtain more and better information on target populations and their habitats. This information provides a more accurate and more complete picture of conditions and trends of populations and habitats. More accurate predictions of the consequences of management options and more precise attainment of management objectives should result.

However, the more information available, the more difficult is the job of integrating the information into a comprehensive picture of conditions and trends. Integrating data on several interacting population and habitat parameters soon becomes a voluminous and frightful bookkeeping problem.

Integration also requires some assumption about relationships between two or more habitat or population characteristics. This assumption is a *model*, simply a mental picture of some processes in an ecosystem. Wildlife managers have always used models. Some have been simple models. The idea that during plant succession following forest disturbance, production of forage for deer increases for a number of years and then declines to predisturbance levels is a simple model involving two factors—forage production and time. Some commonly used models have been more complex. The idea that a high ecological density of deer results in overuse and decline of food supplies, followed by poor nutrition of deer, lower reproductive success, higher mortality rates and fewer deer to harvest, is a more complex model. Both of these models are vague because the relationships between factors are not quantified. Vague models are adequate for extensive management programs because (1) the amount of data available does not justify use of intensive modeling efforts, and (2) management objectives may not require maximization of wildlife production nor precise measurement of conditions and trends of populations or habitats.

However, with intensive management more data are available, and more precisely defined management goals require accurate predictions of the consequences of management options. The problems of handling large amounts of data in quantitatively stated models may be solved using the computer. Computers are relatively new tools for handling data. Computer simulation modeling is a new tool for testing and manipulating quantitatively stated ideas. The advantages of simulation modeling are:

1   Simulation modeling forces quantification of ideas.

2   Simulation modeling permits simultaneous use of many ideas, quantified into complex models. Perhaps the human mind can analyze the complexity of wildlife ecology in no other way.

3   Simulation modeling will not permit simultaneous use of incompatible ideas. Quantification of incompatible ideas into a model generally produces absurd output, not simulating reality, indicating the inadequacy of the ideas.

4   Once an adequate model is produced, the sensitivity of the output, presumably population or habitat information, to changes in input, presumably environmental factors, may be tested. If the output is not very sensitive to changes in, say, the age structure of the harvested animals, then crude but inexpensive methods will suffice for obtaining these data from hunters. This permits use of funds for obtaining precise estimates of other parameters that are more important in determining population or habitat status.

5   If the model is adequate, the results of proposed management activities may be tested in advance. For instance, one may test the effect of harvesting 25 percent of the female animals every other year on population levels during the next 20 years.

EXAMPLE 18.8   Computer Simulation of a Complex Habitat

Giles and Snyder described a model for simulating changes in the combined production of big-game forage on many independently changing habitat units (1970). This example presents their concepts in abbreviated form. Responsibility for any misinterpretation is mine, however.

In many places, production of forage on big-game winter range is primarily determined by plant succession. In general, forage production increases following disturbance such as fire or logging, then decreases to predisturbance levels (Fig. 18.8). However, site characteristics and the intensity of disturbance affect the rate of change in production over time and also the peak levels of production attained during succession. Study of forage production on a variety of sites exhibiting many stages of plant succession permits developing a series of forage production — succession curves (Fig.

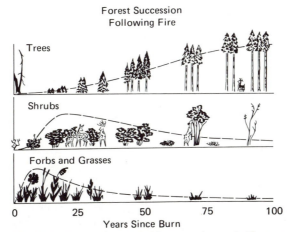

Fig. 18.8   General pattern of succession and effect on forage production by shrubs and herbs. Figure from Lyon 1966.

18.9). Each curve describes forage production during succession on a particular kind of site following a particular intensity of disturbance.

The managed winter range is then divided into a series of units, each unit having relatively uniform site conditions; and supporting vegetation originating from a common disturbance. Each unit is assigned to one of the forage production — succession curves depending on its site conditions. The age of vegetation (time since disturbance) and the acreage of each unit is recorded. This information is used to predict future

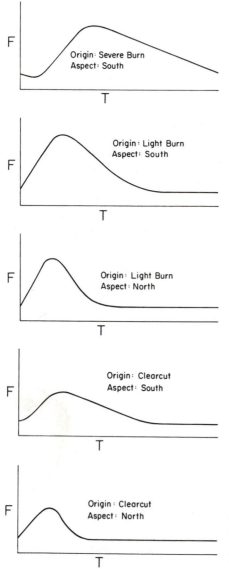

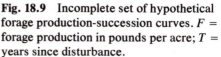

Fig. 18.9 Incomplete set of hypothetical forage production-succession curves. $F =$ forage production in pounds per acre; $T =$ years since disturbance.

production of big-game forage on the unit of range. The combined predictions of production for all units within the winter range simulate the future of total forage production on the entire range (Fig. 18.10). Calculating and summing these predictions for many units of winter range is a large bookkeeping problem, one best handled by computer.

Predictions of total forage production on the entire winter range can be used as a basis for management decisions. If a stable production of big-game forage is desired, but forage production is predicted to decline in 10 years, initiation of new successions by logging, controlled burning, or other planned disturbance will be necessary within the next decade.

PRINCIPLES

P18.1 Selecting a data basis for a management program is one of the management biologist's most important decisions. Selection will be influenced by the availability and precision of methods for measuring population and habitat characteristics and by budget constraints; but the selected data base should have a meaningful relation to management objectives.

P18.2 The types of wildlife measurements are (1) population indices, (2) population censuses, (3) habitat measurements, and (4) indices of ecological

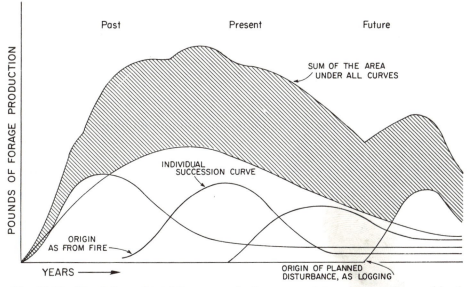

Fig. 18.10 Simulation of total forage production on a winter range as the combined production on several habitat units. For clarity only a few habitat units are illustrated. In practice, many more units are likely to be considered on one winter range. Figure adapted from Giles and Snyder 1970.

density, including population-condition and habitat-condition indices. Population indices and indices of ecological density are most often used in extensive programs of management. Population censuses and habitat measurements are most often used in intensive programs and may serve as bases for population and/or habitat models for predicting the results of various management alternatives.

P18.3   Whenever wildlife measurements involve sampling, samples should be obtained so that statistical analysis can be performed to quantify the precisions of each estimate.

CHAPTER 19

THE ART OF WILDLIFE MANAGEMENT

Remember, nothing that's good works by
itself, just to please you—you've
got to *make* the damn thing work.

Thomas Alva Edison

Wildlife management is the art of making land produce populations of wildlife, for harvest or other values. In simplest terms, wildlife management consists of a series of decisions—whether to have a long hunting season or a short one, whether to plant food patches and pine trees or to manipulate food and cover with fire or herbicides, whether to spend money on a game-check station or on a forage survey, whether to compromise biologically optimum goals with prevailing public opinion or to attempt influencing public opinion, whether to improve existing habitat or to purchase more land, and whether to feed deer during severe winters or to reduce the deer herd or to improve the natural supply of winter foods.

These decisions must be made every year. Failure to reach a decision is, in essence, a decision to do nothing—at least nothing new. Decisions are often based on limited information about how the target wildlife population, its habitat, or the public may respond to management practices. Decisions based on limited information should include provisions for increasing the information base; that is, the response of the target population, of its habitat, or of the public to management practices should be measured.

MANAGEMENT VARIES IN INTENSITY

Ideally, wildlife managers would have unlimited budgets and would know all they needed to know about their target populations and habitats. Tested methods for measuring each population and habitat would be available. Alternatives for treating each population and habitat would be several, and their consequences would be well known. There would be no limits imposed by budgets or lack of knowledge, and very intensive management could be applied (Table 19.1).

Of course, there are always budget and knowledge constraints on wildlife management. The greater the constraints imposed by limited budgets and limited knowledge, the more extensive a management program must be. In the most extensive programs, wildlife managers deal with much uncertainty. There is uncertainty over the status of the target population and its habitat, over public desires for the population and habitat, and over the consequences of management treatments. Extensive programs of management involve a cautious testing of treatments until their consequences have been measured (Table 19.1).

MANAGEMENT IS DYNAMIC

Leopold described the historical development of wildlife management in the United States and elsewhere as following this sequence (1933): (1) restriction of harvest, (2) control of competing predators, (3) establishment of refuges, (4) restocking, game farming, and transplanting, and (5) habitat management. To this list we can add: (6) informing and communicating with the public and other land users. Now, more than ever, with increasing demands on all land resources,

TABLE 19.1 Comparison of Extensive and Intensive Programs for Managing a Public Wildlife Resource

Management Characteristics	Extensive Management	Intensive Management
Budget time, labor, dollars	Small	Large
Knowledge of biota, techniques	Little, empirical, untested	Much, detailed, tested, and reliable
Management units	Large areas, many populations	Small areas, few populations
Goals public needs and desires	Unsure, tested by public response to incremental changes in program	Well-defined, based more on surveys of public desires

Local data
  experience, population and
  habitat data, information on
  user satisfaction
	Little, disjointed	More, some can be integrated into models

Uncertainty of
  population, habitat, or
  status of user satisfaction
	Large	Small

Predictions	Large confidence limits based more on theory, less accurate	Small confidence limits based more on local data, more accurate
Management treatments	Small incremental changes, cautious	Larger incremental changes, bold

wildlife managers need support from an informed public and must work with foresters, ranchers, miners, and others who use the land and alter wildlife habitat.

In this historical sequence, each new technique was added because the preceding set of techniques was found inadequate to cope with new problems caused by human population growth and land development. Control of overharvest was sufficient management in a sparsely settled country. But as numbers of hunters and land users grew, game declined despite restriction of harvest. Predator control has often been proposed as a solution to game scarcity. Most often it has not worked, being based on a limited view of how the abundance of wildlife is determined. Refuges, where harvest was not allowed, were established for migratory and nonmigratory wildlife. Refuge establishment produced mixed results, having been most successful in supporting populations of migratory waterfowl. But some refuges contained poor habitat and produced little wildlife; others, although productive, had only local effects, as nonmobile species failed to repopulate surrounding areas that often had poor habitat. On some refuges, deer populations increased to the point of severe destruction of their forage resources (Flader 1974). Game farming, stocking, and transplanting were the next panaceas. It was, of course, unwise to expect pen-reared wildlife to survive when released into habitats already too poor to support truly wild animals. Game farming and release of birds in the hunting season provided game in the bag, but this was too expensive for broad application. Most transplants of exotic game birds, adapted to environments in other parts of the world, failed. The ring-necked pheasant, Hungarian partridge, and chukar partridge are one notable and two partial exceptions. Realization of the importance and complexity of good habitat came slowly. Habitat management could produce wildlife. But as our population and its demands on the land grew, there was less habitat dedicated to wildlife production. It has become more necessary to promote wildlife production in multiple-use programs and to preserve wildlife habitats through the political process. As a result, the communications aspects of wildlife management have grown in importance.

In developing and testing the six tools of wildlife management, none have been abandoned. Harvest control, refuge establishment, and habitat management are still very important. Stocking, transplanting, game farming, and predator control are used less than in the past but are still useful in local situations.

The historical development of wildlife management is marked by changes over a long period. We expect such trends to continue. Among them will be a greater emphasis on the nongame values of wildlife.

Wildlife managers also deal with change on local levels. Habitats change with land use, disturbance, and biotic succession. Public interests, demands, and goals change. Management budgets are rarely stable. Research produces new knowledge of wildlife and habitats, and new management techniques are developed. The file of data on the target population and habitat grows. Each year requires a new set of decisions. The manager's job is to "fine tune" the management program—that is, to move from extensive management toward more intensive management. Beware of routine. It signals stagnation, which is seldom justified in a changing world.

MANAGEMENT IS GOAL ORIENTED

Management activities are usually designed to change the status of the wildlife resource and/or the satisfaction of resource users from an unsatisfactory condition to another more desirable condition. The more desirable condition is the management goal.

Surprisingly, some wildlife management programs have existed for years without reconsideration of goals and without clearly defined goals. Management goals should be carefully defined in writing. Although goals at first seem to be a simple concern—We'd like to have more deer—they are often surprisingly complex. Is the goal (1) a larger year-round population of deer, (2) a larger annual harvestable surplus, (3) a larger annual harvest of deer, (4) a larger annual harvest of trophy-sized deer, (5) more hunters in the field, regardless of their success or lack of it, (6) quality hunting experiences, (7) more deer in places where tourists can see them, (8) maintenance of the condition of deer habitat, or (9) a minimum of damage to forest or agricultural crops by deer? Sometimes, after careful thought, long-accepted goals are found to be contradictory. Perhaps we cannot have trophy deer and a large annual harvest. Most management programs will have several goals, possibly arranged in priorities. These goals should be reviewed periodically.

Since wildlife is a publicly owned resource, management goals are usually public goals. They are often integrated with other land-use goals, for most land is managed equally, if not primarily, for products other than wildlife. There are diverse public and private interests in how land and wildlife are managed. Communication with many individuals and interest groups is necessary in defining management goals. If this communication can be abundant, management goals for public wildlife resources can be more precisely defined. However, the public's many and changing views are difficult to discern, especially when there is little time and budget for public hearings, as in extensive programs of management. Lindblom noted that in these cases managers of public resources continually test the acceptabilities of their selected goals by measuring public responses to small, incremental changes in management programs (1959). When the public complains, managers learn that they are moving toward unpopular goals, and they proceed in new directions to test other goals. If the public complains long and loud, it may be necessary to intensify contact that enhances public understanding of the resource and its potentials and to gain the public's views on land-use goals.

Sometimes people will accept the goals selected by management but reject its methods. The method of harvesting deer (seasons, limits, mangement areas) may attract more attention than the number of deer to be harvested. Habitat improvement may be accepted but use of prescribed fire or herbicide to manage vegetation may not be. To the public, methods are often indistinguishable from goals.

It is the manager's job to meld diverse public opinions into one set of management goals. If a public employee, the manager's personal views on land-use goals must be submerged, with two exceptions. I have already suggested that he or she uphold the primacy of the goals of maintaining land productivity and environmental diversity.

MANAGEMENT IS A CYCLIC, INCREMENTAL PROCESS

King described wildlife management as a linear process (1941). Ideally, a wildlife manager first obtains a great deal of information about the target population and its habitat through inventory, census, and yield determination (Fig. 19.1). The

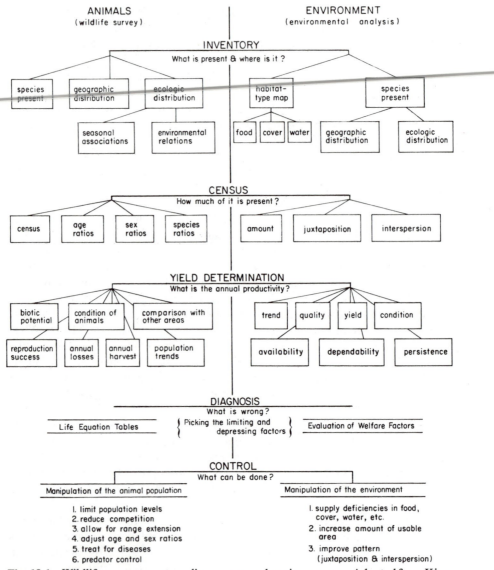

ANIMALS
(wildlife survey)

ENVIRONMENT
(environmental analysis)

INVENTORY
What is present & where is it?

| species present | geographic distribution | ecologic distribution | habitat-type map | species present |

| seasonal associations | environmental relations | food | cover | water | geographic distribution | ecologic distribution |

CENSUS
How much of it is present?

| census | age ratios | sex ratios | species ratios | amount | juxtaposition | interspersion |

YIELD DETERMINATION
What is the annual productivity?

| biotic potential | condition of animals | comparison with other areas | trend | quality | yield | condition |

| reproduction success | annual losses | annual harvest | population trends | availability | dependability | persistence |

DIAGNOSIS
What is wrong?

Life Equation Tables   { Picking the limiting and depressing factors }   Evaluation of Welfare Factors

CONTROL
What can be done?

Manipulation of the animal population

1. limit population levels
2. reduce competition
3. allow for range extension
4. adjust age and sex ratios
5. treat for diseases
6. predator control

Manipulation of the environment

1. supply deficiencies in food, cover, water, etc.
2. increase amount of usable area
3. improve pattern (juxtaposition & interspersion)

Fig. 19.1   Wildlife management as a linear, comprehensive process. Adapted from King 1941.

manager is then prepared to diagnose the situation and select and apply treatments to increase wildlife abundance. No measure of treatment efficacy is necessary. Lindblom termed this method of management *comprehensive*, because it involves a comprehensive analysis of the resource system (1959). He considered the comprehensive method too theoretical and suggested that public resources are usually managed by a cyclic, incremental process described below and in Fig. 19.2, which combines King's ideas and those of Lindblom.

Management almost always begins with some information, however little, about the target wildlife population, its habitat, or about user satisfaction with the population. If the condition or trend of any of these is unsatisfactory, more satisfactory goals are selected. A management treatment that, it is predicted, will change the present condition or trend toward a desired status is then applied. At this point, the value of the management program is unknown. New information concerning the population, habitat, or users must be obtained to evaluate the success of management. This information has been named the data basis of management. The new information then becomes the basis for a new set of decisions concerning goals and whether management treatments should be discontinued, expanded, altered or replaced (Fig. 19.2).

The population and habitat information bases of wildlife management are discussed in Chapter 18. I repeat that getting this local data is the manager's job. For some reason it has been common to assume that any collection of wildlife data is a research job and not the responsibility of management. This is absurd. (When the manager of a supermarket inventories the stock on the shelves, it is not called research.) Management must measure the status of the resource it manages. Without this information, the value of sometimes expensive treatments remains unknown, the success of achieving goals is not measured, and management may be a worthless display of activity.

Management treatments are selected because it is predicted that, by their application, goals will be achieved. The bases of these predictions are (1) major principles of wildlife ecology, (2) empirical knowledge based on local experience, and (3) detailed, local knowledge of the responses of populations or habitats to treatments.

Lacking any local experience on responses of wildlife to treatments, the manager should begin a program with the cautious applicaton of major principles of ecology. The major principles used to predict wildlife responses to management treatments are (1) the broad concept of welfare and limiting factors discussed in Chapter 12, (2) the concept of biotic succession, Chapter 13, and (3) the sigmoid population model, Chapter 15. For example, with these principles a wildlife manager can predict that increased habitat diversity is likely to increase abundance and variety of wildlife; that habitat protection or, conversely, disturbance will favor or inhibit wildlife species according to their successional relationships; or that an uncontrolled, forage-limited population will eventually damage its forage resources, resulting in lower animal quality and changes in reproduction and/or mortality rates. Thus, even in the most extensive management programs, with little local information, some management prescriptions are possible.

Once the management program is under way, local experience—preferably carefully collected local data—on the effectiveness of each management treatment begins to accumulate. Likewise, information on the responses of the target habitat and population to weather variables accumulates. This information

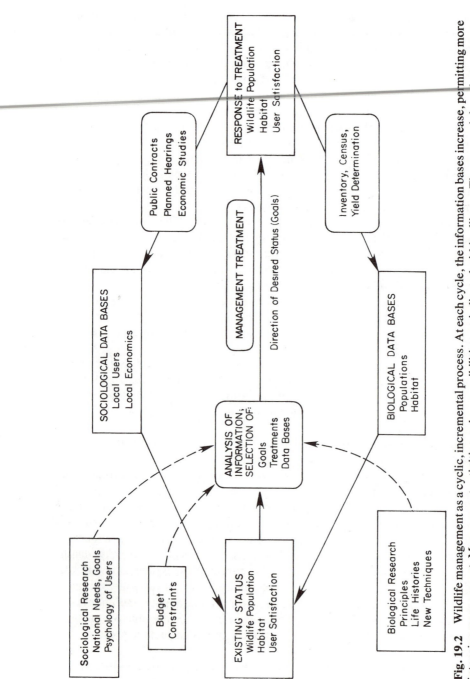

Fig. 19.2 Wildlife management as a cyclic, incremental process. At each cycle, the information bases increase, permitting more intensive management. Management activities and responsibilities are indicated within ellipses. The process is based on concepts in King 1941 and Lindblom 1959.

should be carefully recorded. In too many management programs it has been unrecorded and lost with changes in personnel. This information becomes the basis for intensifying the management program, even *without an increase in the management budget*. It includes local empirical knowledge of what treatments work (i.e. burning 20 percent of the habitat each year produces quail), even if the manager does not know *why* they work (what specific welfare factors for quail are affected). The management program should be designed to enhance accumulation of meaningful local information. Habitat treatments are first tested on small areas. Treatments are located and replicated so that results can be analyzed statistically for interpretation. Responses of hunters to new regulations are tested locally or on a small number of hunters. There is a carefully planned collection of data to evaluate each new managment practice. In this, the wildlife manager uses methods of the research scientist. He or she hypothesizes that a treatment will accomplish certain goals and then tests the hypothesis.

With time, this process is intensified. With each cycle of management, more abundant and more detailed information on habitats and populations is collected. Some data can be integrated into population or habitat models (such as in Example 18.8). The manager's predictions become more precise. Rather than predicting an increase of 10 to 30 percent by a deer herd, one might predict the *number* of additional deer to be expected, by sex and age classes.

Whatever the intensity of management, the process is cyclic and incremental. Management moves forward testing its methods and its goals (Lindblom 1959). The background of experience and data accumulate, permitting more precise and more efficient management at each cycle (Bailey 1982).

SPECIES MANAGEMENT REQUIRES LIFE-HISTORY INFORMATION

Habitat diversity will produce an abundance and variety of wildlife. However, if management goals include increasing or controlling a population of one wildlife species, the wildlife manager's job is to become thoroughly familiar with all that is known of that species. This information is commonly called a species' life history.

This book has presented little information on life histories of wildlife species, and only to illustrate wildlife management principles. However, knowledge of the life histories of species is *essential* to most wildlife management.

The wildlife manager will not find all the needed life-history information in a single book. Some species have been reviewed rather thoroughly (for example, see Bump et al. 1947; Wallmo 1981; Kelsall 1968). But knowledge of life histories is dynamic. New information is being added. Old concepts are being tested and sometimes modified or even discarded. Information on a species in one part of its range often does not apply elsewhere in its range. It is the wildlife manager's job to study the literature on species for which he or she is responsible. Much of this literature is in scientific journals available in major libraries. However, the manager should have some key references in a personal library.

MANAGEMENT IS AN ART

Despite contrary allegations, wildlife management is not a science. Wildlife managers apply the science of biology. They use some methods of science in their work. But management is an art.

Science is any body of organized, tested, and accepted knowledge; or it is research, the process of developing, testing, organizing, and communicating knowledge. Neither of these definitions includes anything about management. As an art, wildlife management is the application of knowledge to achieve goals. Wildlife management is primarily the application of biology, especially ecology, and the wildlife manager is well educated in these sciences. The wildlife manager uses scientific methods to obtain information about populations and habitats. In this, he or she requires the objectivity of a scientist. Wildlife managers also require skills achieved through experience—communications skills and manual skills. They use judgment in making decisions, especially when decisions must be based on limited, often empirical, information. In selecting management goals, they must compare and judge values. Science does not deal in value judgments.

Recent decades have produced some curious ideas concerning the relation-ship between science and wildlife management. Americans have long revered science and, to some extent, scientists. For years we educated our best students for wildlife research; the rest could become wildlife managers. Research posi-tions required graduate degrees and received higher salaries than did manage-ment positions that were open to baccalaureates. This practice was demeaning to the profession of wildlife management. Some failures in wildlife management have been due to this attitude. We produced good wildlife research but often poor or no application.

In the 1960s, science was further exalted with the publicity given aerospace technology and Russian-American competition in research of all kinds. Some tried to put wildlife management on the bandwagon by calling wildlife manage-ment a science. Many university departments changed their names from wildlife management or wildlife conservation to wildlife biology or wildlife science at that time. The movement reinforced ideas that science is something better than management, that it is more difficult and more important, and that it requires better employees. These ideas are wrong. In the long run, research and applica-tion are equally important.

Is wildlife management *more* difficult than wildlife research? Like research, management requires original thinking. It is not just the application of research, as some management handbooks imply. Most research biologists concentrate on parts of ecosystems. Management biologists must consider many ecosystems and many wildlife species. They must consider many land products and many land users. Managers must make decisions every year; they cannot wait for more data. Although wildlife management is not a science, it is both complicated and important. Management deserves some of our best professionals, and they deserve education, respect, and compensation equal to that of research biologists.

WILDLIFE MANAGEMENT IN SUMMARY

Just as there are many ways to manage a farm or to manage a forest, there are many ways to manage a quail population, a deer herd, or a songbird habitat. Factors determining wildlife populations vary continuously in time and space. Wildlife and wildlife habitats possess many values, including some negative values. Public or private policy may dictate emphasis on some values more than others. Thus, management objectives vary. Further, there may be several ways to reach one objective. Each management opportunity is a separate challenge, requiring separate decision making. The manager's job may be hectic, but it is never dull. It is unique.

This text does not tell the student how to manage any wildlife population. This may create some anxiety, because most undergraduates crave absolutes—rules to rely on as a basis for similar management decisions to be repeated from traineeship to retirement. There are no such rules in wildlife management. When the student becomes a wildlife manager, he or she will face new problems and will be responsible for new decisions. This text has described some, hopefully much, of what one must consider in making those decisions. But a biologist must learn much more. Education only begins in college. A biologist should continue to learn and expand his or her basis for management decisions throughout his or her career.

The continuing education of a wildlife management biologist includes three categories: technology, philosophy, and sensitivity. Scientific journals will keep one abreast of technology. One should also strive for a broad philosophical appreciation of the diversity of land values and human uses of the land. This comes from reading literature outside of biology and from dealing with a diversity of people, professionals and laymen. Wildlife managers should learn from foresters, range managers, and farmers; from hunters, bird-watchers, and backpackers. Managers should be aware of their needs and intentions and should be able to communicate effectively with them. Wildlife managers should develop a sensitivity to wildlife values that are personal and unmeasurable. In public hearings, biologists should strive to be equally conversant with the sterile economic and biological facts and the emotional issues surrounding wildlife values. Biologists develop their sensitivities through contact with nonscientific literature, poetry, history, art, music, and, most of all, wild creatures and wild places. If they are always too busy and cannot pause occasionally to enjoy the experience and beauty of the outdoor world, they are neglecting part of the job. If we, the professionals, do not perceive and enjoy the beauty of wild nature, beauty that meets the senses and the mind itself, how can we encourage others toward such experiences? If we do not, will they experience much of their wildlife heritage? And will they care? And will there ultimately be much wildlife left to manage?

Finally, wildlife management is land husbandry. It is a way of experiencing life by participating in the earth's basic processes. Perhaps wildlife management offers this experience more than does any other profession. The experience is rewarding. It leads to a philosophy of life that is necessary to the ultimate survival of technologically developed mankind. It provides some understanding of life, of human ecology, and of mankind's choices on earth. As a result, wildlife biologists have been among the world's leaders in developing an ecologically sound philosophy for man's management of himself.

PRINCIPLES

P19.1   Wildlife management is the art of making land produce valuable populations of wildlife, often in conjunction with other forms of land use. In the United States, wildlife is usually managed according to the desires of a diversity of public interests; but management goals should be carefully defined and frequently reviewed.

P19.2   Management of species populations is based on knowledge of the life histories and habitats of species. This knowledge is found in a growing and evolving literature of scientific publications.

P19.3   In intensive management, limitations of knowledge and budget are comparatively small; a comprehensive understanding of populations, habitats, and public desires for wildlife values can be attained; responses of populations, of habitats, and of the public to management practices can be predicted with comparative accuracy; and a linear process of management may be appropriate. However, most wildlife management is extensive, with comparatively large limitations of knowledge and budget. In these cases, understanding and predictions concerning populations, habitats, and public desires are limited and perhaps inaccurate. Consequently, a more cautious cyclic-incremental process of management is usually appropriate. The key to practicing cyclic incrementalism is in planning to measure responses of populations, habitats, and the public to management practices. Cyclic-incremental management is dynamic, capable of responding to changing habitat and population conditions, the vagaries of public desires, and the development of new knowledge applicable to the management situation.

LITERATURE CITED

Adams, J. T. 1931. *The Epic of America*. Little, Brown and Co., Boston. 405 pp.

Adams, W. H., Jr. 1960. "Population ecology of white-tailed deer in northeastern Alabama." *Ecology* **41**:706–715.

Albl, P. 1971. "Studies on assessment of physical conditions in African elephants." *Biol. Conservation* **3**:134–140.

Albrecht, W. A. 1944. "Soil fertility and wildlife—cause and effect." *Trans. N. Amer. Wildl. Conf.* **9**:19–28.

———. 1956. "Physical, chemical and biochemical changes in the soil community." Pp. 648–673 in *Man's Role in Changing the Face of the Earth,* W. L. Thomas Jr. (Ed.). Univ. Chicago Press, 1193 pp.

———. 1957. "Soil fertility and biotic geography." *Geograph. Review* **47**:86–105.

Alexander, M. M. 1959. "The habitat map: a basis for wildlife management." *N.Y. Fish and Game J.* **6**:103–113.

Allee, W. C., A. E. Emerson, O. Park, T. Park, and K. P. Schmidt. 1949. *Principles of Animal Ecology*. W. B. Saunders, Philadelphia, 837 pp.

Allen D. L. 1943. *Michigan Fox Squirrel Management*. Game Div., Mich. Dept. of Cons., Lansing. 404 pp.

Allen, D. M. and G. B. Lamming. 1961. "Nutrition and reproduction in the ewe." *J. Agric. Sci.* **56**:69–79.

Amann, G. A. 1957. *The Prairie Grouse of Michigan*. Game Div., Mich. Dept. Cons., Lansing, 200 pp.

Anderson, A. E., D. E. Medin, and D. P. Ochs. 1969. Relationships of carcass fat indices in 18 wintering mule deer. *Proc. Western Assoc. Game and Fish Comm.* **40**:329–340.

———, ———, and D.C. Bowden. 1972. Mule deer numbers and shrub yield-utilization. *J. Wildl. Mgmt.* **36**:571–578.

Anderson, R. M. 1965. "Cerebrospinal nematodiasis in North American cervids." *Trans. N. Amer. Wildl. and Nat. Res. Conf.* **30**:156–166.

———, and R. M. May. 1979. "Population biology of infectious diseases: Part I." *Nature* **280**:361–267.

———, H. C. Jackson, R. M. May, and A. M. Smith. 1981. "Population dynamics of fox rabies in Europe." *Nature* **289**:765–771.

Anderson, W. L. 1973. "Chemical elements and the distribution of pheasants in Illinois." *J. Wildl. Mgmt.* **37**:142–153.

———. 1978. "Waterfowl collisions with power lines at a coal-fired power plant." *Wildl. Soc. Bull.* **6**:77–83.

————, and P. L. Stewart. 1969. "Relationships between inorganic ions and the distribution of pheasants in Illinois." *J. Wildl. Mgmt.* **33**:254–270.

Andrewartha, H. G., and L. C. Birch. 1954. *The Distribution and Abundance of Animals.* Univ. Chicago Press, 782 pp.

Anon. 1975. "Can we afford natural regulation?" (Editorial). *Montana Outdoors* **6**:36–37.

Anthony, R. G. 1976. "Influence of drought on diets and numbers of desert deer." *J. Wildl. Mgmt.* **40**:140–144.

Archibald, H. L. 1977. "Is the 10-year wildlife cycle induced by a lunar cycle?" *Wildl. Soc. Bull.* **5**:126–129.

Asdell, S. A. 1964. *Patterns of Mammalian Reproduction.* Constable, London, 670 pp.

Bailey, J. A. 1966. "Crude protein in Adirondack deer browses." Unpubl. Ph.D. thesis. St. Univ. of N.Y. College of Forestry, Syracuse. 151 pp.

————. 1967. "Mineral content of deer browse on the Huntington Wildlife Forest." *N.Y. Fish and Game J.* **14**:76–78.

————. 1967a. "Effects of site exposure and deer browsing upon the quantity and protein-quality of witchhobble browse." *N.Y. Fish and Game J.* **14**:193–198.

————. 1967b. "Sampling deer browse for crude protein." *J. Wildl. Mgmt.* **31**:437–442.

————. 1968. "A weight-length relationship for evaluating physical condition of cottontails." *J. Wildl. Mgmt.* **32**:835–841.

————. 1968a. "Regionwide fluctuations in the abundance of cottontails." *Trans. N. Amer. Wildl. and Nat. Res. Conf.* **33**:265–277.

————. 1969. "Exploratory study of nutrition of young cottontails." *J. Wildl. Mgmt.* **33**:346–353.

————. 1980. "Desert bighorn, forage competition and zoogeography." *Wildl. Soc. Bull.* **8**:208–216.

————. 1982. Implications of "Muddling Through" for wildlife management. *Wildl. Soc. Bull.* **10**:363–369.

Bailey, N. T. J. 1951. "On estimating the size of mobile populations from recapture data." *Biometrika* **38**:293–306.

Balser, D. S., H. H. Dill, and H. K. Nelson. 1968. "Effect of predator reduction on waterfowl nesting success." *J. Wildl. Mgmt.* **32**:669–682.

Bandy, P. J., I. McT. Cowan, W. D. Kitts, and A. J. Wood. 1956. "A method for the assessment of the nutritional status of wild ungulates." *Can. J. Zool.* **34**:48–52.

Bartholomew, G. A. 1958. "The role of physiology in the distribution of terrestrial vertebrates." Pp. 81–95, in *Zoogeography, AAAS Symposium,* C. L. Hubbs (ed.). Publ. No. 51, Amer. Assoc. Adv. Sci., Washington, D.C. 509 pp.

Bartlett, I. H. 1950. *Michigan Deer.* Mich. Dept. Cons., Lansing. 50 pp.

Bartonek, J. C. 1965. "Mortality of diving ducks on Lake Winnipegosis through commercial fishing." *Can. Field-Naturalist* **79**:15–20.

Bauman, T. G. 1978. "Winter ecology of bighorn sheep in the Mummy Range, Colorado." Unpubl. M.S. thesis, Colorado State University, 151 pp.

Beeson, K. C. 1941. "The mineral composition of crops with particular reference to the soils in which they were grown. A review and compilation." Misc. Publ. 369, U.S. Dept. Agr., Washington, D.C. 164 pp.

Beetle, A. A. 1974. "The zootic disclimax concept." *J. Range Mgmt.* 27:30−32.

Bellrose, F. C. 1955. "Housing for wood ducks." Ill. Nat. Hist. Sur. Circ. 45. 48 pp.

―――, K. L. Johnson, and T. V. Meyers. 1964. "Relative value of natural cavities and nesting houses for wood ducks." *J. Wildl. Mgmt.* 28:661−676.

―――, and F. B. McGilvrey. 1966. "Characteristics and values of artificial nesting cavities." Pp. 125−131 in *Wood Duck Management and Research: A symposium,* L. Jahn et al. (Eds.). Wildl. Mgmt. Inst. Washington, D.C. 212 pp.

―――. 1976. *Ducks, Geese and Swans of North America.* Wildl. Mgmt. Inst., Stackpole. Harrisburg, Pa. 540 pp.

Bergerud, A. T. 1970. "Population dynamics of the willow ptarmigan (*Lagopus lagopus alleni L.*) in Newfoundland, 1955 to 1965." *Oikos* 21:299−325.

―――. 1971. "The population dynamics of Newfoundland caribou." *Wildl. Monogr.* Vol. 25. 55 pp.

Birch, L. C. 1958. "The role of weather in determining the distribution and abundance of animals." *Cold Spring Harbor Symposia on Quantitative Biol.* 22:203−215.

Bischoff, A. I. 1954. "Limitations on the bone marrow technique in determining malnutrition in deer." *Proc. West. Assn. St. Game and Fish Comm.* 34:205−210.

Black, H. C. 1958. "Black bear research in New York." *Trans. N. Amer. Wildl. Conf.* 23:443−460.

Bock, C. E. and J. F. Lynch. 1970. "Breeding bird populations of burned and unburned conifer forest in the Sierra Nevada." *Condor* 72:182−189.

―――, and L. W. Lepthien. 1976. "Synchronous eruptions of boreal seed-eating birds." *Amer. Nat.* 110:559−571.

Boulding, K. E. 1968. "The economics of the coming spaceship earth." pp. 275−287, in *Beyond Economics.* Univ. Mich. Press, Ann Arbor. 302 pp.

Branagan, D., and J. A. Hammond. 1965. "Rinderpest in Tanganyika: A review." *Bull. Epizoot. Dis. Afr.* 13:225−246.

Bromley, P. T. 1969. "Territoriality in pronghorn bucks on the National Bison Range, Moiese, Montana." *J. Mamm.* 50:81−89.

Browman, L. G., and H. S. Sears. 1955. "Erythrocyte values and alimentary canal pH values in the mule deer." *J. Mamm.* 36:474−476.

Brown, E. R. 1961. *The black-tailed Deer of Western Washington. Biol. Bull.* 13, Wash. St. Game Dept. 124 pp.

Buechner, H. K. 1961. "Territorial behavior in Uganda kob." *Science* 133:698−699.

Bump, G., R. W. Darrow, F. C. Edminster, and W. F. Crissey. 1947. *The Ruffed Grouse: Life History, Propagation, Management.* N.Y. Cons. Dept., Albany. 915 pp.

Burkholder, B. L. 1959. "Movements and behavior of a wolf pack in Alaska." *J. Wildl. Mgmt.* 23:1−11.

Butler, L. 1953. "The nature of cycles in populations of Canadian mammals." *Can. J. Zool.* 31:242−262.

Calhoun, J. B. 1952. "The social aspects of population dynamics." *J. Mamm.* 33:139−159.

Carl, E. A. 1971. "Population control in arctic ground squirrels." *Ecology* 52:395−413.

Carr, A. F. 1967. *So Excellent a Fische, a Natural History of Sea Turtles.* Natural History Press, N.Y. 248 pp.

Carrick, R. 1963. "Ecological significance of territory in the Australian magpie, *Gymnorhina Tibicen.*" *Proc. Internat. Ornithol. Congr.* **13**:740–753.

Caughley, G. 1966. "Mortality patterns in mammals." *Ecology* **47**:906–918.

———. 1970. "Eruption of ungulate populations, with emphasis on Himalayan thar in New Zealand." *Ecology* **51**:53–71.

———. 1974. "Interpretation of age ratios." *J. Wildl. Mgmt.* **38**:557–562.

———. 1976. "Wildlife management and the dynamics of ungulate populations." Pp. 183–246 in *Applied Biology,* Vol. 1, T. H. Coaker (Ed.). Academic Press, N.Y. 358 pp.

———. 1977. *Analysis of Vertebrate Populations.* John Wiley and Sons, N.Y. 234 pp.

———. 1979. "What is this thing called carrying capacity?" Pp. 2–8 in *North American Elk: Ecology, Behavior and Management,* M. S. Boyce and L. D. Hayden-Wing (Eds.). Univ. Wyoming. 294 pp.

Cayot, L. J., J. Prukop, and D. R. Smith. 1979. "Zootic climax vegetation and natural regulation of elk in Yellowstone National Park." *Wildl. Soc. Bull.* **7**:162–169.

Chadwick, D. H. 1977. "The influence of mountain goat social relationships on population size and distribution." Pp. 74–91 in *Proc. 1st Internat. Mountain Goat Symp.,* W. Samuel and W. G. Macregor (Eds.). 241 pp.

Cheatum, E. L. 1949. "Bone marrow as an index of malnutrition in deer." *N.Y. St. Conservationist* **3**:19–22.

———. 1949a. "The use of corpora lutea for determining ovulation incidence and variations in fertility of white-tailed deer." *Cornell Vet.* **39**:282–291.

———, and C. W. Severinghaus. 1950. "Variations in fertility of white-tailed deer related to range conditions." *Trans. N. Amer. Wildl. Conf.* **15**:170–190.

Chitty, D. 1960. "Population processes in the vole and their relevance to general theory." *Can. J. Zool.* **38**:99–113.

———. 1967. "The natural selection of self-regulating behaviour in animal populations." *Proc. Ecol. Soc. Australia* **2**:51–78.

Christian, J. J. 1964. "Physiological and pathological correlates of population density." *Proc. Royal Soc. for Medicine* **57**:169–174.

———. 1971. "Population density and reproductive efficiency." *Biol. Reprod.* **4**:248–294.

———, and C. D. LeMunyan. 1958. "Adverse effects of crowding on lactation and reproduction of mice and two generations of their progeny." *Endocrinology* **63**:517–529.

———, V. Flyger, and D. E. Davis. 1960. "Factors in the mass mortality of a herd of Sika deer, *Cervus nippon.*" *Chesapeake Sci.* **1**:79–95.

———, and D. E. Davis. 1964. "Endocrines, behavior, and population." *Science* **146**:1550–1560.

Clements, F. E. 1936. "Nature and structure of the climax." *J. Ecol.* **24**:252–284.

Cole, G. F. 1971. "An ecological rationale for the natural or artificial regulation of native ungulates in parks." *Trans. N. Amer. Wildl. and Nat. Res. Conf.* **36**:417–425.

———. 1972. "Grizzly bear-elk relationships in Yellowstone National Park." *J. Wildl. Mgmt.* **36**:556–561.

Cole, L. C. 1954. "Some features of random population cycles." *J. Wildl. Mgmt.* **18**:2–24.

Conant, R., E. S. Thomas and R. L. Rausch. 1945. "The plains garter snake, *Thamnophis radix,* in Ohio. *Copeia* (1945):61–68.

Cooley, R. A. 1963. *Politics and Conservation.* Harper and Row, N.Y. 230 pp.

Cowan, I. M., W. S. Hoar, and J. Hatter. 1950. "The effect of forest succession upon the quantity and upon the nutritive values of woody plants used as food by moose." *Can. J. Res.,* Sec. D. **28**:249–271.

Craighead, F. C., Jr., and R. F. Dasmann. 1965. "Exotic big game on public lands." *Trans. Desert Bighorn Coun.* **9**:19–26.

Crawford, B. T. 1946. "Wildlife sampling by soil types." *Trans. N. Amer. Widl. Conf.* **11**:357–364.

Cringan, A. T. 1957. "History, food habits and range requirements of the woodland caribou of continental North America." *Trans. N. Amer. Wildl. Conf.* **22**:485–501.

———. 1971. "Status of the wood duck in Ontario." *Trans. N. Amer. Wildl. and Nat. Res. Conf.* **36**:296–311.

Curtis, J. T., and R. P. McIntosh. 1951. "An upland forest continuum in the prairie-forest border region of Wisconsin." *Ecol.* **32**:476–496.

Dahlberg, B. L. and R. C. Guettinger. 1956. *The White-tailed Deer in Wisconsin.* Game Div., Wis. Cons. Dept. Tech. Wildl. Bull. 14. 282 pp.

Dale, F. H. 1954. "Influence of calcium on the distribution of pheasant in North America." *Trans. N. Amer. Wildl. Conf.* **19**:316–323.

Darlington, P. J. 1957. *Zoogeography: The Geographical Distribution of Animals.* John Wiley and Sons, N.Y. 675 pp.

Dasmann, R. F. 1964. *African Game Ranching.* Pergamon Press, Oxford. 75 pp.

———. 1964a. *Wildlife Biology.* John Wiley and Sons, N.Y. 231 pp.

———. 1968. *A Different Kind of Country.* Macmillan Co., N.Y. 176 pp.

———, and W. P. Dasmann. 1963. "Mule deer in relation to a climatic gradient." *J. Wildl. Mgmt.* **27**:196–202.

Dasmann, W. P. 1951. "Some deer range survey methods." *Cal. Fish and Game,* **37**:43–52.

Daubenmire, R. 1968. *Plant Communities: a Textbook of Plant Synecology.* Harper and Row, N.Y. 300 pp.

Dauphine, T. C., and R. L. McClure. 1974. "Synchronous mating in Canadian barren-ground caribou." *J. Wildl. Mgmt.* **38**:54–66.

Davis, D. E. 1957. "The existence of cycles." *Ecol.* **38**:163–164.

Day, G. I. 1971. Pp. 153–157 in *Wildlife Research in Arizona, 1970–71.* Ariz. Game and Fish Dept., Phoenix. 283 pp.

Denney, A. H. 1944. "Wildlife relationships to soil types." *Trans. N. Amer. Wildl. Conf.* **9**:316–323.

Dietz, D. R., R. H. Udall, H. R. Shepherd, and L. E. Yeager. 1958. "Seasonal progression in chemical content of five key browse species in Colorado." *Proc. Soc. Amer. Foresters, Salt Lake City,* pp. 117–122.

———, R. H. Udall, and L. E. Yeager. 1962. *Chemical Composition and Digestibility by Mule Deer of Selected Forage Species, Cache la Poudre Range, Colorado.* Tech. Publ. 14, Colo. Game and Fish Dept., Denver. 89 pp.

Dills, G. F. 1970. "Effects of prescribed burning on deer browse." *J. Wildl. Mgmt.* **34**:540–545.

Duncan, O. D. 1959. "Human ecology and population studies." Pp. 678–716 in *The Study of Population*, P. M. Hauser and O. D. Duncan (Eds.). Univ. Chicago Press, 864 pp.

Dyksterhuis, E. J. 1949. "Condition and management of range land based on quantitative ecology." *J. Range Mgmt.* **2**:104–115.

Eberhardt, L. L. 1968. "A preliminary appraisal of line transects." *J. Wildl. Mgmt.* **32**:82–88.

Edwards, R. Y. 1954. "Fire and the decline of a mountain caribou herd." *J. Wildl. Mgmt.* **18**:521–526.

———. 1956. "Snow depths and ungulate abundance in the mountains of western Canada." *J. Wildl. Mgmt.* **20**:159–168.

———. 1957. "Dammed waters in a moose range." *Murrelet*, Jan.–April, pp. 1–3.

———, and C. D. Fowle. 1955. "The concept of carrying capacity." *Trans. N. Amer. Wildl. Conf.* **20**:589–602.

Egler, F. E. 1967. "Wildlife habitat management for the citizen" (Review). *Atlantic Naturalist* **22**:166–169.

Ehrlich, P. R., and A. H. Ehrlich. 1970. *Population, Resources, Environment.* W. H. Freeman and Co., San Francisco. 383 pp.

Einarsen, A. S. 1946. "Crude protein determination of deer food as an applied management technique." *Trans. N. Amer. Wildl. Conf.* **11**:309–312.

Ellig, L. 1975. "Yellowstone elk: curse or blessing." *Montana Outdoors* **6**:26–34.

Ellis, J. A., W. R. Edwards, and K. P. Thomas. 1969. "Responses of bobwhites to management in Illinois." *J. Wildl. Mgmt.* **33**:749–762.

Elton, C. 1924. "Periodic fluctuations in the numbers of animals: their causes and effects." *Brit. J. Exp. Biol.* **2**:119–163.

———. 1942. *Voles, Mice and Lemmings.* Clarendon Press, Oxford. 496 pp.

Enright, C. A. 1971. *A Review of Research on Type C Botulism among Waterbirds.* Colorado Coop. Wildl. Res. Unit, U.S. Bur. Sport Fish. and Wildl., Fort Collins. 22 pp.

Errington, P. L. 1945. "Some contributions of a 15-year local study of the northern bobwhite to a knowledge of population phenomena." *Ecol. Monogr.* **15**:1–34.

———. 1946. "Predation and vertebrate populations." *Quart. Rev. Biol.* **21**:144–177; 221–245.

———. 1956. "Factors limiting higher vertebrate populations." *Science* **124**:304–307.

———. 1963. "The phenomenon of predation." *Amer. Scientist* **51**:180–192.

Erskine, A. J. 1978. *The First Ten Years of the Cooperative Breeding Bird Survey in Canada.* Can. Wildl. Serv. Rpt. Ser. 42., Ottawa. 61 pp.

Flader, S. 1974. *Thinking Like a Mountain.* Univ. Missouri Press. 284 pp.

French, C. E., L. C. McEwen, N. D. Magruder, R. H. Ingram, and R. W. Swift. 1955. *Nutritional Requirements of White-tailed Deer for Growth and Antler Development.* Penn. St. Univ., Coll. of Agr., Exp. Sta. Bull. 600. 49 pp.

Friend, M. and D. O. Trainer, 1974. Experimental DDT-duck hepatitis virus interaction studies." *J. Wildl. Mgmt.* **38**:887–895.

————, M. A. Haegele, and R. Wilson. 1973. "DDE: Interference with extrarenal salt excretion in the mallard." *Bull. Environ. Contam. Toxicol.* **9**:49–53.

Gallizioli, S. 1965. *Quail Research in Arizona.* Ariz. Game and Fish Dept., Phoenix. 12 pp.

Geist, V. 1967. "A consequence of togetherness." *Nat. Hist.* **76**:24–31.

————. 1971. Mountain Sheep, a Study in Behavior and Evolution. Univ. Chicago Press, 383 pp.

————. 1974. "On the evolution of reproductive potential in moose." *Can. Naturalist* **101**:527–537.

————. 1978. "On weapons, combat, and ecology." Pp. 1–30 in *Aggression, Dominance, and Individual Spacing,* L. Krames, P. Pliner, and T. Alloway (Eds.). Plenum Publ. Corp. 173 pp.

————, and F. R. Walther (Eds.). 1974. *The Behavior of Ungulates and Its Relation to Management.* International Union for Conservation of Nature and Natural Resources Publ. 24 (Vols. 1,2), Morges, Switzerland. 940 pp.

Gilbert, P. F., O. C. Wallmo, and R. B. Gill. 1970. "Effect of snow depth on mule deer in Middle Park, Colorado." *J. Wildl. Mgmt.* **34**:15–23.

Giles, R. H., Jr., and N. Snyder. 1970. "Simulation techniques in wildlife habitat management." in *Modelling and Systems Analysis in Range Science,* D. A. Jameson (Ed.). Sci. Series No. 5, Range Sci. Dept., Colo. St. Univ., Fort Collins.

Gleason, H. A. 1939. "The individualistic concept of the plant association." *Amer. Midland Nat.* **21**:92–108.

Goodall, J. 1965. "Chimpanzees of the Gombe Stream Reserve." Pp. 425–473 in *Primate Behavior,* I. DeVore (Ed.). Holt, Rinehart and Winston, Inc. 654 pp.

Goodson, N. J. 1978. "Status of bighorn sheep in Rocky Mountain National Park." Unpubl. M.S. thesis, Colorado State University. 151 pp.

Grange, W. B. 1936. "Some observations on the ruffed grouse in Wisconsin." *Wilson Bull.* **48**:104–110.

————. 1948. *Wisconsin Grouse Problems.* Wis. Conserv. Dept. Pub. 328. 318 pp.

————. 1949. *The Way to Game Abundance.* C. Scribner's Sons, N.Y. 365 pp.

Green, R. G., and C. A. Evans. 1940. "Studies on a population cycle of snowshoe hares on the Lake Alexander area." *J. Wildl. Mgmt.* **4**:220–238; 4:267–278; 4:347–358.

Greenley, J. C., and M. Humphreys. 1964. "The decline in the 1962 mule deer harvest in Nevada." *Proc. West. Assn. St. Game and Fish Comm.* **44**:173–176.

Grieb, J. R. 1973. "Considerations in setting hunting seasons. Pp. 107–111 in *Wildlife and the Environment, Proc. Governor's Conf. on Wildlife, Denver,* E. Decker and G. Swanson (Eds.). 119 pp.

Griffiths, M. E., J. H. Calaby and D. L. McIntosh. 1960. "The stress syndrome in the rabbit." *C.S.I.R.O. Wildl. Res.* **5**:134–148.

Gross, J. 1969, "Optimum yield in deer and elk populations." *Trans. N. Amer. Wildl. and Nat. Res. Conf.* **34**:372–385.

Gulland, J. A. 1970. "The effect of exploitation on the numbers of marine animals." Pp. 450–467 in *Dynamics of Populations,* P. J. den Boer and G. R. Gradwell (Eds.). Centre for Agr. Publ. and Documentation, Wageningen, Netherlands. 611 pp.

Gullion, G. W. 1960. "The ecology of Gambel's quail in Nevada and the arid southwest." *Ecology* **14**:518–536.

——. 1966. "A viewpoint concerning the significance of studies of game bird food habits." *Condor* **68**:372–376.

——, and W. H. Marshall. 1968. "Survival of ruffed grouse in a boreal forest." *The Living Bird* **8**:117–167.

Hailey, T., D. DeArment, and P. Evans. 1964. "Pronghorn decline." *Texas Game and Fish* **22**:22–23.

Hamerstrom, F. N., Jr. 1963. "Sharptail brood habitat in Wisconsin's northern pine barrens." *J. Wildl. Mgmt.* **27**:793–802.

Hancock, N. V. 1964. "The 1963 mule deer harvest decline in Utah." *Proc. West. Assn. St. Game and Fish Comm.* **44**:181–188.

Hansen, H. L. 1966. "Silvical characteristics of tree species and decay process as related to cavity production." Pp. 65–69 in *Wood Duck Management and Research: a Symposium,* L. Jahn et al. (Eds.). Wildl. Mgmt. Inst., Washington, D.C. 212 pp.

Hanson, H. C., and C. W. Kossack. 1963. *The Mourning Dove in Illinois.* Tech. Bull. 2, Ill. Dept. Cons., Springfield. 133 pp.

Hanson, J. C., J. A. Bailey and R. J. Siglin. 1969. "Activity and use of habitat by radio-tagged cottontails during winter." *Trans. Ill. Acad. Sci.* **62**:294–302.

Hanson, W. R., and R. J. Miller. 1961. "Edge types and abundance of bobwhites in southern Illinois." *J. Wildl. Mgmt.* **25**:71–76.

Harper, J. A., and R. F. Labisky. 1964. "The influence of calcium on the distribution of pheasants in Illinois." *J. Wildl. Mgmt.* **28**:722–731.

Harrington, F. A., Jr. 1978. "Ecological segregation of ungulates in alpine and subalpine communities." Unpubl. Ph.D. Thesis, Colorado State Univ., Ft. Collins. 152 pp.

Harris, V. T. 1952. "An experimental study of habitat selection by prairie and forest races of the deermouse, *Peromyscus maniculatus.*" *Univ. Mich. Contr. Lab. Vert. Biol.* (Ann Arbor) **56**:1–53.

Haugen, A. O. (Ed.). 1971. *Snow and Ice in Relation to Wildlife and Recreation Symposium.* Iowa State Univ., Ames. 280 pp.

Hawley, A. H. 1950. *Human Ecology, A Theory of Community Structure.* Ronald Press, N.Y. 456 pp.

Henderson, B. A. 1977. "The genetics and demography of a high and low density of red grouse *Lagopus l. scoticus.*" *J. Animal Ecol.* **46**:581–592.

Herrenkohl, L. R. 1979. "Prenatal stress reduces fertility and fecundity in female offspring." *Science* **206**:1097–1099.

Hewitt, C. G. 1921. *The Conservation of the Wild Life of Canada.* C. Scribner's Sons, N.Y. 344 pp.

Hickey, J. J. 1954. "Mean intervals in indices of wildlife populations." *J. Wildl. Mgmt.* **18**:90–106.

——, and D. W. Anderson. 1968. Chlorinated hydrocarbons and eggshell changes in raptorial and fish-eating birds. *Science* **162**:271–273.

Hildebrand, P. R. 1971. "Biology of white-tailed deer on winter ranges in the Swan Valley, Montana." Unpubl. M.S. Thesis. Univ. Montana. 91 pp.

Hill, E. P., III. 1972. "Litter size in Alabama cottontails as influenced by soil fertility." *J. Wildl. Mgmt.* **36**:1199–1209.

Hirth, D. H. 1977. "Social behavior of white-tailed deer in relation to habitat." *Wildl. Monogr.* Vol. 53. 55 pp.

Hoffman, D. M. 1965. *The Scaled Quail in Colorado: Range, Population, Status and Harvest.* Colo. Dept. Game, Fish and Parks. Tech. Bull. 18. 47 pp.

Hoffman. R. R. 1968. "Comparisons of the rumen and omasum structure in East African game ruminants in relation to their feeding habits." In *Comparative Nutrition of Wild Animals,* M. A. Crawford (Ed.). Academic Press, Inc., N.Y. 427 pp.

Holling, C. S. 1966. "The functional response of invertebrate predators to prey density." *Memoirs Ent. Soc. Can.* **48**:86 pp.

Horvath, J. C. 1974. "Economic survey of Southeastern wildlife and wildlife-oriented recreation." *Trans. N. Amer. Wild. and Nat. Res. Conf.* **39**:187–194.

Houston, D. B. 1971. "Ecosystems of national parks." *Science* 172:648–651.

———. 1982. *The Northern Yellowstone Elk.* Macmillan Publ. Co., N.Y. 474 pp.

Howell, F. C., and F. Bourliere (Eds.). 1963. *African Ecology and Human Evolution.* Aldine Publ. Co., Chicago. 666 pp.

Huffaker, C. B. 1970. "The phenomenon of predation and its roles in nature." Pp. 327–341 in *Proc. Adv. Study Inst. Dynamics of Numbers in Populations,* P. J. den Boer and G. R. Gradwell (Eds.). Oosterbeck, Netherlands. 611 pp.

Hughes, E., and R. Mall. 1958. "Relation of the adrenal cortex to condition of deer." *Cal. Fish and Game* **44**:191–196.

Hundley, L. R. 1959. "Available nutrients in selected deer-browse species growing on different soils." *J. Wildl. Mgmt.* **23**:81–90.

Jackman, S. 1974. *Some Characteristics of Cavity Nesters: Can We Ever Have Enough Snags?* Oregon St. Univ. Infor. Memo 74–36, 8 pp.

Jantzen, R. A. 1964. "Population declines of mule deer in northern Arizona." *Proc. West. Assn. St. Game and Fish Comm.* **44**:158–166.

Jehl, J., and D. Hussell. 1966. "Effects of weather on reproductive success of birds at Churchill, Manitoba." *Arctic* **19**:185–191.

Jenkins, D. H., and I. H. Bartlett. 1959. *Michigan Whitetails.* Mich. Dept. Cons., Lansing. 80 pp.

Jones, G. 1952. "Hail damage to wildlife in southwest Oklahoma." *Wilson Bull.* **64**:166–167.

Jones, R. E. 1963. "Identification and analysis of lesser and greater prairie chicken habitat." *J. Wildl. Mgmt.* **27**:757–778.

Jordan, P. A., D. B. Botkin, and M. L. Wolfe. 1971. "Biomass dynamics in a moose population." *Ecology* **52**:147–152.

Joselyn, G. B., J. E. Warnock, and S. L. Etter. 1968. "Manipulation of roadside cover for nesting pheasants—a preliminary report. *J. Wildl. Mgmt.* **32**:217–233.

Kauffeld, C. 1969. *Snakes, the Keeper and the Kept.* Doubleday and Co., N.Y. 248 pp.

Keith, L. B. 1963. *Wildlife's Ten-year Cycle.* Univ. Wisc. Press, Madison. 201 pp.

———. 1974. "Some features of population dynamics in mammals." *Int. Cong. Game Biol.* **11**:17–58.

————, and L. A. Windberg. 1978. "A demographic analysis of the snowshoe hare cycle." *Wildl. Monographs* Vol. 58. 70 pp.

Kelsall, J. P. 1968. *The Migratory Barren-ground Caribou of Canada*. Queens Printer, Ottawa. 339 pp.

————, and E. S. Telfer. 1971. "Studies of the physical adaptation of big game for snow." Pp. 134–146, in *Snow and Ice in Relation to Wildlife and Recreation Symposium*, A. O. Haugen (Ed.). Iowa State Univ., Ames. 280 pp.

Kendeigh, S. C. 1954. "History and evaluation of various concepts of plant and animal communities in North America." *Ecol.* **35**:152–171.

————. 1974. *Ecology with Special Reference to Animals and Man*. Prentice-Hall, N.J. 474 pp.

King, R. T. 1937. "Ruffed grouse management." *J. For.* **35**:523–532.

————. 1938. "The essentials of a wildlife range." *J. For.* **36**:457–464.

————. 1938a. "What constitutes training in wildlife management?" *Trans. N. Amer. Wildl. Conf.* **3**:548–557.

————. 1941. "Forest zoology and its relation to a wildlife program as applied on Huntington Forest." *Roosevelt Wildl. Bull.* **7**:461–505.

————. 1966. "Wildlife and man." *N.Y. Conservationist* **20**:8–11.

Klein, D. R. 1964. "Range-related differences in growth of deer reflected in skeletal ratios." *J. Mamm.* **45**:226–235.

————. 1968. "The introduction, increase, and crash of reindeer on St. Matthew Island." *J. Wildl. Mgmt.* **32**:350–367.

————. 1970. "Food selection by North American deer and their response to over-utilization of preferred plant species." In *Animal Populations in Relation to their Food Resources*, A. Watson (Ed.). *Brit. Ecol. Soc. Symposium* **10**:25–44.

Klopfer, P. H., and J. P. Hailman. 1962. "Habitat selection in birds." Pp. 279–303 in *Advances in the Study of Behavior*, Vol. I, R. A. Hinde and E. Shaw (Eds.). Academic Press, N.Y.

Kolenosky, G. B. 1972. "Wolf predation on wintering deer in east-central Ontario." *J. Wildl. Mgmt.* **36**:357–369.

Koskimies, J., and L. Lahti. 1964. "Cold-hardiness of the newly hatched young in relation to ecology and distribution in ten species of European ducks." *Auk* **81**:281–307.

Kozicky, E. L., G. O. Hendrickson, and P. G. Homeyer. 1955. "Weather and fall pheasant populations in Iowa." *J. Wildl. Mgmt.* **19**:136–142.

Kozlovsky, D. G. 1974. *An Ecological and Evolutionary Ethic*. Prentice-Hall, Inc., Englewood Cliffs, N.J. 116 pp.

Krebs, C. J., M. S. Gaines, B. L. Keller, J. H. Myers, and R. H. Tamarin. 1973. "Population cycles in small rodents." *Science* **179**:35–41.

Krutilla, J. V. 1974. "Methods for estimating the value of wildlife resources." Pp. 125–136 in *Readings in Wildlife Conservation*, J. Bailey et al. (Eds.). The Wildl. Soc., Washington, D.C. 722 pp.

Lack, D. 1933. "Habitat selection in birds with special reference to the effects of afforestation on the Breckland avifauna." *J. Animal Ecol.* **2**:239–262.

————. 1954. *The natural Regulation of Animal Numbers.* Clarendon Press, Oxford. 343 pp.

Lauckhart, J. B. 1957. "Animal cycles and food." *J. Wildl. Mgmt.* **21**:230–234.

Ledger, H. P. 1968. "Body composition as a basis for a comparative study of some East African mammals." In *Comparative Nutrition of Wild Animals,* M. A. Crawford (Ed.). Academic Press, Inc., N.Y. 427 pp.

Leege, T. A. 1968. "Prescribed burning for elk in northern Idaho." *Proc. Tall Timbers Fire Ecol. Conf.* **8**:235–253.

————. 1969. "Burning seral brush ranges for big game in northern Idaho." *Trans. N. Amer. Wildl. and Nat. Res. Conf.* **34**:429–438.

Leopold, A. 1933. *Game Management.* Charles Scribner's Sons, N.Y. 481 pp.

————. 1943. "Deer irruptions." *Trans. Wisc. Acad. Sci., Arts and Letters* **35**:351–366.

————. 1949. *A Sand County Almanac.* Oxford Univ. Press, N.Y. 226 pp.

————. 1953. *Round River* (L. B. Leopold, Ed.). Oxford Univ. Press, N.Y. 173 pp.

————, L. K. Sowls, and D. L. Spencer. 1947. "A survey of over-populated deer ranges in the United States." *J. Wildl. Mgmt.* **11**:162–177.

Leopold, A. S. 1944. "The nature of heritable wildness in turkeys." *Condor* **46**:133–197.

————. 1953. "Intestinal morphology of gallinaceous birds in relation to food habits." *J. Wildl. Mgmt.* **17**:197–203.

————. 1966. "Adaptability of animals to habitat change." In *Future Environments of North America,* F. F. Darling and J. P. Milton (Eds.). The Conservation Foundation, Doubleday and Co., N.Y. 767 pp.

————, S. A. Cain, C. M. Cottam, I. N. Gabrielson, and T. L. Kimball. 1963. "Wildlife management in the National Parks." *Trans. N. Amer. Wildl. and Nat. Res. Conf.* **28**:29–42.

Leslie, D. M., Jr. and C. L. Douglas. 1979. "Desert bighorn sheep of the River Mountains, Nevada." Wildl. Monogr. Vol. 66. 56 pp.

Lincoln, F. C. 1950. *Migration of Birds.* Circular 16, U.S. Fish and Wildl. Service, Washington, D.C. 102 pp.

Lindblom, C. E. 1959. "The science of 'muddling through.'" *Public Administration Review* **19**:79–88.

Linduska, J. P. (Ed.) 1964. *Waterfowl Tomorrow.* U.S. Fish and Wildl. Service, Washington, D.C. 770 pp.

Lord, R. D., Jr. 1963. *The Cottontail Rabbit in Illinois.* Tech. Bull. No. 3. Ill. Dept. Cons. 94 pp.

Lorimer, F. 1963. "Issues of population policy." Pp. 143–178 in *The Population Dilemma,* P. M. Hauser (Ed.). The American Assembly, Columbia Univ. 188 pp.

Loveless, C. M. 1959. *The Everglades Deer Herd, Life History and Management.* Fla. Game and Fresh Water Fish Comm. Tech. Bull. 6. 104 pp.

Lyon, L. J. 1966. *Problems of habitat management for deer and elk in the northern forests.* U. S. Forest Service, Intermountain. For. and Rge. Expt. Sta., Ogden, Utah, 15 pp.

MacArthur, R. H., and E. O. Wilson. 1967. *The Theory of Island Biogeography*. Princeton Univ. Press, N.J. 203 pp.

Macgregor, W. G. 1964. "Analysis of Great Basin deer decline—California." *Proc. West. Assn. St. Game and Fish Comm.* **44**:167–169.

Malthus, T. 1926. *An Essay on the Principle of Population*. MacMillan Co., London. (Originally published 1798, St. Paul's, London.)

Marcstrom, V. 1960. "Studies on the physiological and ecological background to the reproduction of the Capercaillie (*Tetrao urogallus* Lin.)." *Jaktbiologisk Tidskrift* Band 2, Hafte 1. 85 pp.

Marshall, W. H. 1954. "Ruffed grouse and snowshoe hare populations on the Cloquet Experimental Forest, Minnesota." *J. Wildl. Mgmt.* **18**:109–112.

Martin, P. S. 1970. "Pleistocene niches for alien animals." *Bioscience* **20**:218–221.

May, R. M. 1973. "Time delays versus stability in population models with two and three trophic levels." *Ecology* **54**:315–325.

———, and R. M. Anderson. 1979. "Population biology of infectious diseases: Part II." *Nature* **280**:455–561.

Maynard, L. A., and J. K. Loosli. 1962. *Animal Nutrition*. 5th ed. McGraw-Hill Co., N.Y., 533 pp.

McEwan, E. H., and A. J. Wood. 1966. "Growth and development of the barren-ground caribou. I. Heart girth, hind foot length, and body weight relationships." *Can. J. Zool.* **44**:401–411.

McKean, J. W., and I. D. Luman. 1964. "Oregon's 1962 decline in mule deer harvest." *Proc. West. Assn. St. Game and Fish Comm.* **44**:177–180.

Mech, L. D. 1966. *The Wolves of Isle Royale*. U.S. Nat. Park Service, Fauna Series No. 7. 210 pp.

———. 1970. *The Wolf: the Ecology and Behavior of an Endangered Species*. Doubleday and Co., N.Y. 384 pp.

Merriam, C. H. 1898. *Life Zones and Crop Zones of the United States*. U.S. Dept. Agr., Div. Biol. Surv. Bull. 10. 79 pp.

Milne, A. 1957. "Theories of natural control of insect populations." *Cold Spring Harbor Symp. on Quant. Biol.* **22**:253–271.

Morrow, D. A. 1969. "Phosphorus deficiency and infertility in dairy heifers." *J. Amer. Vet. Med. Assn.* **154**:761–768.

Morton, G. H., and E. L. Cheatum. 1946. "Regional differences in breeding potential of white-tailed deer in New York." *J. Wildl. Mgmt.* **10**:242–248.

Moss, R., G. R. Miller, and S. E. Allen. 1972. "Selection of heather by captive red grouse in relation to age of the plant." *J. Applied Ecol.* **9**:771–781.

Murie, A. 1944. *The Wolves of Mount McKinley*. U.S. Nat. Park Service, Fauna Series No. 5. 238 pp.

Nagy, J. G., H. W. Steinhoff, and G. M. Ward. 1964. "Effects of essential oils of sagebrush on deer rumen microbial function." *J. Wildl. Mgmt.* **28**:785–790.

National Research Council. 1958. *Nutrient Requirements of Dairy Cattle*. Washington, D.C.

Neff, D. J. 1968. "The pellet-group count technique for big game trend, census and distribution: a review." *J. Wildl. Mgmt.* **32**:597−614.

Nicholson, A. J. 1955. "An outline of the dynamics of animal populations." *Aust. J. Zool.* **2**:9−65.

Nobe, K. C., and A. H. Gilbert. 1970. *A Survey of Sportsmen Expenditures for Hunting and Fishing in Colorado, 1968*. Tech. Pub. 24, Colorado Div. Game, Fish and Parks, Denver. 83 pp.

Norman, R. L., L. A. Roper, P. D. Olson, and R. L. Evans. 1975. *Using Wildlife Values in Benefit/cost Analysis and Mitigation of Wildlife Losses*. Colorado Div. Wildl., Denver. 18 pp.

Odum, E. P. 1971. *Fundamentals of Ecology*. W. B. Saunders Co., Philadelphia. 574 pp.

Ogren, H. A. 1965. *Barbary Sheep*. Bull. 11, New Mex. Dept. Game and Fish, Santa Fe. 117 pp.

Oosting, H. J. 1953. *The Study of Plant Communities*. Freeman and Co., San Francisco. 389 pp.

Orr, R. T. 1970. *Animals in Migration*. MacMillan Co., London. 303 pp.

Ozaga, J. J. 1968. "Variations in microclimate in a swamp deeryard in northern Michigan." *J. Wildl. Mgmt.* **32**:574−585.

Pederson, V. C. 1963. "Ulcerative enteritis in the cottontail rabbit." Unpubl. Ph.D. thesis, Univ. of Missouri, Columbia. 96 pp.

Petocz, R. G. 1973. "The effect of snow cover on the social behavior of bighorn rams and mountain goats." *Can. J. Zool.* **51**:987−993.

Picozzi, N. 1968. "Grouse bags in relation to the management and geology of heather moors." *J. Applied Ecol.* **5**:483−488.

Pimlott, D. H. 1967. "Wolf predation and ungulate populations." *Amer. Zool.* **7**:267−276.

Pitelka, F. A. 1973. "Cyclic patterns in lemming populations near Barrow, Alaska." Pp. 199−215 in Tech. Paper 25, Arctic Institute of N. Amer., M. E. Britton (Ed.). 224 pp.

Pruitt, W. O., Jr. 1959. "Snow as a factor in the winter ecology of the barren-ground caribou." *Arctic* **12**:158−180.

Reeves, H. M., H. H. Dill, and A. S. Hawkins. 1968. "A case study in Canada goose management: The Mississippi Valley population." Pp. 150−165 in *Canada Goose Management*, R. L. Hine and C. Schoenfeld (Eds.). Dembar Educ. Res. Services, Inc., Madison, Wis. 195 pp.

Riney, T. 1955. "Evaluating condition of free-ranging red deer with special reference to New Zealand." *N. Zealand J. Sci. and Tech.* **36**:429−463.

———. 1960. "A field technique for assessing physical condition of some ungulates." *J. Wildl. Mgmt.* **24**:92−94.

Risenhoover, K. L., and J. A. Bailey. 1980. "Visibility: an important habitat factor for an indigenous, low-elevation bighorn herd in Colorado." *Proc. Biennial Symp. N. Wild Sheep and Goat Counc.*, Salmon, Idaho, pp. 18−28.

Robbins, C. S., and W. T. Van Velzen. 1969. *The Breeding Bird Survey, 1967 and 1968*. Spec. Sci. Rpt. 124, Bur. Sport Fisheries and Wildlife. U.S.D.I., Washington, D.C. 107 pp.

Rosen, M. N., and A. I. BIschoff, 1952. "The relation of hematology to condition in California deer." *Trans. N. Amer. Wildl. Conf.* **17**:482−496.

Sadlier, R. M. F. S. 1969. *The Ecology of Reproduction in Wild and Domestic Mammals.* Methuen and Co., London. 321 pp.

———. 1973. *The Reproduction of Vertebrates.* Academic Press, N.Y. 180 pp.

Sampson, A. W. 1944. *Plant Succession on Burned Chaparral Lands in Northern California.* Cal. Agr. Expt. Sta. Bull. 685. 144 pp.

———. 1952. *Range Management Principles and Practices.* John Wiley and Sons, N.Y. 570 pp.

Sanderson, G. C. 1966. "The study of mammal movements—a review." *J. Wildl. Mgmt.* **30**:215−235.

Schaller, G. B. 1972. "Predators of the Serengeti: Part 2. Are you running with me, Hominid?" *Natural History* **81**:60−69.

Scheffer, V. B. 1955. "Body size with relation to population density in mammals." *J. Mammal.* **36**:493−514.

Schemnitz, S. D. (Ed.). *Wildlife Management Techniques Manual.* 4th ed. The Wildl. Soc., Washington, D.C. 686 pp.

Schmidt, K. P. 1938. "Herpetological evidence for the postglacial eastward extension of the steppe in North America." *Ecology* **19**:396−407.

Schmidt, R. L., C. P. Hibler, T. R. Spraker, and W. H. Rutherford. 1979. "An evaluation of drug treatment for lungworm in bighorn sheep." *J. Wildl. Mgmt.* **43**:461−467.

Schmidt-Nielson, K. 1964. *Desert Animals: Physiological Problems of Heat and Water.* Clarenden Press, Oxford Univ. Press, Eng. 277 pp.

Schoonveld, G. G., J. G. Nagy, and J. A. Bailey. 1974. "Capability of mule deer to utilize fibrous alfalfa diets." *J. Wildl. Mgmt.* **38**:823−829.

Schultz, A. M. 1969. The tundra as a homeostatic system. Pp. 86−93 in *The Ecosystem Concept in Natural Resource Management,* G. M. Van Dyne (Ed.). Academic Press, N.Y. 383 pp.

Schultz, V. 1951. "Game mortality resulting from a severe snow and ice storm in Tennessee." *Proc. S. E. Assn. Game and Fish Comm.* **5**:1−23.

Schweitzer, A. 1923. *Civlization and Ethics.* Trans. by C. T. Campion. A. and C. Black, London.

Scotter, G. W. 1971. Fire, Vegetation, soil, and barren-ground caribou relations in northern Canada. Pp. 209−230 in C. W. Slaughter, R. J. Barney and G. M. Hansen (Eds.). *Fire in the Northern Environment, A Symposium.* Pacific Northwest For. and Rge. Expt. Sta., U. S. Forest Service, Portland.

Sears, P. B. 1957. *The Ecology of Man.* Condon Lecture, Oregon St. System of Higher Education, Eugene. 61 pp.

Selander, R. K. 1965. "On mating systems and sexual selection." *Amer. Nat.* **99**:129−141.

———. 1966. "Sexual dimorphism and differential niche utilization in birds." *Condor* **68**:113−151.

Selye, H. 1946. "The general adaptation syndrome and the diseases of adaptation." *J. Clin. Endocrinology* **6**:117−230.

————. 1950. *Stress*. Acta, Montreal. 815 pp.

————. 1955. "Stress and Disease." *Science* **122**:625–631.

————. 1956. *The Stress of Life*. McGraw-Hill Co., N.Y. 324 pp.

Seton, E. T. 1911. *The Arctic Prairies*. C. Scribner's Sons, N.Y. 308 pp.

Severinghaus, C. W. 1955. "Deer weights as an index of range conditions in two wilderness areas of the Adirondack region." *N.Y. Fish and Game J.* **2**:154–160.

————. 1972. "Weather and the deer population." *The Conservationist* **27**:28–31.

Shaw, H. 1965. "Investigation of factors influencing deer populations." Pp. 125–143 in *Wildlife Research in Arizona, 1964*. Ariz. Game and Fish Dept., Phoenix. 251 pp.

Shaw, W. W., and J. B. Low. 1971. "Chukars don't need guzzlers." *Utah Wildl.* Sept., p. 93.

Shelford, V. E. 1963. *The Ecology of North America*. Univ. Ill. Press. 610 pp.

Shepherd, H. R. 1971. *Effects of Clipping on Key Browse Species in Southwestern Colorado*. Tech. Publ. 28. Colo. Div. Game, Fish and Parks, Denver. 104 pp.

Siivonen, L. 1956. "The correlation between the fluctuations of partridge and European hare populations and the climatic conditions of winters in south-west Finland during the last thirty years." *Papers on Game Research, Finnish Game Foundation* **17**:1–30.

Simpson, G. G. 1945. *The principles of Classification and a Classification of Mammals*. Amer. Museum. Nat. Hist. Bull., N.Y. 350 pp.

Sinclair, A. R. C. 1977. *The African Buffalo, a study of Resource Limitation of Populations*. Univ. Chicago Press. 355 pp.

Smith, A. 1960. "Hail: great destroyer of wildlife." *Audubon Mag.* **62**:170–171, 189.

Smith, C. C. 1968. "The adaptive nature of social organization in the genus of tree squirrels *Tamiasciurus*." *Ecol. Monogr.* **38**:31–63.

Smith, D. R. 1954. *The Bighorn Sheep in Idaho*. Dept. Fish and Game Wildl. Bull. No. 1, Boise, 154 pp.

Smith, P. W. 1957. "An analysis of post-Wisconsin biogeography of the prairie peninsula region based on distributional phenomena among terrestrial vertebrate populations." *Ecology* **38**:205–218.

Snyder, L. L. 1957. *Arctic Birds of Canada*. Univ. Toronto Press. 310 pp.

Solomon, M. E. 1949. "The natural control of animal populations." *J. Animal Ecol.* **18**:1–35.

————. 1958. "Meaning of density-dependence and related terms in population dynamics." *Nature* **181**:1778–1780.

Squillace, A. E., and R. R. Silen. 1962. *Racial Variation in Ponderosa Pine*. Forest Sci. Monogr. No. 2. Soc. Amer. Foresters, Washington, D.C. 27 pp.

Stahelin, R. 1943. "Factors influencing the natural restocking of high altitude burns by coniferous trees in the Central Rocky Mountains." *Ecology* **24**:19–30.

Stebler, A. M., and S. D. Schemnitz. 1955. "Habitat description and the life-form concept." *Proc. Okla. Acad. Sci.* **36**:154–157.

Steen, M. O. 1944. "The significance of population turnover in upland game management." *Trans. N. Amer. Wildl. Conf.* **9**:331–335.

————. 1955. "Not how much but how good." *Mo. Conservationist* **16**:1–3.

Steinhoff, H. W. 1971. "Communicating complete wildlife values of Kenai." *Trans. N. Amer. Wildl. and Nat. Res. Conf.* **36**:428–438.

Stoddard, H. L. 1932. *The Bobwhite Quail; Its Habits, Preservation and Increase.* Charles Scribner's Sons. N.Y. 559 pp.

———, and R. A. Norris. 1967. "Bird casualties at a Leon County, Florida TV tower: an eleven-year study." *Bull. Tall Timbers Res. Sta.*, No. 8. 104 pp.

Stoddart, L. A. and J. E. Greaves. 1942. *The Composition of Summer Range Plants in Utah.* Utah Agr. Exp. Sta. Bull. No. 305. 22 pp.

———, A. D. Smith, and T. W. Box. 1955. *Range Management,* 3rd ed. McGraw-Hill Co. N.Y. 532 pp.

Stokes, A. W. (Ed.) 1974. *Territory. Benchmark Papers in Animal Behavior,* Vol. 2, Dowden, Hutchinson and Ross, Stroudsburg, Pa. 395 pp.

Storer, R. W. 1966. "Sexual dimorphism and food habits in three North American accipiters." *Auk* **83**:423–436.

Stumpf, W. A., and C. O. Mohr. 1962. "Linearity of home ranges of California mice and other animals." *J. Wildl. Mgmt.* **26**:149–154.

Svardson, G. 1949. "Competition and habitat selection in birds." *Oikos* **1**:157–174.

Svoboda, F. J., and G. W. Gullion. 1974. "Techniques for monitoring ruffed grouse food resources." *Wildl. Soc. Bull.* **2**:195–197.

Swank, W. G. 1956. "Protein and phosphorus content of browse plants as an influence on southwestern deer herd levels." *Trans. N. Amer. Wildl. Conf.* **21**:141–157.

Swift, L. W. 1955. "The need of wildlife for drinking water." Pp. 586–588 in *Water, The Yearbook of Agriculture.* U.S.D.A. 751 pp.

Taber, R. D. 1956. "Deer nutrition and population dynamics in the north coast range of California." *Trans. N. Amer. Wildl. Conf.* **21**:159–172.

———. 1958. "Development of the cervid antler as an index of late winter physical condition." *Proc. Mont. Acad. Sci.* **18**:27–28.

——— and R. Dasmann. 1958. *The Black-tailed Deer of the Chaparral.* Cal. Dept. Fish and Game, Game Bull. 8. 159 pp.

——— K. L. White, and N. S. Smith. 1959. "The annual cycle of condition in the Rattlesnake, Montana, mule deer." *Proc. Mont. Acad. Sci.* **19**:72–79.

Tanner, J. T. 1966. "Effects of population density on growth rates of animal populations." *Ecology* **47**:733–745.

Taylor, W. P. (Ed.) 1956. *The Deer of North America.* Wildl. Mgmt. Inst. Washington, D.C. 688 pp.

Teer, J. G., J. W. Thomas, and E. A. Walker. 1965. "Ecology and management of the white-tailed deer in the Llano Basin of Texas." *Wildl. Monogr.* Vol. 15, 62 pp.

———, and N. K. Forrest. 1968. "Bionomic and ethical implications of commercial game harvest programs." *Trans. N. Amer. Wildl. and Nat. Res. Conf.* **33**:192–202.

Teeri, A. E., W. Virchow, N. F. Colovos, and F. Greeley. 1958. "Blood composition of white-tailed deer." *J. Mamm.* **39**:269–274.

Thomas, J. W., G. L. Crouch, R. S. Bumstead, and L. D. Bryant. 1975. "Silvicultural options and habitat values in coniferous forests." Pp. 272–287 in *Proc. Symposium on*

Management of Forest and Range Habitats for Nongame Birds. U.S.D.A. Forest Service, Gen. Tech. Report WO-1. 343 pp.

Tierson, W. C., E. F. Patric, and D. F. Behrend. 1966. "Influence of white-tailed deer on the logged northern hardwood forest." *J. For.* **64**:801–805.

Transeau, E. N. 1935. "The Prairie Peninsula." *Ecology* **16**:423–437.

Turner, J. C., Jr. 1973. "Water, energy and electrolyte balance in the desert bighorn sheep, *Ovis canadensis.*" Unpubl. Ph.D. thesis, Univ. Cal., Riverside. 138 pp.

Twomey, A. C. 1936. "Climographic studies of certain introduced and migratory birds." *Ecology* **17**:127–132.

Ullrey, D. E., W. G. Youatt, H. E. Johnson, L. D. Fay, B. L. Schoepke, and W. T. Magee. 1970. "Digestible and metabolizable energy requirements for winter maintenance of Michigan white-tailed does." *J. Wildl. Mgmt.* **34**:863–869.

United States Bureau of Sport Fisheries and Wildlife. 1982. *1980 National Survey of Fishing, Hunting and Wildlife-associated Recreation (Initial Findings).* Washington, D.C.

Vance, D. R. 1976. "Changes in land use and wildlife populations in southeastern Illinois." *Wildl. Soc. Bull.* **4**:11–15.

Van Soest, P. J. 1967. "Development of a comprehensive system of feed analyses and its application to forages." *J. Animal Sci.* **26**:119–128.

Verme, L. J. 1962. "Mortality of white-tailed deer fawns in relation to nutrition." *Proc. Natl. Deer Disease Symp.* **1**:15–38.

———. 1965. "Swamp conifer deeryards in northern Michigan." *J. For.* **63**:523–529.

Wagner, F. H. 1969. "Ecosystem concepts in fish and game management." Pp. 259–307 in *The Ecosystem Concept in Natural Resource Management,* G. M. Van dyne (Ed.). Academic Press, N.Y. 383 pp.

———, C. D. Besadny, and C. Kabat. 1965. *Population Ecology and Management of Wisconsin Pheasants.* Wis. Cons. Dept. Tech. Bull. 34. 168 pp.

———, and L. C. Stoddart. 1972. "Influence of coyote predation on black-tailed jackrabbit populations in Utah." *J. Wildl. Mgmt.* **36**:329–342.

Wallmo, O. C. 1973. "Important game animals and related recreation in arid shrublands of the United States." Pp. 98–107 in *Arid Shrublands, Proc. 3rd Workshop U.S./Australia Rangelands Panel,* Tucson, Ariz.

——— (Ed.). 1981. *Mule and Black-tailed Deer of North America.* The Wildl. Mgmt. Institute, Washington, D.C. and Univ. of Nebraska Press, Lincoln. 605 pp.

———, and R. B. Gill. 1971. "Snow, winter distribution, and population dynamics of mule deer in the Central Rocky Mountains." Pp. 1–15 in *Snow and Ice in Relation to Wildlife and Recreation Symposium,* A. O. Haugen (Ed.). Iowa St. Univ., Ames. 280 pp.

———, L. H. Carpenter, W. L. Regelin, R. B. Gill, and D. L. Baker. 1977. "Evaluation of deer habitat on a nutritional basis." *J. Range Mgmt.* **30**:122–127.

Weaver, J. E., and F. E. Clements. 1938. *Plant Ecology.* McGraw-Hill Co., N.Y. 520 pp.

Wecker, S. C. 1964. "Habitat selection." *Sci. Amer.,* **211**(4):109–116.

Welch, C., and A. G. Kettunen. 1939. *Michigan's Deer Herd: A winter Deer Yard Study for 4-H Club Members.* Club Bull. 40, Extension Div., Mich. St. Coll., East Lansing. 30 pp.

Welles, R. E., and F. B. Welles. 1961. *The Bighorn of Death Valley*. U.S. Nat. Park Service, Fauna Series 6. 242 pp.

Wesley, D. E., K. L. Knox, and J. G. Nagy. 1970. "Energy flux and water kinetics in young pronghorn antelope." *J. Wildl. Mgmt.* **34**:908–912.

Whatley, H. E., M. E. Lisano, and J. E. Kennamer. 1977. "Plasma corticosterone level as an indicator of stress in the eastern wild turkey." *J. Wildl. Mgmt.* **41**:189–193.

Whittaker, R. H. 1967. "Gradient analysis of vegetation." *Biol. Rev.* **42**:229.

———. 1975. *Communities and Ecosystems*. 2nd ed. Macmillan Co., N.Y. 385 pp.

Wight, H. M. 1974. "Non-game wildlife and forest management." Pp. 27–38 in *Wildlife and Forest Management in the Pacific Northwest*, H. C. Black (Ed.). School of Forestry, Oregon St. Univ., Corvallis. 236 pp.

Williams, G. R. 1954. "Population fluctuations in some northern hemisphere game birds (*Tetraonidae*)." *J. Animal Ecol.* **23**:1–34.

Willis, A. J. 1973. *Introduction to Plant Ecology*. Allen and Unwin, London. 237 pp.

Wodzicki, K., and H. S. Roberts. 1960. "Influence of population density on the adrenal and body weights of the wild rabbit in New Zealand." *New Zealand J. Sci.* **3**:103–120.

Wood, J. E., R. J. White, and J. L. Durham. 1970. *Investigations Preliminary to the Release of Exotic Ungulates in New Mexico*. Bull. 13, New Mex. Dept. Game and Fish, Santa Fe. 58 pp.

Wright, V. L. 1980. "Use of randomized response technique to estimate deer poaching." *Wildl. Soc. Bull* **8**:342–344.

Wynne-Edwards, V. C. 1965. "Self-regulating systems in populations of animals." *Science* **147**:1543–1548.

Yeatter, R. E. 1943. "The Prairie Chicken in Illinois." *Ill. Nat. Hist. Surv. Bull.* **22**:377–416.

Yocum, C. F. 1950. "Weather and its effect on hatching of waterfowl in eastern Washington." *Trans. N. Amer. Wildl. Conf.* **15**:309–319.

Zarn, M. 1974. *Habitat Management for Unique or Endangered Species*. Rpt. No. 10. Spotted Owl (*Strix occidentalis*). USDI, Bur. Land Mgmt. Tech. Note T-N-242. 22 pp.

PHOTO CREDITS

SOURCES OF CHAPTER OPENING QUOTATIONS

Preface: John Steinbeck, from *The Log from the Sea of Cortez*, Viking Press, 1951. Copyright © by John Steinbeck and Ed Ricketts, Jr.

Chapter 1: Kingman Brewster, Jr., former president of Yale University.

Chapter 2: Aldo Leopold, source unknown.

Chapter 3: Edwin Way Teale, source unknown.

Chapter 4: George A. Bartholomew, from American Association for the Advancement of Science Publ. No. 51, *Zoogeography*, C. L. Hubbs (ed.). Copyright © 1958 by the American Association for the Advancement of Science.

Chapter 5: Durward L. Allen, from *Our Wildlife Legacy*, Funk and Wagnalls, 1962. Copyright © 1962 by D. Allen.

Chapter 6: David Lack, from *The Natural Regulation of Animal Numbers*, Oxford University Press, copyright © 1954.

Chapter 6: John Wesley Powell, from *The Exploration of the Colorado River and its Canyons*, Dover Publications, copyright © 1961; first published by Flood and Vincent, 1895.

Chapter 7: Adolph Murie, from *The Wolves of Mount McKinley*, USDI, National Park Service, Fauna Series 5, 1944.

Chapter 8: Archie Carr, from *So Excellent a Fische*, revised edition, copyright © 1967, 1984, by Archie Carr. Reprinted by permission of Charles Scribner's Sons.

Chapter 9: Julia N. Allen, reprinted by permission.

Chapter 10: Valerius Geist, from *Mountain Sheep and Man in the Northern Wilds*, Cornell University Press, copyright © 1975.

Chapter 11: Charles Darwin, from the *Origin of Species*, 1859.

Page 194: A. G. Tansley, source unknown.

Chapter 12:   Aldo Leopold, from *Game Management*, copyright © 1933 by Charles Scribner's Sons; copyright renewed 1961 by Estella B. Leopold. Used with permission of Charles Scribner's Sons.

Chapter 13:   Lewis Carroll, from *Through the Looking Glass*, 1896.

Chapter 14:   Robert H. Giles, Jr. (paraphrased), from *Wildlife Management*, W. H. Freeman and Co., copyright © 1978, by permission of R. H. Giles, Jr.

Chapter 15:   Paul R. Ehrlich and L. C. Birch, from the "balance of nature" and "population control," *The American Naturalist*, pp. 106—107. Copyright © 1967, by permission of The University of Chicago Press.

Chapter 16:   Graeme Caughley, from "What is this thing called carrying capacity?," *North American Elk: Ecology Behavior and Management*. Copyright © 1979, University of Wyoming.

Chapter 17:   Robert A. McCabe, from *Wildlife's Ten-year Cycle* (by L. B. Keith). Copyright © 1963 by The Board of Regents of the University of Wisconsin System, used by permission of The University of Wisconsin Press.

Chapter 18:   M. J. Moroney, from *Facts from Figures*, Penguin Books, copyright © 1962.

Chapter 19:   Thomas Alva Edison, source unknown.

INDEX

When several references are cited, major discussions or the locations of definitions are cited in **boldface** type. Locations of figures are indicated by f.

367